Global Civil Society
Dimensions of the Nonprofit Sector

Other Project Publications

JOHNS HOPKINS NONPROFIT SECTOR SERIES

The Emerging Nonprofit Sector. Lester M. Salamon and Helmut K. Anheier (Manchester, UK: Manchester University Press, 1996).

Defining the Nonprofit Sector: A Cross-National Analysis. Edited by Lester M. Salamon and Helmut K. Anheier (Manchester, UK: Manchester University Press, 1997).

The Nonprofit Sector in France. Edith Archambault (Manchester, UK: Manchester University Press, 1997).

The Nonprofit Sector in Hungary. Éva Kuti (Manchester, UK: Manchester University Press, 1996).

The Nonprofit Sector in Italy. Edited by Gian Paolo Barbetta (Manchester, UK: Manchester University Press, 1997).

The Nonprofit Sector in Japan. Tadashi Yamamoto (Manchester, UK: Manchester University Press, 1998).

The Nonprofit Sector in Sweden. Tommy Lundström and Filip Wijkström (Manchester, UK: Manchester University Press, 1998).

The Voluntary Sector in the UK. Jeremy Kendall and Martin Knapp (Manchester, UK: Manchester University Press, 1996).

The Nonprofit Sector in the Developing World. Edited by Helmut K. Anheier and Lester M. Salamon (Manchester, UK: Manchester University Press, 1998).

OTHER PUBLICATIONS

The International Guide to Nonprofit Law. Lester M. Salamon (New York: John Wiley & Sons, 1997).

CNP Working Papers. For a list of the CNP working papers, contact the Center for Civil Society Studies (mailing address: CCSS, Institute for Policy Studies, The Johns Hopkins University, 3400 N. Charles Street, Baltimore, MD 21218-2688, USA; e-mail: jh_cnpsp@jhu.edu; fax: 410-516-7818; telephone: 410-516-4523; Web address: http://www.jhu.edu/~ccss/).

The Johns Hopkins Comparative Nonprofit Sector Project

Global Civil Society
Dimensions of the Nonprofit Sector

Lester M. Salamon
Helmut K. Anheier
Regina List
Stefan Toepler
S. Wojciech Sokolowski
and Associates

The Johns Hopkins Center for Civil Society Studies
Baltimore, MD • 1999

Printed in the United States of America
First Printing
Second Printing

ISBN 1-886333-42-4

Production editors: Mimi Bilzor and Regina List
Cover art and design: Doug Hess

Copies of this publication are available for a price of $34.95 each, plus $5.00 for the
first book and $2.00 for each additional book for shipping and handling. Prepayment
is required on all orders. Prices for multiple copies provided on request. Direct all inquiries to the address noted below, or the following: e-mail: jh_cnpsp@jhu.edu; fax:
(410) 516-7818; telephone: (410) 516-4523; www.jhu.edu/~ccss/.

Center for Civil Society Studies
Institute for Policy Studies
The Johns Hopkins University
3400 N. Charles Street
Baltimore, MD 21218-2688, USA

The Johns Hopkins Center for Civil Society Studies (CCSS) seeks to encourage the development and effective operation of not-for-profit, philanthropic, or "civil society" organizations that provide organized vehicles for the exercise of private initiative in the
common good, often in collaboration with government and the business sector. CCSS
is part of the Johns Hopkins Institute for Policy Studies and carries out its work internationally through a combination of research, training, and information-sharing.

Table of Contents

Contributors

SOPHIE ADAM is a research associate at the Centre of Social Economy of the University of Liège. She holds a Masters in Development Management from the University of Liège.

STEPHEN ALMOND is Research Officer at the Personal Social Services Research Unit with half-time posts at the University of Kent at Canterbury and the London School of Economics and Political Science in the U.K. He also teaches in the Economics Department at Kent. He received his Ph.D. in Health Economics and Econometrics from the University of Kent at Canterbury. Recent publications include *Poverty, Disability and the Use of Long Term Care Services*, a Royal Commission report, and *The Costs of Schizophrenia* (Wiley & Sons, 1999).

HELMUT K. ANHEIER was the Associate Director of the Comparative Nonprofit Sector Project until 1998. He is currently the Director of the Centre for Voluntary Organisation at the London School of Economics and Political Science in the U.K. Prior to this, he was Senior Research Associate at the Johns Hopkins Institute for Policy Studies, Associate Professor of Sociology at Rutgers University, and Social Affairs Officer at the United Nations. The author of numerous books and articles and founding editor of the journal *Voluntas,* he holds a Ph.D. in Sociology from Yale University.

ÉDITH ARCHAMBAULT is the Local Associate for France and a Professor at the Sorbonne-University of Paris I in France. She is also Director of the Laboratoire d'Économie Sociale, a 30-person research team acknowledged by the Centre National de la Recherche Scientifique (National Center for Scientific Research). She was the Vice President of the International Society for Third-sector Research (ISTR) from 1994 to 1996. Her most recent publication in English is *The Nonprofit Sector in France* (Manchester University Press, 1997).

ADRIAN BABOI STROE is a researcher at both the Civil Society Development Foundation and the Institute for Educational Sciences in Bucharest, Romania.

NEIDE BERES is an economist with the Instituto Brasileiro de Geografia e Estatística (Brazilian Institute of Geography and Statistics).

BOGDAN BERIANU is a researcher specializing in the Romanian nonprofit sector.

ARY BURGER, co-Local Associate for the Netherlands, is a researcher at the Social and Cultural Planning Office (SCP) in the Netherlands. He studied economic and social history at the Vrije Universiteit Amsterdam and has published on the Dutch nonprofit sector, as well as on Europe's agricultural policy and on international growth and productivity comparisons.

ix

STEFAN CONSTANTINESCU is a sociologist and former member of the Research Program of the Civil Society Development Foundation in Bucharest, Romania. Currently, he works in the business sector.

HANNY CUEVA is an economist, junior professor, and associated researcher at the Universidad del Pacífico in Lima, Peru. She is currently working on social evaluation issues and a broader study of the social and economic impact of third sector activities in Peru.

JACQUES DEFOURNY, co-Local Associate for Belgium, is Professor at the University of Liège and Head of the University's Centre of Social Economy—well-known throughout the world for its research on the third sector. He holds a Ph.D. in Economics from the University of Liège and a Masters in Public Administration from Cornell University.

PAUL DEKKER, Local Associate for the Netherlands, is a political scientist and Research Fellow at the Social and Cultural Planning Office in The Hague. He has published about planning and government, social and political attitudes, and political participation in the Netherlands, often in a cross-national perspective. His present research interests include environmental attitudes, volunteering, and civil society.

FREDA DONOGHUE is the Director of the Policy Research Centre at the National College of Ireland in Dublin. She holds a Ph.D. in Sociology and has worked in, and published on, nonprofit research for several years. She is the chief researcher on the Irish team in the Johns Hopkins Comparative Nonprofit Sector Project and has produced the first systematic data on the size and scope of the nonprofit sector in Ireland. She is a founding member of the Association for Voluntary Action Research in Ireland (AVARI). Her other research areas include women and political participation and the elderly in Ireland.

CARMEN EPURE holds a Masters in Political Philosophy and is a researcher based in Bucharest, Romania.

PAVOL FRIČ, co-Local Associate for the Czech Republic, is a researcher and Lecturer at the Institute of Sociological Studies, Faculty of Social Sciences, Charles University, Prague. Prior to this, he was with the Slovak Academy of Sciences and was the Deputy Director of the Institute for Social Analysis of Komenský University in Bratislava. He holds a Doctorate in Sociology from Komenský University.

MARIE GARIAZZO is Research Assistant at the Laboratoire d'Économie Sociale, Sorbonne-University of Paris I in France.

BENJAMIN GIDRON, the Local Associate for Israel, is Professor of Social Work and the Director of the Israeli Center for Third-sector Research (ICTR) at the Ben-Gurion University of the Negev. He was the Founding President of the International Society for Third-sector Research (ISTR) and has published numerous books and articles on the third sector, philanthropy, and self-help.

ROCHDI GOULLI, a member of the Czech research team, is a researcher and Lecturer of Public Economics at the Institute of Sociological Studies, Faculty of Social Sciences, Charles University, and at the Chair of Public Finance at the University of Economics, Prague. Prior to this, he was a researcher at the Institute of Economics of the Czechoslovak Academy of Science, where he also completed his doctoral studies. He is a member of the Czech Association of Public Economics.

Voitto Helander is Local Associate for Finland and Professor of Public Administration at the Åbo Akademi University in Åbo. He holds a Ph.D. in Political Science.

Leslie C. Hems is Senior Research Associate at the Johns Hopkins Institute for Policy Studies and Principal Associate in the Comparative Nonprofit Sector Project since 1998. Before this, he was Head of Research at the National Council for Voluntary Organisations in the U.K. and Research Associate at the Aston Business School.

Susan Hocking is co-Local Associate for Australia and an economist who has undertaken research into the provision of health and welfare services. In 1994/95 she worked on the Australian Industry Commission Inquiry into Charitable Organisations.

Antonio Jiménez Lara is a researcher on the Spanish project team.

Hagai Katz is a graduate student of Organizational Sociology at the Ben-Gurion University of the Negev in Israel and a researcher at the Israeli Center for Third-sector Research (ICTR).

Jeremy Kendall, co-Local Associate for the U.K., is Research Fellow at the Personal Social Services Research Unit, London School of Economics and Political Science. He received his doctorate, "The role and scope of the UK Voluntary Sector," from the University of Kent at Canterbury in 1996. The editor of *Voluntas—International Journal of Voluntary and Nonprofit Organizations,* his publications include *The Voluntary Sector in the U.K.* (Manchester University Press, 1996) and *The Contract Culture in Public Services: Studies from Britain, Europe and the USA* (Ashgate Publishers, Aldershot, 1997).

Éva Kuti, co-Local Associate for Hungary, is an economist, researcher, and founding member of the Research Project on Nonprofit Organizations, a voluntary association that initiated the study of the nonprofit sector in Hungary. She is Head of the Section on Voluntary Sector Statistics of the Central Statistical Office and the author of several books and articles published in both Hungarian and other languages, including *The Nonprofit Sector in Hungary* (Manchester University Press, 1996). Since 1993, she is also Associate Professor at the Budapest University of Economics, and was Visiting Professor at the Sorbonne in 1997. She is a member of the Editorial Boards of *Voluntas* and the *International Journal of Cultural Policy.*

Harri Laaksonen holds a Masters in Social Sciences with a concentration in National Economy and is a junior researcher in the Finnish project team.

Leilah Landim is Local Associate for Brazil and Professor of Social Anthropology at the Federal University of Rio de Janeiro. She is also a researcher at ISER, the Institute for Religious Studies.

Ewa Leś is Assistant Professor at the Institute of Social Policy, University of Warsaw, and co-Local Associate for Poland. The author of three books and more than 70 articles, reports and commentaries on family sociology, social policy, and the comparative voluntary sector, she has been a visiting scholar at several European, American and Canadian universities and was Philanthropy Fellow at Johns Hopkins University in Baltimore in 1992 and Japan Foundation Fellow in Tokyo in 1996.

Regina A. List is Program Manager and Coordinator for Developing Countries of the Comparative Nonprofit Sector Project. She holds an M.A. in International

Development from the American University and was formerly the Executive Director of the Washington-based Esquel Group Foundation, member of a network of Latin American nonprofit research and advocacy organizations.

SIMONA LUCA is a Romanian lawyer specializing in nonprofit issues.

MARK LYONS is the Local Associate for Australia and Associate Professor in the School of Management at the University of Technology, Sydney. He is also the Director of the University's Centre for Australian Community Organisations and Management (CACOM).

MICHEL MARÉE is a research associate at the Centre of Social Economy of the University of Liège. He holds a Masters in Economics from the University of Paris I (Panthéon-Sorbonne).

SYBILLE MERTENS is a research associate at the Centre of Social Economy of the University of Liège. She holds a Masters in Economics from the Catholic University of Leuven and is a Ph.D. student in Economics at the University of Liège.

SŁAWOMIR NAŁĘCZ graduated from the University of Warsaw, Poland, in 1994 with a Masters in Organizational Sociology. Between 1995 and 1997, he was Research Assistant at the Institute of Philosophy and Sociology of the Polish Academy of Science, carrying out independent research on the institutional changes in education and the health care system in Poland. In 1997, he became a member of the Polish research team of the Comparative Nonprofit Sector Project.

JOZEF PACOLET, co-Local Associate for Belgium, is Professor and Head of the Social and Economic Policy Department at the Higher Institute of Labor Studies (HIVA), Catholic University of Leuven. He holds a Ph.D. in Economics from the Catholic University of Leuven.

ALEXANDRA PETRÁŠOVÁ is the Head of the Governmental and Non-profit Sectors Statistics Unit in the Department of Social Statistics of the Statistical Office of the Slovak Republic. Currently, she also serves as the Acting Director of the Social Statistics Department. Her areas of specialization in social statistics include compulsory social insurance, nonmarket services (central and local government sector and nonprofit sector), social protection, and education statistics. She holds degrees in Theology, Mechanical Engineering (M.Sc.), and a Ph.D. in Technical Cybernetics.

FELIPE PORTOCARRERO, co-Local Associate for Peru, is Research Professor and the Director of the Centro de Investigación de la Universidad del Pacífico in Lima. He is currently working on social policy issues and a broader study of the history of philanthropy among the Peruvian economic elite. He holds a Ph.D. in Sociology from the University of Oxford.

ECKHARD PRILLER is co-Local Associate for Germany and Senior Researcher at the Social Structure and Social Reporting Research Unit of the Social Science Research Center Berlin (WZB). Prior to this, he was a Research Associate with the Institute for Sociology and Social Politics at the Academy of Sciences of the German Democratic Republic and a visiting fellow at several social and economic research institutes in Germany. The author of numerous social reports and publications on the nonprofit sector, he received his doctorate from Humboldt University of Berlin.

MARIO ROITTER, an economist and Local Associate for Argentina, is the co-Director of the Civil Society and Social Development Unit at CEDES, the Center for the

Study of State and Society. He has also worked as consultant for UNDP and UNICEF.

José Ignacio Ruiz Olabuénaga, Local Associate for Spain, is Professor in the Faculty of Sociology at the University of Deusto. He holds doctoral degrees in Sociology, Philosophy, and Educational Sciences. His most recent publication is *El Extranjero en Europa [The Foreigner in Europe]* (University of Deusto, 1997).

Lester M. Salamon is the Director of the Johns Hopkins Comparative Nonprofit Sector Project. A Professor at Johns Hopkins University, he was the founding director of the Johns Hopkins Institute for Policy Studies and currently directs the Johns Hopkins Center for Civil Society Studies. Dr. Salamon previously served as Director of the Center for Governance and Management Research at the Urban Institute in Washington, D.C. and as Deputy Associate Director of the U.S. Office of Management and Budget in the Executive Office of the President. Before that, he taught at Duke University, Vanderbilt University, and Tougaloo College. A pioneer in the empirical study of the nonprofit sector in the U.S. and, more recently, throughout the world, he is the author or editor of numerous books and articles, including *America's Nonprofit Sector: A Primer* and *Partners in Public Service: Government-Nonprofit Relations in the Modern Welfare State* (Johns Hopkins University Press). Dr. Salamon received his B.A. degree in Economics and Policy Studies from Princeton University and his Ph.D. in Government from Harvard University.

Cynthia Sanborn is co-Local Associate for Peru and Research Professor at the Universidad del Pacífico in Lima. Currently, she works on a broader study of government policy towards the nonprofit sector in Peru. She received her Ph.D. in Political Science from Harvard University.

Daniel Saulean is the Local Associate for Romania and the Research Program Coordinator of the Civil Society Development Foundation in Bucharest, Romania. A sociologist by training, he is currently also a Ph.D. candidate at the University of Bucharest.

István Sebestény, a sociologist by training, is co-Local Associate for Hungary. Since 1992, he has worked in the Section on Voluntary Sector Statistics of the Hungarian Central Statistical Office. He is a founding member and current President of the Civitalis Research Association, which served as the local host institution for the Hungarian portion of the second phase of the Johns Hopkins Comparative Nonprofit Sector Project.

Hiroko Shimizu is a doctoral student at the Osaka School of International Public Policy, Osaka University, Japan. She holds an M.A. in International Public Policy from Osaka University and a B.A. in Chinese History from Gakushuin University. She has been conducting research on economic aspects of the Japanese nonprofit sector and on grant-making foundations in Japan.

S. Wojciech Sokolowski is Research Associate and Data Manager with the Comparative Nonprofit Sector Project. He received his Ph.D. in Sociology from Rutgers University, an M.A. in Philosophy from the Lublin Catholic University in Poland, and an M.A. in Sociology from San Jose State University. Before coming to the United States, he was an activist in the Solidarność labor movement in Poland. His publications include the forthcoming *Civil Society and the Professions in Eastern Europe: Social Change and Organizational Innovation in Poland* (Kluwer/Plenum, 1999).

DAN STANCU is former Research Program Coordinator for the Civil Society Development Foundation in Bucharest, Romania, and oversaw the early stages of this project as the initial Local Associate for Romania until 1998. He now works in the private sector.

SUSAN SUNDBACK, Ph.D., is a Docent of Sociology and senior researcher in the Finnish project team.

OANA TIGANESCU is a psychologist and researcher at the Civil Society Development Foundation in Bucharest, Romania. Currently, she serves as the Interim Coordinator of the Foundation's Research Program.

STEFAN TOEPLER is Research Associate and Lecturer at the Center for Civil Society Studies, Johns Hopkins Institute for Policy Studies, where he oversees the Central and Eastern European part of the Johns Hopkins Comparative Nonprofit Sector Project. He holds a doctorate in Economic Sciences from the Free University of Berlin in Germany. Among other publications, his most recent book is *Private Funds, Public Purpose: Philanthropic Foundations in International Perspective* (Kluwer/Plenum, 1999).

ILSE VAN DE PUTTE is a Research Associate at the Higher Institute of Labor Studies (HIVA) of the Catholic University of Leuven. She holds a graduate degree in Applied Economics and Criminology.

GUSTAVO VERDUZCO, the Principal Investigator for this project in Mexico, has been Professor and a researcher at El Colegio de Mexico since 1983 and a member of the Mexican Academy of Sciences since 1987. He was a member of a bi-national research team to study migration from Mexico to the United States (1994–97). He is the author of four books as well as a number of articles published in academic journals and edited volumes. His most recent book is *Una ciudad agrícola: Zamora. [An Agricultural City: Zamora]*.

RODRIGO VILLAR is an independent researcher on the issues of civil society, participation, and advocacy. He has served as a consultant for several national and international organizations. The Local Associate for Colombia, he is based at the Colombian Confederation of NGOs for the purposes of this project.

HELENA WOLEKOVÁ is the Local Associate for Slovakia and Program Director at the Social Policy Analysis Center (S.P.A.C.E. Foundation) in Bratislava, where she conducts research on social welfare and the nonprofit sector. She holds a doctorate in Sociology and also lectures at the Comenius University in Bratislava. Among other publications, she is the co-author of *Social Policy in Slovakia*.

JAN JAKUB WYGNAŃSKI is a sociologist and co-Local Associate for Poland. An activist of the NGO movement in Poland, President of the Forum of Nongovernmental Initiatives, and Board Member of the Stefan Batory Foundation, he has been the Director of the KLON/JAWOR Data Base of Polish NGOs since 1992.

NAOTO YAMAUCHI is co-Local Associate for Japan and Associate Professor of Public Economics at the Osaka School of International Public Policy, Osaka University. Former Senior Economist at the Economic Planning Agency of the Japanese government, he was Visiting Fellow at Yale University from 1997 to 1998. He received a B.A. from Osaka University and a M.Sc. from the London School of Economics. His research focuses on the economic analysis of the nonprofit sector, especially the estimation of the impact of taxation on giving and volunteering, and the study of microeconomic behavior of nonprofit hospitals and schools.

ANNETTE ZIMMER, co-Local Associate for Germany, is Professor of Social Policy and Comparative Politics at the Department of Political Science of the University of Münster in Germany. Prior to this, she taught at the University of Kassel, was Visiting Fellow at Yale University and, most recently, DAAD-Visiting Professor of German and European Studies at the University of Toronto. Author of numerous publications on the nonprofit sector, she received her doctoral degree from the University of Heidelberg.

Preface

This book summarizes the initial results of the second phase of an ambitious project designed to shed important new light on a major social force that has increasingly made itself felt in recent years in countries throughout the world—the thousands of private community groups, health clinics, schools, day care centers, environmental organizations, social clubs, development organizations, cultural institutions, professional associations, consumer groups, and similar entities that comprise what is increasingly coming to be known as the private nonprofit or "civil society" sector.

Despite their considerable diversity and the variations that characterize them in different countries, these entities also share some important features that justify treating them as a distinguishable social "sector": they are all organizations that operate outside the state apparatus, that do not distribute profits, and that citizens are free to join or not join to pursue common purposes.

The work that we have undertaken in the Johns Hopkins Comparative Nonprofit Sector Project, and that is partially covered in the present volume, seeks to answer three basic questions about this important set of institutions:

1. *What is their basic scale, structure, and revenue base and how does this vary from country to country?*
2. *What accounts for the differences that exist in the scale, structure, and revenue base of this set of institutions from place to place? What factors seem to encourage or retard their development?*
3. *Finally, what difference do these entities seem to make? What are their special contributions?*

The present book presents the answers that have emerged to the first of these questions in 22 out of a total of 42 countries now covered by this project. Included are countries in Western Europe, Central Europe, Asia, Latin America, and North America where work on the current phase of our project got under way the earliest.[1] Subsequent products will fill in the descriptive data for the remaining countries and then explore the answers to the other two questions, those relating to the *causes* of the patterns we are uncovering and the *contributions* that this set of institutions is making.[2]

My hope is that this volume will constitute the first in a biennial series of reports that will document the scale and structure of the nonprofit sector throughout the world and thus provide the authoritative source of basic information that has long been needed in this field.[3]

The information presented in this volume is the product of the collaborative effort of nearly 150 researchers and over 300 advisors throughout the world. Local Associates in each of the project countries took an active part in the development of the basic definition that determined the focus of the work, helped devise the guidance and information-collection protocols, and then had primary responsibility for applying these protocols and interpreting the results in their respective countries. The result, I believe, is a body of material that is systematically comparative but that still retains its sensitivity to local realities and circumstances.

As overall director of this project, I want to express my gratitude to the extraordinary team of researchers that has worked with me on this project both at the Johns Hopkins Center for Civil Society Studies and in the various project countries. This includes Dr. Helmut K. Anheier, Ms. Regina List, Dr. Stefan Toepler, and Dr. Wojciech Sokolowski at Johns Hopkins and the network of Local Associates in the project countries recorded in Appendix E and in the authorship credits for the individual chapters.

I also want to express my appreciation to the extraordinary array of funding agencies that came together to make this project possible. Included here were well over 50 foundations, government agencies, and corporations in five of the seven continents of the world. A list of these funders can be found inside the back cover. Thanks are also due to the distinguished International Advisory Committee to the Project and to the national advisory committees made up of nonprofit, foundation, corporate, and government leaders in each of the project countries (see Appendix D). Finally, I am grateful for the critical assistance of Mimi Bilzor, who coordinated the production of this book; for the energies of Amanda Briggs, Armen Carapetian, Doug Hess, Susan Mitchell, Toni Nunes, and Wendell Phipps, without whom the book would not have been brought together; and for the design and production work of Brushwood Graphics of Baltimore, Maryland.

No project of this scope and complexity can reasonably aspire to being the "last word" on a topic as vast as the one this book addresses, particularly given the rudimentary nature of knowledge in this field in many of the countries covered. While we have attempted to be thorough and precise, therefore, we are also well aware of the limitations that nevertheless attend work of this sort at this stage of the development of this field. Thus, for example, while we have attempted to cover the informal parts of the nonprofit sector as well as the formal ones, and designed special surveys of individual giving and volunteering in order to capture it, financial limitations in some sites made it impossible to treat this dimension of civil society activity as fully as we would have liked in all countries. Similarly, while we sought to include religious worship institutions within the project's focus, practical considerations often made this impossible in particular sites. Even for the formal portions of the sector and the more explicit dimensions of activity, moreover, frustrating gaps in coverage often posed difficult methodological challenges.

In view of these challenges, we have presented our data in a way that offers maximum flexibility to readers. Thus, for example, we report employment with and without volunteers. Similarly, we present the sector with and without the religious worship activities. Readers can therefore choose for themselves which definition of the sector, and which dimensions, are of greatest relevance bearing in mind the different levels of coverage we were able to attain for the different variables.

Even with the best of intentions, however, errors doubtless remain. As overall director of the effort, responsibility for any such errors is ultimately mine alone. I accept it gladly knowing that future work in this field can benefit as much from the errors we may have made as by the breakthroughs we may have achieved.

Lester M. Salamon
Director, Johns Hopkins Comparative
Nonprofit Sector Project
Baltimore, Maryland
June 29, 1999

ENDNOTES

1. An initial phase of this project covered eight countries in depth and another five countries only partially. For a summary of the findings of this phase of project work, see: Lester M. Salamon and Helmut K. Anheier, *The emerging nonprofit sector: An overview* (Manchester, U.K.: Manchester University Press, 1996).

2. At least one project publication exploring the reasons for the variations in scope and structure of the nonprofit sector in different countries is already available. See: Lester M. Salamon and Helmut K. Anheier, "Social Origins of Civil Society: Explaining the Nonprofit Sector Cross-Nationally," *Voluntas,* Vol. 9, No. 3 (September 1998), pp. 213–248.

3. To facilitate this process, the United Nations Statistics Division has invited the Johns Hopkins Comparative Nonprofit Sector Project to assist in the formulation of a Handbook for possible distribution to statistical offices throughout the world to guide regular national data gathering on this sector. For a discussion of this project, see: "Project Announcement: Toward an Official Global Economic Data System on Nonprofit Institutions." *Review of Income and Wealth,* Vol. 44, No. 4 (December 1998), 593–5.

PART 1

Comparative Overview

The following chapter presents an overview of the scope, size, structure, and funding base of the nonprofit sector in twenty-two countries in North America, South America, Europe, Asia, and the Middle East. In addition, it documents recent trends in sector size and composition in a subset of these countries.

Among other things, the results demonstrate that the nonprofit sector is a far more significant economic force around the world than is commonly understood, that substantial differences exist in both the overall size and the composition of this sector in different countries, that private philanthropy plays a far less significant role in the financing of this sector than either fees or public sector support, and that the sector has grown substantially in recent years in most of the countries for which trend data are available.

CHAPTER 1

Civil Society in Comparative Perspective[1]

Lester M. Salamon, Helmut K. Anheier, and Associates

BACKGROUND

Recent years have witnessed a considerable surge of interest throughout the world in the broad range of social institutions that operate outside the confines of the market and the state. Known variously as the "nonprofit," the "voluntary," the "civil society," the "third," or the "independent" sector, this set of institutions includes within it a sometimes bewildering array of entities—hospitals, universities, social clubs, professional organizations, day care centers, environmental groups, family counseling agencies, sports clubs, job training centers, human rights organizations, and many more. Despite their diversity, however, these entities also share some common features.[2] In particular, they are:

- *Organizations,* i.e., they have an institutional presence and structure;
- *Private,* i.e., they are institutionally separate from the state;
- *Not profit distributing,* i.e., they do not return profits to their managers or to a set of "owners";
- *Self-governing,* i.e., they are fundamentally in control of their own affairs; and

Global Civil Society: Dimensions of the Nonprofit Sector by Lester M. Salamon, Helmut K. Anheier, Regina List, Stefan Toepler, S. Wojciech Sokolowski and Associates. Baltimore, MD: Johns Hopkins Center for Civil Society Studies, 1999.

- *Voluntary,* i.e., membership in them is not legally required and they attract some level of voluntary contribution of time or money.

The "global associational revolution"

That these organizations have attracted so much attention in recent years is due in large part to the widespread "crisis of the state" that has been underway for two decades or more in virtually every part of the world, a crisis that has manifested itself in a serious questioning of traditional social welfare policies in much of the developed North, in disappointments over the progress of state-led development in significant parts of the developing South, in the collapse of the experiment in state socialism in Central and Eastern Europe, and in concerns about the environmental degradation that continues to threaten human health and safety everywhere. In addition to stimulating support for market-oriented economic policies, this questioning of the state has focused new attention, and new expectations, on the civil society organizations that operate in societies throughout the world.

Also contributing to the attention these organizations are attracting is the sheer growth in their number and scale. Indeed, a veritable "global associational revolution" appears to be underway, a massive upsurge of organized private, voluntary activity in literally every corner of the world.[3] Prompted in part by growing doubts about the capability of the state to cope on its own with the social welfare, developmental, and environmental problems that face nations today, this growth of civil society organizations has been stimulated as well by the communications revolution of the past two decades and by the striking expansion of educated middle class elements who are frustrated by the lack of economic and political expression that has confronted them in many places.

Finally, a new element has surfaced more recently to increase further the attention that has been focused on nonprofit or civil society organizations. This is the growing questioning of the "neo-liberal consensus," sometimes called the "Washington consensus," that has guided global economic policy over the past two decades. This consensus essentially held that the problems facing both developed and developing societies at the present time could most effectively be approached through the simple expedient of unleashing and encouraging private markets. In the wake of the worldwide financial crisis and continuing social distress in many regions, however, this consensus has come under increasingly severe attack, even from some of its most ardent advocates. As World Bank Chief Economist Joseph Stiglitz recently put it:

"The policies advanced by the Washington consensus . . . are hardly complete and sometimes misguided . . . It is not just economic policies and human capital, but the quality of a country's institutions that determine economic outcomes."[4]

Reflecting this, political leaders in many parts of the world have begun searching for alternative ways to combine the virtues of the market with the advantages of broader social protections, a search that is evident in Mr. Tony Blair's emphasis on a "Third Way" in the U.K., Gerhard Schröder's "New Middle" in Germany, and French Prime Minister Lionel Jospin's summary declaration: "Yes to a market economy, no to a market society."

Because of their unique position outside the market and the state, their generally smaller scale, their connections to citizens, their flexibility, their capacity to tap private initiative in support of public purposes, and their newly rediscovered contributions to building "social capital," civil society organizations have surfaced as strategically important participants in this search for a "middle way" between sole reliance on the market and sole reliance on the state that now seems to be increasingly underway.

The Johns Hopkins Comparative Nonprofit Sector Project

The nonprofit sector's ability to participate in this search as a full-fledged partner has been seriously impeded, however, by a gross lack of basic information about this sector and how it operates. Despite some considerable improvement over the past five years, including the completion of the first phase of the present project and the launching of empirical studies by Eurostat in response to the Commission of the European Union, the nonprofit sector remains the "lost continent" on the social landscape of modern society, invisible to most policymakers, business leaders, and the press, and even to many people within the sector itself.

- **Objectives.** It was to fill this gap in basic knowledge and put the non-profit sector on the economic map of the world that the project reported on here was undertaken. More specifically, this project seeks to:

  Document the scope, structure, financing, and role of the nonprofit sector for the first time in solid empirical terms in a significant number of countries scattered widely throughout the world;

  Explain why this sector varies in size from place to place and identify the factors that seem to encourage or retard its development;

  Evaluate the impact these organizations are having and the contribution they make;

Publicize the existence of this set of institutions and increase public awareness of them; and

Build local capacity to carry on this work into the future.

- **Approach.** To pursue these objectives, this project adopted an approach that embodies six key features:

It is comparative, covering a wide assortment of countries. A first phase of the project, completed in 1994, focused in-depth on eight countries (the U.S., the U.K., France, Germany, Italy, Sweden, Hungary, and Japan).[5] The current phase is updating information on many of these original countries and has extended the analysis to 28 countries in all. Of these, 22 have completed the basic data-gathering and are covered in this volume, including nine Western European countries, four other developed countries, four Central and Eastern European countries, and five Latin American countries (see Table 1.1).[6]

It is collaborative, enlisting local analysts in each country to carry out the data gathering and analysis (see Appendix E). Altogether, approximately 150 researchers have been involved in the effort.

It is consultative, utilizing an International Advisory Committee of prominent nonprofit, philanthropic, and business leaders (see Appendix D) and relying on local advisory committees in each country to help interpret and publicize the results. Altogether, more than 300

Table 1.1 Country coverage of Phase II of the Johns Hopkins Comparative Nonprofit Sector Project

Western Europe		Central and Eastern Europe
Austria	Ireland	Czech Republic
Belgium	Netherlands	Hungary
Finland	Spain	Romania
France	United Kingdom	Slovakia
Germany		

Other Developed	Latin America
Australia	Argentina
Israel	Brazil
Japan	Colombia
United States	Mexico
	Peru

nonprofit, philanthropy, government, and business leaders are taking part in the project through these committees.

It utilizes a common definition worked out in collaboration with the local associates and focused on the common features outlined above. Included, therefore, is a broad range of organizations spanning a wide assortment of fields, as outlined in Table 1.2 and Appendix A.

It utilizes a common information-gathering approach based on a set of collaboratively developed field guides. This modular approach relies heavily on existing national income data sources such as employment surveys, estimates of the relationship of expenditures to wages by industry, and other similar data (for more information on data assembly, see Appendix C).

It is quantitative, seeking not just general impressions but solid empirical data on this set of organizations, including data on employment, volunteers, expenditures, and revenues.

- **Coverage.** The present chapter summarizes some of the major results of this second phase of project work, focusing on the major empirical findings of the descriptive portion of the effort in 22 countries. Subsequent publications will include data on the remaining countries and go behind the basic descriptive statistics to explain the patterns that are apparent and to evaluate the contributions that nonprofit organizations are making.

Unless otherwise noted, all data here relate to 1995, and monetary values are expressed in U.S. dollars. In most countries, data were collected on both the formal and informal dimensions of nonprofit activity, and results are reported separately for paid staff only and for paid staff *and* volunteers. Similarly, both secular and religiously based or affiliated organizations, including religious congregations, were covered in most countries. When denominational organizations were mainly

---

Table 1.2   Fields of nonprofit activity covered by Phase II of the Johns Hopkins Comparative Nonprofit Sector Project

1. Culture	7. Civic and advocacy
2. Education and research	8. Philanthropy
3. Health	9. International
4. Social services	10. Religious congregations
5. Environment	11. Business and professional, unions
6. Development	12. Other

devoted to human service provision, they were assigned to the appropriate service field (e.g. health, education, social services), along with the secular service providers. The organizations engaged primarily in religious worship or promotion of religion *per se* (e.g., parishes, synagogues, mosques, shrines) were allocated to a special "religion" category (ICNPO Group 10). Data on the latter were not available for all of the countries covered here and are therefore reported separately in the discussion that follows.

PRINCIPAL FINDINGS

The major findings emerging from this work on the scope, structure, financing, and role of the nonprofit sector internationally can be grouped under five major headings.

1. A major economic force

In the first place, aside from its social and political importance, the nonprofit sector turns out to be a significant economic force in most of the regions examined, accounting for significant shares of employment and of national expenditures. More specifically:

- **A $1.1 trillion industry.** Even excluding religious congregations, the nonprofit sector in the 22 countries we examined is a $1.1 trillion industry that employs close to 19 million full-time equivalent paid workers. Nonprofit expenditures in these countries thus average 4.6 percent of the gross domestic product,[7] and nonprofit employment is nearly 5 percent of all nonagricultural employment, 10 percent of all service employment, and 27 percent of all public sector employment (see Table 1.3).

Table 1.3   The nonprofit sector in 22 countries, 1995

$1.1 trillion in expenditures
 — 4.6 percent of GDP

19.0 million paid employees
 — 5 percent of total nonagricultural employment
 — 10 percent of total service employment
 — 27 percent of public employment

Source: The Johns Hopkins Comparative Nonprofit Sector Project

- **The world's eighth largest economy.** To put these figures into context, if the nonprofit sector in these countries were a separate national economy, it would be the eighth largest economy in the world, ahead of Brazil, Russia, Canada, and Spain (see Table 1.4).
- **More employees than in largest private firms.** Put somewhat differently, nonprofit employment in these countries easily outdistances the combined employment in the largest private business in each country by a factor of six (19.0 million nonprofit employees vs. 3.3 million combined employees in the largest private enterprise in each of these 22 countries) (see Figure 1.1).
- **Outdistances numerous industries.** Indeed, more people work in the nonprofit sector in these 22 countries than in the utilities industry, the

Table 1.4 If the nonprofit sector were a country . . .

Country	GDP (trillion $)
U.S.	$7.2
Japan	5.1
China	2.8
Germany	2.2
France	1.5
U.K.	1.1
Italy	1.1
Nonprofit Expenditures (22 countries)	**1.1**
Brazil	0.7
Russia	0.7
Spain	0.6
Canada	0.5

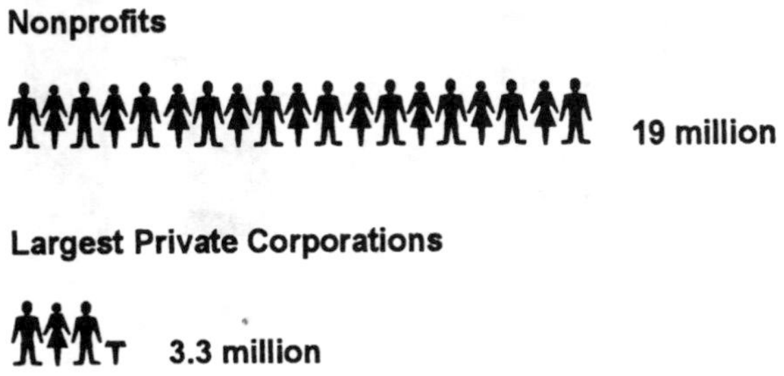

Nonprofits

19 million

Largest Private Corporations

3.3 million

Figure 1.1 Employment in nonprofits vs. largest firm (22 countries)
Source: The Johns Hopkins Comparative Nonprofit Sector Project

textile manufacturing industry, the paper and printing industry, or the chemical manufacturing industry in these same countries, and almost as many work in the nonprofit sector as work in transport and communications (see Figure 1.2).

- **Volunteer inputs.** Even this does not capture the full scope of the non-profit sector, for this sector also attracts a considerable amount of *volunteer effort*. Indeed, an average of 28 percent of the population in these countries contributes their time to nonprofit organizations. This translates into another 10.6 million full-time equivalent employees, which boosts the total number of full-time equivalent employees of nonprofit organizations to 29.6 million. With volunteers included, the nonprofit sector thus represents, on average, 7 percent of the total nonagricultural employment in these countries, 14 percent of the service employment, and a striking 41 percent of the public sector employment (see Figure 1.3).

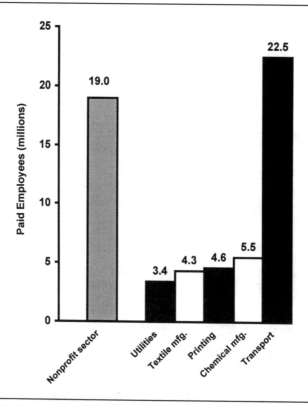

Figure 1.2   Nonprofit employment in context, 1995

Source: The Johns Hopkins Comparative Nonprofit Sector Project

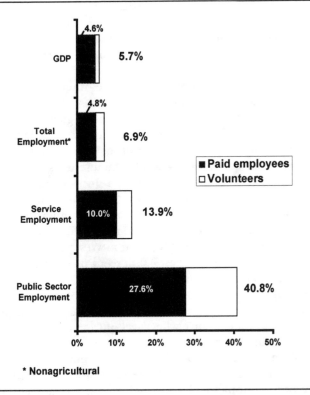

Figure 1.3   Nonprofits with and without volunteers, 1995, as a % of . . .
Source: The Johns Hopkins Comparative Nonprofit Sector Project

- **Religion.** The inclusion of religious congregations, moreover, would boost these totals further. Thus, in the 16 countries for which we were able to compile data on the activities of religious congregations (all but Hungary, Belgium, Spain, Colombia, Mexico, and Peru), the inclusion of these data adds approximately 1.5 million paid full-time equivalent employees to the nonprofit sector, an increase of roughly 7.5 percent over the amounts without religion.[8] With this religious employment included, the nonprofit share of total nonagricultural employment in these 16 countries increases from 5.3 percent to 5.6 percent. With religious volunteering included as well, the share rises from 7.8 percent to 8.5 percent.

2. Great variations in size among countries and regions

While the nonprofit sector is a significant economic force, it neverthe-less varies considerably in size from place to place.

- **Larger in more developed countries.** Generally speaking, the nonprofit sector is larger in the more developed countries and much less in evidence in Latin America and Central and Eastern Europe. Thus, compared to an average of 4.8 percent for all the countries, nonprofit organizations account for about 7 percent of the nonagricultural labor force in Western Europe and in the other developed countries this project examined, but only 2.2 percent in Latin America and 1.1 percent in Central and Eastern Europe (see Figure 1.4). Evidently, the scale of the nonprofit sector may have as much to do with the availability of resources as the presence of social or economic needs.

- **Margins widen with volunteers.** This picture does not change much, moreover, when volunteers are added. Indeed, to some extent the margin widens, at least between the developed countries and Latin America, and between Western Europe and other developed countries. Thus, with volunteers included, nonprofit organizations account for 10.3 percent of total employment in Western Europe, 9.4 percent in other developed countries, 3.0 percent in Latin America, and 1.7 percent in Central Europe (see Figure 1.4). Viewed in perspective, therefore, with volunteers included, Western Europe emerges as the region with the most highly developed voluntary and nonprofit sector. Also striking is the relatively low level of formal volunteering the data reveal in Latin America.

- **End of the myth of U.S. dominance.** This point is even more apparent in Figure 1.5, which records the level of nonprofit employment as a share of total nonagricultural employment for each country. As this figure shows, several Western European countries (the Netherlands, Ireland, and Belgium), as well as one other developed country (Israel), have larger nonprofit sectors measured as a share of total employment than does the United States. In other words, the United States, long regarded as the seedbed of nonprofit activity, does not have the world's largest nonprofit sector after all, at least when measured as a share of total employment.[9] At the same time, while a number of Western European countries exceed the United States and the all-country average in nonprofit employment as a share of total employment, several others (Finland, Austria, Spain, Germany, and France) and at least one other developed country (Japan) fall very near or below the all-country average.[10]

- **Impact of volunteers.** The inclusion of volunteers would lift two of the Western European countries (France and Germany) further above the all-country average, but the rest of this pattern would remain largely the same.

- **Inclusion of religious worship activities.** The inclusion of the worship activities of religious congregations does not change this overall picture

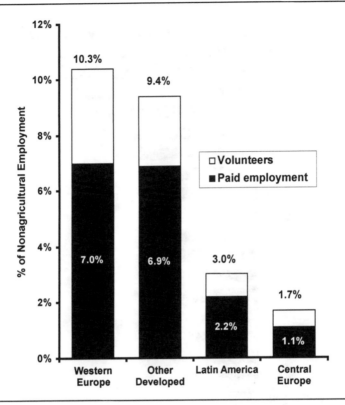

Figure 1.4   Nonprofit share of employment, with and without volunteers, by region, 1995

Source: The Johns Hopkins Comparative Nonprofit Sector Project

either. Although such employment boosts the nonprofit share of total employment by 1 percentage point in the U.S. (from 7.8 percent to 8.8 percent), elsewhere the change is much smaller. Even so, with religious worship included, U.S. nonprofit employment still remains below the level in the Netherlands (12.7 percent), Ireland (12.2 percent), and Israel (9.3 percent). When volunteering in religious congregations is factored in, the overall picture changes only slightly, though under these circumstances the U.S. moves ahead of Israel (11.1 percent) but remains behind the Netherlands (19.4 percent) and Ireland (15.0 percent).

- **Government social welfare spending and nonprofit size.** One possible explanation for these variations is the presence or absence of sizable government social welfare protections. According to a popular line of thought, the greater the scale of government social welfare protections,

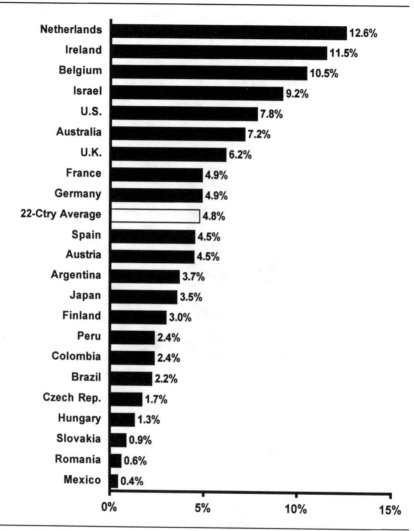

Figure 1.5 Nonprofit share of total paid employment, by country, 1995
Source: The Johns Hopkins Comparative Nonprofit Sector Project

the smaller the nonprofit sector that can be expected. In fact, however, data on the 22 countries studied give no support to this theory. Among the eleven countries with relatively high levels of government social welfare spending (i.e., above the 22-country mean), five had relatively small nonprofit sectors (i.e., lower employment than the 22-country average) while six had relatively large ones. On the other hand, among the 11

Table 1.5 Relationship between government social welfare spending and nonprofit size

Government Social Welfare Spending	Nonprofit Share of Employment (No. of countries)	
	Small	Large
High	5	6
Low	8	3

▩ Outcome predicted by theory

Source: The Johns Hopkins Comparative Nonprofit Sector Project

countries that have relatively low levels of government welfare protections, eight had relatively small nonprofit sectors. By contrast, only three had relatively large nonprofit sectors. Thus, as shown in Table 1.5, in more than half of these cases the outcome contradicts the theory. Evidently, something more complex than the relationship posited in this theory is determining the variation in nonprofit scale from place to place.[11]

3. Welfare services dominate

Despite differences in scale from place to place, the nonprofit sector has certain broad similarities in internal structure and composition, though these, too, differ somewhat from place to place.

- **Two-thirds of employment in three fields.** In the first place, it turns out that two-thirds of all nonprofit employment is concentrated in the three traditional fields of welfare services: education, with 30 percent of the total; health, with 20 percent; and social services, with 18 percent (see Figure 1.6). The field of recreation and culture, moreover, is not far behind with 14 percent of total nonprofit employment.
- **Pattern shifts with volunteers.** This pattern changes considerably when volunteer inputs are factored in. Nearly three-fifths (55 percent) of volunteer time goes into two principal fields: recreation, including sports; and social services. In addition, environment, civic, and development organizations attract a significant share of the time of volunteers. With volunteers included, therefore, the proportion of all nonprofit

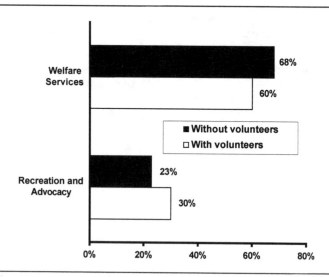

Figure 1.6   Share of nonprofit employment in selected fields, with and without volunteers, 1995 (22-country average)

Source: The Johns Hopkins Comparative Nonprofit Sector Project

employment in the three fields of health, education, and social services falls from 68 percent to under 60 percent while the share in culture and recreation, environment, development, and advocacy increases from 23 percent to 30 percent (see Figure 1.6).

- **Significant variations by region.** Despite some general similarities, the composition of the nonprofit sector also seems to vary considerably by region. Thus, as shown in Figure 1.7:

In *Western Europe,* the dominance of welfare services in nonprofit employment is particularly marked. On average, three-fourths of all nonprofit employees in the Western European countries examined work in education, health, or social service organizations. This reflects the historic role that the Catholic and Protestant churches have long played in the education and social service fields in Western Europe. In Ireland, for example, where Catholic influence is particularly strong, employment in nonprofit schools alone accounts for 6 percent of the nonagricultural employment in the country. Elsewhere, the Catholic Church-inspired doctrine of "subsidiarity," coupled with strong worker pressures for expanded social welfare protections, helped shape the evolution of social policy. Under this concept, which is especially influential in Germany, the Netherlands, Belgium, and, to a lesser extent, Austria and Spain, nonprofit associations are assumed to be the first line of defense for coping with social welfare problems,

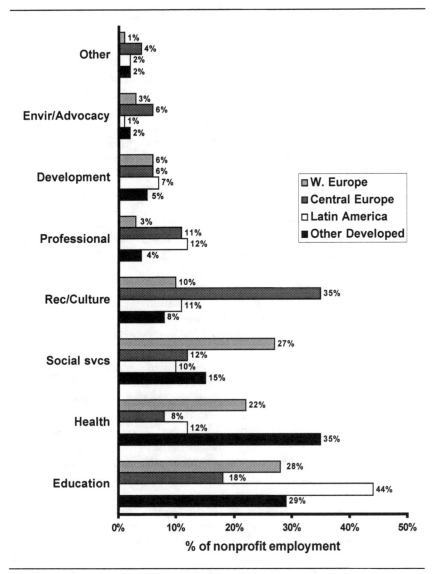

Figure 1.7 Composition of nonprofit employment, by region, 1995
Source: The Johns Hopkins Comparative Nonprofit Sector Project

and state involvement, when it occurs, is expected to take place with and through such groups to the extent possible. Significant nonprofit organizations have consequently grown up in these fields, many of them affiliated with religious groups, and in some places, the workers' movement. While nonprofit organizations operate in other fields as well, such as culture and recreation, environment, development, advocacy, and business and professional, their share of total nonprofit employment in these fields in this region is considerably smaller (for further detail, see Appendix B: Table 1).

With volunteers factored in, however, the welfare services dominance declines somewhat in Western Europe. This reflects the substantial involvement of volunteers in sports and recreation, as well as in civic and advocacy activities in this region. Thus, with volunteers included, the welfare services share of total nonprofit employment declines from 77 percent to 62 percent, while the culture and recreation share nearly doubles from 10 percent to 19 percent and the environment/civic and advocacy share goes from 3.3 percent to 6.1 percent.

In *Central Europe,* a quite different dynamic seems to be at work. In this region, recreation and culture play a much more important part in the employment base of the nonprofit sector. As shown in Figure 1.7, more than a third of the full-time equivalent workers in the nonprofit sector in these countries is employed in culture and recreation associations. This very likely reflects the heavy subsidization of such associations during the Communist era. The resulting organizations thus had a comparative advantage in making the transition to the post-Communist era. Indeed, they have often managed to retain their prior state assets. Also notable is the sizable 11 percent of all nonprofit employment in Central and Eastern Europe in business and professional associations, again partly a reflection of the Communist past, when the state subsidized writers' unions, engineers' associations, and many other professional groups. Finally, Central Europe is also notable for the significant scale of employment in nonprofit environmental and advocacy organizations. These seem to be newer organizations that emerged as part of the transition to democracy and attracted Western funding. Many of the earliest nonprofit organizations in this region, in fact, were environmental groups mobilizing mass support to deal with the deteriorating environmental conditions in the region. By contrast, the traditional welfare services—health, education, and social services—still engage much smaller shares of the nonprofit workforce in Central and Eastern Europe. This is because the state remains a much more favored vehicle for social welfare provision in this region and the tradition of subsidiarity so evident in Western Europe retains only a faint echo in Central Europe.

When volunteers are factored into the equation, this Central and Eastern European pattern changes only marginally. This is so because a third of the volunteer input goes into culture and recreation organizations, which also absorb the largest single part of the paid workers.

The one major deviation is in the area of social services, which absorbs 28 percent of the volunteer time in the region as compared with only 12 percent of the paid employment. With volunteers included, therefore, the social services share of nonprofit employment in Central and Eastern Europe rises from 12 percent to 18 percent, close to what it is, as a share of the total, though not in absolute scale, in the U.K. and Japan.

In *Latin America,* education dominates the employment base of the nonprofit sector, whereas nonprofit employment in the other fields of social welfare is more limited (see Figure 1.7). This reflects again the prominent role of the Catholic Church in the education field in this region, but also the middle and upper-class tilt to the more formal components of the nonprofit sector in the region, since private education has tended to be heavily financed by fees and therefore available mostly to the upper and middle classes. The unusually large share of nonprofit employment in professional, business, and labor organizations also supports this interpretation.

At the same time, an above-average component of development organizations is also evident in the Latin American data. What is more, with volunteering included, this component turns out to be even larger. Thus, on average, 44 percent of all volunteer time in the Latin American countries we examined goes for social service activities, some of it through religiously affiliated assistance agencies, but increasingly through community-based development organizations. Another 17 percent of volunteer time goes into development organizations *per se*. With volunteer time included, therefore, the social service share of total nonprofit employment increases from 10 percent to 17 percent, and the development share increases from 7 percent to 10 percent. What this suggests is a dualistic nonprofit sector in this region, with a more formal component oriented to middle class professionals, and a smaller, more informal segment oriented toward the poor.

Finally, in the *other developed countries* covered by this project (the United States, Japan, Australia, and Israel), the major area of nonprofit employment is in the health field, which accounts, on average, for 35 percent of the total, followed closely by education with 29 percent. This result is largely a reflection of the situation in the U.S. and Japan, in both of which nonprofit activity is heavily concentrated in health and higher education. Thus in both of these countries, health alone accounts for nearly half (46 and 47 percent, respectively) of all nonprofit employment, and education, mostly at the higher education level, for another 22 percent. By contrast, the social service field, which accounts for 27 percent of nonprofit employment in Western Europe, absorbs only 14 to 17 percent in the U.S. and Japan. This suggests a fairly strong amenities and middle-class orientation to the nonprofit sector in these two countries. The situation in the other two countries included in this grouping—Israel and Australia—differs somewhat from this U.S. and Japanese pattern. In Israel, the relative positions of education and health in the employment base of the nonprofit sector are reversed, with education—mostly elementary and secondary—accounting for 50 percent and health for 27 percent. In Australia, the social welfare complex also dominates the nonprofit scene, but here the three main components—health, education, and social services—are closely balanced, with 19 to 23 percent of the total employment embraced within each.

With volunteers included, the amenities focus of the nonprofit sector, particularly in the U.S., is moderated considerably. Nearly 40 percent of the considerable volunteer activity that takes place in the United States flows to the social services area, and another 10 percent to civic and advocacy activity. With volunteers included, therefore, the health dominance of the American nonprofit sector declines somewhat and social services emerges as the second largest type of nonprofit activity as measured by full-time equivalent employment. Australia, too, exhibits a substantial amount of social service volunteering, but here sports and recreation absorbs the largest share of volunteer time.

- **Five patterns.** More generally, it is possible to discern five more or less distinct patterns of nonprofit structure among the 22 countries examined, as reflected in Table 1.6. To some extent, these patterns follow regional lines. But they also reflect special national particularities that go beyond regional norms. In particular:

Education-dominant model. Perhaps the most common pattern of nonprofit activity is that embodied in the "education dominant" model. Eight of the 22 countries adhered to this model, including 4 of the 5 Latin American countries as well as Belgium, Ireland, Israel, and the U.K. The distinctive feature of this model is the heavy concentration of nonprofit employment in the education sphere. An average of 48 percent of all nonprofit employment is in this field among these countries. For the Latin American countries as well as Belgium and Ireland, this reflects the prominent presence of the Catholic Church and its involvement in elementary and secondary education. Religiously affiliated education also explains the substantial nonprofit presence in the education field in Israel, though here it is Judaism rather than Catholicism that is responsible. In the U.K., by contrast, the concen-

Table 1.6   Patterns of nonprofit structure, by country

Pattern*	Country	
Education-Dominant	Argentina	Israel
	Belgium	Mexico
	Brazil	Peru
	Ireland	U.K.
Health-Dominant	Japan	
	Netherlands	
	U.S.	
Social Services-Dominant	Austria	
	France	
	Germany	
	Spain	
Culture/Recreation-Dominant	Czech Republic	
	Hungary	
	Romania	
	Slovakia	
Balanced	Australia	
	Colombia	
	Finland	

*Based on paid employment
Source: The Johns Hopkins Comparative Nonprofit Sector Project

tration of nonprofit employment in the education field occurs at the higher education level and reflects the recent transformation of significant segments of the U.K. higher education system from public into private, nonprofit status during the Thatcher era.

While the countries that adhere to this pattern share a common concentration of nonprofit employment in the education field, they differ in terms of where the balance of nonprofit employment is concentrated. For the U.K., for example, culture and recreation absorbs a quarter of the employment. For Ireland, Israel, and Belgium, however, health accounts for 27 to 30 percent of the employment. And for Mexico, business and professional organizations are the second largest field of nonprofit action. In short, while these countries have some key features in common, they also diverge along other dimensions.

Health-dominant model. A second distinguishable model of nonprofit structure is that evident in the United States, Japan, and the Netherlands. What distinguishes this model is the extent of nonprofit employment in the health field. On average, 45 percent of nonprofit employment is concentrated in this field in these countries. This reflects the unusual private character of health care in these countries. In addition, these three countries also share a sizable nonprofit presence in the field of education, though this is largely in higher education in the U.S. and Japan, and in elementary and secondary education in the case of the Netherlands.

Social services-dominant model. A third pattern of nonprofit activity finds expression in the four Western European countries of Austria, France, Germany, and Spain. These countries, too, share a common background of extensive Catholic influence. However, for a variety of reasons, religious influence has been weakened in the education sphere and remains strong chiefly in the field of personal social services. On average, about 44 percent of all nonprofit employment is thus in the social services field in these countries, though in two of the countries (France and Spain) a sizable nonprofit presence is also evident in education, and in a third (Germany) health almost equals social services as a focus of nonprofit employment.

Culture/recreation-dominant model. Much different yet is the model of nonprofit structure evident in the four Central European countries examined. As noted above, the largest portion of nonprofit employment in these countries is concentrated in culture and recreation. This reflects the heritage of the Communist era in these countries, during which sport and recreational associations were actively encouraged. This pattern also grows out of the transformation of cultural funds into foundations in the immediate aftermath of Communist control in several of these countries. The largest and most established nonprofit organizations in many of these countries, therefore, are traditional organizations with roots in the old order.

Balanced model. Finally, three countries exhibit a more "balanced" pattern of nonprofit employment, with no subsector clearly in the ascendance. In each of these countries (Australia, Colombia, and Finland), anywhere from 14 to 26 percent of total nonprofit employment is dedicated to the three fields of education, health, and social services; but no one of the fields claims more than 26 percent of the total.

- **No fundamental change with inclusion of religious worship activities.** The overall profile of the nonprofit sector does not change much, moreover, when the religious worship activities of religious congregations are included. As reflected in Figure 1.8, religious congregations account for approximately 6 percent of nonprofit employment on average in the 16 countries for which such data were compiled. With reli-

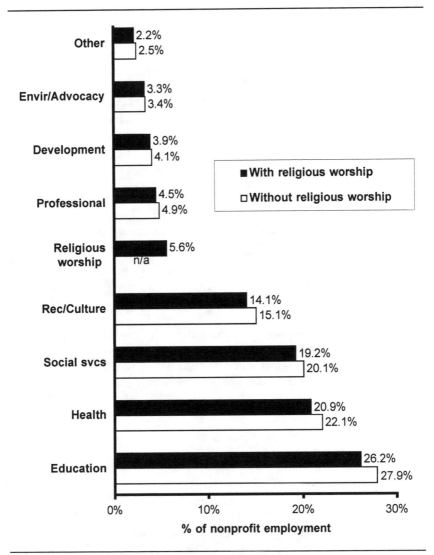

Figure 1.8   Nonprofit employment by field, with and without religious worship activities, 16 countries

Source: The Johns Hopkins Comparative Nonprofit Sector Project

gious worship included, therefore, the relative share of education, health, and social services in the employment base of the nonprofit sector declines somewhat from 70 percent to 66 percent—but it remains clearly dominant. Even in the United States, where religious congregations account for a larger share of total nonprofit employment than elsewhere (11 percent), health, education, and social services still remain the dominant fields when religious worship is included, accounting for 72 percent of the total sector employment.

In short, the nonprofit sector is not a single thing. Rather, it takes different forms in different places reflecting the particular constellation of cultural, historical, political, and economic forces that are at work. At the same time, these patterns are not wholly random. Rather, they take definable shapes where circumstances are similar.[12]

4. Most revenue from fees and public sector, not philanthropy

Not only does the nonprofit sector take different forms in different places, it also has a distinctive revenue structure. However, this structure differs from what conventional thinking often assumes. In particular:

- **Limited support from philanthropy.** Private philanthropy is hardly the major source of nonprofit sector income. To the contrary, as Figure 1.9 shows, private philanthropy—from individuals, corporations, and foundations combined—accounts for only 11 percent of nonprofit income on average.
- **Fees and public support.** By contrast, the major sources of nonprofit income are fees and public support. Fees and other commercial income alone account for nearly half (49 percent) of all nonprofit revenue, while public sector payments account for 40 percent (see Figure 1.9).

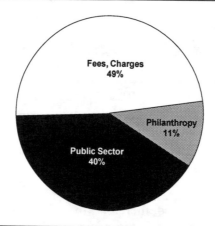

Figure 1.9 Sources of nonprofit revenue, 1995 (22-country average)
Source: The Johns Hopkins Comparative Nonprofit Sector Project

- **Variation among countries.** This general pattern holds up across most of the countries this project examined, though some significant variations are also apparent. In particular, as shown in Figure 1.10:

  Fee-dominant countries. Fee income is the dominant source of income for 13 of the 22 countries. The fee share of total revenue in these countries ranged from a high of 85 percent in Mexico to 47 percent in the Czech Republic. Generally speaking, fee income was especially important in Latin America, in Central and Eastern Europe, and in some of the developed countries outside of Western Europe (Australia, Japan, and the U.S.).

  This reflects, in part, the composition of the nonprofit sector, as will be noted more fully below. Under these circumstances, the scale of

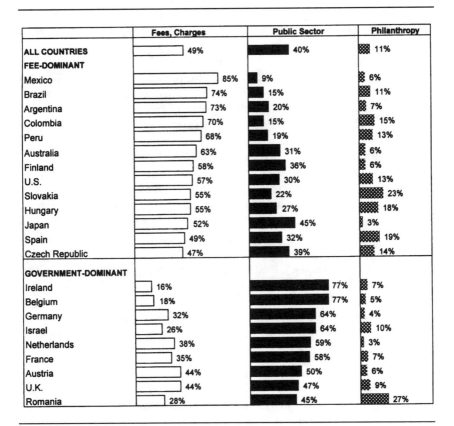

	Fees, Charges	Public Sector	Philanthropy
ALL COUNTRIES	49%	40%	11%
FEE-DOMINANT			
Mexico	85%	9%	6%
Brazil	74%	15%	11%
Argentina	73%	20%	7%
Colombia	70%	15%	15%
Peru	68%	19%	13%
Australia	63%	31%	6%
Finland	58%	36%	6%
U.S.	57%	30%	13%
Slovakia	55%	22%	23%
Hungary	55%	27%	18%
Japan	52%	45%	3%
Spain	49%	32%	19%
Czech Republic	47%	39%	14%
GOVERNMENT-DOMINANT			
Ireland	16%	77%	7%
Belgium	18%	77%	5%
Germany	32%	64%	4%
Israel	26%	64%	10%
Netherlands	38%	59%	3%
France	35%	58%	7%
Austria	44%	50%	6%
U.K.	44%	47%	9%
Romania	28%	45%	27%

Figure 1.10 Sources of nonprofit revenue, by country, 1995 (22 countries)

Source: The Johns Hopkins Comparative Nonprofit Sector Project

the nonprofit sector comes to depend on the scope of a private market for the services that nonprofits can provide.

A fee-dominant revenue structure is thus consistent with both relatively large and relatively small nonprofit sectors. Where the market is small, as in Central Europe and Latin America, dependence on fees translates into a small nonprofit sector. Where the market is large, as in Australia and the U.S., the nonprofit sector can be relatively large even though fees are the major source of income. To the extent that this model prevails, however, it puts serious limitations on the scope and nature of the nonprofit sector, pushing it in the direction of market forces.

Public sector-dominant countries. A significantly different pattern of nonprofit finance is apparent in the remaining nine countries (see Figure 1.10). In these countries the major source of nonprofit revenue is not fees and payments but public sector grants and contracts. Included here are third-party payments from public sector social security and health programs. Every one of the Western European countries except for Spain and Finland exhibits this pattern. As noted earlier, this reflects the tradition of subsidiarity built into European social policy, a tradition that acknowledges the important role of the state in financing social welfare services, but turns extensively to private, nonprofit organizations to deliver many of the services that result.

A similar pattern is also evident in Israel, where publicly enforced health benefits are channeled to essentially private health care providers. While similar relationships are evident in other countries (e.g., in the federally operated health insurance program for the elderly in the United States), the relative scope is far more extensive in these countries, where the public sector share of nonprofit revenues tends to exceed 50 percent, and often 60 percent, of the total. Significantly, moreover, the countries that have the largest nonprofit sectors seem to adhere universally to this pattern. This is true, for example, of Ireland, the Netherlands, Belgium, and Israel, the four countries that surpass the United States in the relative scope of nonprofit activity. Evidently, public sector support is a critical factor in the growth of nonprofit action.

Private philanthropy. Significantly, in no country is the nonprofit sector supported chiefly by private philanthropy. At the same time, private giving is quite important in a number of settings. Interestingly, this is particularly true in Central and Eastern Europe, where private giving generally accounts for about 21 percent of nonprofit revenue, considerably higher than for other regions. This paradoxical result likely reflects the residue of a long tradition of enterprise financing of key services for employees under the Communist era and the relatively limited scale of other support for nonprofit action in this region. Also at work in all likelihood is a significant level of outside philanthropic support to the incipient Central European nonprofit sector. Among the more developed countries, private giving is higher in the U.S. and Israel than in most of the other countries, but even here it does not exceed 13 percent of total income.

• **Variations among fields.** That the pattern of nonprofit finance varies among countries is at least partly a result of the fact that revenue sources vary considerably among different fields of nonprofit action, and these different fields are more or less prominent in different places. In particular:

Fee-dominant fields. In six of the 10 fields examined in depth, fees and service charges are the dominant source of nonprofit income (see Figure 1.11). This is understandable enough in the cases of business and professional organizations and recreation and culture. In the case of the development organizations, the explanation lies in the substantial number of housing organizations that are included within this category. So far as foundations are concerned, the chief source of revenue is earnings on endowments, which are treated here as earnings. The significant fee income for environmental organizations likely reflects the membership fees often collected by such organizations. Finally,

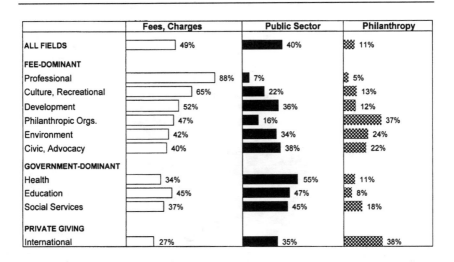

	Fees, Charges	Public Sector	Philanthropy
ALL FIELDS	49%	40%	11%
FEE-DOMINANT			
Professional	88%	7%	5%
Culture, Recreational	65%	22%	13%
Development	52%	36%	12%
Philanthropic Orgs.	47%	16%	37%
Environment	42%	34%	24%
Civic, Advocacy	40%	38%	22%
GOVERNMENT-DOMINANT			
Health	34%	55%	11%
Education	45%	47%	8%
Social Services	37%	45%	18%
PRIVATE GIVING			
International	27%	35%	38%

Figure 1.11   Sources of nonprofit revenue, by field, 1995

Source: The Johns Hopkins Comparative Nonprofit Sector Project

civic and advocacy organizations generate slightly more income from fees, including, for example, fees for legal services or membership dues, than from the public sector.

Public sector-dominant fields. In three of the 10 major fields of nonprofit action that were examined, by contrast, the major source of nonprofit income is not fees and charges but public sector support. This is especially true of the major fields of social welfare—health, education, and social services—where public sector support ranges anywhere from 45 percent to 55 percent of the total.

Private philanthropy-dominant fields. In at least one field—international assistance—private philanthropy is the dominant source of income, though it is a close second in one other—philanthropic intermediaries. What is more, private giving is also the principal source of income of religious congregations.

- **Revenue structure with volunteers.** The pattern of nonprofit revenue portrayed here changes significantly when volunteers are factored into the picture. Although the relative ranks of the three major sources of income do not change with volunteers included, the philanthropy proportion increases substantially, from 11 percent to 27 percent, and the fee and public sector proportions decline proportionally, to 41 percent and 32 percent, respectively, as shown in Figure 1.12. Because much of the volunteer input flows to sports and recreation organizations, the relative rankings of funding sources do not change significantly among the

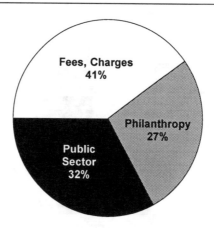

Figure 1.12   Sources of nonprofit revenue with volunteers, 1995 (22 countries)
Source: The Johns Hopkins Comparative Nonprofit Sector Project

different fields. At the same time, the fee dominance of the culture and recreation field declines significantly, from 65 percent to 48 percent, while the private giving share grows from 13 percent to 38 percent. In addition, four other fields become philanthropy-dominant once volunteers are included: environment, civic and advocacy, philanthropic intermediaries, and social services.

- **Modest change with inclusion of religious worship.** With the worship activities of religious congregations included, the general picture of nonprofit finance painted here changes only slightly. With regard to cash revenue, the inclusion of religious worship and religious congregations boosts the private philanthropy share of total revenue from an average of 10 percent in the 16 countries for which there are data to 12 percent. With congregational volunteers included as well, the philanthropy share of the total goes from 28 percent to nearly 32 percent—still behind fees (36 percent) and public sector support (almost 33 percent), though somewhat closer. Only in the United States does the inclusion of religious worship and religious congregations make a major change in the nonprofit revenue picture, boosting private philanthropy from 13 percent to 21 percent when only cash income is considered, and from 27 percent to 37 percent when volunteers are included as well.

5. A major employment generator

Not only is the nonprofit sector a larger economic force than commonly recognized, but also it has been an unusually dynamic one in recent years, outdistancing the general economies in most project countries in generating employment growth.

- **Nonprofit vs. overall employment growth.** Nonprofit employment in the eight countries for which time-series data were available grew by an average of 24 percent, or more than 4 percent a year, between 1990 and 1995 (see Figure 1.13). By comparison, overall employment in these same countries grew during this same period by a considerably slower 8 percent, or less than 2 percent a year. The nonprofit sector therefore outpaced the overall growth of employment in these countries by nearly 3 to 1.[13]
- **Nonprofit contribution to employment growth especially significant in Western Europe.** The growth of nonprofit employment between 1990 and 1995 was even stronger in Europe than elsewhere, moreover. Nonprofit employment expanded by an average of 24 percent in the four European countries for which longitudinal data were available (France, Germany, the Netherlands, and the U.K.), thus accounting

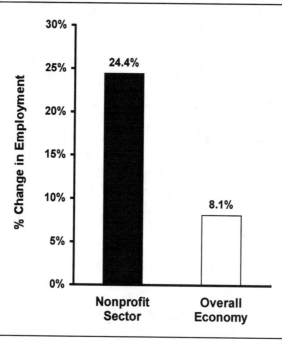

Figure 1.13   Growth in nonprofit employment vs. total employment, 1990–1995
(8 countries)

Source: The Johns Hopkins Comparative Nonprofit Sector Project

for 40 percent of total employment growth (3.8 million new FTE jobs). In the three other developed countries for which there were employment data (Israel, Japan, and the U.S.), the increase averaged 21 percent, though this accounted for a somewhat smaller 11 percent of the 16 million new FTE jobs.

- **Health and social services the dominant sources of nonprofit growth.** The overwhelming majority of nonprofit job growth between 1990 and 1995 took place in two fields: health and social services. The former of these absorbed 40 percent of the job growth and the latter 32 percent (see Figure 1.14). This exceeded substantially the shares of total employment with which these fields started the period. Nonprofit education organizations also absorbed a considerable share of employment growth, though here the share was smaller than the one with which these organizations began the period. Finally, development organizations accounted for 5 percent of the nonprofit job growth.
- **Social services the dominant source of growth in Western Europe.** The composition of nonprofit job growth in Western Europe deviated sig-

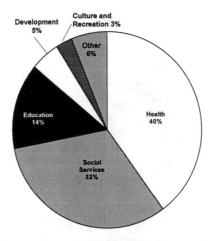

Figure 1.14 Areas of nonprofit job growth, by field, 1990–1995
Source: The Johns Hopkins Comparative Nonprofit Sector Project

nificantly from the overall average. Instead of health, social services accounted for the largest share of nonprofit job growth in Western Europe (50 percent vs. 15 percent). In addition, development organizations in Western Europe experienced a 38 percent increase in employment and accounted for 11 percent of the nonprofit job growth. In all likelihood, these figures reflect the investment that the European Commission, as well as national governments, have been putting into job training and development programs in the European region.

- **"Marketization."**[14] More generally, the growth in nonprofit employment evident in these figures has been made possible not chiefly by a surge in private philanthropy or public-sector support, but by a substantial increase in fee income. As shown in Figure 1.15, in the six countries for which there were comparable revenue data going back to 1990, fees accounted for 52 percent of the real growth in nonprofit income between 1990 and 1995. By comparison, the public sector accounted for 40 percent and private giving 8 percent. This means that the fee share of the total increased over what it was earlier, whereas both the philanthropic and public sector shares declined.

To be sure, this general trend was not evident everywhere. In Israel, Hungary, and the U.K., for example, substantial increases took place in the levels of public sector support to nonprofit organizations. In the three other countries, however, such support, while growing in absolute terms, nevertheless declined as a share of total nonprofit

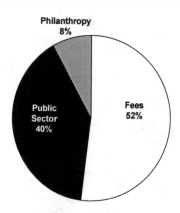

Figure 1.15   Sources of nonprofit revenue growth, 1990–1995
Source: The Johns Hopkins Comparative Nonprofit Sector Project

revenue, forcing nonprofit organizations to turn more extensively to fees and other commercial income. Moreover, this marketization trend was not only apparent in the United States, where it has long been in evidence, but also in Western Europe. In both France and Germany as well, fees and service charges grew faster than overall nonprofit income and thus boosted their share of total income.

- **Tepid growth of private giving.** The record of private giving during this period was varied. Some growth in private giving occurred in every country, and in at least three (the U.S., Hungary, and France) the growth was substantial, exceeding 10 percent. Because of the small base from which such growth is measured, however, it still did not add very much to overall nonprofit revenue. Indeed, in five of the six countries for which time-series data were available, the philanthropy share of total nonprofit income actually declined during this period, and even in France where it gained ground, the absolute growth in fee income outpaced the absolute growth in philanthropic support by 4:1.

CONCLUSIONS AND IMPLICATIONS

The nonprofit sector thus emerges from the evidence presented here as a sizable and highly dynamic component of a wide assortment of societies throughout the world. Not only does this set of institutions serve important human needs, it also constitutes a major, and growing, economic force and is a significant contributor to economic as well as social life. At the same time, this sector is hardly equally developed everywhere. While it has taken its place as a full-fledged partner with government and the business sector in many countries, in far more it remains a highly fragile organism whose future is very insecure. Thus, no single set of implications will apply equally in all places. Under these circumstances, it may be appropriate to outline the implications that seem to flow from the discussion here, and from the broader evidence this project is generating, for the different regions examined.

Central and Eastern Europe: An ambiguous sector

Ambiguity is perhaps the principal characteristic that emerges from the picture of the nonprofit sector that these data reveal in Central and Eastern Europe. To be sure, the period since the fall of Communism in 1989 has been aptly termed the "rebirth of civil society," but this rebirth has not been without its delivery pains and the offspring, despite some remarkable energy, has hardly attained full maturity. Indeed, one of the more striking features of the post-Communist nonprofit sector as it appears in the data the project has assembled is how fully it still reflects the Communist legacy, as evidenced by the comparatively strong position of culture and recreation and professional organizations and unions, the two main types of activities that were tolerated and even supported by the Communist regimes. This coexistence of the old and the new creates a pervasive tension that has hardly been addressed, let alone overcome. At the same time, and in striking contrast to the developed world, nonprofit activities in the core welfare state areas of social services, health, and education are still limited. This reflects the expectation that Central and Eastern European citizens still have about the state's obligation to provide for citizen welfare, an expectation that is all the more paradoxical in view of the abuses of state power under the Communist regimes. This persisting ambiguity suggests the need for continued concerted effort to nurture a truly effective private, nonprofit sector in Central and Eastern Europe. Among the tasks that must be addressed, moreover, three seem especially important:

- **Fostering legitimacy.** The persistent ambiguity of the Central and Eastern European nonprofit sector is due in important part to the legitimacy problems that the sector continues to face. For better or worse, the early evolution of the sector in the immediate aftermath of the fall of Communism produced a limited, but highly publicized, number of scams and scandals in many countries. These were due, in many instances, to early loopholes and uncertainties in the law, which enabled unscrupulous operators to utilize the nonprofit form for personal financial gain. Fortunately, many countries across the region have since passed new legal frameworks that spell out the functions and purposes of various types of nonprofit organizations more clearly; and some have also improved the tax treatment of both organizations and donations. Indeed, in many ways, the new legal frameworks emerging in the region appear to be superior to those in the West, which developed in a far more haphazard fashion. Nevertheless, public attitudes still lag behind this legal development, and the public at large seems disillusioned with the promise of the sector. To overcome this, a significant investment in public education will be needed along with the development of effective codes of conduct among nonprofit organizations themselves.

- **Capacity building.** A second key conclusion that emerges from the data presented here concerns the time frame required to build a truly viable and self-sustaining nonprofit sector. Despite considerable growth, the nonprofit sector in Central and Eastern Europe, five years after the fall of Communism, remains a pale reflection of its counterparts elsewhere in the world, including Latin America as well as Western Europe. To grow and nurture a sustainable nonprofit sector and civil society obviously takes more than just a few years of investment. Accordingly, it seems crucially important to continue the training and capacity building efforts that marked the first years of Western assistance at significant levels in the foreseeable future. So, too, are the efforts to build an institutional infrastructure for this sector in the region to facilitate training efforts and information-sharing and provide a unified voice vis-à-vis the government, especially at the national level. Such efforts have made important headway, but they regularly run into resistance on the part of nonprofit leaders fearful of "umbrella organizations" that seem to resemble what existed under the previous regime.

- **Resource development.** Finally, as elsewhere, there remains a significant need to create a sustainable financial base for the sector in this region. In part, this will require nurturing a culture of philanthropy and giving. Fortunately, there is a long tradition of enterprise giving, but this has yet to translate into sizable individual donations capable of freeing these organizations from dependence on fees and corporate support. In addition, however, progress is also needed in allowing nonprofit organizations to tap into public funding, which has been a significant engine of nonprofit growth elsewhere in Europe.

Latin America: The problem of duality

If ambiguity is the central reality of the nonprofit sector in Central and Eastern Europe, "duality" is the central feature in Latin America. In a sense, two separate nonprofit sectors exist in this region—one of them composed of more traditional charitable organizations and other agencies linked to the social and economic elite and the other associated with the relatively newer forms of grassroots organizations and so-called "nongovernmental organizations" (NGOs) that support them. As shown previously in this chapter, the former of these remains quite prominent so far as the formal picture of the sector is concerned, but the latter is clearly gaining ground and comprises an increasingly prominent "informal" or less formal component. Given this situation, the challenges facing the Latin American nonprofit sector therefore take the following forms:

- **Making "sector" a reality.** In the first place, serious steps are needed to bridge this divide between the two major components of the Latin American nonprofit sector and foster a common understanding of a "sector" sharing common interests and needs. The emergence of the concept of "civil society" has been useful in this regard, but much more dialogue and interaction will be required.
- **Capacity building.** One way to foster a sense of a distinctive nonprofit sector in Latin America is to invest in the capacity of this sector through improved training and infrastructure organizations. Although considerable effort has been put into training nonprofit personnel in this region, indigenous capacity to provide such training, and indigenous infrastructure organizations, have been lacking until recently. Building these capabilities thus seems a high priority for the region. Equally important is encouraging indigenous philanthropic institutions to buttress the financial foundation of the sector. In short, with the significant base that has now been built, Latin America is ripe for a major nonprofit sector capacity-building campaign to bring the less formal part of the region's civil society sector more fully into a position to operate on a par with the more traditional part, and with partners in government and the business sector.
- **Building partnerships with government and business.** Government has emerged in recent years as an important source of support for nonprofit organizations in many parts of Latin America. At the same time, the relationships between the nonprofit sector and the state remain strained. In part, this reflects the lack of transparent procedures for regularizing contacts between these two sectors and the long tradition of clientelistic politics under which the funding and operation of nonprofit organizations are subjected to the whims of local or national political elites. A significant priority for the future, therefore, is to build a firmer foundation for cooperation between these two sectors to ensure a reasonable degree of autonomy for the nonprofit partners.

Similarly, the nonprofit sector must find ways to build cooperative ties with the business sector in the region if for no other reason than as a counterpoise to excessive dependence on the state.

- **Making room in the public space.** One way to foster a greater partnership between nonprofit organizations and the state is to ensure nonprofit organizations a more secure place at the table in the so-called "public space" that is opening in most countries in the region, in which dialogue among social and political actors should occur. Clearly, advances have been made in many countries in bringing nonprofit organizations into the process of public policy formulation and implementation, but much has yet to be done.

Developed countries: The challenge of renewal

If basic capacity building and resourcing are the central challenges facing the nonprofit sectors in Central Europe and Latin America, in the more developed regions of the world the central challenge is one of "renewal." The 1990s, as shown in these data, was a period of considerable growth for the nonprofit sector. A heightened demand for social services of all kinds and a generally reduced role for governments, among other factors, increased the importance of the nonprofit sector. At the same time, however, this growth has not been without its challenges, though the challenges have been as much to the heart of the sector as to its stomach. Long accustomed to significant levels of public support, and enticed by the promise of greater fee income, nonprofit agencies in the developed world are in heightened danger of losing touch with their citizen base. On the one hand, many of these organizations have long since been transformed into large bureaucracies seemingly indistinguishable from the government bureaus with which they interact; on the other hand, they face a growing danger of becoming evermore like the business firms with which they frequently compete. Negotiating the dual dangers of over-bureaucratization and over-commercialization becomes thus the true challenge for nonprofit managers and policy-makers in these areas.

- **A renewal strategy.** To help preserve and regain the sector's true identity and core values, serious effort needs to be made to reinvigorate the nonprofit sector on a regular basis. This can be done through regular strategic planning, through improved training and management models that reflect the central values this set of institutions is supposed to promote, and through a critical dialog that engages a wide range of societal actors in a discussion of the sector's appropriate social role. Clearly, citizens cannot be expected to defend this sector's worth if the sector does not make itself worthy of their support.

- **Accountability and effectiveness.** In order to ensure their claims on citizen loyalties, nonprofits also need to be able to demonstrate the worth of what they do, and to operate both efficiently and effectively in the public interest. This will require something more than traditional management training, or the wholesale adoption of management techniques imported from the business or government sector. Rather, continued effort must be made to forge a distinctive mode of nonprofit management training that takes account of the distinctive values and ethos of this sector while ensuring the effectiveness of what it does. Important progress has been made along these lines in a number of countries, but significant steps remain to be made in building up the training capability in numerous places, especially in Western Europe.

- **Expanding philanthropy.** Important as the development of organizational and leadership capacities are for the future of the nonprofit sector, the expansion of private philanthropy continues to be vital to ensure a meaningful level of independence from both government and business. Yet, such support is marginal in many countries. What is more, it has not kept pace with the overall growth even in the countries where it historically has been more substantial. Over the long run, therefore, serious efforts are needed to encourage private philanthropy. The recent increases in the number of grant-making foundations in many developed countries suggest a positive trend toward greater philanthropic input into the nonprofit sector—a trend that needs the active encouragement of policy-makers and nonprofit leaders. Moreover, changes in demographics and the labor force suggest that in many countries large reservoirs of potential volunteers remain "untapped" for the expansion of the philanthropic share of nonprofit operations. However, this will require public education efforts on the part of the sector's leadership, and creative models for combining paid and unpaid work, particularly in countries with high levels of unemployment.

- **International integration and globalization.** For the European countries, greater efforts toward integration and harmonization are under way that will certainly increase the role transnational governments play in nonprofit sector affairs. Yet institutions like the European Union have been hesitant in their approach towards the nonprofit sector and civil society. The recent publication of an official *Communication,* which benefited much from the work done in the initial phase of this project, is a step in the right direction. Yet much more remains to be done—on the part of the European Commission as well as nonprofit leaders—to make sure that this set of institutions can develop its full potential in and for the New Europe. More generally, the worldwide trend towards globalization hardly excludes the nonprofit sector. Policy-makers and nonprofit leaders thus face the challenge to build adequate legal environments for cross-national nonprofit action while protecting legitimate national interests at the same time.

Conclusion

More generally, the discussion here points up the vital need to improve the general awareness of this set of institutions in virtually every part of the world, and to monitor the trends affecting it on a more pervasive, and more sustained, basis. The existence of a vibrant nonprofit sector is increasingly being viewed not as a luxury, but as a necessity, for peoples throughout the world. Such institutions can give expression to citizen concerns, hold governments accountable, promote community, address unmet needs, and generally improve the quality of life. Putting this sector firmly on the mental map of the world is therefore a matter of some urgency. However incomplete, if the work reported here and in the chapters that follow has contributed to this goal, it will have served its purpose well.

ENDNOTES

1. This chapter was published previously as a stand-alone report under the title, *The Emerging Sector Revisited: A Summary, Revised Estimates* (Baltimore, MD: Center for Civil Society Studies, 1999). It has been modified slightly for this volume. Copies of the original can be obtained from the Center for Civil Society Studies at the address provided on the back of the title page.

2. For further detail on the derivation of this "structural-operational definition" of the nonprofit sector, see: *Defining the Nonprofit Sector: A Cross-national Analysis* (Manchester, U.K.: Manchester University Press, 1997).

3. Lester Salamon, "The Rise of the Nonprofit Sector," *Foreign Affairs*, vol. 74, No. 3 (July/August 1994).

4. Joseph Stiglitz, 1998 Wider Lecture, Helsinki (January 1998).

5. For a summary of the results of Phase I of project work, see: Lester M. Salamon and Helmut K. Anheier, *The Emerging Sector: An Overview* (Baltimore, MD: Johns Hopkins Institute for Policy Studies, 1994), republished as *The Emerging Nonprofit Sector*, Vol. 1 in the Johns Hopkins Nonprofit Sector Series (Manchester: Manchester University Press, 1996). More detailed results are available in a series of books published in the Johns Hopkins Nonprofit Sector Series by Manchester University Press. For a complete list of the products of the Johns Hopkins Comparative Nonprofit Sector Project, please contact the Center for Civil Society Studies as noted on the back of the title page.

6. Chapters on all but one of these countries, Austria, are included in the body of this volume. In addition, as this volume went to press, preliminary data became available on an addi-

tional Central European country, Poland. A chapter on Poland is therefore included here but the Polish data are not incorporated in the summary figures presented in this chapter.

7. Technically, the more precise comparison is between nonprofit contribution to "value added" and gross domestic product. For the nonprofit sector, "value added" in economic terms essentially equals the sum of wages and the imputed value of volunteer time. On this basis, the nonprofit sector in our 22 countries account for $840 billion in value-added, which represents, on average, 3.5 percent of the gross domestic product. This still leaves the nonprofit sector, if it were a country, as the eighth largest economy in the world.

8. These personnel engaged principally in religious worship activities are in addition to the employees of religiously affiliated service organizations (e.g. hospitals, social service agencies, soup kitchens), which, as noted above, are already included in the data reported earlier.

9. Given the overall size of the U.S. economy, the U.S. nonprofit sector is still larger in absolute terms, of course. Thus, of the 18.98 million full-time-equivalent nonprofit employees we have identified in the 22 countries examined here, 8.6 million, or 45 percent, are in the U.S. alone. By comparison, the nine countries of Western Europe included in our data set account for 5.6 million nonprofit employees, or 30 percent of the total; Japan accounts for 2.1 million, or 11 percent of the total; the five Latin American countries account for 1.9 million employees, or 10 percent of the total; the other developed countries (Australia and Israel) account for 0.5 million employees, or 3 percent of the total; and the four Central and Eastern European countries account for 0.2 million employees, or 1 percent of the total. These figures are summarized in Appendix B: Table 1.

10. In the case of Germany, this outcome is very likely a result of the inclusion of East Germany in the data. Without former East Germany, the German figure would probably be close to 5.5 percent, or well above the all-country average.

11. For more detailed analysis of the forces that give shape to the nonprofit sector in different settings, and the resulting patterns that emerge, see: Lester M. Salamon and Helmut K. Anheier, "Social Origins of Civil Society: Explaining the Nonprofit Sector Cross-Nationally," *Voluntas*, Vol. 9, No. 3 (September 1998) pp. 213–248.

12. For further elaboration of the alternative patterns, see endnote 9.

13. These data do not include the shift in structure of the U.K. higher education field that occurred during the Thatcher period, since we did not have comparable data for these organizations in both 1990 and 1995. We also note that German data for 1990 include only West German organizations. Therefore, a part of the reported growth of the German nonprofit sector is due to the country's 1990 unification.

14. For a discussion of this concept in the context of the United States, see: Lester M. Salamon, "The Marketization of Welfare: Nonprofit and For-Profit Roles in America's Welfare State," *Social Service Review*, Vol. 67, No. 1 (March 1993) pp. 16–39.

PART 2

Western Europe

One of the notable discoveries of the work reported in this book is the immense scale of the nonprofit sector in much of Western Europe. This outcome is a byproduct, in important part, of the partnership arrangements between the state and nonprofit organizations that formed in many parts of Western Europe during the expansion of the welfare state. In the process, a distinctive Western European pattern took shape that, with important variations from country to country, features a large and well-developed nonprofit sector that is heavily financed by the public sector and significantly engaged in the provision of core welfare services in the fields of education, health, and social services. The major deviation from this pattern is in the Nordic countries, where less reliance is placed on nonprofit organizations to deliver welfare services, but where these organizations still play a vital role in civic and cultural life.

This sizable Western European nonprofit sector has long been overshadowed by the rise of the welfare state. Now, however, it is attracting increased attention as a potentially important part of the solution to the significant unemployment and social cohesion problems currently plaguing Western European societies, and as contributors as well to a revitalization of Western European democracy.

CHAPTER 2

Belgium

Sybille Mertens, Sophie Adam, Jacques Defourny,
Michel Marée, Jozef Pacolet, and Ilse Van de Putte

BACKGROUND

The Belgian nonprofit sector, among the largest of those described in this volume, is in great measure a product of the unique welfare state model the country adopted in the immediate post-World War II period. This model, a combination of the principle of subsidiarity and centralized public administration, facilitates cooperation between "associations without profit purposes," as many nonprofit organizations are known in Belgium, and government agencies to provide social welfare services such as health care and education. Thus, like much of Western Europe but unlike most other countries, Belgium's nonprofit sector relies on government sources for the majority of its revenue. Still, volunteers, who make up more than a third of the sector's total human resource pool, are crucial to the sector's activity and impact.

These findings result from work carried out by a Belgian inter-university research team based at the *Centre d'Economie Sociale* (Center for Social Economy) of Liège University and the *Hoger Instituut voor de Arbeid* (Higher Institute of Labor) of the *Katholieke Universiteit Leuven* (Leuven Catholic University) as part of the Johns Hopkins Comparative Nonprofit Sector Project's collaborative international inquiry.[1] It thus offered excellent opportunities

Global Civil Society: Dimensions of the Nonprofit Sector by Lester M. Salamon, Helmut K. Anheier, Regina List, Stefan Toepler, S. Wojciech Sokolowski and Associates. Baltimore, MD: Johns Hopkins Center for Civil Society Studies, 1999.

both to capture local Belgian circumstances and peculiarities and to compare and contrast them with those in other countries in Western Europe and elsewhere in a systematic way.[2] The result is the first empirical overview of the Belgian nonprofit sector, the first systematic comparison of Belgian nonprofit realities to those elsewhere in the world, and a first step toward bringing the Belgian nonprofit sector into focus in national statistics.

The present chapter reports on just one set of findings from this project, those relating to the size and structure of the nonprofit sector in Belgium and elsewhere. Subsequent publications will fill in the historical, legal, and policy context of this sector and also examine the impact that this set of institutions is having. Most of the data reported here have been extrapolated from a detailed pilot face-to-face survey of organizations.[3] Information about hospitals and schools was obtained from the relevant government ministries. (For a more complete statement of the sources of data, see the references section of this chapter and Appendix C.) Unless otherwise noted, financial data are reported in U.S. dollars at the 1995 average exchange rate.

PRINCIPAL FINDINGS

1. The weight of the nonprofit sector in the national economy

At the start, it is important to highlight one of the most significant findings revealed by the survey.[4] As shown in Table 2.1, of every ten Belgian "associations without profit purpose" (AWPPs) maintaining formal legal personalities in 1995, four had ceased all activity without necessarily publishing a formal dissolution, four operated with the participation of only voluntary workers, and two employed paid staff. Consequently, it is estimated that, of the 82,000 nonprofit organizations registered with the National Register for Legal Entities, just over 50,000 associations were actually in operation in 1995. And as only about one-third of these active nonprofit organizations (approximately 18,000 associations) employed paid staff, the majority of nonprofit organizations relied entirely on volunteers.

Employment in the nonprofit sector.   There are several basic indicators of the significance of the nonprofit sector in the economic life of the country. One of these indicators is the sector's contribution to employment. During the course of 1995, nearly 470,000 paid workers were employed by nonprofit associations in Belgium. This workforce can also be expressed as the equivalent of 359,000 full-time jobs,[5,6] or approximately 10.5 percent of nonagricultural full-time equivalent (FTE) paid employment,[7] 12.7 percent of FTE paid employment in the private sector, and 14.7 percent of

Table 2.1   The nonprofit sector in Belgium, 1995

AWPPs recognized as legal personalities	82,123
— In operation	50,773
— With paid workers	18,100
— Without paid workers	32,673
— Inactive	31,350
Labor force in AWPPs	
— Paid employment	
— Head count	468,764
— Full-time equivalent	358,852
— As % of nonagricultural paid employment	10.5%
— Volunteering	
— Full-time equivalent	100,687
Cash resources of the AWPPs	
— Millions U.S. dollars	25,688
Wage bill of the AWPPs	
— Millions U.S. dollars	15,200
— As % of GDP	5.6%
— As % of GDP (including volunteers)	7.1%

Sources: See References section and Appendix C.

FTE paid employment in the service sector. Although paid employment in the nonprofit sector represents a considerable contribution to the economy, it cannot be forgotten that one of the particularities of this sector is the fact that volunteering constitutes the equivalent of 100,000 additional full-time jobs.[8]

The contribution of the nonprofit sector to gross domestic product.   The total monetary resources raised by all nonprofit associations amounts to more than $25 billion (750 billion Belgian francs), an amount equivalent to 9.5 percent of the gross domestic product (GDP). On the basis of data relative to paid employment, the wage bill of the sector is estimated to be $15 billion (about 450 billion Belgian francs),[9] and the sector's added value as a percentage of the GDP to be the equivalent of nearly 6 percent.[10] If the imputed value of volunteer input is factored in, the nonprofit sector's value added exceeds 7 percent of the GDP.[11] These figures represent the extent to which Belgian nonprofit associations contributed to the growth of national wealth in 1995. If one takes into account that this is the equivalent of one quarter of the contribution of industry to GDP, it is evident that this result is far from insignificant.[12]

2. The nonprofit sector's composition

In order to grasp the diversity within the nonprofit sector, it is fitting to venture beyond the aggregates and turn attention to its components. One of the most common methods of breaking down the analysis consists of subdividing the whole according to the main activity of the organizations of which it is composed. Unfortunately, the classification of activity used by official statistical organizations does not cover the diversity of activities pursued by nonprofit associations. In order to fill this gap, the international team of researchers involved in the Johns Hopkins project put together the International Classification of Nonprofit Organizations (ICNPO), which is a common classification more adapted to the activities of nonprofit organizations. (For more information on the ICNPO, see Appendix A.)

As shown in Table 2.2 below, two-thirds of all Belgian associations studied (including hospitals and schools) are concentrated in three fields of activity: culture and recreation, education and research, and social services. Notably, the distribution of associations with paid labor differs significantly from that of organizations relying solely on volunteers. In fact, 70 percent of the associations with paid employment are in the fields of education and research, culture and recreation, and social services. The associations without paid employment are mainly concentrated in the field of culture and recreation (more than 50 percent) and professional associations (13 percent).

Table 2.2 also reveals that the vast majority of associations active in the health field and most of the associations in education and research and social services employ paid staff. This would seem to indicate that these activities demand a higher degree of professional competence than in other fields. It also indicates that major political decisions to allocate significant public funding for these activities may have contributed to this professionalism.

Nonprofit sector employment.   As noted previously, the nonprofit labor force includes more than 350,000 FTE paid workers and over 100,000 FTE volunteers.[13] Paid workers are principally found in three fields: education and research (38.7 percent of total nonprofit FTE employment, including nonprofit private schools), health (30.4 percent, including hospitals), and social services (13.8 percent).

Volunteers represent more than one-third of the total human resources pool engaged in nonprofit associations, even if volunteers in hospitals and schools are excluded. Volunteer work is evident throughout the whole

Table 2.2 Structure of Belgian nonprofit associations, by field, 1995

ICNPO groups	Organizations with paid employment (No.)	(%)	Organizations without paid employment (No.)	(%)	All organizations (No.)	(%)
1. Culture and recreation	4,611	25.5	16,434	50.3	21,045	41.4
2. Education and research*	3,950	21.8	2,348	7.2	6,298	12.4
3. Health**	1,938	10.7	196	0.6	2,134	4.2
4. Social services	3,610	19.9	2,543	7.8	6,153	12.1
5. Environment	282	1.6	587	1.8	869	1.7
6. Dvlp and housing	1,606	8.9	1,565	4.8	3,172	6.2
7. Civic and advocacy	429	2.4	978	3	1,407	2.8
8. Philanthropy	208	1.2	1,174	3.6	1,382	2.7
9. International activities	208	1.2	1,565	4.8	1,774	3.5
10. Religion***	282	1.6	978	3	1,260	2.5
11. Professional associations	975	5.4	4,304	13.2	5,279	10.4
Total	18,100	100	32,673	100	50,773	100

* including nonprofit private schools

** including hospitals

*** The Belgian team's definition of religious worship differs from that adopted by the Johns Hopkins project.

Sources: See References section and Appendix C.

group of associations, even if only through the voluntary presence of administrators on boards of directors. Volunteerism can be considered, therefore, a vital component of the Belgian nonprofit sector. Two fields of activity are characterized especially by their capacity to mobilize voluntary work: social services, which absorbs 55 percent of FTE volunteers, and cultural and recreational activities, which attract 33 percent.[14]

As also shown in Table 2.3, associations in different fields of activity rely to varying extents on paid and volunteer workers. Whereas paid employment is predominant in the fields of environment, development and housing, and civic and advocacy, volunteering constitutes more than half of committed human resources in associations that provide services to their members, such as those in the field of culture and recreation. In social service organizations, activities are carried out in about the same proportions by paid staff and volunteers.

The nonprofit sector's revenues. In 1995, total cash revenues for the nonprofit organizations covered in this study in Belgium amounted to more than $25 billion (758 billion BEF), as shown in Table 2.4. Public sector

Table 2.3 Nonprofit sector employment in Belgium, by field, 1995

ICNPO groups	Paid employment (No. of workers)	(%)	(FTE)	(%)	Volunteering (FTE)	(%)
1. Culture and recreation	40,973	8.7	17,546	4.9	33,391	33.2
2. Education and research*	26,096	5.6	8,332	2.3	614	0.6
3. Health**	71,991	15.4	48,991	13.7	439	0.4
4. Social services	60,841	12.9	49,429	13.8	55,422	55.0
5. Environment	2,029	0.4	1,922	0.5	551	0.5
6. Dvlp and housing	37,887	8.1	35,357	9.9	2,526	2.5
7. Civic and advocacy	1,410	0.3	1,324	0.4	988	1.0
8. Philanthropy	643	0.1	573	0.2	716	0.8
9. International activities	705	0.1	594	0.2	1,018	1.0
10. Religion***	1,319	0.3	1,051	0.3	1,587	1.6
11. Professional associations	4,024	0.9	3,293	0.9	3,434	3.4
Subtotal	247,558	52.8	168,411	46.9	100,687	100
Nonprofit private schools	152,932	32.6	130,565	36.4	n.a.	n.a.
Hospitals	68,274	14.6	59,876	16.7	n.a.	n.a.
Total	468,764	100.0	358,852	100.0	n.a.	n.a.

*Nonprofit schools reported separately.

**Hospitals reported separately.

***The Belgian team's definition of religious worship organizations differs from that adopted by the CNP.

Sources: See References section and Appendix C.

Table 2.4 Nonprofit cash revenues in Belgium, by field and by source, 1995

ICNPO groups	Total cash revenues (millions U.S. dollars)	Public sector subsidies (%)	Sales (%)	Dues (%)	Private giving (%)
1. Culture and recreation	1,901	41	40.8	6.1	12.0
2. Education and research*	445	53.9	39.2	3.8	3.1
3. Health**	3,544	58.2	38.0	0.1	3.7
4. Social services	3,133	65.8	11.0	10.8	12.4
5. Environment	103	93.6	1.7	2.4	2.3
6. Dvlp and housing	1,955	47.4	46.5	1.4	4.7
7. Civic and advocacy	72	84.0	4.2	6.6	5.2
8. Philanthropy	119	1.4	32.4	0.6	65.6
9. International activities	266	32.7	8.7	0.5	58.1
10. Religion***	112	13.9	49.7	0.0	36.4
11. Professional associations	392	6.7	35.3	32.7	25.2
Subtotal	12,042	52.8	31.6	5.3	10.2
Nonprofit private schools	7,280	100.0	0.0	0.0	0.0
Hospitals	6,366	94.4	5.6	0.0	0.0
Total	25,688	76.5	16.2	2.5	4.8

* Nonprofit schools reported separately.

** Hospitals reported separately.

*** The Belgian team's definition of religious worship activities differs from that adopted by the CNP.

Sources: See References section and Appendix C.

resources account for more than three-quarters (76.5 percent) of total non-profit revenues, while private sales and membership dues together account for 18.7 percent. Private donations only provide 4.8 percent of the financial means available to associations. These results have been greatly influenced by the funding structure of nonprofit private schools and hospitals. These two categories of organizations mobilize a little more than half of all the resources available to the sector and are mainly financed by public funding.

Without hospital and school revenues, total cash income for the sector is just over $12 billion. In this scenario, public sector funds represent only 52.8 percent, whereas sales represent 31.6 percent of cash resources. Private giving and membership fees constitute 10.2 percent and 5.3 percent of the total, respectively. Nevertheless, these aggregates must not mask the great diversity of funding mechanisms used by Belgian nonprofit associations.

As might be expected, public sector resources play a large role in the provision of quasi-collective services offered by associations. The public sector is almost the sole source of income for hospitals, nonprofit private schools,[15] and environmental protection associations, and provides 84 percent of the income of civic and advocacy organizations. In the first two cases, this reflects the fact that these associations have been integrated into the well-established national system along with public service providers, such as public hospitals and official state schools. The extent of public funding allocated to environmental, human rights, and advocacy organizations can be explained by the fact that their activities cannot easily be paid for, even in part, by the beneficiaries.

In other fields, market resources complement public funds. Even when the state has decided to intervene in the associations' favor, the resources fail to cover all of the organizations' production costs. To the extent the services they offer can be individualized, some costs can be recovered from the service users, depending on the circumstances. This practice can be observed in the cultural and recreational sector, in the field of education and research (apart from nonprofit private schools), in health care (apart from hospitals), and in associations involved in local development.

It is also interesting to note that private giving comprises an important source of income in the fields that receive little or no support from the government, such as professional associations, as well as those that have managed to convince the population that "institutional solidarity" can be complemented by a more "citizen-based" solidarity (philanthropic intermediaries, associations involved in international relations, or in religious activities). While religious worship associations also receive a significant share of their income from private giving, their main source is fees for services, especially rental fees charged for use of their space for cultural and other activities. Finally, membership fees represent a particularly high proportion of the resources of professional associations. This is not surprising since it concerns organizations that are, above all, at the service of their members.

Table 2.5 shows the distribution of public sector subsidies according to ICNPO groups. The resulting proportions demonstrate the decision of the Belgian collectivity to support certain activities that it does not wish to see governed solely by market laws. Hospitals and nonprofit private schools benefit from the lion's share by "capturing" nearly 70 percent of the public resources allocated to the nonprofit sector. The rest is shared among other health services, social services, local development, and cultural and recreational activities.

Hospitals receive resources mainly from the National Institute for Disease and Disability Insurance (INAMI). However, for other associations, government contributions largely take the form of partial or total reimbursement of remuneration related to certain work posts. In certain cases, the government takes direct financial responsibility without the employer first having to pay the salary to be later reimbursed. These reimbursements

Table 2.5 Distribution of public sector subsidies in Belgium, 1995

ICNPO groups	(%)
1. Culture and recreation	3.97
2. Education and research*	1.22
3. Health**	10.50
4. Social services	10.49
5. Environment	0.49
6. Dvlp and housing	4.71
7. Civic and advocacy	0.31
8. Philanthropy	0.01
9. International activities	0.44
10. Religion***	0.08
11. Professional associations	0.13
Subtotal	32.37
Nonprofit private schools	37.05
Hospitals	30.58
Total	100.00

* Nonprofit schools reported separately.

** Hospitals reported separately.

*** The Belgian team's definition of religious worship differs from that adopted by the CNP.

Sources: See References section and Appendix C.

or state payments often exist within the framework of unemployment benefit programs. These programs have increased the financial means of associations over the last two decades, and have also contributed to the reinforcement of professionalism in their activities.

Giving and volunteering.   In Belgium, the contribution of the civil society to the nonprofit sector is manifested through both cash donations and voluntary action. If a cash value were ascribed to the voluntary work contributed by the Belgian populace,[16] it would amount to $4 billion (125 billion BEF), about three times the amount collected through monetary donations.

As shown in Table 2.6, civil society involves itself to a great extent in social services and in cultural and recreational activities both in terms of FTE volunteering and in terms of donations paid to the associations. Not only does the social services field absorb more voluntary labor (55 percent) than any other, it also attracts the most cash donations (31.5 percent). The culture and recreation field also accounts for significant shares of both volunteering (33.2 percent) and private giving (18.6 percent), but still quite a bit less than social services.

Table 2.6   Giving and volunteering in the nonprofit sector in Belgium, by field, 1995 (excluding hospitals and nonprofit private schools)

ICNPO groups	Giving (millions U.S. dollars)	(%)	Volunteering (FTE)	(%)
1. Culture and recreation	229	18.6	33,391	33.2
2. Education and research*	14	1.1	614	0.6
3. Health**	130	10.5	439	0.4
4. Social services	389	31.5	55,422	55.0
5. Environment	2	0.2	551	0.5
6. Dvlp and housing	92	7.5	2,526	2.5
7. Civic and advocacy	4	0.3	988	1.0
8. Philanthropy	78	6.3	716	0.7
9. International activities	154	12.5	1,018	1.0
10. Religion	41	3.3	1,587	1.6
11. Professional associations	99	8.0	3,434	3.4
Total	1,232	100.0	100,687	100.0

* excludes schools

** excludes hospitals

Sources: See References section and Appendix C.

Education and research activities, as well as health care, are largely controlled by the government, which has ensured for a long time that these sectors are run in a professional manner. As they feel less directly responsible for these groups, citizens tend not to donate as much time or money to these services. Fundraising campaigns are essentially concentrated on philanthropic activities, social services, or development aid. This probably explains why these latter fields have had such good results in capturing private giving resources.

3. The teachings of an international comparison

Participation in the Johns Hopkins Project has been advantageous for the Belgian nonprofit sector, resulting in an improved macroeconomic description of nonprofit associations in Belgium. Moreover, comparing the Belgian nonprofit sector with the nonprofit sector in other countries in accordance with a common criterion of definitions and classifications has contributed to a greater understanding of the private non-market sector from a global perspective. Specifically, it has contributed to a greater understanding and appreciation of the Belgian nonprofit sector and its position and character in relation to the nonprofit sector in other countries throughout Europe and the world.[17]

The third largest nonprofit sector. The Belgian nonprofit sector, which employs 10.5 percent of the paid nonagricultural workforce, [18,19] is the third largest among the 22 studied in the Johns Hopkins project (see Figure 2.1). Although the three countries with the largest nonprofit sectors (Netherlands, Ireland, and Belgium) are aligned with the "welfare" model, key sectors such as education and health are not covered by a unified public service. In other "welfare state" countries, such a unified service tends to reduce the presence of associations in these sectors. These three countries, in contrast, have opted for co-existing public and private nonprofit structures to which they have delegated an often large share of public service provision.

Development of the welfare state in Belgium. According to the Johns Hopkins study, the paid labor force of nonprofit organizations in the 22 project countries is concentrated in three fields of activity: education, health, and social services. An analysis by region indicates that the model in which welfare-type services dominate is more prevalent in the Western European countries than in the others.

In Belgium, the predominance of these welfare associations can be explained by the development of the welfare state in the context of a pillarized

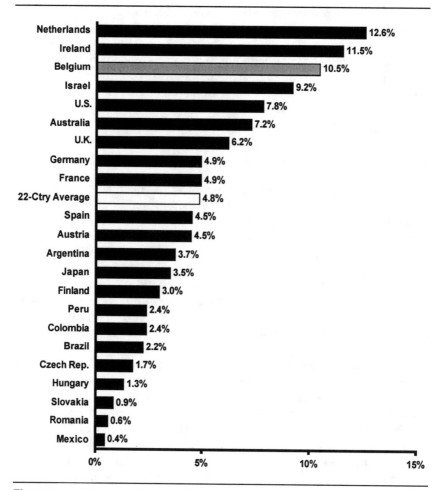

Country	Percentage
Netherlands	12.6%
Ireland	11.5%
Belgium	10.5%
Israel	9.2%
U.S.	7.8%
Australia	7.2%
U.K.	6.2%
Germany	4.9%
France	4.9%
22-Ctry Average	4.8%
Spain	4.5%
Austria	4.5%
Argentina	3.7%
Japan	3.5%
Finland	3.0%
Peru	2.4%
Colombia	2.4%
Brazil	2.2%
Czech Rep.	1.7%
Hungary	1.3%
Slovakia	0.9%
Romania	0.6%
Mexico	0.4%

Figure 2.1   Nonprofit share of total employment, by country, 1995

society.[20] As in most other Western European countries, the immediate post-World War II period saw the birth of the modern welfare state. The structure that has taken shape in Belgium is, in reality, a skillful combination of two models. The Belgian nonprofit sector is shaped, on one hand, by the French model which focuses on a foundation of centralized public action and the development of public institutions. On the other hand, it is also based on the German model centered on the principle of subsidiarity that implies a delegation of public services to nonprofit organizations.

These two tendencies have been supported in Belgium by the main constitutive socio-political "pillars," namely, on the one hand, organizations of a socialist character and, on the other, the corresponding Christian organizations. Whereas the socialist movement has generally privileged the establishment and development of public institutions, the Christian-inspired entities have been more concerned with defending the option to provide collective services outside of the state environment. As major participants in the Belgian political arena since the end of World War II, these two pillars have gradually built up the institutional framework for the welfare state as it is today, always reserving an important place for private nonprofit organizations alongside public agencies.

Even though a multitude of associations are active in the cultural, recreational, or international relations sectors, the Belgian nonprofit sector is, among its most institutionalized components, a sector that is essentially involved in the production of collective services. These services, especially health, education, and social work, are delegated and sanctioned in part by the state. Public service providers and the nonprofit associations share responsibility in these particular areas. As shown in Table 2.7, in hospitals, schools, and homes for the elderly, there is a significant share of service providers outside the public sphere. This can be explained, in part, by the fact that governmental authorities allocate nearly equal funding to all active organizations within a given field, whether private or public.

The importance of public funding. As highlighted previously, the recognition of the role of Belgian nonprofit organizations as providers of quasi-collective services can be found in the sector's revenue structure. More than three-quarters of nonprofit revenues come from public funds (grants, funding of work posts, refund of benefits, etc.), and much of the remainder is generated from private fees and charges.

This model of funding is mainly a characteristic of Western European countries. They are, for the most part, grouped together in Figure 2.2 un-

Table 2.7 Output shares in Belgian hospitals, schools, and homes for the elderly, 1995

Fields	Criteria	Nonprofit sector	Public sector	For-profit sector
Hospitals	Number of days	66%	34%	0%
Schools	Number of students	61%	39%	0%
Homes for the elderly	Number of homes	23%	22%	55%

Source: Institut National de Statistique [1994], *Annuaire de statistiques régionales*, Bruxelles

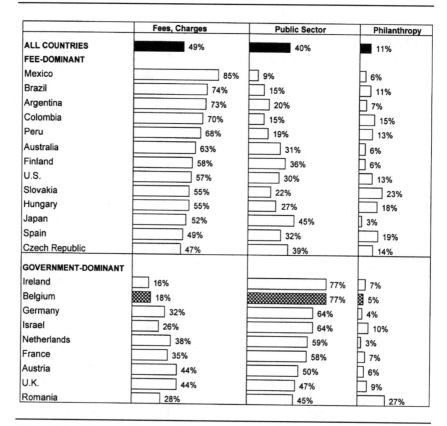

	Fees, Charges	Public Sector	Philanthropy
ALL COUNTRIES	49%	40%	11%
FEE-DOMINANT			
Mexico	85%	9%	6%
Brazil	74%	15%	11%
Argentina	73%	20%	7%
Colombia	70%	15%	15%
Peru	68%	19%	13%
Australia	63%	31%	6%
Finland	58%	36%	6%
U.S.	57%	30%	13%
Slovakia	55%	22%	23%
Hungary	55%	27%	18%
Japan	52%	45%	3%
Spain	49%	32%	19%
Czech Republic	47%	39%	14%
GOVERNMENT-DOMINANT			
Ireland	16%	77%	7%
Belgium	18%	77%	5%
Germany	32%	64%	4%
Israel	26%	64%	10%
Netherlands	38%	59%	3%
France	35%	58%	7%
Austria	44%	50%	6%
U.K.	44%	47%	9%
Romania	28%	45%	27%

Figure 2.2   Sources of nonprofit revenue, by country, 1995

der the category "government-dominant."[21] This is not the case in other countries where funding depends to a much greater extent on sales and membership fees. Finally, it should be noted that everywhere in the world, like Belgium, private giving makes up only a minor, even negligible, fraction of the nonprofit organizations' cash resources.

PERSPECTIVES

Through comparison with the other countries included in the Johns Hopkins project, it became increasingly evident that the Belgian nonprofit sector comprises a considerable component in the nation's economy: it employs over 10 percent of the paid workers, contributes to the gross domestic product (6 percent), mobilizes more than $25 billion (750 billion

BEF), and has recourse to a contingent of volunteer staff whose working hours amount to the equivalent of 100,000 full-time jobs.

Conscious of the lack of statistical evidence about the activities of these associations, the European Union has recently obliged its member-states to elaborate national accounts according to the latest version of the European System of National Accounts (ESA).[22] This version makes explicit space for the construction of a sector for "Nonprofit Institutions Serving Households" (NPISH). Toward this end, since 1997, the Belgian Institute of National Accounts has conducted a broad annual survey of AWPPs (nonprofit associations) that employ paid staff. Although this is a significant first step, the conventions in effect in the 1995 version of the ESA will not permit a satisfactory exploitation of the collected data. In fact, they will prevent researchers from answering in a sufficiently pertinent manner the following simple questions: "In the nonprofit sector, who produces what and how?"; "Who finances what?"; and "Who is the consumer of what?"

In order to give the most adequate description of this little-known component of the economy, the construction of a satellite account certainly constitutes a promising course of action. In use outside of Belgium for a number of years, satellite accounts form a flexible framework, particularly well-adapted to non-market activities. The construction of such a satellite account for the nonprofit sector has already been envisaged at an international level and constitutes one of the next items on the agenda of the Johns Hopkins Comparative Nonprofit Sector Project. In this respect, Belgium would appear to be at an advantage since an ongoing collaboration with the Institute for National Accounts may enable the construction of the first satellite account for nonprofit associations before the year 2001.[23]

If a better quantitative global knowledge of associations is desirable, the diversity of the fields studied should, however, cause researchers to act with prudence and suggest that the global statistical approach be complemented with field-related analyses, with case studies, and with more qualitative approaches inspired by a multi-disciplinary enlightenment. Statistics, and more particularly global statistics, are only tools, albeit useful ones, whose limits should also be taken into consideration. The other components of the Johns Hopkins project, i.e., the historical, legal, and policy analyses and the impact analysis, recognize those limits and thus can make a significant contribution to furthering research on the nonprofit sector in Belgium and elsewhere.

Finally, the joint presence of associations and public providers in the fields of collective services pleads in favor of a broader study of the non-market sector in its entirety. Belgian participation in the Johns Hopkins project can be considered a first stage in this research. It took the time necessary to study the private component of the non-market sector (the nonprofit sector) leaving aside the public component (public services).

REFERENCES

Hospitals

Institut National de Statistique (1994), *Annuaire de statistiques régionales,* Bruxelles.

Ministère de la santé publique et de l'environnement (1991), *Personnel occupé dans les hôpitaux (situation au 1 janvier 1991),* Bruxelles.

Ministère des Affaires Sociales, de la Santé publique et de l'environnement (1995), *Annuaire statistique des hôpitaux, parties 2 et 3 (situation au 1er janvier 1995),* Bruxelles.

Ministère de l'emploi et du travail (1997), *La population active en Belgique (situation au 30 juin 1995),* Bruxelles.

Schools

Institut National de Statistique (1994), *Annuaire de statistiques régionales,* Bruxelles.

Ministère de la Communauté française (1997), *Statistiques du personnel de l'enseignement, Annuaire 1995–1996,* Bruxelles.

Ministère de la Communauté française (1998), *Statistiques générales de l'enseignement et de la formation, Annuaire 1995–1996,* Bruxelles.

Ministère de la Communauté germanophone (1998), *Statistik Stand Januar 1996,* document de travail interne, Service Organization des Etudes.

Ministerie van de Vlaamse Gemeenschap (1998), *Statistisch jaarboek van het Vlaams onderwijs + addendum, schooljaar 1996/1997,* Brussel.

OCDE (1997), *Regards sur l'Education, les indicateurs de l'OCDE,* Paris.

Global statistics

Eurostat (1997), *Enquête sur les forces de travail—Résultats 1994,* Luxembourg.

Institut des Comptes Nationaux (1996), *Comptes nationaux 1995,* Service statistiques financières et économiques, Banque Nationale de Belgique, Bruxelles.

Institut National de Statistique (1994), *Annuaire de statistiques régionales,* Bruxelles.

Ministère de l'emploi et du travail (1997), *La population active en Belgique (situation au 30 juin 1995),* Bruxelles.

ENDNOTES

1. The work in Belgium is the first stage in a larger study of the non-market sector in Belgium. This part was coordinated by Jacques Defourny of the Centre d'Economie Sociale of Liège University and Josef Pacolet of the Hoger Instituut voor de Arbeid of Leuven. Assisting them were S. Mertens, S. Adam, M. Marée, and I. Van de Putte. Others who contributed significantly to this effort include Pascale Dubois (CIRIEC-Ulg), Nathalie Jauniaux (Ministry of the French-speaking population), Ides Nicaise and Els Plevoet (HIVA-KUL), Jacques Ouziel (Ministry of Work and Employment), Bénédicte Perrone (Wallonia Region), Michel Simon (CES-Ulg), Béatrice Thiry (National Bank of Belgium), Theresa Tilquin (Translator), Ilse Vleugels (HIVA-KUL), and Françoise Wagner (IRES-UCL). The team was aided, in turn, by a

local advisory committee (see Appendix D for a list of committee members). The Johns Hopkins Project was directed by Lester M. Salamon and Helmut K. Anheier. Financed in its preliminary stages by the SSTC (The Prime Minister's Scientific Affairs Technical and Cultural Services) and by the European Commission (DGXXIII), this study has also received the financial support of the King Baudouin Foundation, the Confederation of Non-market Sector Companies, and the Belgian Authorities.

2. The definitions and approaches used in the Johns Hopkins project were developed collaboratively with the cooperation of the Belgian researchers and researchers in other countries and were designed to be applicable to Belgium and the other project countries. For a full description of the Johns Hopkins project's definition of the nonprofit sector and the types of organizations included, see Appendix A. For a full list of the other countries included, see Chapter 1 above and Lester M. Salamon and Helmut K. Anheier, *The Emerging Sector Revisited: A Summary* (Baltimore, MD: The Johns Hopkins Center for Civil Society Studies, 1999). For the larger Belgian study, nonprofit organizations are a subset of the non-market sector, i.e., the sector made up of the organizations that, because of their non-lucrative nature, have exclusive or non-negligible recourse to non-market resources, i.e., resources other than those coming from the sale of their goods and services at a price expected to cover the cost of their production. For more information, see M. Marée (1998), *Le Secteur non marchand, essai de définition dans le contexte belge,* working note, Liège University.

3. Liège University (Centre for Social Economy) and the Katholieke Universiteit Leuven (Hoger Instituut Voor de Arbeid). For an initial and partial development of these surveys, see J. Defourny, P. Dubois and B. Perrone (1997), *La Démographie et l'emploi rémunéré des A.S.B.L. en Belgique,* Centre d'Economie Sociale, Liège University.

4. Insofar as the surveys depended on the use of samples, we should (if one considers the hypothesis of representativeness of the geographical areas studied) present the result as confidence intervals. Out of concern for their legibility we have restricted ourselves here to giving the mean values of these intervals.

5. These results are very similar to those presented in J. Defourny, P. Dubois and B. Perrone (1997), *op. cit.* The differences observed can be attributed to a revision of certain hypotheses at the time of extrapolation at a national level.

6. This number is slightly lower than that obtained if one calculates by "headcount," i.e., the numbers of workers. This is simply due to the relatively high proportion of part-time work in the associations.

7. Official statistics on employment in Belgium do not publish employment information in FTE. Thus, the Belgian estimates are based on the average of full-time equivalents from data concerning part-time work.

8. This result does not include voluntary work done in hospitals or that done within the private nonprofit school network.

9. We evaluated the wage bill by multiplying paid labor force (expressed in FTE) by the average labor cost in non-market sectors, in other words 1.25 million BEF. In fact, this estimation should be considered as the lower limit since the average cost was calculated using the number of workers and not as a measure of FTE. However, if we multiply this cost by the number of workers, we risk overestimating the wage bill because of the high proportion of part-time work in certain categories of AWPP's.

10. In previous research regarding the non-market sector in Belgium [J. Defourny, S. Mertens, M. Salamé (1996), "Le non-marchand, frein ou moteur pour la croissance", 12th Congress of Belgian economists of the French language, Charleroi], it was demonstrated that the wage bill made up 97 percent of the sector's added value, and thus, the wage bill can be considered a first approximation of the added value generated by the activity of the associations. Note that the work of volunteers was not taken into account when calculating the added

value, in accordance with conventions in effect in the European System of National Accounts (ESA). In 1995, the current GDP at market prices amounted to 7,936 billion BEF. Institut des Comptes Nationaux (1996), *Comptes Nationaux 1995, Partie 1—Agrégats et Comptes*, Brussels.

11. Robert Eisner, *The Total Incomes System of Accounts, Survey of Current Business*, January 1985, pp 26–34.

12. One might be surprised to note that 10 percent of paid workers only achieve 6 percent of the added value of the Belgian economy. This remark refers us back to the question of worker productivity. Rather than hastily concluding that people working in associations demonstrate lower productivity, one must remember that the apparent productivity of a worker also depends on the other factors of production that are called into play in addition to the worker himself. Therefore, a worker with a machine at his disposal will have an apparently higher productivity than a worker without a machine. In fact, the associations use few other factors besides the work itself. In associations, apparent work productivity can therefore be assimilated to all practical purposes with its real productivity (in other words, a measure of the productivity that manages to remove the positive effect of the other factors), which is not the case of capital intensive industries within which there are fewer associations.

13. This result does not include volunteering in schools and hospitals. The pilot survey did not cover these organizations and the official statistics agencies do not issue information on the extent of volunteering in these structures. Even though we do not possess data on volunteering in hospitals, it is particularly active. The presence of volunteer staff is a complement to the paid nursing staff, the duties of which are becoming more and more technically oriented. Nor are there any data concerning volunteering in schools, which often takes the form of parent participation.

14. A finer analysis of volunteering would without doubt enable us to distinguish the specific motivations for each type of activity. In the social services, volunteers are probably led by the pursuit of general interest whereas for the more recreational activities it is probably the mutual interest of its members that is the guiding force.

15. Even though our legislation requires that schooling be free of charge, in fact the financial participation of parents in nonprofit private schools is not insignificant. We do not have access to data allowing us to quantify this participation and thus to evaluate the share of non-public resources in the funding of nonprofit private schools.

16. 100,687 FTE (volunteering in all the ICNPO groups with the exception of hospitals and nonprofit private schools) multiplied by 1.25 million BEF (average labor cost in non-market sectors) = 125.8 billion BEF. Once again, this estimation constitutes the lower limit because we have multiplied the average labor cost by volunteering expressed in FTE and not in the number of volunteers.

17. Further details on the results of the research project can be found in Chapter 1 of this volume and L.M. Salamon, H.K. Anheier and Associates [1999], *op.cit.*

18. The Belgian result shown in Figure 2.1 differs from that shown in Table 2.3 because the Belgian team's definition of what is included in "religious worship" differs from that used by the Johns Hopkins project for international comparison. Therefore, the Johns Hopkins estimates do not include this component in its data on Belgium.

19. If we take into account both volunteers and paid employees, Belgium's international position remains unchanged.

20. Pillarization appears in Belgium as early as the 19th century. It can be observed in the constitution of groups with differing political and philosophical tendencies. As time passed, these associations that were active in various fields of community life (health, mutual aid, education, etc.) eventually formed real families, or "pillars," of which the most important are those of socialist and Christian inspiration, respectively. Today, each pillar includes a union branch, a cooperative branch, a health insurance branch, a political branch, etc.

21. See endnote number 18.

22. The European System of National Accounts (ESA) is the European version of the System of National Accounts of the United Nations.

23. For further information on the limits of the national accounts in grasping the nonprofit sector and on the advantage of a satellite account for the nonprofit sector, see S. Mertens (1999), *Du traitement des associations par les appareils statistiques officiels à la nécessaire construction d'un compte satellite,* Centre of Social Economy, Liège University.

CHAPTER 3

Finland

Voitto Helander, Harri Laaksonen, Susan Sundback,
Helmut K. Anheier, and Lester M. Salamon

BACKGROUND

Unlike Belgium and the rest of Western Europe, Finland adopted quite different arrangements for attending to the social welfare and other needs of its society. A "Nordic-type" government social welfare system based on the principle of universal coverage and a strong tradition of popular social movements has greatly influenced the development of the Finnish nonprofit sector. As of the mid-1990s, therefore, the Finnish nonprofit, or "third," sector was relatively small in terms of paid employment, with a lower concentration of employees in social welfare fields than in most other countries. Reflecting this, the sector has been less reliant overall on public sector payments than its counterparts elsewhere in Western Europe. The picture changes dramatically, however, when account is taken of the involvement of volunteers in Finnish social movement organizations. This involvement has been substantial, making the third sector in Finland a far more significant social, political, and economic force than the data on paid employment alone would suggest. In addition, at the close of the 20th century, the Finnish nonprofit sector faces tremendous challenges as citizens, politicians, and public officials look for alternative ways to provide for societal needs.

Global Civil Society: Dimensions of the Nonprofit Sector by Lester M. Salamon, Helmut K. Anheier, Regina List, Stefan Toepler, S. Wojciech Sokolowski and Associates. Baltimore, MD: Johns Hopkins Center for Civil Society Studies, 1999.

These and other findings reported in this chapter result from work carried out by a Finnish research team based at the Department of Public Administration of the Åbo Akademi as part of the Johns Hopkins Comparative Nonprofit Sector Project.[1] This work sought both to analyze Finnish nonprofit circumstances and to compare and contrast them to those in other countries both in Western Europe and elsewhere in a systematic way.[2] The result is the first empirical overview of the Finnish nonprofit sector and the first systematic comparison of Finnish nonprofit realities to those elsewhere in the world.

The present chapter reports on just one set of findings from this project, those relating to the size and structure of the nonprofit sector in Finland (as of 1996) and elsewhere. Subsequent publications will fill in the historical, legal, and policy context of this sector and also examine the impact that this set of institutions is having. Most of the data reported here were drawn from a comprehensive survey of local-level associations complemented by a survey of national-level associations and data on private foundations. These field data were supplemented with data from official Finnish statistics and special studies on associations. (For a more complete statement of the sources of data, see Appendix C.) Unless otherwise noted, financial data are reported in U.S. dollars using the 1996 exchange rate for Finland and the 1995 exchange rate for other countries.

PRINCIPAL FINDINGS

Five major findings emerge from this work on the scope, structure, financing, and role of the nonprofit sector in Finland.

1. A sizable economic force

In the first place, despite the presence of a highly developed "welfare state," Finland has a sizable nonprofit sector that, though smaller than its counterparts elsewhere in Western Europe, still accounts for significant shares of national expenditures and employment.

More specifically:

- **A $4.7 billion industry.** Even excluding its religion component, the nonprofit sector in Finland had operating expenditures of $4.7 billion in 1996, or 3.8 percent of the country's gross domestic product, a significant amount.[3]
- **A major employer.** Behind these expenditures lies a sizable workforce that includes the equivalent of 63,000 full-time equivalent paid workers. This represents 3 percent of all nonagricultural workers in the

country, 9.5 percent of service employment, and the equivalent of nearly one-eighth as many people as work for government at all levels-national, provincial, and municipal (see Table 3.1).

- **More employees than in the largest private firm.** Put somewhat differently, nonprofit employment in Finland outdistances the employment in the largest private business in the country by a ratio of 3:2. Thus, compared to the 63,000 paid workers in Finland's nonprofit organizations, Finland's largest private corporation, Nokia, employs 44,000 workers, only 19,000 of whom work in Finland (see Figure 3.1).

- **Outdistances numerous industries.** Indeed, more people work in the nonprofit sector in Finland than in some entire industries in the country. Thus, as shown in Figure 3.2, nonprofit employment in Finland outdistances employment in the country's paper making and food industries that employ 45,000 and 39,000 persons, respectively.[4]

- **Volunteer inputs.** Paid employment does a particularly inadequate job of capturing the full reality of the nonprofit sector in Finland, however, because this sector plays less of a service delivery than policy advocacy role. As such, it attracts a considerable amount of *volunteer*

Table 3.1   The nonprofit sector in Finland, 1996

$4.7 billion in expenditures
— 3.8 percent of GDP

62,848 paid employees
— 3.0 percent of total nonagricultural employment
— 9.5 percent of total service employment
— 12.9 percent of public sector employment

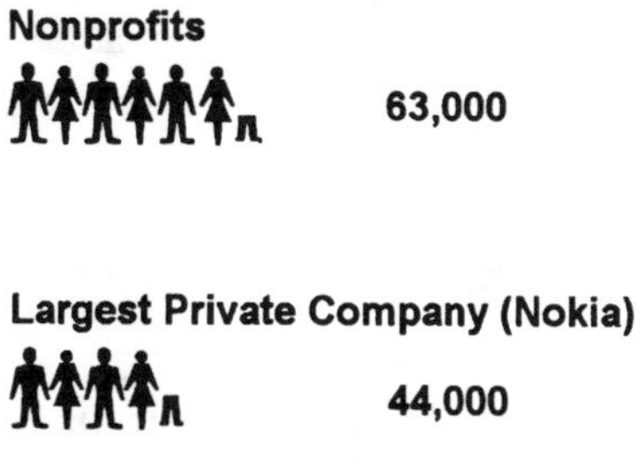

Nonprofits

63,000

Largest Private Company (Nokia)

44,000

Figure 3.1   Employment in nonprofits vs. largest firm in Finland, 1996

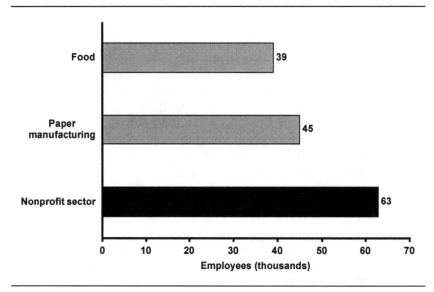

Figure 3.2   Nonprofit employment in Finland in context, 1996

effort. Indeed, an estimated 12.6 percent of the Finnish population reports contributing their time to nonprofit organizations. This translates into another 75,000 full-time equivalent employees, which more than doubles the total number of full-time equivalent employees of nonprofit organizations in Finland to 138,000, or 6.3 percent of total employment in the country (see Figure 3.3).

- **Religion.** The inclusion of religion (but not state-sponsored churches), moreover, would raise these totals by another 3,000 paid employees and 2,000 full-time equivalent volunteers. With religion included, nonprofit paid employment therefore rises modestly from 3.0 to 3.1 percent of the total; factoring in both paid and volunteer employment increases this share from 6.3 to 6.4 percent. Religion also increases operating expenditures by $176 million, thus bringing total expenditures to $4.9 billion, the equivalent of 3.9 percent of the gross domestic product.

2. One of the smallest nonprofit sectors in Western Europe

Although the size of the Finnish nonprofit sector is considerable relative to the Finnish economy, it is small relative to its counterparts in other Western European countries included in this study, though still above the level in most countries outside of Europe.

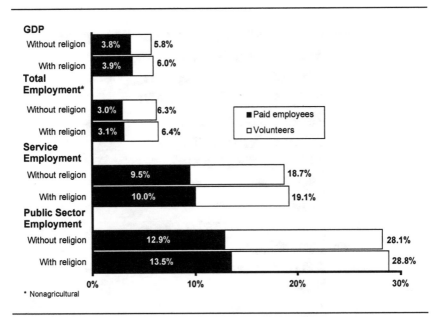

Figure 3.3 Nonprofits in Finland, with and without volunteers and religion, 1996, as a % of . . .

- **Below the international average.** As Figure 3.4 shows, the relative size of the nonprofit sector varies greatly among countries, from a high of 12.6 percent of total nonagricultural employment in the Netherlands to a low of less than 1 percent of total employment in Mexico. The overall 22-country average, however, was 4.8 percent. This means that Finland, at 3.0 percent without religion, falls considerably below the global average.
- **Considerably below the Western European and other developed countries averages.** Nonprofit employment as a share of total employment is also considerably lower in Finland than it is elsewhere in Western Europe and other developed countries. However, nonprofit employment in Finland is still higher than in Central Europe and Latin America. Thus, as shown in Figure 3.5, full-time equivalent employment in nonprofit organizations in Finland, at 3 percent of total employment, is less than half the Western European and other developed countries averages of 6.9 percent. However, in relation to her nearest neighbor-country, Sweden, the Finnish figure is comparable. The nonprofit sector employment share for Sweden in 1992 was a little lower than that in Finland.[5]

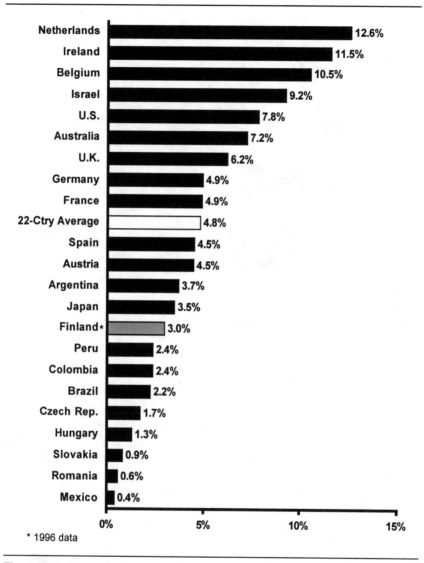

Figure 3.4 Nonprofit share of total employment, by country, 1995

- **Margin narrows significantly with volunteers.** As noted above, with volunteer time included, nonprofit organizations account for 6.3 percent of total employment in Finland. Thus, although the employment share is still less than the Western European regional average of 10.3 percent, the margin narrows considerably (see Figure 3.5).

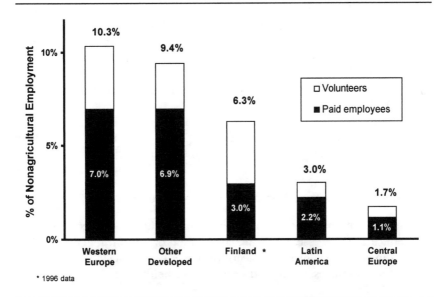

Figure 3.5 Nonprofit share of employment, with and without volunteers, Finland and four regions, 1995

3. A limited history of nonprofit activity

That the nonprofit sector is relatively small in Finland is very likely a product of the country's social and political structure. The following features in particular seem to have shaped the Finnish nonprofit sector:[6]

- *A traditional cultural homogeneity* has favored egalitarian ideals and equal treatment for all citizens in public policies and administration. Thus private schools, private hospitals, and other agencies that cater to particular population groups have been seen as problematic, possibly promoting inequity.
- Also limiting the incentives to form nonprofit organizations has been an ancient tradition of strong *local government* which, with the help of the Lutheran parishes, survived through periods of centralized power. This tradition of local self-government gives individuals and groups confidence that local politicians will represent their interests.
- The Finnish population has turned actively to private associations as vehicles for social movements seeking to provide health and social benefits, among other things. Such social movements were crucial to Finland becoming an independent state in 1917 and have played a

central political role in the country's development into a Nordic-type welfare state. The resulting organizations historically have been content to leave the service delivery functions to government and to perform more of an advocacy and watchdog function themselves.

- The tax-financed universal welfare system has *high legitimacy* among the population but criticism and increasing needs for alternative solutions have recently surfaced.
- The old social movements are suffering from institutionalization, an aging membership, and recruitment problems and *tend to distrust* changes that are contrary to their own traditional ideals.

4. A balanced composition of the nonprofit sector

Similar to other Western European countries and the all-country average, education and research is the largest field of nonprofit activity in Finland as measured by its share of nonprofit employment. However, unlike most other countries, in Finland several other fields rival it in size.

- **One-quarter of nonprofit employment in education and research.** Of all the types of nonprofit activity, the one that accounts for the largest share of nonprofit employment in Finland is education and research. As shown in Figure 3.6, 25 percent of all nonprofit employment in Finland is concentrated in the education field, mainly in vocational and other adult education organizations. This is comparable to the Western European average of 28.1 percent; however, the share of employment in education and research does not dominate the sector in Finland as it does in many other societies. Its relative weight within the Finnish nonprofit sector very likely reflects the fact that the education field employs many professionals, especially in the subfield of adult education.
- **Sizable nonprofit employment shares in other social welfare fields.** Another sizable portion of total nonprofit employment in Finland is found in the health and social services fields. As shown in Figure 3.6, the health field accounts for 23 percent of nonprofit employment and social services comprises 17.8 percent. Altogether, the three core welfare fields (education, health, and social services) account for 65.8 percent of all nonprofit employment in Finland. Although this share is slightly less than the 22-country average for these three fields (68.1 percent) and significantly less than the Western European average (77.1 percent), the core social welfare functions in Finland remain an important generator of paid work among nonprofit organizations.
- **Relatively large share of nonprofit employment in civic and advocacy.** The civic and advocacy field absorbs by far a larger share of nonprofit

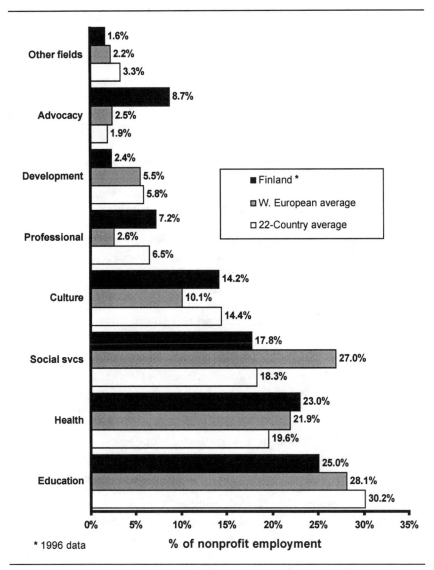

Figure 3.6 Composition of the nonprofit sector, Finland, W. Europe, and 22-country average, 1995

employment in Finland than in any of the other 21 countries studied. Thus, while civic and advocacy associations within the 22 countries studied absorb 1.9 percent of nonprofit employment on average, they account for a much larger 8.7 percent of nonprofit employment in Finland. This very likely reflects the traditionally important roles that civic and political associations have played at both national and local levels. Political associations such as youth, women, and pensioner organizations that belong to the "party family" without being political party organizations proper, are strong organizations with numerous salaried officials. Several other multifunctional organizations act at the same time as both service organizations and interest organizations. Since they define their functional focus as interest mediation in relation to public authorities, they are classified as civic and advocacy organizations.

- **Pattern shifts significantly with volunteers.** This pattern changes considerably when volunteer inputs are factored in. In particular, as shown in Figure 3.7, with volunteers included, the weight of nonprofit employment shifts dramatically to the field of culture and recreation. With volunteers, the share of employment in cultural and recreational activities rises from 14.2 percent to 32.6 percent, making it by far the largest field. This reflects the ability of organizations in this field, particularly sports, to capture nearly one half of all nonprofit sector volunteering. The civic and advocacy field takes second place, with its share rising from 8.7 percent without volunteers to 16.8 percent with them. As in the case of culture and recreation, this increase is based on the great voluntary input that constitutes almost one-fourth of all volunteering.

In summary, in terms of paid employment, the Finnish nonprofit sector is relatively small, in fact the smallest in relation to those in the other Western European countries. Although social welfare services absorb nearly two-thirds of paid nonprofit employment in Finland, their combined share is not as significant as elsewhere in Western Europe where nonprofit organizations are much more engaged in service delivery. Rather, these social welfare fields are more in balance with other fields of nonprofit activity, such as culture and recreation, civic and advocacy, and professional associations that have more to do with social mobilization than services. When volunteering is factored in, the share of nonprofit employment more than doubles in relation to total employment. Furthermore, the profile of the nonprofit sector changes dramatically so that activities other than social welfare take on much larger shares of the total.

5. Most revenue from private fees, not philanthropy or public sector

Consistent with its relative smallness, its strong reliance on voluntary work, and its more balanced composition, the Finnish nonprofit sector receives the bulk of its cash revenue not from private philanthropy or the public sector, but from private fees and charges.

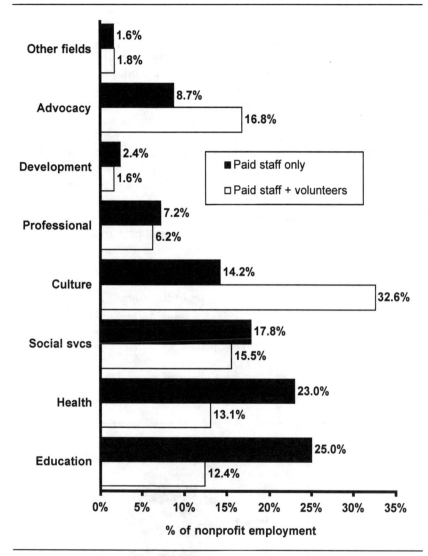

Figure 3.7   Share of nonprofit employment in Finland, with and without volunteers, by field, 1996

- **Fee income dominant.** The dominant source of income of nonprofit organizations in Finland is fees and charges for the services that these organizations provide, as well as membership dues. As reflected in Figure 3.8, this source alone accounts for nearly three-fifths, or 57.9 percent, of all nonprofit revenue in Finland.

- **Limited support from philanthropy and the public sector.** By contrast, private philanthropy and the public sector provide much smaller shares of total revenues. Thus, as Figure 3.8 shows, private philanthropy—from individuals, corporations, and foundations combined—accounts for only 5.9 percent of nonprofit income in Finland, while public sector payments account for 36.2 percent.
- **Revenue structure with volunteers.** This pattern of nonprofit revenue changes dramatically when volunteers are factored into the picture. In fact, as shown in Figure 3.9, private philanthropy swells by a factor of approximately 6 once volunteers are included, jumping from 5.9 percent of total revenue without volunteers to 34.6 percent with them, thereby moving ahead of public sector financing (25.2 percent). Although private fees and charges remain the dominant source of income at 40.3 percent, their dominance is reduced significantly.
- **Revenue structure with religion.** The overall pattern of nonprofit finance in Finland changes only modestly when account is taken of religious institutions, such as churches and synagogues, but not the official churches of the state. Such religious institutions account for approximately 4 percent of the total revenue of the Finnish nonprofit sector. With religion included, therefore, the philanthropic share of total nonprofit revenue in Finland rises from 5.9 percent to 7.1 percent. With volunteers included as well, the private giving share rises to 35.6 percent (see Figure 3.10).
- **Different from other Western European countries.** The pattern of nonprofit finance evident in Finland is quite different from that else-

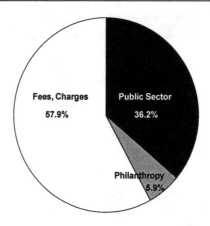

Figure 3.8   Sources of nonprofit revenue in Finland, 1996

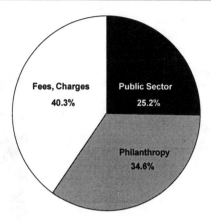

Figure 3.9 Sources of nonprofit revenue in Finland, with volunteers, 1996

where in Western Europe. Thus, as shown in Figure 3.11, unlike Finland, the nonprofit organizations in the Western European countries included in this project, on average, derived the overwhelming majority of their revenues from the public sector. Thus, in contrast to Finland's 36.2 percent, the share of total nonprofit income coming from the public sector stood at 55.6 percent on average for all nine Western European countries. The fees and private giving shares of nonprofit

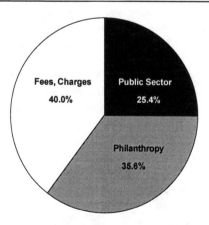

Figure 3.10 Sources of nonprofit revenue in Finland, with volunteers and religious worship, 1996

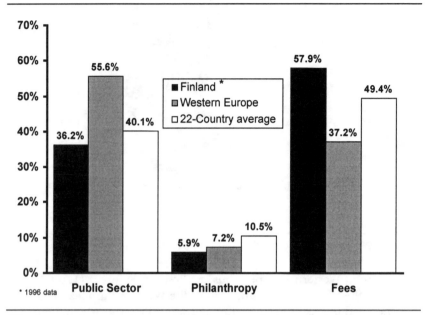

Figure 3.11   Sources of nonprofit cash revenue, Finland, W. Europe, and 22-country average, 1995

revenue in Finland deviated considerably from the Western European regional average, with fees and charges much stronger in Finland than elsewhere in the region (57.9 percent in Finland compared to an average of 37.2 percent for all nine Western European countries) and philanthropy somewhat weaker (5.9 percent as compared to 7.2 percent).

- **More like the global average.** While the revenue structure of the Finnish nonprofit sector differs from that elsewhere in Western Europe, it generally mirrors that evident elsewhere in the world. However, as Figure 3.11 also shows, although fees and charges are the dominant element in the financial base of the nonprofit sector globally, their dominance is less pronounced elsewhere than in Finland (49.4 percent of total revenue compared to 57.9 percent in Finland). By contrast, public sector payments comprise a larger share of nonprofit income in these other countries on average (40.1 percent as compared to 36.2 percent in Finland). Quite clearly, a different pattern of cooperation has taken shape between nonprofit organizations and the state in these other countries. Evidently, the Nordic-type welfare system adopted by Finland, in which the state directly provides

In summary, the overall composition of the German nonprofit sector with its overwhelming dominance of core welfare services, especially social care and health, closely reflects the cooperative relationships between the state and crucial parts of the nonprofit sector. Indeed, Germany provides a prime example of a corporatist regime, largely driven by the adoption of the principle of subsidiarity by the state in the social policy realm. By contrast, the German nonprofit sector seems relatively underdeveloped in service areas such as education and culture, where this principle has not taken root and where state provision remains the rule.

5. Most revenue from the public sector, not philanthropy or fees

Consistent with the principle of subsidiarity, the German nonprofit sector receives the bulk of its revenue not from private philanthropy or fees, but from public sector sources. In particular:

- **Public sector income dominant.** The overwhelmingly dominant source of income of nonprofit organizations in Germany is public sector payments. As reflected in Figure 5.8, this source alone accounts for almost two-thirds, or 64 percent, of all nonprofit revenue in Germany.
- **Limited support from philanthropy and private fees and charges.** By contrast, private philanthropy and fees provide much smaller shares of total revenues. Thus, as Figure 5.8 shows, private philanthropy—from individuals, corporations, and foundations combined—accounts for only 3 percent of nonprofit income in Germany, while fees and charges account for nearly one-third.

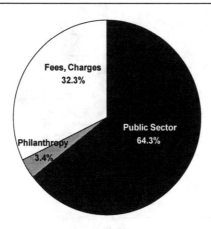

Figure 5.8   Sources of nonprofit revenue in Germany, 1995

- **Revenue structure with volunteers.** This pattern of nonprofit revenue changes significantly when volunteers are factored into the picture. In fact, as shown in Figure 5.9, private philanthropy increases substantially from 3 percent to 36 percent, thereby clearly overtaking fees and charges (21 percent) though still falling short of the level of public sector support (43 percent).
- **Similar to other Western European countries.** The pattern of nonprofit finance evident in Germany is quite similar to that elsewhere in Western Europe, although this pattern is even more pronounced in the German case. Thus, as shown in Figure 5.10, like Germany, the nonprofit organizations in the other Western European countries included in this project (Austria, Belgium, Finland, France, Ireland, the Netherlands, Spain, and the U.K.) derived on average the overwhelming majority of their revenues from public sector sources. Thus, compared to Germany's 64 percent, the share of total nonprofit income coming from the public sector stood at 56 percent for the other Western European countries. Although similar in tendency, the philanthropy and fee shares of nonprofit revenue in Germany deviated from the regional average, with philanthropy weaker by half in Germany than elsewhere in the region (3 percent vs. 7 percent on average) and fees also somewhat weaker (32 percent vs. 37 percent). Interestingly, the share of philanthropy in Germany remains low even when the "quasi-voluntary" income from the church tax is taken into account. The church tax is a levy on the income tax of church members, collected by the government revenue service on behalf of the main

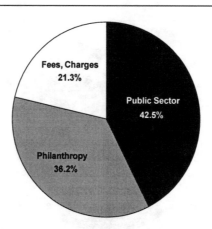

Figure 5.9   Sources of nonprofit revenue in Germany, with volunteers, 1995

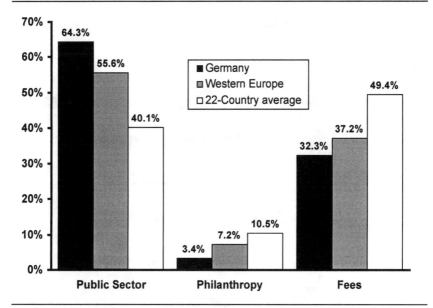

Figure 5.10   Sources of nonprofit cash revenue, Germany, Western Europe, and 22-country average, 1995

churches. Adding the church tax income would increase the philanthropy share by approximately one percent.

- **Deviation from the global average.** While the revenue structure of the German nonprofit sector generally mirrors that elsewhere in Western Europe, it differs considerably from that evident elsewhere in the world. Thus, as Figure 5.10 also shows, public sector payments account for a considerably larger share of nonprofit income in Germany than in these other countries on average (64 percent vs. 40 percent). By contrast, fees and charges account for a considerably smaller share (32 percent vs. 49 percent). Evidently, the subsidiarity-based partnership between the state and the nonprofit sector in Germany has allowed German nonprofits to escape the dependence on the market so evident elsewhere.
- **Variations by subsector.** Even this does not do full justice to the complexities of nonprofit finance in Germany, however. This is so because important differences exist in the finances of nonprofit organizations by subsector. In fact, two quite distinct patterns of nonprofit finance are evident among German nonprofits, as shown in Figure 5.11:

  Public sector-dominant fields. In six fields (health, education, social services, civic, development, and international activities) government

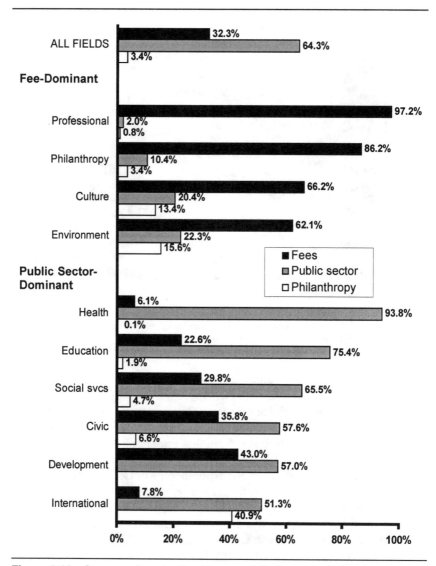

Figure 5.11   Sources of nonprofit cash revenue in Germany, by field, 1995

plays the dominant role in financing nonprofit action in Germany. For the most part, the dominance of this support derives from third-party payments of public health and social insurance systems, of which the health and social care parts of the nonprofit sector are primary beneficiaries. In education, government support results from subsidies for elementary and secondary education. In the civic and advocacy area, the state supports advocacy and support organizations for certain social groups, such as the elderly or disadvantaged families. In development, municipalities have come to finance nonprofit job training programs for young and long-term unemployed in the context of combating high unemployment levels. Particularly in East Germany, organizations offering job opportunities in community work or the environment are highly subsidized. Finally, the policy field of foreign aid and international activities is another prime example of "third-party government" in Germany.[5] While the state keeps a relatively low profile, nonprofit organizations affiliated with the main churches and the political parties, as well as the Red Cross, play a significant role in channeling government funds for international disaster relief and development aid.

Fee-dominant fields. Fee income is the dominant source of income in four fields of nonprofit action for which data were gathered. Professional associations and unions are almost exclusively financed through membership dues. Membership dues also explain the high degree of fee income in the environmental field. In culture and recreation, the fee income is comprised of a combination of dues (sport and social clubs) and admission and ticket sales in the arts. The philanthropy area, in turn, is essentially financed out of investment and similar income.

- **State dependency?** The relatively high government support share of total nonprofit sector cash revenue frequently has led to criticism of the sector's growing dependence on the state. As shown above, however, the share of government support varies greatly by field and shrinks considerably when volunteer labor is factored in. Shifting the unit of analysis from the sectoral to the organizational level, moreover, yields still another view: Of the organizations that responded to the project's organizational survey, only 23 percent reported receiving more than half of their revenues from direct public sector payments and subsidies, and another 10 percent reported deriving more than half of their revenues from third-party payments of public sickness funds. The finding that only about one-third of all nonprofit organizations in Germany receive the majority of their funding from the public sector thus raises important doubts about the validity of the wide-spread state-dependency thesis despite the relatively high overall share of government support in nonprofit finance in Germany.

6. Growth and change in the sector (1990–1995)

Not only does the German nonprofit sector carry significant economic weight, but it has also been been growing in importance.[6] Whereas

nonprofit organizations in the former West Germany had expenditures of
$54 billion in 1990, total expenditures amounted to $94 billion in 1995 for
the whole country. Expressed as a percentage of GDP, however, nonprofit
expenditures remained constant at 3.9 percent. In terms of its employment
contributions, the West German nonprofit sector boasted approximately
one million full-time equivalent jobs in 1990, which translated into a 3.7
percent share of total employment. With the former East Germany included, the number of full-time equivalent nonprofit jobs exceeded 1.4
million in 1995, constituting a substantially increased share of total employment of nearly five percent (see Table 5.2).

This expansion of the German nonprofit sector between 1990 and 1995
was due to the continued growth of the West German nonprofit sector, but
also, to a significant degree, to the formation of nonprofit organizations in
the former East Germany after the end of socialist rule. Although a rudimentary nonprofit sector existed in these parts early on, it was not possible
to capture it statistically in 1990. In 1995, nonprofit organizations in the
area of the former East Germany accounted for an estimated 20 percent of
the German nonprofit sector's size.

Interestingly, however, the evolution of the East German nonprofit sector differed significantly from the development path of nonprofit organizations in other post-socialist societies, since it mostly followed West German
patterns. While the East German nonprofit sector has therefore generally
become a mirror image of its West German counterpart, the characteristics
of its evolution nevertheless influenced certain aspects of the structure and
financing of the German nonprofit scene as a whole. This becomes evident
when changes in the composition of the sector are taken into account. As
borne out in Table 5.3, the high demand especially for social services in
the East boosted the relative share of social service employment in total
nonprofit employment from 32 percent in 1990 to 39 percent in 1995. By
the same token, the greater reliance on the state in the East to provide
health, educational, and cultural services—as a persisting remnant of the

Table 5.2 Change in the German nonprofit sector, 1990–1995

	1990	1995
Operating expenditures (in billions)	$54	$94
as % of GDP	3.9%	3.9%
Paid FTE employment (in millions)	1.02	1.44
as % of total nonagricultural employment	3.7%	4.9%

Source: Johns Hopkins Comparative Nonprofit Sector Project/Germany

Table 5.3   Changes in the employment composition of the German nonprofit
sector, 1990–1995

	1990	1995
Culture and recreation	6.3%	5.4%
Education and research	12.9%	11.7%
Health	35.8%	30.6%
Social services	32.3%	38.8%
Environment	0.2%	0.8%
Development and housing	5.9%	6.1%
Civic and advocacy	1.3%	1.6%
Philanthropy	0.3%	0.4%
International	0.5%	0.7%
Professional associations and unions	4.4%	3.9%
Total	100%	100%

Source: Johns Hopkins Comparative Nonprofit Sector Project/Germany

socialist era—slowed down the development of these fields for the German nonprofit sector as a whole (e.g., health employment as a share of total nonprofit employment dropped from 36 percent in 1990 to less than 31 percent in 1995).

In terms of changes in the revenue composition, the substantial public start-up funding that supported the development of the nonprofit sector in the East over the first few years helped offset the overall trend of declining government support in relative terms. Whereas the share of public sector support in total nonprofit revenues stood at 68 percent for (West) Germany in 1990, it only accounted for 64 percent for the unified Germany in 1995. Without the substantial public investment in the East German nonprofit infrastructure, therefore, the relative share of government support in 1995 would have been considerably lower.

CONCLUSIONS AND IMPLICATIONS

The nonprofit sector thus emerges from the evidence presented here as both a sizable and a rather complex set of institutions in German society. Not only does this set of institutions serve important human needs, it also constitutes a major economic force and a significant contributor to political as well as social life.

The complexity derives mainly from the fact that the German nonprofit sector almost divides into two more or less distinct parts, which has impeded the development of a unified sector identity in the past. One part of the sector is comprised of nonprofit activities in areas such as culture, recreation and sports, and the environment, which show a remarkable degree of civicness and rely heavily on membership dues and volunteer input to finance their activities. The other part consists of nonprofit organizations primarily active in the health and social services fields, which are an integral part of the German welfare state and where the principle of subsidiarity is most forcefully in place. Health and social service organizations are highly professionalized, thus perceived as less civic, and rely primarily on income from social insurance payments and direct state subsidies. Nonprofits in these fields, as well as in some other highly subsidized areas, such as international activities and local development, cooperate very closely with the public sector. Although, as noted above, the state dependency thesis cannot be generalized over the whole German nonprofit sector, it is especially in these fields that nonprofit organizations appear to be quasi-governmental and almost indistinguishable in their operations from the encompassing German state bureaucracy.

These structural particularities of the nonprofit sector were essentially transferred to East Germany after the unification in 1990. The unification treaty included a provision extending the subsidiarity principle in health and social services to the new German states, and the federal government provided substantial seed money to support the establishment of a nonprofit infrastructure in the core welfare service areas. Financial support was also granted to emerging nonprofit organizations in sports, recreation, and culture, but to a significantly lesser degree. With the availability of job subsidies for nonprofits, in addition to the considerable direct public investment, the East German nonprofit sector began to grow at a remarkable pace after unification compared to both the overall economic growth in East Germany and the growth of the nonprofit sector in other post-communist transition countries in Central Europe. In fact, today there are hardly any significant differences between the East and West German nonprofit sectors with respect to size and societal importance.

By the same token, however, East Germany also inherited the many problems of the West German sector, most of which are closely related to the legacy of subsidiarity. Specifically, the highly subsidized and professionalized parts of the sector are looked upon as "public" entities and thus fail to attract volunteers or private giving to any significant degree. This lack of civic or societal embeddedness is perhaps even a little more pronounced in the Eastern parts of the country, where these organizations essentially emerged as a product of an institutional transfer from the West without having any roots in the local communities.

While the principle of subsidiarity has thus generally been both benefi-
cial and problematic for the development of the German nonprofit sector,
its future is anything but assured. In fact, the privileged position that it ac-
cords to parts of the nonprofit sector is at odds with the market-driven
logic at the European Union level. At present, it seems rather unlikely that
German nonprofits will be able to protect their market shares in health
and social services in the future due to the European deregulation procedures. In accordance with the European integration rules, recent German
legislation has already begun to loosen the rigidity of the subsidiarity principle in some areas. In the context of the recently introduced long-term
care insurance, for example, all service providers regardless of their organizational form are treated on equal footing. Thus, nonprofits have not
been able to capture significant market shares in the relatively new personal social care market. More generally, there is little doubt that Brussels
will gain in importance in the future as far as the legal regulation and
funding procedures and sources are concerned. Already, a number of EU
programs providing infrastructure and financial support are leaving their
marks on German nonprofit organizations, especially in fields such as arts
and culture and education and job training.

Whatever else the future of the EU integration might entail, the German
nonprofit sector is already facing a turbulent environment, particularly
with respect to the possibility of legal reforms at the national level. Currently being discussed are possible changes in the legal treatment of foundations, the tax deductibility of corporate and individual giving, and the
treatment of earned income and business activities of nonprofits. With the
new Social-Democratic government just beginning to "discover" the nonprofit sector as the fastest growing segment of the country's service industry, major legal changes in these areas might indeed become a reality. Any
loosening of the earned income and business activity rules would perhaps
have the most far-reaching ramifications, as the current rules have so far
impeded the ability of the German nonprofit sector to follow the global
trend of commercialization and monetarization. Selected results from the
project's organizational survey already indicate that German nonprofits
are getting ready to substitute a stronger market orientation for their traditional "state dependency." How far such a trend will proceed is an open
question at this writing. Clearly, however, data of the sort presented here
will be crucial in charting the evolution.

ENDNOTES

1. The work in Germany was coordinated by Eckhard Priller of the Wissenschaftszentrum
Berlin für Sozialforschung (WZB) and Annette Zimmer of the Westf. Wilhems-Universität

Münster, who acted as local associates to the project. Assisting them were Klaudia Sauer, Sigrid Glowka, Jana Rückert, Nicole Schneider, Thorsten Hallmann, André Zimmermann, Georg Albers, Stefan Modlich, and Ingo Benitz. The team was aided, in turn, by a local advisory committee made up of more than 20 prominent philanthropic, government, academic, and business leaders (see Appendix D for a list of committee members). The Johns Hopkins project was directed by Lester M. Salamon and Helmut K. Anheier.

2. The definitions and approaches used in the project were developed collaboratively with the cooperation of the German researchers and researchers in other countries and were designed to be applicable to Germany and the other project countries. For a full description of this definition and the types of organizations included, see Appendix A. For a full list of the other countries included, see Chapter 1 above and Lester M. Salamon and Helmut K. Anheier, *The Emerging Sector Revisited: A Summary* (Baltimore, MD: The Johns Hopkins Center for Civil Society Studies, 1999).

3. Technically, the more precise comparison is between nonprofit contribution to "value added" and gross domestic product. For the nonprofit sector, "value added" in economic terms essentially equals the sum of wages and the imputed value of volunteer time. On this basis, the nonprofit sector in Germany accounted for 4.5 percent of total value added, a somewhat higher amount.

4. Helmut K. Anheier and Wolfgang Seibel, "Germany," in Lester M. Salamon and Helmut K. Anheier, *Defining the Nonprofit Sector: A Cross-national Analysis*, Vol. 4 in the Johns Hopkins Nonprofit Sector Series (Manchester: Manchester University Press, 1997), p.129.

5. See Lester M. Salamon, "Rethinking Public Management: Third-Party Government and the Changing Forms of Government Action, " *Public Policy*, Vol. 29 (Summer 1981), pp. 255–275.

6. See Eckhard Priller, Annette Zimmer, and Helmut K. Anheier, "Der Dritte Sektor in Deutschland: Entwicklungen, Potentiale, Erwartungen." *Aus Politik und Zeitgeschichte*, B9/99, February 26, 1999, pp.12–21.

CHAPTER 6

Ireland

Freda Donoghue, Helmut K. Anheier, and
Lester M. Salamon

BACKGROUND

Attention is being focused more and more on the voluntary and community sector in Ireland—its role in local development and in service provision, its significance in the area of anti-poverty action, and its importance in the growth of Irish society as a whole. Such interest, however, runs the risk of mere platitude if it is not supported by substantial evidence of the sector's value and worth. Lack of information on the sector has been a factor in debates on the sector up until recently, and much research to date on the voluntary sector has been issue-focused, applied, or prescribed as responses to specific questions.[1] In order to address this fundamental gap in current knowledge of the sector, an Irish research team based at the Policy Research Centre of the National College of Ireland took the opportunity to map the Irish nonprofit sector in a systematic, solid, and empirical way through the Johns Hopkins Comparative Nonprofit Sector Project (CNP).[2]

Spurred by a lack of basic data on the sector and a desire to measure this "lost continent" (Salamon, Anheier and Associates 1999: 2), CNP has sought to deepen existing knowledge of the sector by measuring its size, structure,

Global Civil Society: Dimensions of the Nonprofit Sector by Lester M. Salamon, Helmut K. Anheier, Regina List, Stefan Toepler, S. Wojciech Sokolowski and Associates. Baltimore, MD: Johns Hopkins Center for Civil Society Studies, 1999.

income, and composition. This chapter presents the Irish data and, for the first time, the economic contribution of the nonprofit sector in Ireland. Subsequent publications will fill in the historical, legal, and policy context of this sector and also examine the impact that this set of institutions is having.

The definitional question

In Ireland the nonprofit sector is usually referred to as the voluntary sector. More recently, however, the "voluntary and community sector" as a term has come into vogue, although the boundaries of this voluntary and community sector have not been clearly defined (see Department of Social Welfare 1997). Indeed, various definitions of the sector and its components abound depending on the different agencies or actors that use the term.

One way to address the definitional question has been the application of the structural-operational definition of CNP to define the parameters of this non-state, non-profit-making sector in Ireland (see Donoghue 1998a).[3] The benefits of the structural-operational definition are that a) the main types of voluntary organizations in Ireland are included, b) voluntary organizations recognized as charities for tax purposes are included, and c) the definition complies with other criteria applied to organizations seeking the limited tax treatments and benefits that are available (see Cousins 1997). The nonprofit sector in Ireland, therefore, covers organizations that are non-statutory and not part of the market sector, such as arts, recreation and sports organizations, social service voluntary organizations, charities, community groups, voluntary-run hospitals and schools, area-based partnerships, trade unions, and nongovernmental organizations. The "nonprofit sector" data reported here also include religious worship organizations such as churches.

Furthermore, in order to highlight the contribution made by the community-based organizations that have become the focus of attention and debate over the past decades, information is provided separately on the "voluntary and community sector." As noted above, there is no common agreement on what organizations and activities would be included in this subsector. However, for the purpose of this chapter, the voluntary and community sector includes all organizations meeting the same structural-operational criteria as the "nonprofit" organizations, but excludes hospitals, hospices, primary and secondary schools, and higher education establishments that are not usually perceived in Ireland as being community-based.

With the definitional question resolved, the data were assembled from a variety of sources. The principal data source was the 1996 Population Census, which, with the aid of officials at the Central Statistics Office, became a font of information on employment by industry. Income sources were derived from published national expenditure accounts for 1995. These basic data were complemented with information from various government-level reports, as well as population surveys on giving and volunteering practices. (See Appendix C for more information.)

The historical and policy context

The Irish nonprofit sector has a long history, elements of which are seen clearly in the findings on the sector's income, size, and composition today. This history includes:

- A significant lay Protestant and Quaker presence in efforts to attend to medical and other needs of the poor before the Catholic Emancipation Act of 1829.
- An expansive set of health, education, and social welfare services set up following the 1829 Emancipation by Catholic religious orders. These service-providing nonprofit organizations have operated under the principle of subsidiarity, under which the government recognizes the autonomy of the organizations (see also Chapter 5, "Germany"). In the last few decades, government has also provided these organizations with an increasing measure of public sector financing.
- A strong tradition of self-help and local initiative exemplified by the founding of *Muintir na Tire* (People of the Land) in the 1930s. *Muintir* focused on the revival of community spirit through cooperative efforts and was a key force in rural life in Ireland until the 1960s.
- Passage of the Health Act in 1953, which established statutory public sector support for most hospitals and "Section 65" discretionary grants offered to nonprofit organizations providing social welfare services "ancillary" to those provided by government. This Act formalized the government-voluntary sector partnership in the health field.
- The establishment in the 1960s of a new educational system that provided public sector funding for voluntary-run secondary schools. Now, over three-quarters of secondary school students receive their education in these voluntary schools. As early as the 19th century, Ireland already had set up a system of "national schools," whereby landowners (mainly clergy) donated land and upkeep services, while the government built the schools and paid teachers' salaries. The national and secondary schools, along with the religious-run industrial schools set up to "reform" troubled youth, operate as autonomous voluntary organizations.
- Increased activism on the part of community and advocacy groups during the 1980s, particularly on the issues of unemployment and

related social problems. In the 1990s, this has led to their inclusion in the development of economic and social policy initiatives at the national level, such as the policy-oriented National Economic and Social Forum (NESF) and the National Anti-Poverty Strategy.

Despite the sector's long history, however, research in the area is relatively recent. The area of nonprofit research in Ireland is now thriving, like the sector, and it is hoped that this chapter, which provides the first profile of the size and economic significance of the sector in Ireland, will be a valuable contribution to it.

INCOME OF THE IRISH NONPROFIT SECTOR

Funding of the nonprofit sector in Ireland is a constant theme both in public debate and in the literature. Paying homage to the importance of this issue for the sector in Ireland, this chapter looks first at income to the sector. In 1995, the nonprofit sector's income amounted to $5.15 billion, or 8.2 percent of gross domestic product and 9.3 percent of Ireland's gross national product.[4] This funding came through three main sources, namely the public sector (which includes central and local government funding, European Union funding, national lottery monies and various third party payments such as funding through the Community Employment Program, Combat Poverty Agency and the National Social Service Board), private sources (individual donations and foundations), and money earned through fees, sales, or membership dues.

By far the most important source of income, as Figure 6.1 shows, is the public sector, which accounted for almost three-quarters of the nonprofit sector's income ($3.81 billion) in 1995. The shares of both private giving and earned income are less significant than publicly funded sources, amounting to 10.3 percent ($529.1 million) and 15.2 percent ($803.67 million), respectively. Most of the private giving originates with individuals (Ruddle and O'Connor 1993, Ruddle and Mulvihill 1995, 1999), which is noteworthy given the limited incentives for giving that exist.

In view of the definitional issue discussed earlier in this chapter, it must be asked where this funding goes and who the main beneficiaries are of this large slice of Ireland's GDP. Not surprisingly, given the history of the nonprofit sector in Ireland, there are two main groups that receive the bulk of the revenue, as Table 6.1 shows. Of the $3.8 billion received from public sector sources, over half (56 percent) went to education and research and a further 29 percent went to health. The 6.6 percent of public sector sources that went to development and housing is a sign of that category's growing importance in public policy implementation, particularly

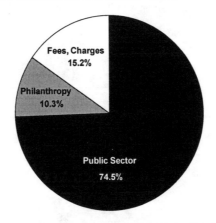

Figure 6.1 Sources of nonprofit revenue in Ireland, 1995

when compared to other groups such as culture and recreation and social services, each of which received about 3 percent of public funds (3.1 percent and 2.7 percent, respectively) or environment, which received under two percent of public sector money (1.7 percent).

The distribution of income from private sources shows a completely different pattern from the one presented by the distribution of income from public sector sources. Religion received just over one-third of all income from private sources (34.6 percent). Health and social services also gained from private giving (18.5 percent and 17.5 percent, respectively), while international organizations received 9 percent of the income to the sector from this source. In addition, it is most likely that income from fees is underestimated, as data on fee sources were not available for several of the groups comprising the nonprofit sector in Ireland (as can be seen in Table 6.1). If patterns elsewhere in the world (Salamon, Anheier and Associates 1999) are to be believed, however, this is a source of revenue that is probably likely to grow in the future.

It is also of use to examine the importance of these income sources for each ICNPO group (see Table 6.2). What this exercise does is measure the relative importance of these sources and possibly highlight areas that are problematic for fundraisers (Donoghue in press). For example, as Table 6.2 shows, social services, international organizations, and religious organizations rely quite heavily, the latter completely, on private sources, essentially individual donors, for their funding (Faughnan and Kelleher 1993, Mulvihill 1993). The various social welfare services are an area well known to rely upon public sector grants like "Section 65," which is discretionary

Table 6.1   Sources of cash income to ICNPO Groups

ICNPO Group	Public sector (%)	Private giving (%)	Fee sources (%)	Total income (%)
Culture & recreation	3.1	7.7	9.0	4.5
Education & research	56.0	4.4	74.3	53.5
Health	28.9	18.5	4.4	24.1
Social services	2.7	17.5	1.5	4.1
Environment	1.7	0.7	0	1.3
Development & housing	6.6	2.2	0	5.2
Civic and advocacy	0.3	1.3	0	0.4
Philanthropic	0.1	0.1	0	0.1
International	0.4	8.9	0	1.2
Religion	0	34.6	0	3.5
Professional associations	0.1	0	10.8	1.7
NEC*	0	4.1	0	0.4
TOTAL	**100**	**100**	**100**	**100**

*Respondents to survey stated they 'forgot' to which organization they donated money (Ruddle and Mulvihill 1999)

funding. When public sector sources of income for social services are viewed in comparison with cash from other sources, however, they are almost matched by funding from private sources, which is principally income from individuals (44.2 percent of all income to social services). This finding serves to provide evidence to back previous assumptions that social services organizations are very dependent on non-government sources for their survival (Faughnan and Kelleher 1993, Mulvihill 1993).

As also shown at the bottom of Table 6.2, the set of organizations that make up the "voluntary and community sector" has a revenue structure closer to that of the social services field than that of the nonprofit sector as a whole. Thus, just more than half (52.7 percent) of cash income to this subsector comes from the public sector, more than one-third (40.1 percent) from private giving, and only 7.3 percent from private fees and charges. This subsector is therefore much more reliant on philanthropy than the Irish nonprofit sector as a whole.

Fundraising has been identified as the most frequent activity in which volunteers are engaged. Moreover, the most often cited problem for the future viability of organizations tends to be the issue of funding. These data confirm what has been indicated by previous research, therefore, and

Table 6.2 Amount and relative importance of cash income sources in Ireland, by field, 1995

ICNPO Group	Public sector ($'000)	%	Private giving ($'000)	%	Fees ($'000)	%	Total ($'000)
Culture	120,450	51.9	40,867	17.6	70,600	30.4	231,917
Education	2,149,259	78.0	23,474	.9	583,779	21.2	2,756,512
Health	1,111,200	89.4	97,809	7.9	34,443	2.8	1,243,452
Social services	105,139	50.3	92,373	44.2	11,494	5.5	209,007
Environment	64,576	94.4	3,853	5.6	—	—	68,430
Development	254,284	95.6	11,757	4.4	—	—	266,041
Advocacy	13,287	66.3	6,758	33.7	—	—	20,045
Philanthropic	2,437	79.6	624	20.4	—	—	3062
International	14,582	23.6	47,198	76.4	—	—	61,780
Religion	—	—	182,866	100	—	—	182,866
Professional	2,269	2.6	—	—	85,396	97.4	87,665
NEC*	—	—	21,538	100	—	—	21,538
TOTAL	**3,837,483**	**74.5**	**529,117**	**10.3**	**785,714**	**15.2**	**5,152,315**
Voluntary and community sector		52.7		40.1		7.3	1,147,955

*Respondents to survey stated they 'forgot' to which organization they donated money (Ruddle and Mulvihill 1999)

suggest the wider ramifications of this issue. These data, for example, raise issues for fundraisers such as the saturation of different funding sources and the dependence of nonprofit organizations on a relatively limited number of sources of finance.

What the data presented so far do not show is the value of volunteering as a source of in-kind income. As has been suggested elsewhere, volunteering is a very important source of income to the Irish nonprofit sector (Ruddle and O'Connor 1993, Ruddle and Mulvihill 1995, 1999, Ruddle and Donoghue 1995). As Table 6.3 below indicates, in-kind revenue from volunteering is particularly important for some ICNPO groups. In 1995, the imputed value of volunteering was worth $747.9 million to the nonprofit sector in Ireland (calculated by applying average wage figures to volunteer time in each ICNPO group). Volunteering is, therefore, worth more than cash income from private sources, and amounts to almost the same value as cash income from fees and earnings.

When factored in with income from cash sources, the imputed value of volunteering alters the balance between the various sources of revenue as

Table 6.3   Imputed value of volunteering in Ireland, by field, 1995

ICNPO Group	Imputed value ($'000)	%
Culture and recreation	126,500	16.9
Education and research	38,477	5.1
Health	69,830	9.3
Social services	341,415	45.6
Environment	5,607	.7
Development and housing	82,632	11.0
Civic and advocacy	5,607	.7
Philanthropic	21,310	2.8
International	5,607	.7
Religion	39,084	5.2
Not elsewhere classified*	11,874	1.6
TOTAL	**747,947**	**100**

*Respondents to survey stated they 'forgot' for which type of organization they volunteered (Ruddle and Mulvihill 1995)

Figure 6.2 shows below. Privately funded income to the nonprofit sector now amounts to over one-fifth of total income (21.6 percent), while income from public sector sources is reduced to 65 percent, and income from fees and earned sources is reduced to 13.3 percent. The inclusion of volunteering brings the total income of the Irish nonprofit sector in 1995 to $5.8 billion, or 9.5 percent of GDP and 10.7 percent of GNP.

The importance of volunteering is greater for some groups within the nonprofit sector than for others; Table 6.3 demonstrates the significance of volunteering for social services, for example. As Table 6.4 shows, when volunteering is included with other forms of privately funded sources, social services receive almost 80 percent of their funding from these sources. Similarly, volunteering is also important for other components of the nonprofit sector such as culture and recreation, civic and advocacy, and foundations. Table 6.4 shows the way in which the balance between the various sources of income is shifted once volunteering is included as a form of inkind income. Indeed, for culture and recreation, social services, and philanthropic intermediaries, private giving now becomes the most important source of revenue. Furthermore, with volunteer input included, social services receives the third highest income in the Irish nonprofit sector.

As shown at the bottom of Table 6.4, the inclusion of volunteering also has a major impact on the subset of "voluntary and community sector" organizations. When the value of volunteer labor is added, private giving's

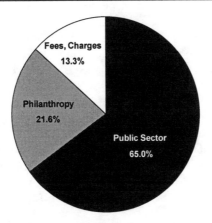

Figure 6.2 Sources of nonprofit revenue in Ireland, with volunteers, 1995

Table 6.4 Total (cash and in-kind) nonprofit income in Ireland, by field and source, 1995

ICNPO Group	% from public sector	% from private giving	% from fees and earnings	Total income (cash and in-kind) ($'000)
Culture	33.6	46.7	19.7	358,419
Education	76.9	2.2	20.9	2,794,992
Health	84.6	12.8	2.6	1,313,281
Social services	19.1	78.8	2.1	550,423
Environment	87.2	12.8		74,037
Development	72.9	27.1	—	348,672
Advocacy	51.8	48.2	—	25,652
Philanthropic	10.0	90.0	—	24,372
International	21.6	78.4	—	67,389
Religion	—	100.0	—	221,951
Professional	2.6	—	97.4	87,663
NEC*	—	100.0	—	33,415
TOTAL	**65.0**	**21.6**	**13.3**	**5,900,271**
Voluntary and community sector	33.1	62.4	4.6	1,828,321

*Respondents to survey stated they 'forgot' for which type of organization they volunteered or to which organization they donated money (Ruddle and Mulvihill 1995, 1999) share of total income rises to 62.4 percent, a 50 percent increase over its share without volunteers (see Table 6.2).

Not only do these data indicate the importance of volunteering for certain groups within the nonprofit sector, they also indicate the economic significance of volunteering *per se*. This issue will be returned to when employment data are examined later.

EXPENDITURE OF THE IRISH NONPROFIT SECTOR

In 1995, nonprofit operating expenditures in Ireland amounted to $5.24 billion, 8.6 percent of GDP or 9.5 percent of GNP for that year.[5] Table 6.5 below indicates, similar to the profile emerging on income to the sector, that the two largest components were education (52.7 percent) and health (24.1 percent).

More than three-quarters of the total expenditures of the nonprofit sector is spent by education and health service organizations. This finding deserves some contextualization in order to shed light on the greater economic worth of these two categories. As noted previously in the historical context section, education in Ireland is provided, in the main, by nonprofit organizations, that is, organizations that are institutionally separate from the state, non-profit-distributing, and self-governing. The state has provided the vast majority of funding for several decades in support of both educational and health services. Significantly, when the hospitals and

Table 6.5 Operating expenditure of the nonprofit sector in Ireland, 1995

ICNPO Group	$ ('000)	%
Culture and recreation	179,448	3.4
Education and research	2,778,275	52.7
Health	1,269,067	24.1
Social services	266,243	5.1
Environment	59,488	1.1
Development and housing	257,961	4.9
Civic and advocacy	15,691	.3
Foundations	10,964	.2
International	29,514	.6
Religion	328,223	6.2
Professional associations	72,920	1.4
TOTAL	**5,267,800**	**100.0**
Voluntary and community sector	1,334,792	25.3

schools that account for the majority of expenditures in the health and education fields are excluded, the remaining organizations that make up the voluntary and community sector spend approximately $1.3 billion, or about one-quarter of total sector expenditures.

The revenue data have shown the significance of volunteering as an in-kind form of income and its particular significance for certain ICNPO categories, and the expenditure data show the contribution of the nonprofit sector to the Irish economy. The latter, however, take no account of the input from volunteering. An imputed value can be ascribed to volunteering by calculating what nonprofit organizations would have paid in labor costs if volunteers were full-time equivalent (FTE)[6] paid employees. Adding the ascribed value of volunteer labor to operating expenditures (Table 6.6) shows that volunteering in 1995 contributed a value-added equivalent of $747.9 million. Table 6.6 shows the imputed value of volunteers added to operating expenditure, which now gives a total of $6,015 million contributed to the Irish economy by the nonprofit sector in 1995. This contribution is equivalent to 11 percent of GNP and 9.5 percent of GDP.[7] The voluntary and community subsector alone accounts for $2 billion, or one-third, of the nonprofit sector's expenditures when volunteers are included.

Table 6.6   Nonprofit operating expenditure in Ireland with imputed value of volunteers, by field, 1995

ICNPO Group	$ ('000)	%
Culture and recreation	305,949	5.1
Education and research	2,816,755	46.8
Health	1,338,897	22.3
Social services	607,659	10.1
Environment	65,096	1.1
Development and housing	340,592	5.7
Civic and advocacy	21,298	.4
Foundations	32,274	.5
International	35,121	.6
Religion	367,308	6.1
Professional associations	72,920	1.2
Not elsewhere classified*	11,874	.2
TOTAL	**6,015,749**	**100**
Voluntary and community sector	2,017,016	33.5

*Respondents to survey stated they 'forgot' for which type of organization they volunteered
(Ruddle and Mulvihill 1995)

Table 6.7 Contribution to Irish economy, by industry, 1995

Sector	Expenditure 1995 ($m)
Industry	21,140
Other domestic	19,717
Distribution, transport, and communications	9,090
Nonprofit sector including volunteers	*6,016*
Nonprofit sector	*5,268*
Agriculture and fishing	4,520
Public administration and defense	2,783
Voluntary and community sector including volunteers	*2,017*

Source: 1995 data taken from Central Statistics Office (1997): *National Income and Expenditure 1996*, Dublin: Stationery Office

The contribution of the nonprofit sector to the Irish economy can also be seen in other ways. Table 6.7 shows the economic contribution to the economy by sectors in 1995. As can be seen, the nonprofit sector is more economically significant than either agriculture and fishing, or public administration and defense. Furthermore, when the imputed value of volunteers is factored in, the nonprofit sector's value is more than twice that of public administration and defense. Even the subset of "voluntary and community sector" agencies makes a notable economic contribution. With the imputed value of volunteers included, this subsector's contribution amounts to three-quarters that of public administration and almost half that of agriculture and fishing.

EMPLOYMENT IN THE NONPROFIT SECTOR IN IRELAND

This section presents findings on employment in the nonprofit sector in 1995. Both paid and volunteer employment data are detailed. A comparison is then drawn between the nonprofit sector and other industries in the Irish economy.

Paid employment

In 1995 there were 125,584 paid employees (full-time equivalent, or FTE) in the Irish nonprofit sector. Education and health employed over three-quarters of paid workers in the Irish nonprofit sector (see Table 6.8). The remainder of paid workers were employed by culture and recreation (5.7 percent), religion (5.5 percent), social services (4.3 percent) and develop-

Table 6.8   Paid, volunteer, and total employment in the Irish nonprofit sector, by field, 1995

ICNPO Group	Paid employment No. FTE	%	Volunteers No. FTE	%	Total employment No. FTE	%
Culture	7,150	5.7	8,619	25.6	15,770	9.9
Education	63,731	50.7	896	2.7	64,627	40.6
Health	32,739	26.1	2,329	6.9	35,068	22.0
Social services	5,343	4.3	14,265	42.3	19,607	12.3
Environment	1,070	0.9	234	0.7	1,304	0.8
Development	5,079	4.0	3,453	10.2	8,531	5.4
Advocacy	459	0.4	234	0.7	693	0.4
Foundations	133	0.1	890	2.6	1,023	0.6
International	370	0.3	234	0.7	604	0.4
Religion	6,921	5.5	2,040	6.1	8,961	5.6
Professional	2,590	2.1	0	0.0	2,590	1.6
NEC*	0	0.0	496	1.5	496	0.3
TOTAL	**125,584**	**100**	**33,690**	**100**	**159,274**	**100**
Voluntary and community sector contribution to total	32,136	25.6	31,919	94.7	64,055	40.2

* Respondents to survey stated they 'forgot' for which type of organization they volunteered. (Ruddle and Mulvihill 1995)

ment and housing (4 percent).[8] The voluntary and community subcomponent employs approximately one-quarter of the sector's paid workers.

Unpaid, in-kind, or volunteer employment

As Table 6.8 indicates, volunteer employment shows a different pattern from paid employment. Altogether 33,690 (FTE) people worked as volunteers in Ireland in 1995. Of most importance here is the area of social services, in which 42.3 percent of volunteers were located. This is followed by culture and recreation, which absorbs over one-quarter of the FTE volunteers (25.6 percent). Development and housing comes third (10.2 percent of volunteers), while health comes fourth (6.9 percent of volunteers).

The contribution of volunteer employment alters the balance among the different components of the nonprofit sector, as Table 6.8 shows. For

Table 6.9   Paid employment in Ireland, by industry, 1995 (FTE)*

Industry	No. (FTE '000)
Manufacturing	247.5
Agriculture, forestry and fishing	210.2
Professional services	192.6
Nonprofit sector (paid and in-kind employment)	*159.3*
Retail distribution	147.9
Nonprofit sector (paid employment)	*125.6*
Personal services	83.7
Building and construction	82.8
Insurance, financial and business services	77.6
Transport, communications and storage	77.5
Voluntary and community sector (paid and in-kind employment)	*64.1*
Wholesale distribution	46.9
Public administration and defense	34.9
Voluntary and community sector (paid employment)	*32.1*
Other industrial not elsewhere stated	26.0
Electricity, gas and water	13.2
Mining, quarrying and turf	5.6

* FTE was calculated by applying a ratio based on the average number of hours worked in one week for each sector compared with the average number of hours per week for the total labor force. (Source: Central Statistics Office (1996): *Labour Force Survey 1995,* Dublin: Stationery Office.)

example, when FTE volunteers are added to paid employment, the proportion of employees in education and health is reduced from 51 percent to 41 percent and from 26 percent to 22 percent, respectively. Social services moves up from fifth to third place with 12 percent of total employment, and the proportion employed in culture and recreation increases from almost 6 percent to just under 10 percent of total nonprofit employment. Finally, paid plus volunteer employment figures in both development and religion increase but to a lesser degree than in the other categories above.

Overall, volunteers make up one-fifth of total employment in the nonprofit sector and volunteering emerges clearly as a significant form of employment. The contribution of volunteers, moreover, is far greater in some ICNPO categories than in others. This contribution can be seen most clearly in social services and also in culture and recreation. The former category employs only 4 percent of paid employees. Yet 42 percent of all volunteers and 12 percent of all employees in the sector (paid plus volunteer) work in social services. Culture and recreation, on the other hand, employs almost 6 percent of paid workers, one quarter of volunteers, and 10 percent of all employees in the sector.

The impact of volunteering is most notable for the "voluntary and community" set of organizations. In fact, this subsector attracts nearly 95 percent of all FTE volunteers. Thus, its share of nonprofit employment rises from 25.6 percent without volunteers to 40.2 percent with them. Thus, paid and unpaid employment in the Irish nonprofit sector is sizable. Paid employment in the nonprofit sector, for example, amounts to 12 percent of the nonagricultural workforce. The inclusion of in-kind or volunteer employment brings total employment in the nonprofit sector to 15 percent of nonagricultural employment. Indeed, as Table 6.9 shows, paid employment in the Irish nonprofit sector is more than half that in all branches of manufacturing, and exceeds that in personal services, building and construction, and transport and communications. In the context of media trumpeting about the importance of the financial services sector and the "Celtic Tiger" economy—which had begun roaring in 1995—it is relevant to note that nonprofit paid employment also surpasses that in insurance, financial, and business services. Furthermore, once volunteering is added in, employment in the nonprofit sector is more than twice as great as in these services. The voluntary and community subsector also compares favorably with other industries in Ireland. Paid and volunteer employment in this subsector together amount to 6 percent of total nonagricultural employment. This means that there are more people working in the voluntary and community sector than are employed in the wholesale distribution industry, for example.

IRELAND AND THE REST OF THE WORLD

So far, this chapter has presented the Irish findings solely within an Irish context. This section examines the economic significance of the Irish nonprofit sector within the international situation drawing on findings from the entire Comparative Nonprofit Sector Project. As Table 6.10 shows, not only is the Irish nonprofit sector sizable in its own right, it also compares favorably to nonprofit sectors around the world.[9] Paid employment, at 12.2 percent of the nonagricultural workforce, means that the Irish nonprofit sector is the second largest after the Dutch nonprofit sector (12.7 percent). The size of the Irish nonprofit workforce is well above the Western European average (7 percent) and the international average (5.5 percent). When volunteers are included as a form of in-kind employment, Ireland's position remains unchanged at second place (15 percent), although its differential with the Netherlands (19.4 percent) widens quite considerably (see Table 6.10).

Indeed, the international findings show that although volunteering is significant in the Irish context, volunteers make up a smaller proportion of the nonagricultural workforce in Ireland than is the case in most other

Table 6.10   Paid and in-kind employment in the nonprofit sector internationally as proportion of nonagricultural labor force, 1995*

Country	Paid employment (%)	In-kind (volunteer) employment (%)	Paid and in-kind employment (%)
Netherlands	12.74	6.63	19.36
Ireland	**12.22**	**2.79**	**15.00**
U.S.	8.82	5.67	14.50
U.K.	6.45	6.35	12.80
Israel	9.32	1.82	11.14
Australia	7.48	3.50	10.98
France	4.97	5.12	10.09
Germany	5.06	3.78	8.84
Argentina	4.35	3.38	7.73
Finland	3.12	3.30	6.42
Austria	4.67	1.19	5.86
Japan	3.74	1.32	5.06
Brazil	2.45	0.70	3.15
Czech Rep	1.84	1.04	2.88
Romania	0.61	0.78	1.39
Slovakia	1.01	0.38	1.39
Total average	**5.5**	**3.0**	**8.5**
EU average	**7.02**	**4.16**	**11.18**

*Includes religion.

Source: Salamon, Anheier and Associates (1999)

countries in the international study. On average, volunteers in the seven Western European countries for which religion data are available make up 4.2 percent of the nonagricultural workforce compared with 2.8 percent in Ireland. Indeed, only one-fifth of the Irish population volunteers (in a formal capacity), compared to 33 percent in the EU and 30 percent internationally. Despite this, the significance of volunteering for certain fields within the Irish nonprofit sector stands up to international comparison. As shown earlier, volunteering is most important in social services, and is also important in culture and recreation, development, and foundations, and the proportion of volunteers in these groups in Ireland is above the international average.

The expenditure of the Irish nonprofit sector (see Table 6.11) is also above both the EU and international averages. Eight percent of GDP is spent by the Irish nonprofit sector, compared to six percent in the EU and

Table 6.11 Operating expenditure of nonprofit sectors internationally as proportion of GDP, 1995*

Country	Op. exp (excl volunteers) %	Op. exp (incl volunteers) %	Value added** %
Netherlands	15.3	19.2	11.9
Israel	12.6	13.6	7.3
Ireland	**8.4**	**9.5**	**6.6**
U.K.	6.8	9.5	5.4
U.S.	7.5	9.5	5.5
Australia	5.4	6.8	4.2
France	3.8	6.6	5.3
Germany	4.0	6.3	5.0
Argentina	5.1	6.3	3.7
Finland	3.9	6.0	4.0
Japan	5.0	5.5	2.8
Austria	3.0	3.6	2.5
Czech Rep	1.7	2.1	1.2
Brazil	1.5	1.7	1.0
Slovakia	1.4	1.5	0.5
Romania	0.3	0.7	0.6
Total average	**5.4**	**6.8**	**4.2**
EU average	**6.4**	**8.7**	**5.8**

* Includes religion.

** Wages + imputed value of volunteer labor as percentage of GDP.

Source: Salamon, Anheier and Associates (1999)

five percent internationally. When volunteers are included, however, non-profit expenditure increases in Ireland to 9.5 percent of GDP. The differential with other countries closes, however, although Ireland is still above both the EU and international averages.

Finally, revenue data show that the Irish nonprofit sector is the most reliant of all other countries in the international study on public sector support (see Table 6.12). What Table 6.12 also shows, however, is the relative importance of private giving in Ireland, in comparison with other EU countries. As noted previously, individual giving comprises the vast majority of the private giving in Ireland (99 percent), which means that the Irish population's image of itself as a nation of givers (Donoghue in press) now has some empirical basis, even if the level of individual donations in recent years has not kept pace with the booming Irish economy (Ruddle and Mulvihill 1999).

Table 6.12   Share of cash revenue of nonprofit sectors internationally, 1995

Country	Public sector (%)	Private giving (%)	Fees and earnings (%)
Ireland	74.5	10.3	15.2
Germany	64.8	3.4	31.8
Israel	63.5	10.5	26.0
Netherlands	58.8	2.7	38.6
France	57.1	8.5	34.4
Austria	47.3	5.7	47.0
U.K.	45.2	11.3	43.5
Romania	45.1	26.5	28.4
Japan	40.9	3.6	55.5
Czech Rep	39.5	15.0	45.6
Finland	36.0	7.1	56.8
Australia	29.9	9.2	60.9
U.S.	27.4	21.2	51.3
Slovakia	22.1	23.7	54.2
Argentina	17.2	18.6	64.2
Total average	44.6	11.8	43.6
EU average	54.8	7.0	38.2

Source: Salamon, Anheier and Associates (1999)

In other countries, particularly the U.S., but also the U.K., there are more incentives to encourage different forms of private giving. The level of individual giving in Ireland, therefore, appears to compare quite favorably with levels of private giving elsewhere. Table 6.12 also demonstrates the relatively low level of cash income from fees and earned sources in Ireland. For the majority of other countries in the study, income from these sources represents a sizable proportion of their total cash income. It is probable, however, that the Irish figures reported here underestimate the actual situation; moreover, if the international trend is followed, fees and earned income may become a more important source of revenue in the future.

CONCLUSIONS AND IMPLICATIONS

Points arising

The findings presented here demonstrate that the Irish nonprofit sector is a thriving, vibrant entity. It is probably of little wonder, therefore, that the relationship between the state and the nonprofit sector needs attention, because the sector is a sizable and significant force in the Irish economy. A number of key points can therefore be seen to emerge from the findings, as described below.

- **The nonprofit sector in Ireland is economically important.** The nonprofit sector is a major economic force. It makes a sizable contribution to both GDP and GNP, and is a large employer. It covers a broad range of activities from grassroots activities (experienced and having an impact at the local and community level) to activities that either supplement or complement state activity (such as in mainstream health and education provision). Nonprofit providers have played a huge role in these areas for many years (see Donoghue 1998a, Ruddle and Donoghue 1995, Faughnan and Kelleher 1993, Mulvihill 1993).
- **The voluntary and community sector makes a significant economic contribution.** Even though it is smaller than the nonprofit sector as a whole, the voluntary and community sector is still a significant economic player. If compared to data on nonprofit sectors internationally, bearing in mind that such data have been collected on the "broader" nonprofit sector, the voluntary and community sector in Ireland is a bigger employer of paid and volunteer workers than the nonprofit sectors in Austria, Japan, and Brazil (see Table 6.10).

  It has already been noted in the literature (Ruddle and Donoghue 1995) that community-based organizations are of increasing importance. Their importance can also been seen in the amount of money that such organizations received from the EU and in their inclusion in the recent Green Paper (Department of Social Welfare 1997), as well as the inclusion of the community "voice" in consultation on national forums such as the National and Economic Social Forum and the National Anti-Poverty Strategy (Donoghue 1998b). The findings presented here give added weight to that importance.
- **Private giving is an important source of income.** Private giving, while amounting to significantly less than cash support from the public sector and from fee sources is, at ten percent of cash income, an important source of revenue for the Irish nonprofit sector. Furthermore, it represents an even more significant source of income for the voluntary and community sector, where it could be said that a "philanthropy" model rather than a "government-dominated" model (see Salamon, Anheier and Associates 1999) begins to emerge. The importance of individual giving in Ireland gets some credibility when placed in an international context where it can be seen that, despite the relatively larger number of private sources of giving available in other countries, the proportion of income coming from such sources is not greatly different from the profile presented for Ireland. Indeed, in

comparison with the rest of the EU, individual giving is far more important in Ireland.

- **Volunteering is significant but there is scope for growth.** The significance of volunteering, particularly for the voluntary and community sector, underlines the importance of philanthropy in Ireland. While the contribution to the Irish economy is significant, there is possibly scope for numbers in volunteering to increase given its relatively lesser importance in comparison with volunteering internationally.

Roles, responsibilities, and relationships

A number of issues can be identified from the findings presented. These have been divided into sections below for policy-makers, practitioners, and researchers, although these categories are by no means mutually exclusive. Broadly, these issues can be conceptualized as centered on the role of the nonprofit sector in Ireland, the responsibilities that the nonprofit sector and the state have, and the relationship between both sectors.

Thoughts for policy-makers. The nonprofit sector is a significant employer or economic player and, given its economic worth, it deserves recognition. This recognition needs to take place on several fronts. First, there needs to be greater recognition at the policy-making level. Although this has started to happen with representation on the National and Economic Social Forum, for example, other developments are needed, and there is scope for increased bargaining power. All nonprofit organizations need to feel that their worth has been recognized and that this is being given greater value in the planning process. The lack of a single body representing the sector is possibly one factor that has prevented this in the past.

Recognition of the worth of the sector could also inform and possibly lead to greater emphasis on the relationship between the state and the sector, which needs to be further addressed. According to the data presented here, the nonprofit sector is not insignificant and, as such, does not need to be a "lesser" party in its relationship with the state.

Thoughts for practitioners. The sector itself needs to engage in some recognition of both its worth and its boundaries or, what is referred to in Chapter 1 as "making the sector a reality." Links between different parts of the sector could be useful if only to recognize similarities and possible common goals. Recognition could also lead, however, to the development of a voice, or a number of voices for the sector, which could help in the realization of the sector's potential and power.

The employment data indicate that there are a number of potential issues requiring attention. First, the management of different kinds of staff who are employed (whether in a paid full-time, paid part-time or unpaid in-kind capacity) is of vital importance. This leads to another issue, that of capacity building within the sector and the role that management training could play in that. Third, given the economic value of the sector, issues in relation to its effectiveness and the link between that and employment potential must be considered.

Volunteers and paid employees represent the "might" of the nonprofit sector. Questions must be asked about how they are used, the skills that they have, ways in which to measure their effectiveness, and ways to value their input into the sector. These questions also relate to management, mentioned above, and to the industrial relations environment. Questions could be raised, for example, about the recognition by trade unions of volunteers as employees.

The issue of funding is also raised by these data. Different sources of funding, and a possible over-dependence on one source, as well as the discretionary and insecure nature of some state funding, are issues for the sector. Financing structures and mechanisms that are more structured are required; but at the same time, there should be a recognition that the autonomy of the sector does not have to be compromised, which is a fear expressed by representatives of the sector when the issue of funding is raised.

The sector is of a significant size and receives major financing from the government. This may raise concerns about its accountability. This is an issue both within the sector and in the relationship between the state and the sector. The sector, as a whole, is vulnerable to public perceptions about its accountability, and there is a need to address this issue so that nonprofit organizations do not become victims of their own success.

Thoughts for researchers. As the data show, and as is also evident from the historical context, religious agencies are still a large part of the nonprofit sector and their role cannot be ignored. Religious organizations are important as employers and service providers in education, health, and social services. They also play a role in social commentary, whether this is on the liberal side (such as the Conference of Religious in Ireland, for example) or in the advocacy of traditional conservative values. There are at least two ways in which the role of religion deserves greater attention. The first is in relation to the role of religious organizations as providers of many nonprofit services in Ireland. The second is the role of religion as a motivation in either giving or volunteering. For example, internationally, Ireland ranks third in the importance of giving to religion (after Argentina at 64.7 percent and the U.S. at 45.6 percent of total giving). Volunteering in religious causes is less important, however, at only six percent in Ireland, compared with almost 60 percent in Brazil and 33 percent in the U.K. There is clearly scope for greater investigation of those areas.

The view that the Irish hold of themselves as a nation of generous donors is given some basis in this chapter. Furthermore, although Irish people do not donate as much time in voluntary activities as people in other countries, volunteering is still of great economic significance within Ireland. This importance can be seen in areas such as social services where other forms of financial support are not as significant. Philanthropy in Ireland, therefore, deserves further exploration. Issues to be explored could include motivation, already mentioned above, and the impact of volunteering in some of the sub-groups within the nonprofit sector. This also raises issues related to the "might" of volunteers, such as their power in numbers and the benefits they can bring to the sector or to groups within the sector. Other related issues such as training, support, and the management of different kinds of employees, including volunteers, are also worth investigating.

More information is required on funding sources, as there is a lack of data on some areas. Corporate donations do not receive the same encouragement in Ireland as they do, for example, in the U.S. Although no data are reported on corporate support here, this is clearly an area that requires some attention, and which has just begun to be given some consideration in the legislation.

The lack of available data in the public arena impedes research but is also a constraint on the sector, for the sector is only gradually beginning to recognize itself and realize its own economic worth. This chapter has attempted to fill some of the voids that have existed in our knowledge of the sector to date, but it also highlights the difficulties involved in trying to "uncover" the sector. These difficulties raise issues related to the data collection and reporting at national accounts level. Data that help the sector recognize and acknowledge itself, and become known by others, can only aid in contributing to its might; the power of knowledge can then be put to good use. Data collection, data reporting, and data sources need to be improved so that the sector is informed about itself, can inform others, and can also be empowered through having the tools for policy, planning, and negotiation.

Data collection and reporting need to happen in a systematic, regulated manner and to be part of the national data collection systems and procedures. This would then allow research to move from basic data collection to addressing in more detail and depth the nature of the sector and its impact, which would further the field of study not only for academics but for policy-makers and practitioners as well.

REFERENCES

"Budget 98," *Irish Times,* 4 December 1997.

Coopers and Lybrand (1994): *The Employment and Economic Significance of the Cultural Industries in Ireland, Summary Report,* Dublin: Temple Bar Properties.

Cospoir (1994): *The Economic Impact of Sport in Ireland,* Department of Education.

Cousins, Mel (1997): "Republic of Ireland," in Lester Salamon (ed.), *International Guide to Nonprofit Law,* New York: Wiley and Sons.

Department of Education (1996): personal communication, November.

Department of Social Welfare (1997): *Supporting Voluntary Activity. A Green Paper on the Community and Voluntary Sector and its Relationship with the State.* Dublin: Stationery Office.

Department of Social Welfare (1996): *Statistical Information on Social Welfare Services 1996,* Dublin: Stationery Office.

Department of Social Welfare (1989): *Statistical Information on Social Welfare Services 1988,* Dublin: Stationery Office.

Donoghue, Freda (1998a): "Defining the Nonprofit Sector: Ireland," *Working Papers of the Johns Hopkins Comparative Nonprofit Sector Project,* No. 28, edited by Lester M. Salamon and Helmut K. Anheier, Baltimore: The Johns Hopkins Institute for Policy Studies.

Donoghue, Freda (1998b): *The Politicisation of Poverty in the Republic of Ireland: the role of the third sector,* paper presented at International Society for Third Sector Research, Geneva, July.

Donoghue, F. (in press): "Fundraising Profile of Ireland," in Thomas Harris (ed.), *International Guide to Fundraising Practices,* New York: John Wiley & Sons.

FAS (1997) personal communication, October.

Faughnan, Pauline and Kelleher, Patricia (1992): *The Voluntary Sector and the State: a Study of Organisations in One Region,* Dublin: Community Action Network/Conference of Major Religious Superiors.

Gaelic Athletics Association (1997) *Annual Report 1996,* Dublin: GAA.

Government of Ireland (1994): *Report of the Registrar of Friendly Societies 1993,* Dublin: Stationery Office.

Government of Ireland (1996): *Annual Report of the Comptroller and Auditor General and Appropriation Accounts 1995,* Dublin: Stationery Office.

Government of Ireland (1997): *Sharing in Progress. National Anti-Poverty Strategy,* Dublin: Stationery Office.

Harvey, Brian (1995): *The National Lottery: Ten Years On,* Dublin: Policy Research Centre.

Harvey, Brian (1998): "The Voluntary Sector in Europe," *Poverty Today,* Dublin: Combat Poverty Agency.

ICOS (1996): *101st Annual Report 1995.* Dublin: Irish Co-Operative Organization Society Limited.

IPA (1996): *Yearbook and Diary 1997.* Dublin: Institute of Public Administration.

Irish Times (1999): "State's Role in Church Wrongs," 27 April.

Kendall, Jeremy and Knapp, Martin (1996): *The Voluntary Sector in the UK,* Manchester: Manchester University Press.

Kendall, Jeremy and Almond, Steve (1998): *The U.K. Voluntary (Third) Sector in Comparative Perspective: Exceptional Growth and Transformation,* Kent: PSSRU at University of Kent at Canterbury.

Lee, Joe (forthcoming) *History of Ireland's Nonprofit Sector,* paper presented to the Johns Hopkins Comparative Nonprofit Sector Project, Phase II.

Luddy, Maria (1995): *Women and Philanthropy in Nineteenth Century Ireland.* Cambridge: Cambridge University Press.

McInerney, Chris (1998): "A Test of Partnership," *Poverty Today.* No. 38, Dublin: Combat Poverty Agency.

Mulvihill, Ray (1993): *Voluntary-Statutory Partnerships in the Care of the Elderly,* Dublin: National Council for the Elderly.

National Social Services Board (1996): Directory of National Voluntary Organisations, Social Services Agencies and Other Useful Public Bodies, Dublin: NSSB.

Nolan, John and Burke, Andrew (1991): *The Financing of Catholic Secondary Schools in the Free Education System.* Dublin: Council of Managers of Catholic Secondary Schools.

O Morain, Padraig (1999): "ISPCC backs staff as Garda continues finances inquiry," *Irish Times,* 23 January.

O'Sullivan, Roddy (1999): "List details bodies with charitable tax status," *Irish Times,* 23 January.

Peillon, Michel (1998): "The Power of Inclusion: An analysis of the Green Paper on supporting voluntary activity, " *Poverty Today.* No. 38. Dublin: Combat Poverty Agency.

Rehab Foundation (1996): *The Not for Profit Sector: Its Role and Its Funding,* Submission to Advisory Group on Fundraising Legislation, May.

Revenue Commissioners. 1998. Personal Communication, April.

Ruddle, Helen and Donoghue, Freda (1995): *The Organisation of Volunteering,* Dublin: Policy Research Centre.

Ruddle, Helen and Mulvihill, Ray (1999): *Reaching Out: Charitable Giving and Volunteering in the Republic of Ireland,* Dublin: Policy Research Centre.

Ruddle, Helen and Mulvihill, Ray (1995): *Reaching Out: Charitable Giving and Volunteering in the Republic of Ireland. The 1994 Study,* Dublin: Policy Research Centre.

Ruddle, Helen and O'Connor, Joyce (1993): *Reaching Out: Charitable Giving and Volunteering in the Republic of Ireland,* Dublin: Policy Research Centre.

Salamon, L. and Anheier, H.K. (1994): *The Emerging Sector: An Overview,* Baltimore: Johns Hopkins University.

Salamon, Lester M. and Anheier, Helmut K. (1996a): "The International Classification of Nonprofit Organizations: ICNPO-Revision 1, 1996," *Working Papers of the Johns Hopkins University Comparative Nonprofit Sector Project, No. 19,* edited by Lester M. Salamon and Helmut K. Anheier, Baltimore: The Johns Hopkins Institute for Policy Studies.

Salamon, Lester M. and Anheier, Helmut K. (1996b): "Social Origins of Civil Society: Explaining the Nonprofit Sector Cross-Nationally." *Working Papers of the Johns Hopkins University Comparative Nonprofit Sector Project, No. 22,* edited by Lester M. Salamon and Helmut K. Anheier, Baltimore: The Johns Hopkins Institute for Policy Studies.

Salamon, Lester M. and Anheier, Helmut K. (1997): *Defining the Nonprofit Sector: A Cross-National Analysis.* Manchester: Manchester University Press.

Salamon, Lester M., Anheier, Helmut K. and Associates (1999): *The Emerging Sector Revisited: A Summary, Revised Estimates,* Baltimore: The Johns Hopkins Institute for Policy Studies.

Weisbrod, Burton (1977): *The Voluntary Nonprofit Sector,* Lexington MA: Lexington Books.

ENDNOTES

1. Recent research to date has focused on volunteering and giving (Ruddle and O'Connor 1993, Ruddle and Mulvihill 1995, 1999, Ruddle and Donoghue 1995, Lucey, Donnelly-Cox and O'Regan 1997), management and organizational behavior of voluntary organizations (Jaffro 1996, Hayes 1996, Donnelly-Cox and O'Regan 1998), policy (Donnelly-Cox 1998, Williamson 1998), sector-state relationships (Mulvihill 1993, Faughnan and Kelleher 1993, O'Sullivan 1998), and civil society (Powell and Guerin 1997, 1998), to name just a few examples (see also Donoghue (1998c).

2. The work in Ireland is coordinated by Freda Donoghue of the Policy Research Centre (PRC) at the National College of Ireland (NCI). Others who contributed significantly to this effort in Ireland include Justin Johnston, Lecturer in Economics at NCI, Helen Ruddle, Senior Research Officer at the PRC, Ray Mulvihill at the PRC, and Ger Hennessy and Elizabeth Harrington, both administrative assistants at the PRC. The team was aided, in turn, by a local advisory committee made up of 9 prominent philanthropic, government, academic, and business leaders, and chaired by Joyce O'Connor, President of NCI (see Appendix D for a list of committee members). The Johns Hopkins project was directed by Lester M. Salamon and Helmut K. Anheier.

3. The definitions and approaches used in the Johns Hopkins project were developed collaboratively with the cooperation of the Irish researchers and researchers in other countries and were designed to be applicable to Ireland and the other project countries. For a full description of the Johns Hopkins project's definition of the nonprofit sector, the types of organizations included, and the International Classification of Nonprofit Organizations (ICNPO), see Appendix A. For a full list of the other countries included, see Chapter 1 above and Lester M. Salamon and Helmut K. Anheier, *The Emerging Sector Revisited: A Summary, Revised Estimates* (Baltimore, MD: The Johns Hopkins Center for Civil Society Studies, 1999).

4. Data are given for GNP as well as GDP since GNP is the usual economic indicator used in Ireland because of the amount of monies repatriated by foreign multinationals ($6.35 billion or £4 billion in 1995).

5. The difference between cash income and operating expenditure figures (2.2 percent comparing Tables 6.2 and 6.5), while not statistically significant, may be explained by the lack of data on corporate donations and incomplete data on fees and foundations. The extent of support from such sources is not fully known and may not make a large difference in view of the fact that income from public sources is so great.

6. Full-time equivalence (FTE) was obtained from the census figures by using ratios supplied by the Central Statistics Office. Ratios for each ICNPO category were obtained (for FTE/headcount numbers) by dividing FTE by headcount (see Appendix C for further details).

7. The gross value added (GVA) contribution was 6.6 percent. Gross value added is calculated using the sum of wages, plus the imputed value of volunteering as a proportion of GDP, plus the imputed value of volunteering. The contribution of the Irish nonprofit sector is, therefore, still sizable.

8. The smaller proportion of employment in international activities may be explained in several ways. Firstly, employees with overseas organizations may regard themselves as "volunteers" rather than employees because that is how many are referred to and defined by those

organizations even if they are in receipt of a nominal wage. Secondly, these employment figures are based on a Census of Population, which means that to be included respondents must be resident in the country on the night of the Census. "Volunteers" or many of the "employees" with overseas organizations would, therefore, be out of the country on that night.

9. Findings from 15 other countries are presented here. Although 22 countries reported findings for Phase II of the Comparative Nonprofit Sector Project (see Chapter 1 and Salamon, Anheier and Associates 1999) only 16 presented data on religious worship organizations. As data on religious organizations have been included in this chapter so far, the term "international" refers to these 16 countries only.

CHAPTER 7

The Netherlands: Key Features of the Dutch Nonprofit Sector

Ary Burger, Paul Dekker, Stefan Toepler,
Helmut K. Anheier, and Lester M. Salamon

BACKGROUND

Nonprofit organizations in the Netherlands are traditionally referred to as "private initiatives" or the "societal midfield," and—as the data reported here will show—Dutch society features a "midfield" of quite substantial proportions. While the Dutch nonprofit scene matches the overall Western European pattern quite well in terms of structure, composition, and financing, it greatly exceeds most of its Continental European counterparts in terms of size. In fact, in relative terms, the Netherlands boasts the largest nonprofit sector among all countries included in this study. For the most part, this reflects the deeply rooted Dutch tradition of subsidiarity accommodating different religious and ideological camps by leaving the provision of crucial services to nonprofit organizations affiliated with such groups. In a process that has come to be known as *pillarization,* the state largely restricted its role to the financing of services provided by the nonprofit sector. This division of labor, however, was not the result of a master plan or grand design, but of a slow and incremental process. First of all, the existence of private organizations in many areas of social life reflects the long and rich tradition of private initiatives. Secondly, the guiding

Global Civil Society: Dimensions of the Nonprofit Sector by Lester M. Salamon, Helmut K. Anheier, Regina List, Stefan Toepler, S. Wojciech Sokolowski and Associates. Baltimore, MD: Johns Hopkins Center for Civil Society Studies, 1999.

principle of subsidiarity kept the profile of the state low and created a prosperous environment for the growth and development of nonprofits. Thirdly, gradual increases in public support to nonprofit activities, most notably in education, health care, and social services, in combination with the postwar growth of the welfare state, boosted the economic significance of the nonprofit sector.

These conclusions emerge from a body of work carried out by a Dutch research team at the Social and Cultural Planning Office (SCP) as part of the Johns Hopkins Comparative Nonprofit Sector Project.[1] It thus offered ample opportunities both to capture local Dutch circumstances and peculiarities and to compare and contrast them to those in other countries both in Western Europe and elsewhere in a systematic way.[2] The result is a comprehensive empirical overview of the Dutch nonprofit sector and a systematic comparison of Dutch nonprofit realities to those elsewhere in Western Europe and the rest of the world.

The present chapter reports on just one set of findings from this project, those relating to the size and structure of the nonprofit sector in the Netherlands and elsewhere. Subsequent publications will fill in the historical, legal, and policy context of this sector and also examine the impact that this set of institutions is having. The data reported here draw heavily on industry reports from the Dutch Statistics Office, various data sources from umbrella organizations, and annual reports from individual agencies. Unless otherwise noted, financial data are reported in U.S. dollars at the 1995 average exchange rate. (For a more complete statement of the sources of data, see Appendix C. For a more complete statement of the types of organizations included, see Chapter 1 and Appendix A).

PRINCIPAL FINDINGS

Five major findings emerge from this work on the scope, structure, financing, and role of the nonprofit sector in the Netherlands:

1. A major economic force

In the first place, aside from its social and political importance, the nonprofit sector turns out to be a huge economic force in the Netherlands, accounting for substantial shares of national expenditures and employment. More specifically:

- **A $60 billion industry.** Even excluding its religion component, the nonprofit sector in the Netherlands had operating expenditures of

$60.4 billion in 1995, or 15 percent of the country's gross domestic product, a quite substantial amount.[3]

- **A major employer.** Behind these expenditures lies an important workforce that includes the equivalent of nearly 653,000 full-time equivalent paid workers. This represents 12.6 percent of all nonagricultural workers in the country, 28 percent of service employment, and the equivalent of nine-tenths of the government employment at all levels—federal, state, and municipal (see Table 7.1).

- **More employees than in the largest private firm.** Put somewhat differently, nonprofit employment in the Netherlands easily surpasses the employment in the largest private business in the country, and does so by a factor of 2 to 1. Thus, compared to the 653,000 paid workers in the Dutch nonprofit organizations, the largest private corporation in the Netherlands, Unilever, employs only 308,000 workers (see Figure 7.1).

- **Outdistances numerous industries.** Indeed, more people work in the nonprofit sector in the Netherlands than in many entire industries in the country. Thus, as shown in Figure 7.2, nonprofit employment in

---

Table 7.1 The nonprofit sector in the Netherlands, 1995

$ 60.4 billion in expenditures
  — 15.3 percent of GDP

652,800 paid employees
  — 12.6 percent of total nonagricultural employment
  — 27.9 percent of total service employment
  — 89.8 percent of public employment

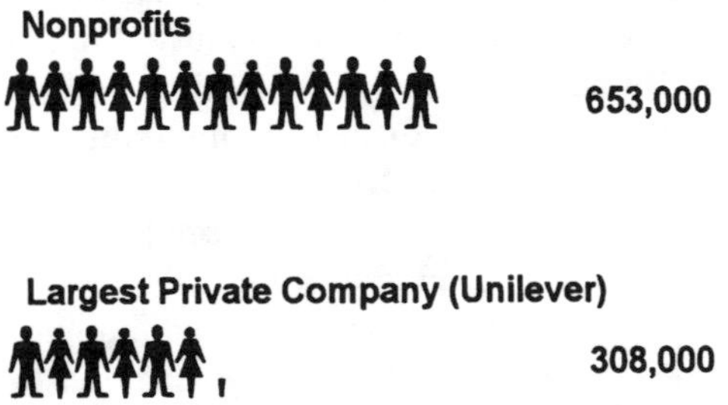

Nonprofits

653,000

Largest Private Company (Unilever)

308,000

Figure 7.1   Employment in nonprofits vs. largest firm in the Netherlands, 1995

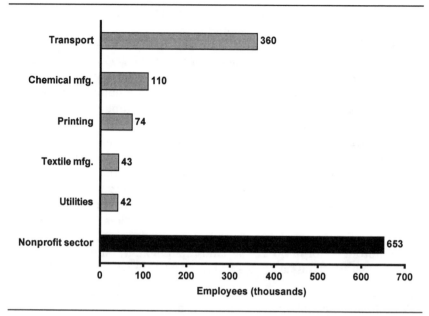

Figure 7.2   Nonprofit employment in the Netherlands in context, 1995

the Netherlands outdistances employment in the country's utilities, textiles, printing, chemical, and transport industries. Indeed, employment in the nonprofit sector in the Netherlands slightly exceeds employment in all of these industries combined.

- **Volunteer inputs.** Even this does not capture the full scope of the nonprofit sector in the Netherlands, for this sector also attracts a considerable amount of *volunteer effort*. Indeed, according to various surveys, the share of the Dutch population that reports contributing a portion of their time to nonprofit organizations ranges between 30 percent and 50 percent. Using the more conservative estimate of 30 percent, this translates into another 390,000 full-time equivalent employees, which boosts the total number of full-time equivalent employees of nonprofit organizations in the Netherlands to one million, or 19 percent of total employment in the country (see Figure 7.3).
- **Religion.** The inclusion of religion would add to these totals another 7,500 paid employees and 35,000 full-time equivalent volunteers. With religion included, nonprofit paid employment rises to 12.7 percent of the total and paid plus volunteer employment to 19.4 percent. Religion also increases the operating expenditures slightly by $540 mil-

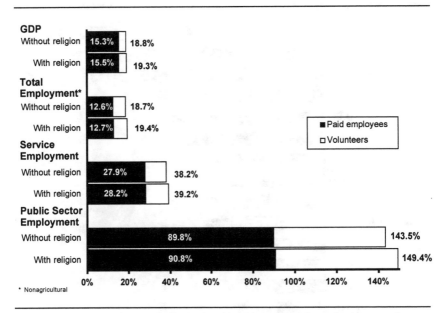

Figure 7.3   Nonprofits in the Netherlands, with and without volunteers and religion, 1995, as a % of . . .

lion, thus bringing total expenditures to $61 billion, the equivalent of 15.5 percent of gross domestic product.

2. One of the largest nonprofit sectors in Western Europe and the world

Not only is the Dutch nonprofit sector large in relation to the Dutch economy, but it is also very large relative to its counterparts elsewhere in Western Europe and world-wide.

- **Largest nonprofit sector world-wide in relative terms.** As Figure 7.4 shows, the relative size of the nonprofit sector varies greatly among countries. The Netherlands, however, outdistances all the other countries studied in the relative size of its nonprofit sector. In fact, the Dutch nonprofit sector's 12.6 percent share of total nonagricultural employment is two-and-a-half times the overall 22-country average of 4.8 percent.

- **Also considerably above the Western European and other developed countries averages.** While it is about two-and-a-half times the 22-country

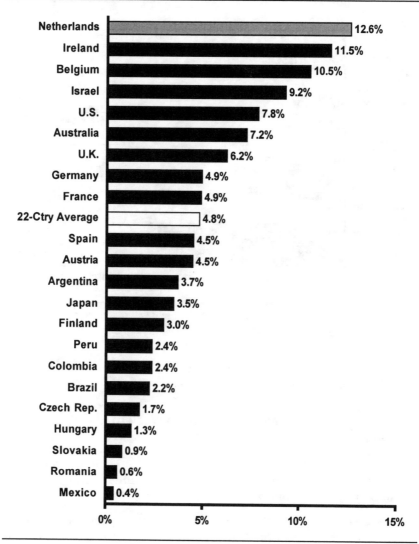

Figure 7.4   Nonprofit share of total employment, by country, 1995

average, moreover, nonprofit employment as a share of total employment is also considerably higher in the Netherlands than it is elsewhere
in Western Europe and in other developed countries. Thus, as shown in
Figure 7.5, full-time equivalent employment in nonprofit organizations
in the Netherlands, at 12.6 percent of total employment, is still 1.8 times

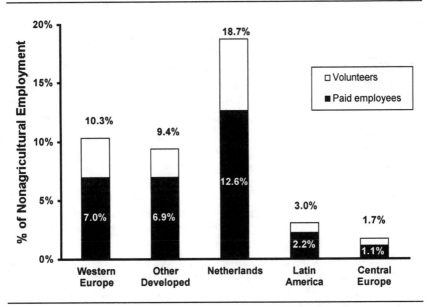

Figure 7.5   Nonprofit share of total employment, the Netherlands and four regions, 1995

the averages of Western Europe and other developed countries (6.9 percent). However, there are two other Western European countries with similar highly developed nonprofit sectors—Ireland with 11.5 percent and Belgium with 10.5 percent.

- **Margin does not change with volunteers.** This margin does not change, moreover, when volunteers are added. Thus, with volunteer time included, nonprofit organizations account for close to 19 percent of total employment in the Netherlands, as compared to the Western European average of 10 percent (see Figure 7.5)—still about twice as large.

3. A rich history of nonprofit activity

That the nonprofit sector is relatively highly developed in the Netherlands reflects the long and rich history that such institutions have had in this country.[4] This history includes:

- A long tradition of private initiatives and the absence of a centralist state. Since its independence, the Netherlands has been predominantly a burghers' country, or bourgeois society. In this environment, private initiative thrived and met little opposition from the state. On the contrary, the state often endorsed and supported nonprofits.

- The process of "pillarization," which further boosted nonprofit activities beginning in the latter half of the 19th century. The segmentation of society along religious and political lines, typically referred to as pillarization, led to the creation of large numbers of religiously or ideologically affiliated nonprofit organizations including schools, hospitals, political parties, labor unions, broadcasters, and welfare organizations.
- The numerous nonprofit organizations that originated in non-pillarized and non-sectarian activities, which also have a long and diverse history.
- A widespread pattern of public funding to core nonprofit activities, which first emerged in primary education, but later spread to health and social services. The extension of the welfare state thus boosted nonprofit action in the Netherlands.
- The long-standing and deeply engrained preference for private over state provision, which finally ensured and safeguarded the pivotal position of nonprofit organizations even as Dutch society began to de-pillarize starting in the 1960s.

4. Social service dominance

Unlike other Western European countries, health clearly dominates the nonprofit scene in the Netherlands.

- **Forty-two percent of nonprofit employment in health.** Of all the types of nonprofit activity, the one that accounts for the largest share of nonprofit employment in the Netherlands is health. As shown in Figure 7.6, 42 percent of all nonprofit employment in the Netherlands is in this field. While this greatly exceeds even the Western European average of 22 percent, it is also more than twice the 22-country average of 20 percent. This reflects a deliberate functional division of labor in health care provision with institutional care largely left to the nonprofit sector. As health institutions mostly take the nonprofit form, nonprofits account for 70 percent of total employment in health overall. In turn, about 70 percent of patients receive treatment in nonprofit hospitals. Government institutions are clearly in the minority, and decreasing as well. For-profit activities are restricted to the medical professions such as general practitioners, medical specialists, and dentists.
- **Large nonprofit presence in education.** Another sizable portion (28 percent) of total nonprofit employment in the Netherlands is in the

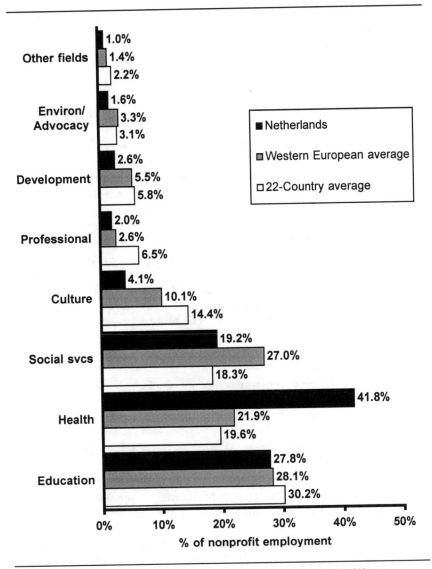

Figure 7.6 Composition of the nonprofit sector, the Netherlands, Western Europe, and 22-country average, 1995

education field. This is exactly on par with the Western European average and only slightly below the 22-country average of 30 percent. This reflects for the most part the fact that education has been one of the main areas of pillarization in Dutch society. Confessional schools still dominate private education, despite the fact that the majority of their pupils, staff, and teaching practices no longer reflect the original denominations.

- **Relatively large share of nonprofit employment in social services.** Compared to the overall 22-country average, the social services field absorbs a slightly larger share of nonprofit employment in the Netherlands. Thus, while social services absorbs about 18 percent of nonprofit employment on average, it accounts for 19 percent of nonprofit employment in the Netherlands. However, the social service share in the Netherlands is only about two-thirds of the Western European average of 27 percent. Compared to education and health, social services is a smaller field of both nonprofit and total activities.

- **Limited nonprofit development and advocacy employment.** Compared to the employment in nonprofit health, education, and social welfare organizations, the share of Dutch nonprofit employment in the development field and in the related fields of advocacy and environmental protection is less pronounced. Altogether, these fields absorb only 4 percent of all nonprofit employment in this country, or considerably less than the 22-country average of 9 percent. An additional approximately 7 percent of nonprofit employees fall into other categories, including culture and recreation (4.1 percent) and professional associations and unions (2 percent). However, while the shares of these groups in nonprofit employment are modest in comparative perspective, it should be kept in mind that they represent shares of—in relative terms—a very large nonprofit employment total. Indeed, in relation to other indicators, such as total nonagricultural employment, nonprofit involvement in these fields may still be larger than in many other countries.

- **Pattern shifts with volunteers.** This pattern changes considerably, however, when volunteer inputs are factored in. In particular, as shown in Figure 7.7, with volunteers included, the relative share of health and education in nonprofit employment declines considerably from about 70 percent of paid employment to only a little more than half of combined paid and volunteer employment. While social services gains slightly, the culture and recreation share almost quintuples from 4.1 percent to 17.3 percent, largely due to sports-related volunteering. The advocacy and environment share also increases significantly from less than 2 percent to 5 percent.

In sum, core welfare services overwhelmingly dominate the composition of the Dutch nonprofit sector, with nine out of every ten paid employees working in the health, education, and social services fields. Even with volunteer labor added, these three fields account for almost three-quarters of

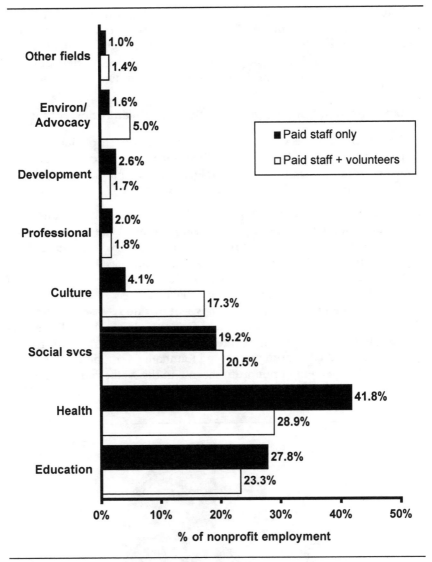

Figure 7.7   Share of nonprofit employment in the Netherlands, with and without volunteers, by field, 1995

combined paid and volunteer employment. This closely reflects the cooperative relationships between the state and crucial parts of the nonprofit sector that have emerged in Dutch society in the pillarization context since the latter half of the 19th century. All other nonprofit activities account for only 10 percent of employment and 17 percent of expenditures, but for almost 54 percent of volunteers. This shows that Dutch nonprofit organizations outside the welfare area depend less on paid labor, are able to attract more direct citizen involvement, and are generally less professionalized and monetarized than nonprofit welfare service providers.

5. Most revenue from the public sector, not philanthropy or fees

Consistent with the state-nonprofit sector relationships that resulted from pillarization, the Dutch nonprofit sector receives the bulk of its revenue not from private philanthropy or fees, but from public sector sources. In particular:

- **Public sector income dominant.** The overwhelmingly dominant source of income of nonprofit organizations in the Netherlands is public sector payments. As reflected in Figure 7.8, this source alone accounts for almost 60 percent of all nonprofit revenue in this country. Public sector income is comprised of direct government support and health insurance payments in equal measure.
- **Limited support from philanthropy and private fees and charges.** By contrast, private philanthropy and fees provide much smaller shares of total revenues. Thus, as Figure 7.8 shows, private philanthropy—from individuals, corporations, and foundations combined—accounts for only 3 percent of nonprofit income in the Netherlands, while fees and charges account for 38 percent.

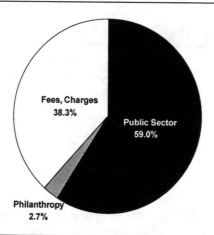

Fees, Charges
38.3%

Public Sector
59.0%

Philanthropy
2.7%

Figure 7.8   Sources of nonprofit revenue in the Netherlands, 1995

- **Revenue structure with volunteers.** This pattern of nonprofit revenue changes significantly when volunteers are factored into the picture. In fact, as shown in Figure 7.9, private philanthropy increases substantially from 3 percent to 24 percent with the inclusion of volunteers. However, it still remains behind fees and charges (30 percent) and public sector support (46 percent).
- **Revenue structure with religion.** The overall pattern of nonprofit finance in the Netherlands changes only slightly when account is taken of religious institutions, such as churches. Such religious institutions account for approximately one percent of the total revenue of the Dutch nonprofit sector. With religion included, therefore, the philanthropic share of total nonprofit revenue in the Netherlands rises from 2.7 percent to 3.4 percent. With volunteers included as well, private giving further increases to 26 percent, compared to 29 percent for fees and charges and 45 percent for public support (see Figure 7.10).
- **Similar to other Western European countries.** The pattern of nonprofit finance evident in the Netherlands is quite similar to that elsewhere in Western Europe. Thus, as shown in Figure 7.11, like the Netherlands, the nonprofit organizations in the other Western European countries included in this project (Austria, Belgium, Finland, France, Germany, Ireland, Spain, and the U.K.) derived on average the overwhelming majority of their revenues from public sector sources. Thus, compared to 59 percent in the Netherlands, the share of total nonprofit income coming from the public sector stood at

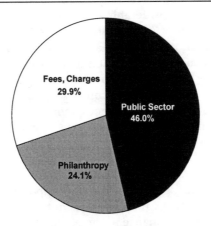

Figure 7.9   Sources of nonprofit revenue in the Netherlands, with volunteers, 1995

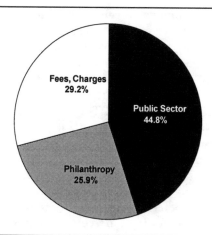

Figure 7.10   Sources of nonprofit revenue in the Netherlands, with volunteers and religious worship, 1995

56 percent for all Western European countries. Although similar in tendency, the philanthropy share of nonprofit revenue in the Netherlands deviates from the regional average, with this source considerably weaker than elsewhere in the region (3 percent vs. 7 percent on average). Fees account for about the same share in the Netherlands as on average (38 percent vs. 37 percent).

- **Deviation from the global average.** While the revenue structure of the Dutch nonprofit sector generally mirrors that elsewhere in Western Europe, it differs considerably from that evident elsewhere in the world. Thus, as Figure 7.11 also shows, while fees and charges are the dominant element in the financial base of the nonprofit sector globally, their dominance is considerably more pronounced than it is in the Netherlands (49 percent of total revenue compared to 38 percent). By contrast, public sector payments comprise a considerably smaller share of nonprofit income in these other countries on average (40 percent vs. 59 percent in the Netherlands). Quite clearly, a different pattern of cooperation has taken shape between nonprofit organizations and the state in these other countries. Evidently, the pillarization-based partnership between state and nonprofit sector in the Netherlands has led to a substantial reliance on public sector support by nonprofits.

- **Variations by subsector.** Even this does not do full justice to the complexities of nonprofit finance in the Netherlands, however. This is so because important differences exist in the finances of nonprofit organizations by subsector. In fact, two quite distinct patterns of nonprofit finance are evident among Dutch nonprofits, as shown in Figure 7.12:

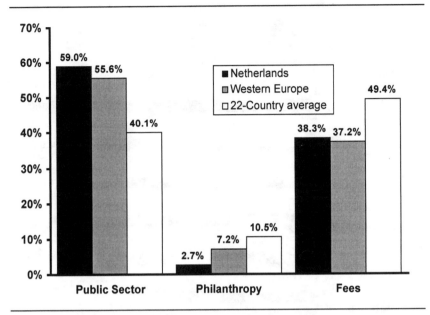

Figure 7.11   Sources of nonprofit cash revenue, the Netherlands, Western
Europe, and 22-country average, 1995

Fee-dominant fields. Fee income is the dominant source of income in
six fields of nonprofit action for which data were gathered, ranging
from philanthropy, where fees and charges (e.g. sales of lottery tickets
and endowment income) account for 97 percent of total revenue, to
the environmental field with a fee share of 61 percent. In the development field, the dominance of fee income largely results from rental income in the housing subgroup of this field. In professional associations and unions, as well as cultural and recreational organizations,
membership dues turn out to be the most important revenue source.

Public sector-dominant fields. In four fields (health, education, social services, and international activities) the public sector plays the dominant role in financing nonprofit action in the Netherlands. In health,
public payments with 96 percent are virtually the sole revenue source,
and this is almost true as well for education, where public support accounts for 91 percent of revenues. Government support is somewhat
less pronounced in the social services (66 percent), where fee income
accounts for about one-third of revenues. Although nonprofit relief
agencies receive only a small part of the 0.8 percent of GNP that the
Dutch government spends on international assistance, public sector
support is the largest revenue source in this field as well.

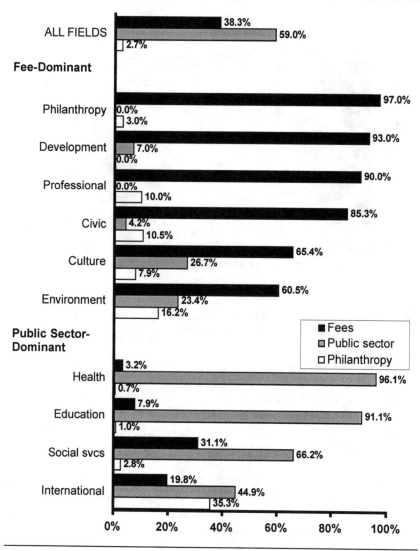

Figure 7.12   Sources of nonprofit cash revenue in the Netherlands, by field, 1995

CONCLUSIONS AND IMPLICATIONS

The nonprofit sector thus emerges from the evidence presented here as both a sizable and rather complex set of institutions in Dutch society. In fact, with its 12.6 percent share of nonagricultural employment, it is the largest nonprofit sector in the group of 22 countries. The structure and financing of the sector show the dominance of collectively organized solidarity over private charity. The welfare services of health, education, and social services are the largest fields of nonprofit activity. Public sources of revenue account for 59 percent of the sector's income, while private fees and private giving account for 38 percent and 3 percent, respectively. In the Netherlands, the role of the nonprofit sector goes beyond delivery of social welfare services alone; its activities in culture, leisure, advocacy, international solidarity, environment, religion, philanthropy, and volunteering also contribute to a vibrant social life. The realm outside the welfare state services is the home of most civil society organizations. Public discourse, community-building, and citizen participation are important but difficult to isolate and measure.

The nonprofit sector's key features such as its size, structure, and revenue base are a clear reflection of its long and rich history: the tradition of private initiatives, the process of pillarization, and the scheme of private delivery and public funding. In the years ahead, nonprofits will struggle to find a new balance among sources of income. With public support under pressure, attention will shift to more market income and private giving.

It is of utmost importance to recognize the nonprofit sector not only as a major economic force, but also as an institutional reality. The sector is private and nongovernmental, yet vulnerable to changes in public policies and support. Issues such as measurement, accounting, autonomy, and accountability deserve better attention. The significance of nonprofits is, if at all, generally recognized at the field level only. The next step is to enhance awareness at the sector level and to show that the sector is more than simply the sum of its parts.

ENDNOTES

1. The work in the Netherlands was coordinated by Paul Dekker and Ary Burger of the Social and Cultural Planning Office (SCP), who acted as local associates to the project. Important contributions, however, were also made by Vic Veldheer (SCP) on history, Tymen van der Ploeg and Wino van Veen (Vrije Universiteit) on legal issues, Peter Hupe and Lucas Meijs (Erasmusuniversiteit) on the impact work, Jan van Heemst on international organizations, and Joep de Hart (SCP) on advocacy organizations. The team was aided, in turn, by a local advisory committee made up of eight prominent philanthropic, government, academic, and nonprofit leaders (see Appendix D for a list of committee members). The Johns Hopkins Project was directed by Lester M. Salamon and Helmut K. Anheier.

2. The definitions and approaches used in the project were developed collaboratively with the cooperation of the Dutch researchers and researchers in other countries and were designed to be applicable to the Netherlands and the other project countries. For a full description of this definition and the types of organizations included, see Appendix A. For a full list

of the other countries included, see Chapter 1 above and Lester M. Salamon and Helmut K. Anheier, *The Emerging Sector Revisited: A Summary, Revised Estimates* (Baltimore, MD: The Johns Hopkins Center for Civil Society Studies, 1999). For a Dutch discussion of the application of the definition in the Netherlands, see Ary Burger and Paul Dekker, "De grootste non-profit sector ter wereld," *Economisch Statistische Berichten*, vol. 83, No. 4181 (11 December 1998).

3. Technically, the more precise comparison is between nonprofit contribution to "value added" and gross domestic product. For the nonprofit sector, "value added" in economic terms essentially equals the sum of wages and the imputed value of volunteer time. On this basis, the nonprofit sector in the Netherlands accounted for 11.2 percent of total value added, still a quite significant amount.

4. For a more detailed discussion, see Ary Burger, Paul Dekker, Tymen van der Ploeg, and Wino van Veen, "Defining the Nonprofit Sector: The Netherlands." *Working Papers of the Johns Hopkins Comparative Nonprofit Sector Project, No. 23.* (Baltimore, MD: Johns Hopkins Center for Civil Society Studies, 1997).

CHAPTER 8

Spain

José Ignacio Ruiz Olabuénaga, Antonio Jiménez Lara,
Helmut K. Anheier, and Lester M. Salamon

BACKGROUND

Like many of its counterparts in Western Europe, the Spanish nonprofit sector focuses a significant portion of its human and financial resources in the social welfare fields, especially social services. However, contrary to much of the rest of the Western European region, Spain's nonprofit organizations rely more heavily on private fees and charges for their income than on government grants and payments. What distinguishes Spain's nonprofit sector even more is a relatively high level of private giving in the revenue mix.

These findings are the result of pioneer work carried out in Spain by a research team at the Fundación Banco Bilbao Vizcaya (FBBV) in conjunction with the Johns Hopkins Comparative Nonprofit Sector Project.[1] The comparative endeavor thus offered ample opportunities both to capture local Spanish circumstances and peculiarities and to compare and contrast them to those in other countries in Western Europe and elsewhere in a systematic way.[2] The result is the first comprehensive empirical overview of the Spanish nonprofit sector and the first systematic comparison of Spanish nonprofit realities to those elsewhere in Western Europe and the rest of the world.

Global Civil Society: Dimensions of the Nonprofit Sector by Lester M. Salamon, Helmut K. Anheier, Regina List, Stefan Toepler, S. Wojciech Sokolowski and Associates. Baltimore, MD: Johns Hopkins Center for Civil Society Studies, 1999.

The present chapter reports on just one set of findings from this project, those relating to the size and structure of the nonprofit sector in Spain and elsewhere. Subsequent publications will fill in the historical, legal, and policy context of this sector and also examine the impact that this set of institutions is having. The principal data sources used were from the *Instituto Nacional de Estadística* (National Statistics Institute-INE), in addition to data available from various government ministries and sociological surveys, both population and organization-based. Unless otherwise noted, financial data are reported in U.S dollars at the 1995 average exchange rate. (For more information on the sources of data, see Appendix C.)

PRINCIPAL FINDINGS

Five major findings emerge from this work on the scope, structure, financing, and role of the nonprofit sector in Spain:

1. A growing economic force

In the first place, aside from its social and political importance, the nonprofit sector appears to be an important and growing economic force in Spain, accounting for significant shares of national expenditures and employment.

More specifically:

- **A $22.6 billion industry.** Even excluding its religion component, the nonprofit sector in Spain had operating expenditures in 1995 of $22.6 billion (2.8 trillion pesetas), or the equivalent of 4.0 percent of Spain's gross domestic product, quite a significant amount.[3]
- **A major employer.** Behind these expenditures lies an important workforce that includes 475,179 full-time equivalent paid workers. This represents 4.5 percent of all nonagricultural workers in Spain, 6.8 percent of service employment, and nearly one-quarter (22.9 percent) as many people as work for government at all levels: national, autonomic (regional), and municipal (see Table 8.1).
- **More employees than in the largest private firm.** Put somewhat differently, nonprofit employment in Spain easily outdistances the employment in the largest private business in Spain, and does so by a factor of almost 7. Thus, compared to the 475,179 paid workers in Spain's nonprofit organizations, Spain's largest private corporation, Telefónica, employs only 68,380 workers (see Figure 8.1).
- **Outdistances numerous industries.** Indeed, as shown in Figure 8.2, more people work in the nonprofit sector in Spain than in many en-

Table 8.1 The nonprofit sector in Spain, 1995

$22.6 billion in expenditures
— 4.0 percent of GDP

475,179 paid employees
— 4.5 percent of total nonagricultural employment
— 6.8 percent of service employment
— 22.9 percent of public sector employment

tire industries in the country, including transport and communication; food, beverages, and tobacco; metal processing; textiles; and chemical manufacturing industries.

- **Volunteer inputs.** Even this does not capture the full scope of the nonprofit sector in Spain, for this sector also attracts a considerable amount of *volunteer effort*. Indeed, an estimated 9.8 percent of the adult Spanish population reports contributing their time to nonprofit organizations. This translates into another 253,599 full-time equivalent employees, which boosts the total number of full-time equivalent employees of nonprofit organizations in Spain to 728,778, or 6.8 percent of total nonagricultural employment in Spain (see Figure 8.3).

2. An average-sized nonprofit sector

Although the Spanish nonprofit sector is large in relation to the Spanish economy, it is slightly below average relative to some of its counterparts elsewhere in Europe.

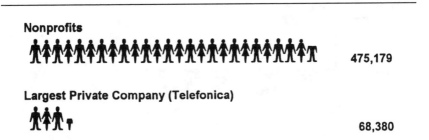

Nonprofits

475,179

Largest Private Company (Telefonica)

68,380

Figure 8.1 Employment in nonprofits vs. largest firm in Spain, 1995

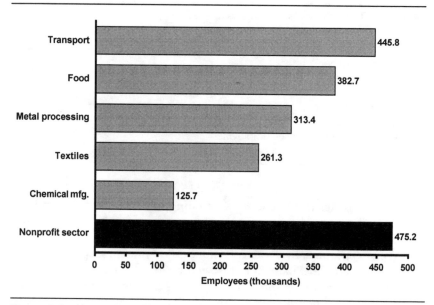

Figure 8.2   Nonprofit employment in Spain in context, 1995

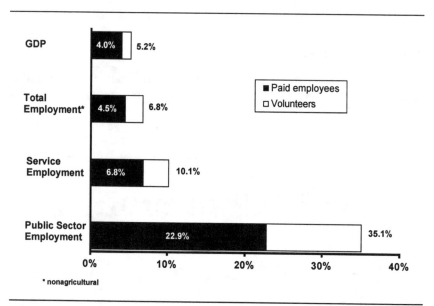

Figure 8.3   Nonprofits in Spain, with and without volunteers, 1995, as a % of . . .

- **Slightly below the international average.** As Figure 8.4 shows, the relative size of the nonprofit sector varies greatly among countries, from a high of 12.6 percent of total nonagricultural employment in the Netherlands to a low of less than 1 percent of total employment in Mexico. The overall 22-country average, however, is 4.8 percent. This means that Spain, at 4.5 percent, falls somewhat below the global average.

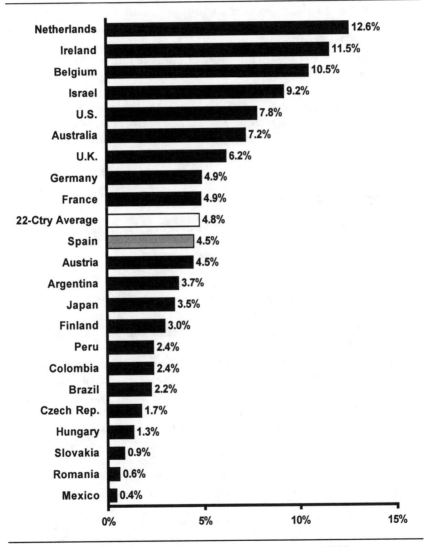

Figure 8.4 Nonprofit share of total employment, by country, 1995

However, it still exceeds Finland and Austria (although only slightly), and comes close to France and Germany (both 4.9 percent).

- **Considerably below the Western European average.** While it is nearly even with the 22-country average, nonprofit employment as a share of total employment is still considerably lower in Spain than it is elsewhere in Western Europe. Thus, as shown in Figure 8.5, full-time equivalent employment in nonprofit organizations in Spain, at 4.5 percent of total employment, is proportionally 35 percent less than the European Union's average of 7.0 percent. This is explained in part by the fact that, although the number of organizations is high (253,000), most Spanish nonprofit entities are rather small and generate limited employment.
- **Margin widens with volunteers.** This margin widens slightly, moreover, when volunteers are added. Thus, with volunteer time included, nonprofit organizations account for 6.8 percent of total employment in Spain, well behind the Western European average of 10.3 percent (see Figure 8.5).

3. A complex history of nonprofit activity

That the Spanish nonprofit sector is smaller in size than its Western European counterparts is the result of several long-term factors as well as more recent developments. Highlights include:

- The long and complicated history of Spain, with the prominent role of the Catholic Church and the late development of industrialization and modern state administration, all of which left many unresolved tensions between church and state power on the one hand, and emergent civil society on the other.
- The strong corporatist policies of the Franco dictatorship from the late 1930s to the mid-1970s and the suppression of civil liberties that reduced the social and political space potentially available for many types of nonprofit organizations, and at the same time, maintained the social services and educational establishments of the Catholic Church.
- The transition from authoritarianism to democracy that brought with it a boom in associational life, as political space for nonprofit activities was freed up and claimed by emerging social movements and citizen action.
- The rapid economic development of Spain since 1975, which has created many new demands for social services. These are supplied, at least in part, by an expanding nonprofit sector. Thus, in the last quar-

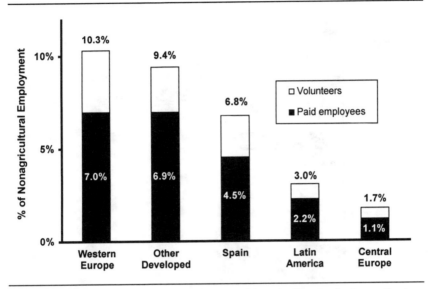

Figure 8.5   Nonprofit share of employment, with and without volunteers, Spain and four regions, 1995

ter of a century, the Spanish nonprofit sector has managed to gain ground.

4. Social services dominance

Similar to other Western European countries, but unlike the all-country average, social services clearly dominates the nonprofit scene in Spain.

- **Nearly 32 percent of nonprofit employment in social services.** Of all the types of nonprofit activity, the one that accounts for the largest share of nonprofit employment in Spain is social services. As shown in Figure 8.6, 31.8 percent of all nonprofit employment in Spain is in this field. This is higher than the Western European average of 27.0 percent, and it greatly exceeds the 22-country average of 18.3 percent. This situation very likely reflects the prominence of three large networks of nonprofit organizations—ONCE (*Organización Nacional de Ciegos*/National Organization for the Blind), the Red Cross, and Caritas—that play a major role in service provision and financing throughout Spain. For example, ONCE alone employs nearly 40,000 paid workers (8.4 percent of all nonprofit employment).

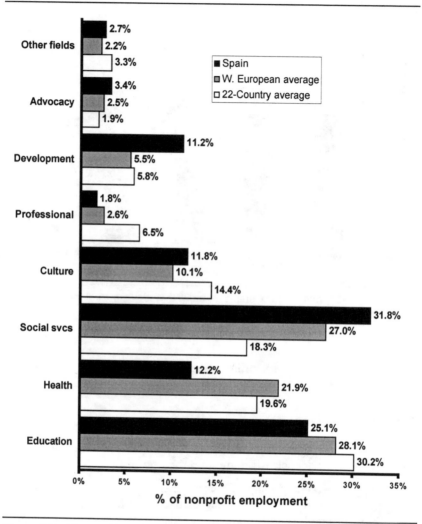

Figure 8.6   Composition of the nonprofit sector, Spain, W. Europe, and 22-country average, 1995

- **Sizable, but smaller shares of nonprofit employment in education, health, and culture and recreation.** Compared to the overall 22-country average, education, health, and culture and recreation absorb sizable, but relatively smaller shares of nonprofit employment in Spain. Thus, while these three fields absorb 64.2 percent of nonprofit employment on average for the 22 countries and 60.1 percent for Western Europe, they account for only 49.1 percent of nonprofit employment in Spain. This reflects, in part, the sector's modest role—relative to the public sector—in the provision of health care services. At the same time, Spain still has a sizable nonprofit presence in these fields, represented most prominently by the education and research field, which accounts for 25.1 percent of nonprofit employment.

- **Unusually large share of employment in development and advocacy.** A relatively large portion of total nonprofit employment in Spain is found in the fields of development and advocacy. Together, these two fields account for 14.6 percent of all nonprofit employment, of which 11.2 percent is in development and 3.4 percent in advocacy. This reflects, in part, the role of nonprofit organizations in the political transition from dictatorship to democracy and their contributions to social and economic development.

- **Limited nonprofit employment in professional organizations and other fields such as environment and international activities.** Compared to the employment in nonprofit social services, education, health, culture, and development, the share of nonprofit employment in professional organizations and in other fields, including environment and international activities, is considerably smaller. Altogether, these fields absorb 4.5 percent of all nonprofit employment in Spain, less than half the 22-country average of 9.9 percent.

- **Pattern shifts with volunteers.** This pattern changes when volunteer inputs are factored in. In particular, as shown in Figure 8.7, with volunteers included, the share of full-time equivalent employment in the culture and sports, civic and advocacy, and "other" fields rises, whereas that in the traditional social welfare fields of education, health, and social services, as well as community development and housing, declines proportionally.

5. Most revenue from fees and charges, not philanthropy

Although fees and charges are the principal income source for the Spanish nonprofit sector, private giving accounts for a larger share than in any other European Union country included in this study.

- **Fee income dominant.** The dominant source of income of nonprofit organizations in Spain is fees and charges for services. As reflected in Figure 8.8, this source alone accounts for 49.0 percent of all nonprofit revenue in Spain.

- **Pronounced support from philanthropy.** Private philanthropy provides a much smaller, but still significant, share of total revenues.

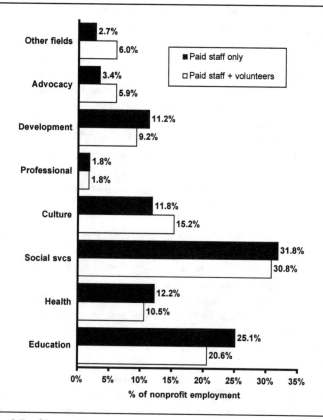

Figure 8.7   Share of nonprofit employment in Spain, with and without volunteers, by field, 1995

Thus, as Figure 8.8 shows, private giving—from individuals, corporations, and foundations combined—accounts for 18.8 percent of nonprofit income in Spain.

- **Limited public sector support.** The public sector share of income (32.1 percent) is significantly less than that of fees and charges, but still greater than private giving.
- **Revenue structure with volunteers.** This pattern of nonprofit revenue changes significantly when volunteers are factored into the picture. In fact, as shown in Figure 8.9, with the value of volunteering included, private philanthropy increases substantially from 18.8 percent to 36.3 percent, thereby surpassing the public sector's contribution, which decreases from 32.1 percent to 25.2 percent. Although the share of

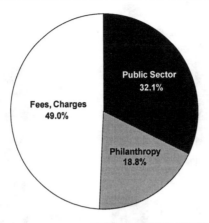

Figure 8.8   Sources of nonprofit revenue in Spain, 1995

fee income also declines from 49.0 percent to 38.5 percent with volunteers included, it remains the major revenue source in Spain.

- **Different from other Western European countries.** The pattern of nonprofit finance evident in Spain is quite different from that elsewhere in Europe. Thus, as shown in Figure 8.10, nonprofit organizations in the other Western European countries included in the project derived the overwhelming majority of their revenues on average from the public sector. Thus, compared to Spain's 32.1 percent, the average

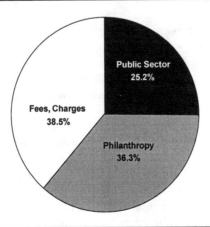

Figure 8.9   Sources of nonprofit revenue in Spain, with volunteers, 1995

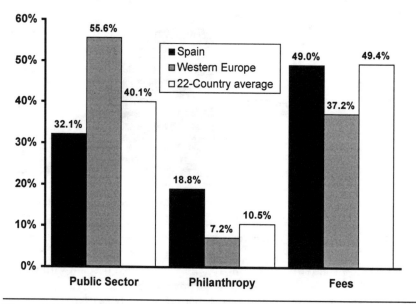

Figure 8.10   Sources of nonprofit cash revenue, Spain, W. Europe, and 22-country average, 1995

share of total nonprofit income coming from public sector payments stood at 55.6 percent for all nine Western European countries. The fees and charges share of nonprofit revenue was much stronger in Spain than elsewhere in Europe (49 percent vs. 37.2 percent on average) and philanthropy significantly more important (18.8 percent vs. 7.2 percent). The relative strength of private giving in the Spanish nonprofit sector's revenue structure is due at least in part to a unique financing scheme. Under this arrangement, a portion of the proceeds from a lottery run by ONCE is devoted to the ONCE Foundation, which supports an entire network of organizations serving the needs of people with disabilities.

- **Closer to the global average.** While the revenue structure of the Spanish nonprofit sector differs from that elsewhere in Europe, its fee dominance mirrors the global average. Thus, as Figure 8.10 also shows, fees and charges are the dominant element in the financial base of the nonprofit sector both globally and in Spain (about 49 percent of total revenue). However, the similarity stops there. Public sector payments comprise a considerably larger share of nonprofit income in these countries on average (40.1 percent vs. 32.1 percent in Spain), whereas philanthropy accounts for a much smaller share globally than in Spain (10.5 percent vs. 18.8 percent). Quite clearly, a different pattern of co-operation has taken shape between nonprofit organizations and the state in the other countries. To some extent, this could be explained by the late development of the welfare state in Spain, and the dominant presence of the Catholic Church in the nonprofit sector throughout Spain's history.

- **Variations by subsector.** Even this does not do full justice to the complexities of nonprofit finance in Spain, however. This is so because important differences exist in the finances of nonprofit organizations by field. In fact, three quite distinct patterns of nonprofit finance are evident among the various fields of nonprofit activity in Spain, as shown in Figure 8.11.

  Fee-dominant fields. Fee income is the dominant source of income in the fields of development and housing and professional associations (both 70.0 percent).

  Private philanthropy-dominant fields. While private philanthropy is not the dominant source of nonprofit income in Spain overall, it turns out to be the dominant source of income for environmental groups, civic/advocacy organizations, and philanthropic intermediaries. These three subsectors are rather new and, consequently, they have not yet established strong ties with the public administration.

  Balanced fields. In five fields, there is no absolutely dominant revenue source, but rather a major source providing between 40 and 60 percent of total income and a minor source providing between 30 and 40 percent. This is the case for health where fees and charges (50.6 percent of revenue) are the senior partner to the public sector (36.7 percent). In the culture and recreation field, likewise, fees are slightly dominant (40.9 percent), but are more in balance with private giving (34.8 percent) and public sector payments (24.3 percent). In the other two traditional welfare fields of education and social services, public sector payments (53.1 percent and 48.6 percent, respectively) take the lead over private payments (40.6 percent and 31.4 percent, respectively). Finally, government funding (56.2 percent of revenue) is the major revenue source for nonprofits in the international activities field, but private philanthropy (35.9 percent) is also significant.

- **This general picture changes if the input of volunteers to each of the fields is taken into account.** Philanthropic resources remain dominant in the same three fields mentioned above, but, with volunteers included, philanthropy becomes the senior partner with state-allocated public funding in both social services (48.0 percent philanthropy vs.

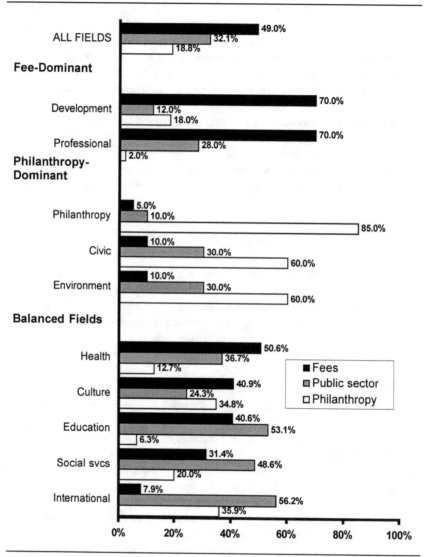

Figure 8.11   Sources of nonprofit cash revenue in Spain, by field, 1995

31.6 percent public sector) and international activities (63.5 percent philanthropy vs. 32.0 percent public sector). Additionally, philanthropy overtakes private fees to become the major source of income in the field of culture and recreation (51.0 percent philanthropy vs. 30.7 percent private fees).

CONCLUSIONS AND IMPLICATIONS

The evidence presented here shows that the Spanish third sector is a sizable set of institutions, with a social significance never before acknowledged by scholars in Spain or elsewhere. Although the size and composition of the Spanish nonprofit sector is quite similar to that of other Western European countries, its financial structure is quite different. In particular, the nonprofit sector's reliance on government financial support is much lower in Spain than elsewhere in Europe. However, it is the elevated level of importance of private philanthropy that emerges as a signature element of the Spanish nonprofit sector.

Given these circumstances, no single set of implications will apply equally to Spain and to the rest of the Western European countries studied. While, like much of Western Europe, Spain does face the fundamental challenges outlined in Chapter 1 of constructing a systematic renewal strategy, evaluating and preserving the accountability and effectiveness of the nonprofit sector, and striving toward integration and globalization of the sector, there exists an important difference between the challenges that face Spain and those with which the rest of Western Europe is presented. Because private philanthropy is already a vital resource for the Spanish nonprofit sector, it is not the development of philanthropy, but rather the expansion of volunteering that remains an important goal for the Spanish nonprofit sector.

Important as the development of organizational and leadership capacities are for the future of the nonprofit sector, the expansion of volunteering continues to be vital to ensure a meaningful level of independence from both government and business. Specifically, changes in demographics and the labor force suggest that in Spain, as elsewhere, large reservoirs of potential volunteers remain "untapped" for the expansion of the philanthropic share of nonprofit operations. However, this will require public education efforts by the sector's leadership, and creative models for combining paid and unpaid work, particularly in countries like Spain with high levels of unemployment.

While much has been achieved in Spain since the democratization process of the mid-1970s opened the way for the development of the modern Spanish nonprofit sector, much remains to be done. Importantly, and in contrast to most other European countries, Spain does not have an established policy of government-nonprofit sector relationships. Indeed, distrust and misunderstanding about how the other sector functions are frequently found among representatives of both government and the nonprofit sector. This lack of awareness of each other's strengths and weaknesses may well prevent symbiotic relationships from developing. A high-level and broad-based commission on the role and future of the nonprofit sector in Spain may offer the platform best suited to set in motion an ongoing policy dialogue that is clearly needed—particularly in the light of further European integration. To this end, the next pressing research task is to get a better understanding of the social contribution that the nonprofit sector does and could make to European societies—a task that is in progress and forms an important part of what this study seeks to achieve.

ENDNOTES

1. The work in Spain was coordinated by Dr. José Ignacio Ruiz Olabuénaga, who acted as local associate for the project. Assisting Dr. Olabuénaga were Antonio Jiménez Lara, Demetrio Casado, José Luis Orella, Carmen Labrador, Mikel Mancisador, and María Angeles Oyarzabal. The team was aided, in turn, by a local advisory committee chaired by María Luisa Oyarzabal. The Johns Hopkins project was directed by Dr. Lester M. Salamon and Dr. Helmut K. Anheier, who also oversaw the Western European work.

2. The definitions and approaches used in the project were developed collaboratively with the cooperation of the Spanish researchers and researchers in other countries included in the project. They were designed to be applicable to Spain and the other project countries. For a full description of this definition and the types of organizations included, see Appendix A. For a full list of the other countries involved in the project, see Chapter 1 above and Lester M. Salamon, Helmut K. Anheier and Associates, *The Emerging Sector Revisited: A Summary, Revised Estimates* (Baltimore, MD: The Johns Hopkins Center for Civil Society Studies, 1999).

3. Technically, the more precise comparison is between nonprofit contribution to "value added" and gross domestic product. For the nonprofit sector, "value added" in economic terms essentially equals the sum of wages and the imputed value of volunteer time. On this basis, the nonprofit sector in Spain accounted for 3.3 percent of total value added, still a quite significant amount.

CHAPTER 9

United Kingdom[1]

Jeremy Kendall and Stephen Almond

INTRODUCTION

It is perhaps now a cliché to comment that organizations operating between the market and the state are increasingly having their multifarious contributions to U.K. society rediscovered by politicians, academics, and the media. Once a rather shadowy enclave at the periphery of the mental maps of most policy-makers and policy-shapers, the third sector has increasingly moved to center stage in their minds as they grapple with the social and economic problems of our time. The diagnoses are many and familiar, and include:

- Disillusionment with private market solutions for their lack of attention to the needs of the disadvantaged and their chronic vulnerability to the erratic movements of the economic cycle and financial markets;
- Mounting distrust of politician-dominated approaches, and skepticism about the capacity of often cash-starved state-controlled agencies to deliver public services able to match spiraling user expectations and increasingly diverse citizen aspirations;
- A positive endorsement of the actual and potential contributions of voluntary organizations to the "good society" both by offering choice

Global Civil Society: Dimensions of the Nonprofit Sector by Lester M. Salamon, Helmut K. Anheier, Regina List, Stefan Toepler, S. Wojciech Sokolowski and Associates. Baltimore, MD: Johns Hopkins Center for Civil Society Studies, 1999.

and responsiveness in services and by providing opportunities for generating trust, civic virtue, and "social capital" via participation in community and public life. This is increasingly seen not only as of intrinsic value, but as being deeply connected with local, national, and international economic success, and—controversially—as even constituting a core ingredient of a "third way" in the political domain.

As a contribution to the developing debate, this chapter provides new empirical data on one very important aspect of the third sector's role in British society: its growing, but at the same time changing, contribution to *economic* life. This is an update and extension of an earlier study that pioneered the comprehensive and systematic measurement of the U.K. sector's financial and human resources,[2] within the context of the Johns Hopkins Comparative Nonprofit Sector Project.[3] Parallel research still underway explores aspects of the third sector's *social* and *political* roles in more detail. This analysis, which includes an exploration of the sector's impact and effectiveness, will be released at a later date.

Box 9.1

Definitions of the third sector used in this chapter

The *broad nonprofit sector* (BNS) includes all entities that are formal organizations having an institutionalized character; constitutionally independent of the state and self-governing; non-profit-distributing; and involving some degree of volunteerism. This definition has been reached though a process of consensus-building within the framework of the Comparative Nonprofit Sector Project and is relevant for international comparisons while representing a relatively inclusive definition compared to traditional U.K. usage.

The *broad voluntary sector* (BVS) includes all organizations in the BNS as identified above, other than political parties and religious congregations. This definition is the basis for broad comparisons between 1991 and 1995 in what follows, since statistical estimates relating to political parties and religious congregations are only available for 1995.

The *narrow voluntary sector* (NVS) includes all organizations in the BVS, less organizations not traditionally thought of as being part of the voluntary sector in the U.K. This is primarily because they are seen as effectively being part of the state despite their constitutional status, and/or because they are thought not to be sufficiently altruistic or public benefit oriented. Excluded on this basis are all universities, schools, sports and social clubs, and trade union and business associations.

Finally, the term "third sector" is used as cross-cutting shorthand and when generalizations are sustainable across all three definitions.

The following chapter will offer a description of the overall size and composition of the third sector in the mid-1990s, as well as demonstrate how its composition and resource base have changed over time. The U.K. experience will be considered in a comparative context by showing how the sector compares with the equivalent set of institutions in other parts of the world. In order to do this accurately, while at the same time taking seriously the contested nature of the "sector" idea in the U.K., three slightly different definitions for this set of institutions are used: a *broad nonprofit sector* (BNS) that corresponds to the one used in the Johns Hopkins Project; a *broad voluntary sector* (BVS) that excludes a portion of those institutions not normally considered part of this sector in the U.K. context; and a *narrow voluntary sector* (NVS) that excludes even more of these institutions to fit U.K. notions of the voluntary sector. The coverage of each of these definitions is outlined in more detail in Box 9.1. The term "third sector" is used as a cross-cutting shorthand.

THE CONTRIBUTION OF THE U.K. THIRD SECTOR TO THE ECONOMY

In 1995 the U.K. broad nonprofit sector (BNS) employed just under 1.5 million full-time equivalent paid workers (Table 9.1). These employees account for just over 6 percent of activity in the economy as a whole, meaning that the BNS now employs considerably more paid staff than the U.K.'s largest single institutional employer, the National Health Service (NHS). This had 1.1 million workers in that year. In fact, for every four people employed directly by the public sector as a whole in the U.K. there is now one employee in the BNS. Even if a much narrower definition of the sector is used (*NVS*, see Box 9.1), over half a million people were employed by voluntary organizations, representing some 2.2 percent of all paid employment, and with nearly one worker in the (narrow) sector for every two employed in the NHS.

While the sector's contribution to paid employment is therefore of considerable significance, volunteering remains the primary labor input for the sector as a whole. When all the hours of the BNS's 16 million volunteers are aggregated, this amounts to the equivalent of 1.7 million full-time voluntary employees, slightly more than its 1.5 million paid employees (Table 9.1). And if these voluntary organizations' volunteers are included in the overall workforce calculations, the BNS emerges as providing some 12.3 percent of the formal economy's human resources (where the comparator includes volunteering across all organizational sectors).

The sector's contribution to the economy can also be compared with the nation's gross domestic product (GDP). In total, the BNS expended $74.9

Table 9.1   The overall economic contribution of the U.K. third sector in 1995

Economic indicator	BNS	NVS
Volunteer headcount ('000s)	16,311	7,852
FTE volunteers ('000s)	1,664	774
FTE paid employment ('000s)	1,473	503
Percent of economy-wide paid employment	6.3	2.2
Total FTE paid and unpaid employment ('000s)	3,137	1,277
Percent of economy-wide employment including volunteering (all formal sectors)	12.3	5.0
Total expenditure (TE)	$74.9 billion	$24.5 billion
TE as percent of GDP	6.6	2.2
TE including volunteers[a]	$107.5 billion	$39.6 billion
As percent of volunteer-adjusted GDP[a,b]	9.2	3.4

Notes:

[a] Assuming volunteer hours can be valued using mean nonagricultural private sector wage.

[b] Denominator includes value of volunteering in all sectors (including private, public, third and informal).

Sources: See Appendix C.

billion (£47.1 billion) in 1995, some 6.6 percent of GDP. However, this does not take into account the value of volunteering. The appropriate route to valuing this input in monetary terms is the subject of some dispute, but using reasonable assumptions would suggest that volunteering in the BNS generates a monetary "value added" equivalent to between $25 billion (£15.7 billion) and $32.6 (£20.5 billion).[4] If this is compared to the GDP, in turn itself adjusted to include the value added of all informal and formal volunteering on a similar basis, the activities of the BNS emerge as representing between 8.7 percent and 9.2 percent of (volunteer-adjusted) GDP.

Composition of the third sector in 1995

Like the public and private (for-profit) sectors, the third sector is characterized by a staggering variety of organizational types, structures, and activities.[5] One helpful way of capturing some of this diversity, borrowed and adapted from the ways in which economic data on the former sectors are routinely analyzed, is to break the sector down according to field of activity or "industry." Table 9.2 shows how both paid employees and unpaid volunteers are distributed across these different activities.

The analysis reveals that most paid employment in the third sector under the broadest definition is concentrated in just three fields: education

Table 9.2 Distribution of paid and unpaid employment, by "industry," U.K. BNS, thousands, 1995

Field of activity (ICNPO)*	FTE paid employment No.	(%)	FTE volunteers No.	(%)	Total employment No.	(%)
Culture & recreation	347	(23.8)	351	(21.1)	698	(22.2)
Education & research	587	(44.3)	58	(3.5)	645	(20.6)
Health	60	(4.2)	143	(8.6)	203	(6.5)
Social services	185	(12.7)	221	(13.3)	406	(12.9)
Environment	18	(1.6)	44	(2.6)	62	(1.9)
Development & housing	108	(7.7)	210	(12.6)	318	(10.1)
Law, advocacy & politics	10	(0.7)	35	(2.1)	45	(1.4)
Philanthropic intermediaries	10	(0.7)	22	(1.3)	32	(1.0)
International activities	54	(3.7)	7	(0.4)	61	(1.9)
Religious congregations	58	(4.0)	544	(32.7)	602	(19.2)
Professional associations, trade unions, etc.	37	(2.6)	0	(0.0)	37	(1.2)
Not elsewhere classified	0	(0.0)	29	(1.8)	29	(0.9)
Total BNS	**1,473**	**(100)**	**1,664**	**(100)**	**3,137**	**(100)**

* International Classification of Nonprofit Organizations (ICNPO).[6]

Sources: See Appendix C.

and research, culture and recreation, and social services, which collectively account for some three-quarters of *BNS* activity. These are the same three fields that dominated the sector economically in 1990 (see below). If the narrow approach is used, which by definition excludes most of education as well as culture and recreation, then a slightly different grouping comes to prominence: social services as well as development and housing together account for 58 percent of all *NVS* employment, with other fields lagging some way behind.

When volunteer input is taken into account, culture and recreation push ahead of education and research. Furthermore, when volunteers are factored in, the relative significance of the religion field, in which the greatest single concentration of volunteers is to be found, is brought into focus. What emerges overall is a distinctive patterning by field according to the relative importance of volunteers:

- Health, environment, community development, advocacy, and religion are volunteer-rich fields, with unpaid workers heavily outnumbering their paid counterparts;

- In education and research, housing, international activities, and professional associations, etc., paid staff are the dominant human resource; and
- In culture and recreation and social services, paid and unpaid employees are involved to a similar extent.

THE CHANGING SIZE AND COMPOSITION OF THE THIRD SECTOR

Not only does the third sector currently make a major contribution to the economic life of the nation, but it has also grown significantly during the course of the 1990s. Figure 9.1 shows that between 1990 and 1995, the *BVS's* paid employment increased from 4.0 to 6.1 percent of economy-wide full-time equivalent paid employment. Moreover, most of this growth took place—at least in the case of "general charities"—between 1990 and 1993,[7]

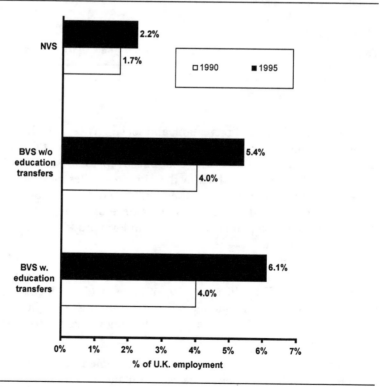

Figure 9.1   Growth in paid employment in the U.K. nonprofit sector, 1990–1995

precisely when the U.K. economy was experiencing significant recessionary pressures. (Real GDP did not regain its 1990 level until 1994.)[8]

This extraordinarily high rate of growth is in part explained by the transformation of educational institutions formerly directly controlled by local government into self-governing, nonprofit institutions operating within the state system.[9] Since this cannot be said to represent genuine growth, the figure also reports this trend with this transfer excluded. The result is still striking, with an increase of 33 percent in absolute numbers employed. As a proportion of employment in the economy as a whole, the figure is slightly higher, at 35 percent, because the U.K. labor force has actually shrunk over this period.[10]

Focusing on the less inclusive *NVS* basis reveals a slightly lower growth rate, with employment increasing by 29 percent from 390,000 to 503,000. This is similar to the annual growth rate of employment in the banking and insurance sector.[11] Until the recent (1998) financial crisis, this field was routinely held up as one of the most dynamic areas of growth of the British economy, alongside computing and technology.

As the third sector has grown, its resource base has changed. Figure 9.2 compares the funding sources for both the *BVS* and *NVS* in 1990 and 1995. In both cases, a marked overall increase in reliance upon public sources can be seen. For the first time the third sector, using both definitions, now has income from the state as its most important single source of income. (This includes all direct funding through grants, contracts, and service level agreements, but does not include the value of indirect support through tax advantages. Including the latter would of course further amplify the importance of state funding to the sector increasing annual support by around $1.6 billion.[12]) This reflects the extent to which the new interest of policy-makers in the sector has already been converted into real resource flows into the sector from government.

The figure also shows a decline in the relative importance, though not the absolute size, of private giving for recipient organizations. This is consistent with a growing body of other evidence from the givers' side. Most well charted has been the fall off in donations from individuals, both in terms of the amount of resources given, and the rate of participation,[13] although this still remains by far the most important single source of monetary private gifts for the sector. The data suggest a slight real increase in the total receipts from donations for the *BVS*—at $4.3 billion in 1995 compared to $2.3 billion in 1990 ($4 billion compared to $3.3 billion for the *NVS*). However, because the sector has grown so rapidly in overall size, private giving from individuals now represents a lower *proportion* of income than before, falling from 6.6 to 5.6 percent of total *BVS* revenue (14.6 to 13.3 percent of total *NVS* revenue). Corporate giving has even fallen in absolute terms according to the project data, although this trend should be interpreted with caution, because of definitional complexities. The only source of donative income to keep pace with the sector's overall growth was revenue from grant-making trusts and foundations. This grew quickly enough to maintain its share of third sector total revenue (from 2.4 to 2.5 percent for the *BVS*, growing from 3.4 to 4.0 percent for the *NVS*).

Finally, the project research provides evidence concerning the extent to which the U.K. third sector has become more "commercial" in character. This trend has been well documented in the U.S. "nonprofit" sector in recent years.[14] In the U.K. case, however, it appears that like private donations, private earned income (primarily accounted for by users' fees and sales, and income from investments) has grown slightly in absolute terms—but has only marginally increased (in the case of *BVS* and *NVS* fees and sales) or fallen (in the case of *BVS* and *NVS* private earned income overall) as a *proportion* of total income. This is shown clearly in Figure 9.2.

Compositional effects

The overall trends described here mask significant differences between contrasting types of organizations. Distinguishing between "industries" is particularly important, because organizations in each area inhabit different "issue networks" and sometimes "policy communities" depending upon their goals and activities, and are therefore subject to a different range of pressures and opportunities. Most obviously, some organizations operate almost completely untouched by the activities of the public sector (other than through the provision of a legal structure and benefiting from tax breaks by virtue of their legal form). Others are closely involved in policy design and implementation, and their development is therefore closely bound up with the funding and other decisions of the public sector that, in turn, may vary according to the particular field in question.[15]

Table 9.3 contrasts the trends by "industry" in terms of employment, while Figure 9.3 shows how sources of finance have altered. The latter shows a remarkably consistent trend across most industries: the sector-wide trend in finance noted above—increased dependence on the state and less recourse to private donations—is not the result of isolated trends in one or two dominant fields, but has happened across broad swathes of the sector.

However, there are important differences in the drivers for and character of change in each industry. As Table 9.3 indicates, the largest absolute change in employment—accounting for over half of all employment growth—has occurred in education and research. In large part, this growth reflects a redistribution by sector of ownership within this field, primarily the outcome of "migration" of institutions from direct state control to

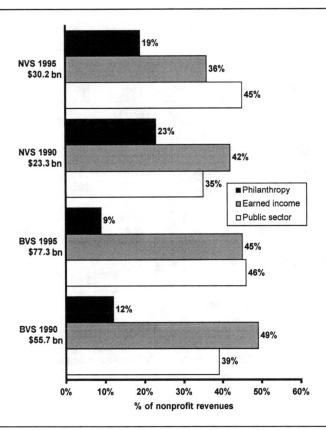

Figure 9.2 Sources of nonprofit revenue in the U.K., 1995

quasi-independent status *within* a state-regulated and (largely) state-funded system.

Two particular policy developments are relevant: firstly, the *en masse* transformation mandated by central government in 1993 to shift tertiary and other education colleges from local-authority-controlled institutions into self-governing charitable corporations (which followed the much higher profile reconstitution of local-authority-controlled polytechnics as independent "new universities" that had already taken place in 1989); secondly, the growth in the number of secondary, and to a much lesser extent, primary schools that decided to "opt out" of direct local authority control into the third sector, following school-by-school parental ballots—an option presented to schools following government reforms of the education system in the late 1980s. Both broad types of reinvented "hybrid" institution now

Table 9.3 Trends in U.K. *BVS* paid employment, by "industry," thousands, 1990–1995

Field of activity	FTE 1990 No.	FTE 1990 (%)	FTE 1995 No.	FTE 1995 (%)	Absolute change
Culture & recreation	262	(27.7)	347	(24.6)	84*
Education & research	330	(34.9)	587	(41.6)	257
Health	43	(4.5)	60	(4.2)	17
Social services	146	(15.4)	185	(13.1)	39
Environment	17	(1.8)	18	(1.3)	1
Development & housing	74	(7.8)	108	(7.6)	34
Civic & advocacy	9	(1.0)	7	(0.5)	–2
Grant-making trusts	7	(0.7)	10	(0.7)	3
International activities	23	(2.4)	54	(3.8)	31
Professional associations, trade unions, etc.	35	(3.7)	37	(2.6)	2
Total *BVS*	**946**	**(100)**	**1,412**	**(100)**	**467**
Total *BVS* excluding 1990–95 education transfers and recreation	**739**		**962**		**273**

* This trend should be treated with caution, as the 1990 estimate for recreation may be unreliable.

Sources: See Appendix C.

operate alongside the *BVS*'s traditional nonprofit providers, the universities, maintained (state-funded) church and other voluntary schools, and charitable "independent" (privately funded) schools.

This growth at the definitional borders of the *BVS* is then unambiguously government-led. Focusing on the *NVS*, however, one finds a more mixed picture. The personal social services field as a whole has been the most rapidly growing component of the *NVS* during this time period. This has been buoyed by a combination of government enthusiasm for, and the provision of resources to, independently provided (as opposed to in-house) community-based care—in response to the aging of the population, antipathy towards public sector direct provision, and a host of other social, political, and economic factors. Figure 9.3 shows that this has fed through into the development of a sector that is markedly more dependent upon state funding. However, the main beneficiary of the new public priority attached to social services has been the private (nominally for-profit) sector, populated mainly by small businesses.[16] Particularly in the case of care for older people, which accounts for the lion's share of re-

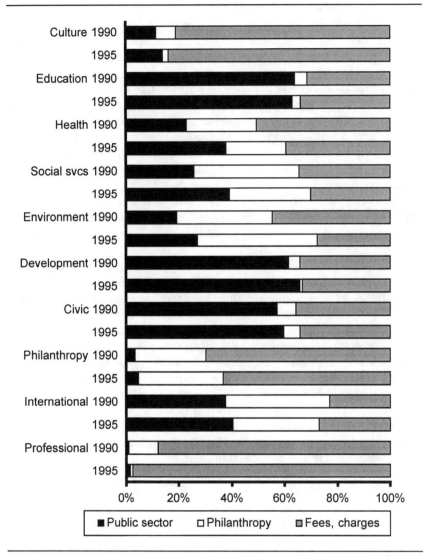

Figure 9.3   Changes in finance in the U.K. nonprofit sector, by field, 1990–1995

sources in this field, the latter has grown much more rapidly than the voluntary sector, first in residential care and more recently in the provision of home care services. A similar pattern—that is, voluntary sector growth, but even greater expansion by private sector providers—can also be found in some other maturing welfare "quasi-markets." Health care, particularly mental health and nursing care, are perhaps the best examples.

The two other main areas of *NVS* growth shown in Table 9.3 are development and housing, and international activities. In the former case, expansion has been led by housing associations (registered social landlords), whose specialist market niche in social housing has remained relatively insulated from private sector competition (although government financial support has itself become both more business-like and, since 1995, more scarce). In the latter case, European as well as domestic government funding has been an important catalyst for growth. British-based agencies are leading actors in the European Commission's overseas development policy community—a uniquely mature field of EU-third sector joint working.[17] Furthermore, unlike most other fields, private earned income has increased significantly here, too. It is likely that this is connected to a range of interdependent economic, social, and political factors often now grouped together under the banner of "globalization"[18] and provides evidence that the voluntary sector is no more immune to these influences than the government and private sector.

Also noteworthy is that an area where decline might have been anticipated—the category covering trade unions—has instead witnessed stability or marginal growth. However, this conceals divergent trends *within* this field. Trade union activity did continue to decline in the U.K. in the early 1990s, following the well-documented trend—but a less well-known expansion of professional associations has offset this effect. Finally, civic and advocacy activity appears to be the only "industry" to experience negative growth during the early 1990s. This is a worrying trend, although it should be noted that the two-dimensional classificatory framework being used here does not really capture the diversity of the sector's "advocacy" contribution. In the U.K. as elsewhere, much of this is not undertaken by the organizations treated in this category. Rather, it tends to be conducted alongside service delivery and membership-oriented activities picked up in other fields, such as environment and health, and is subsumed in our data within these other categories.[19]

THE U.K. THIRD SECTOR IN COMPARATIVE CONTEXT

Because the research reported here was undertaken using the common definitions and classifications developed in the Johns Hopkins project, the U.K. situation can be directly compared with that prevailing in 21 other countries. This section will identify just three of the most striking findings from a U.K. perspective.

The preliminary results of the international study, using paid employment as the basis for comparison, are set out in Figure 9.4. The definition for the numerator used here includes all organizations meeting the struc-

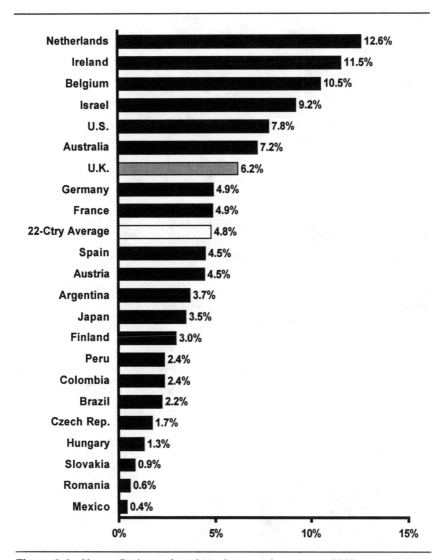

Figure 9.4 Nonprofit share of total employment, by country, 1995

tural-operational definition (what was referred to above, in the U.K. case, as the BNS), other than religious congregations, for which data were not available for all participating countries. In addition, the denominator differs because it includes all economy-wide employment other than agricultural workers. (In fact, only 2 percent of the U.K. labor force are now employed in agriculture and fishing, so the effect is quite small; in other countries in the study, particularly from the developing world, the impact is much greater.)

The U.K. sector: relatively large in a global context; relatively small for a developed democracy

As Figure 9.4 shows, the U.K. third sector turns out to be relatively large in relation to the entire sample of countries but relatively small for a developed democracy. At 6.2 percent, the U.K. third sector is ranked seventh by overall size, accounting for around 1 percent more of economy-wide employment than the 22-country average. Although the figure does not show it, if educational transfers are excluded this does not change the situation enough to alter this ranking, since this would reduce the U.K. figure to 5.3 percent—still some distance ahead of France and Germany.

However, as the figure also shows, developing and newly democratic countries tend to have relatively small sectors by this measure, and developed democracies relatively large sectors (with the exceptions being Finland and Japan). As shown in Figure 9.5, when the U.K. is compared to the Western European average (at 7 percent) and other developed country av-

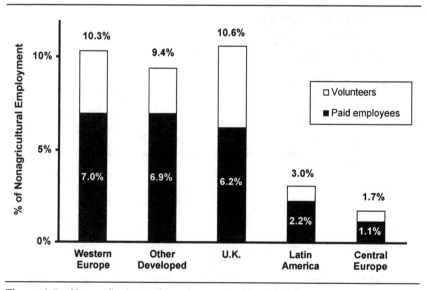

Figure 9.5   Nonprofit share of employment, with and without volunteers, U.K. and four regions, 1995

erage (6.9 percent), the U.K. third sector (at 6.2 percent) actually appears relatively limited in its scope.

These data also allow for the comparison of the U.K.'s third sector to those of other countries in terms of the composition of paid employment. Among a wide range of contrasts that could be drawn, three are particularly striking. First, as illustrated in Figure 9.6, the U.K. has one of the smallest independent nonprofit health sectors in relative terms, reflecting the continued dominance in the field of acute hospital provision of the public sector National Health Service (NHS). (While providers in this area operate as self-governing "trusts" in an internal market, unlike the education institutions that have been discussed, these are not charitable corporations, and their boards are appointed directly by the Secretary of State for health.)

Second, one of the clearest contrasts with other EU countries is the *relatively* limited extent to which social services in the U.K. are provided in the third sector. In this case, as previously noted, in the U.K. it is the private sector that has responded most rapidly to the expanding community care market, although the third sector remains a significant actor and has indeed grown in absolute terms. In other parts of the EU, by contrast, the private sector appears to have had a relatively limited role to play to date, with care services instead dominated by the public and informal sectors, and increasingly, the third sector.

Finally, international activities is the single area in which the U.K.'s third sector is significantly larger, compared to other fields, than that of any other country on which data for this field are available. As noted above, this is one of the fields in which the U.K. sector appears to have grown most significantly between 1990 and 1995.

A relatively high rate of growth between 1990 and 1995

While the U.K. third sector may be relatively small in overall size, it seems to have grown more rapidly than elsewhere—the 35 percent growth over the five year period previously noted (excluding education transfers) compares with an eight-country average of 24 percent, and an EU average (for Belgium, Germany, France, and the U.K.) of 24 percent. Even if recreation is excluded (for which 1990 estimates must be treated with caution), with an increase in employment of 30 percent, the U.K. sector has grown at a faster rate than the EU average.

A comparatively turbulent environment

Finally, the previous section emphasized how the U.K. sector's growth has been accompanied by a dramatic shift in its resource base—most

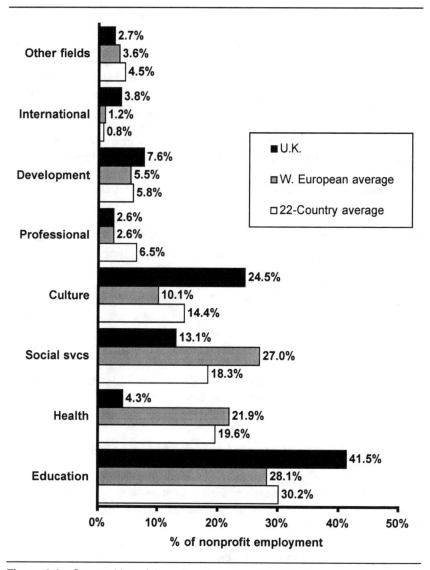

Figure 9.6 Composition of the nonprofit sector, U.K., W. Europe, and
22-country average, 1995

noticeably, a marked move towards reliance on public sector funding. Figure 9.7 shows how the U.K. compared in 1995 to the 21 other countries
participating in the study for which revenue data were available. Countries
are grouped into two broad categories: those for which private earned in-

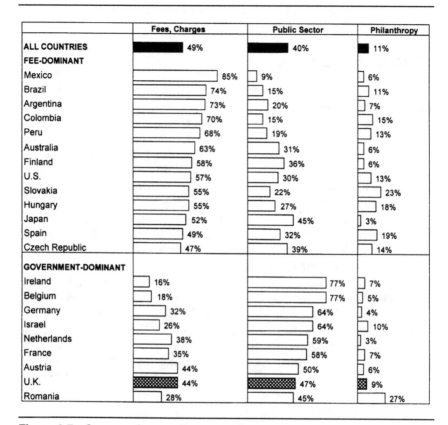

	Fees, Charges	Public Sector	Philanthropy
ALL COUNTRIES	49%	40%	11%
FEE-DOMINANT			
Mexico	85%	9%	6%
Brazil	74%	15%	11%
Argentina	73%	20%	7%
Colombia	70%	15%	15%
Peru	68%	19%	13%
Australia	63%	31%	6%
Finland	58%	36%	6%
U.S.	57%	30%	13%
Slovakia	55%	22%	23%
Hungary	55%	27%	18%
Japan	52%	45%	3%
Spain	49%	32%	19%
Czech Republic	47%	39%	14%
GOVERNMENT-DOMINANT			
Ireland	16%	77%	7%
Belgium	18%	77%	5%
Germany	32%	64%	4%
Israel	26%	64%	10%
Netherlands	38%	59%	3%
France	35%	58%	7%
Austria	44%	50%	6%
U.K.	44%	47%	9%
Romania	28%	45%	27%

Figure 9.7   Sources of nonprofit revenue, by country, 1995

come is the largest single source of income (fee-dominant), and those for which public finance dominates (government-dominant).

The U.K. sector's reliance on the public sector as its primary source of funding is a pattern shared with just under half of these countries. Moreover, this dependency is actually the dominant model for the EU, also applying to Germany, France, Belgium, and the Netherlands. The key point on which the U.K. differs, however, is in the extent to which this represents a new development. In 1990, private earned income was the primary source of income of the U.K. third sector (Figure 9.2). This makes the U.K. the only case—of the countries included in both Phase I and Phase II of this study—in which the resource base has been transformed rapidly enough for it to move from primary reliance on private giving to primary reliance on public sector funding; the positions of other EU countries in the government-dominant group represent continuity with, rather than change from, the recent past.

CONCLUDING COMMENT

Thanks to the efforts of Charities Aid Foundation, the National Council for Voluntary Organizations, the National Center for Volunteering, the Office for National Statistics, and others, the U.K. is now relatively fortunate compared to many other countries in the breadth and depth of statistical information that is available on its third, voluntary, or nonprofit sector. By undertaking secondary analysis of these data and undertaking original research, this study has sought to offer a descriptive overview of the third sector's contribution to the U.K. economy, and to locate it in an international comparative context. Perhaps two of the most striking findings of this work can be underlined. First, the sector as a whole is now evenly balanced in the extent to which it relies upon paid workers and volunteers. Moreover, factoring the latter into calculations of the sector's contribution to the economy makes a major difference in its apparent economic significance. This sector-wide picture, however, conceals significant variations among fields in the relative importance of volunteers and paid employees.

Second, in recent years, the third sector in the U.K. has relied increasingly on the public sector for its financial support. This probably will not surprise most of those involved with the third sector. What is striking in these data, however, is the *rate* at which change has occurred. Moreover, this trend is not limited to a handful of fields of third sector activity: it has happened systematically across most of the domains in which the third sector operates.

However, some of the most important new insights that this research can add derive from its positioning within a larger international study, some of whose preliminary headline findings have been presented here. Even a look at one or two summary indicators makes it clearer than ever that the U.K. third sector is not alone in making a major economic contribution and displaying tremendous richness and diversity. At the same time, the financial data underline how pace of change in the U.K. case in the early 1990s does seem to be rather high compared to other parts of the developed world.

The U.K. certainly appears difficult to categorize. On the one hand, its new positioning in the public sector-dominant funding category suggests the sector increasingly fits the model prevalent in Western Europe. The U.K. sector clearly now differs sharply from the country with which it is often grouped—the U.S. One of the most important factors is that the U.K. sector has not had to respond to systemic public "de-funding" of welfare services[20] by massively extending its reliance on fees and charges.

On the other hand, the U.K. third sector clearly stands distinct from the European "corporatist" model. This is both in terms of the historical legacy of third sector-state relations, which strongly conditions the way these sectors interact, and in terms of the reality of the current environment. This chapter ends with a comment on each.

Relations between the U.K. third sector and government traditionally have developed in a pragmatic and ad hoc way, varying tremendously by field and even subfield. This seems to defy any overall labeling or to be animated by any single organizing principle. This sets the U.K. apart from much of Northern Europe especially, where the concept of subsidiarity, with deep roots in Catholic social doctrine, has played a key role in determining the sectoral division of labor in the delivery of human services, giving special advantages to religiously based social service agencies. Although these advantages have declined somewhat, they remain important and differentiate these countries from the U.K.[21]

The contrast regarding the current environment is important to stress, because it is becoming increasingly difficult to conceptualize the position and role of the third sector in the U.K. purely in terms of its relationship with the state. Of great significance is the extent to which private, for-profit provision has rapidly also come to occupy a pivotal role in welfare provision—both publicly funded and otherwise. In operating alongside, and sometimes competing directly with, the private sector in a turbulent and competitive environment, the U.K. third sector does seem to resemble its U.S. cousin more than its continental neighbors.

ADDITIONAL REFERENCES

Almond, S. and Kendall, J. (1998) "A comparison of employment characteristics and low pay in the voluntary, private and public sectors, with a particular focus on the impact of a minimum wage," *Discussion Paper 1437*, Personal Social Services Research Unit, University of Kent at Canterbury, Canterbury.

Davis Smith, J. (1998) *The 1997 National Survey of Volunteering*, Institute for Volunteering Research, London.

Laing and Buisson (1996) *Laing's Review of Private Health Care*, Laing and Buisson, London.

Zimmeck, M. (1998) *To Boldly Go: The Voluntary Sector and Voluntary Action in the New World of Work*, RSA, London.

ENDNOTES

1. This chapter is a slightly modified version of a report published previously under the title "The U.K. Voluntary (Third) Sector in Comparative Perspective: Exceptional Growth Transformation," by Jeremy Kendall with Stephen Almond. Copies of the original report can be obtained from Maureen Weir at PSSRU, LSE (telephone # 44-955-6238; fax # 44-171-955-6131; e-mail M.Weir@lse.ac.U.K.).

2. Kendall, J. and Knapp, M.R.J. (1996). *The Voluntary Sector in the U.K.*, Manchester University Press, Manchester.

3. The U.K. study was undertaken within the framework of the Johns Hopkins Comparative Nonprofit Sector Project (Phase II), coordinated from Baltimore, USA, and led by Lester Salamon and Helmut Anheier. The findings reported here are from a research study currently being conducted by the Personal Social Services Research Unit (PSSRU), London School of Economics, and supported by the Charities Aid Foundation, the Joseph Rowntree Foundation, and the PSSRU itself. The chapter was written by Jeremy Kendall based on statistics collated and synthesised jointly by Stephen Almond and Jeremy Kendall. In addition, Lucia Wilson of the Northern Ireland Council of Voluntary Action (NICVA) led research which helped the PSSRU team to develop estimates relating to that part of the U.K., which have fed into the overall U.K. estimates reported here. The U.K. research team was aided by a local advisory committee chaired by Ian Bruce, RNIB (see Appendix D for a list of committee members).

4. Using the mean nonagricultural non-public-sector wage ($11 per hour) (£7 per hour) and the median voluntary sector wage ($8.50 per hour) (£5.35 per hour) respectively.

5. Kendall, J. and Knapp, M.R.J. (1995). "Boundaries, Definitions and Typologies: A Loose and Baggy Monster," in J. Davis Smith et al. *An Introduction to the Voluntary Sector*, Routledge, London.

6. Salamon, L. and Anheier, H. (eds) (1997). *Defining the Nonprofit Sector: A Cross-National Analysis*, Manchester University Press, Manchester.

7. Hems, L. and Passey, A., *The U.K. Voluntary Sector Almanac 1998/99* (1998). NCVO publications, London.

8. *United Kingdom National Accounts: The Blue Book 1997 (1997).* HMSO, London.

9. See discussion of compositional effects below. By 1990, one group of educational institutions, the polytechnics, had already been transferred into the sector. Excluding employment in these from the *BVS* in 1990 would have reduced its share of employment in 1990 from 4.0 per cent, as shown in figure 1, to 3.8 percent.

10. *Social Trends, 27* (1997). Office for National Statistics, London.

11. *Labour Force Survey Historical Supplement* (1997). HMSO, London.

12. Williams, S. (1998) "The cost of charity tax relief to the Exchequer," in Hems and Passey, *op. cit.*, pp.139–141.

13. Pharoah, C. and Smerdon, M. (eds) *Dimensions of the Voluntary Sector 1998.* Charities Aid Foundation, West Malling; Hems and Passey, op. cit.; and Kendall, J. and Knapp, M.R.J. (1996), *op.cit.*, chapter 5.

14. Salamon, L. (1995). *Partners in Public Service.* Johns Hopkins Press, Baltimore; "The nonprofit sector in crisis," *Voluntas*, 10, 1, forthcoming.

15. Kendall, J. and Knapp, M.R.J. *op. cit.*

16. Wistow, G., Knapp, M.R.J., Hardy, B., Forder, J., Kendall, J. and Manning, R. (1996). *Social Care Markets: Progress and Prospects*, Open University Press, Buckingham.

17. Kendall, J. and Anheier, H. (1998). "The third sector and the European policy process: an initial evaluation." Paper presented at the third biennial conference of the International Society for Third Sector Research, Geneva.

18. Waters, M. (1995). *Globalization*, Routledge, London.

19. Evers, A. (1996). "Part of the welfare mix: the third sector as an intermediate area between market economy, state and community," *Voluntas*, **6**, 2, 159–182.

20. Pierson, P. (1994). *Dismantling the Welfare State? Reagan, Thatcher and the Politics of Retrenchment*, Cambridge University Press, Cambridge. Also, Evans, M., Glennerster, H. and Hills, J. (eds) (1998). *The State of Welfare II: The Economics of Social Spending*, Oxford University Press, Oxford.

21. This is not to deny the huge influence of the churches on the historical development of the U.K. third sector, but rather to suggest that the principle of subsidiarity has not operated

as a cross-cutting organizing principle in determining the sectoral division of labor in this country. The only field of nonprofit activity where the principle of subsidiarity could be argued to have decisively influenced state policy towards the third sector in the U.K. is in primary and secondary education, as realized in the "dual system." This was the accommodation between the central state, local state, and Catholic and Anglican churches in place from the late nineteenth century until the education reforms of the late 1980s. However, even here, the notion of subsidiarity seems to have been implicit rather than explicit, and there are good reasons more generally to doubt the accuracy of portraying relations here as "corporatist."

PART 3

Other Developed Countries

The nonprofit sectors in the four other developed countries covered in this volume (Australia, Israel, Japan, and the United States) resemble the Western European countries by virtue of their heavy engagement in the provision of social welfare services, though they differ among themselves in terms of which of these services dominates.

Beyond this, the nonprofit sectors in these countries diverge from the Western European pattern in their revenue structure. Only Israel follows the Western European pattern of significant public sector support for nonprofit activities. In contrast, the Australian, Japanese, and U.S. nonprofit sectors rely mainly on fees and charges.

CHAPTER 10

Australia

Mark Lyons, Susan Hocking, Les Hems, and
Lester M. Salamon

BACKGROUND

Nonprofit organizations play an important part in Australian life and have done so since almost the beginning of European settlement, over 200 years ago. They came in the intellectual luggage of the United Kingdom migrants who settled and transformed the country. However, the importance of a nonprofit sector is not widely acknowledged in Australia. Most people do not see a single nonprofit sector but rather a disparate gaggle of organizations: charities, clubs, private schools, churches, associations, lobby groups, unions and the like, gathered between the two powerful pillars of government and business.

Over its two centuries of existence, Australia's nonprofit sector has shaped many important institutions in every aspect of Australian life. Yet from time to time it has been challenged; and over the years, the fields of greatest nonprofit activity have changed. Eighty years ago, for example, nonprofit hospitals and friendly societies played a far greater role in health care than today. In times past, nonprofits faced the possibility of being taken over by governments; today, the threat is from the business sector. Australia's nonprofit sector now faces another period of transformation and, if it is to maintain a

Global Civil Society: Dimensions of the Nonprofit Sector by Lester M. Salamon, Helmut K. Anheier, Regina List, Stefan Toepler, S. Wojciech Sokolowski and Associates. Baltimore, MD: Johns Hopkins Center for Civil Society Studies, 1999.

strong presence, it will need to develop a wider public recognition as a distinct and important sector.

The data reported here should help to develop such a recognition. They were collected as part of the Australian Nonprofit Data Project (ANDP) by a small team of researchers from the University of Technology, Sydney, with considerable support from the Australian Bureau of Statistics (ABS),[1] and as part of Phase II of the Johns Hopkins Comparative Nonprofit Sector Project, thus ensuring that Australian data were collected in a manner that permitted detailed comparisons with other participating countries.[2]

This chapter reports just one set of findings from the project, comparing the size and structure of the nonprofit sector in Australia to that elsewhere. Details of the legal environment of nonprofit organizations in Australia have already been published,[3] and subsequent publications will illuminate the history and policy context of the sector as well as its impact. The data reported here come mainly from industry surveys conducted by the ABS, together with other ABS collections and from data collected by several other Australian government agencies. A fuller account of data sources is provided in Appendix C. A more complete statement of the types of organizations included can be found in Chapter 1 and Appendix A.

PRINCIPAL FINDINGS

Five major findings emerge from this work on the scope, structure, financing, and role of the nonprofit sector in Australia:

1. A substantial economic force

In the first place, aside from its social and political importance, the nonprofit sector turns out to be a major economic force in Australia, accounting for significant shares of national expenditures and employment.

More specifically:

- **A $19 billion industry.** The nonprofit sector in Australia had operating expenditures of $19 billion in 1995–96, or 5.2 percent of the country's gross domestic product, a significant amount.[4]
- **A major employer.** Behind these expenditures lies a sizable workforce that includes the equivalent of nearly 403,000 full-time equivalent (FTE) paid workers. This represents 7.2 percent of all nonagricultural workers in the country, 15.3 percent of service employment, and the equivalent of 31.2 percent of the people who work for government at all levels: federal, departmental, and municipal (see Table 10.1).

Table 10.1   The nonprofit sector in Australia, 1995

$ 19.0 billion in expenditures
  — 5.2 percent of GDP

402,574 paid employees
  — 7.2 percent of total nonagricultural employment
  — 15.3 percent of total service employment
  — 31.2 percent of public sector employment

- **Many more employees than in the largest private firm.** Put somewhat differently, nonprofit employment in Australia outdistances the employment in the largest private business in the country by a factor of four. Thus, compared to the 403,000 full-time equivalent paid workers in Australia's nonprofit organizations, Australia's largest private corporation, Coles Myer, employs about 100,000 workers.
- **Outdistances numerous industries.** In fact, more people work in the nonprofit sector in Australia than in most industries. Thus, nonprofit employment exceeds that in the communication services industry (which in 1995–96 employed 142,900 FTE workers), the transport and storage industry (300,500), the construction industry (317,900), and the provision of public utilities (67,200).
- **Volunteer inputs.** Even this does not capture the full scope of the nonprofit sector in Australia, for this sector also attracts considerable *volunteer effort.* Indeed, an estimated 9.3 percent of the Australian population reports contributing their time to nonprofit organizations. This translates into another 177,148 full-time equivalent employees, which boosts the total number of full-time equivalent employees of nonprofit organizations in Australia to nearly 580,000, or 10.1 percent of all nonagricultural workers in the country (see Figure 10.1).
- **Religion.** The inclusion of operating expenditures by religious worship organizations (about $1 billion) would boost the nonprofit sector's total operating expenditures to $20 billion, equivalent to 5.4 percent of GDP, as shown in Figure 10.1. Similarly, the inclusion of religion would increase FTE employment by 13,000 workers and FTE volunteers by 41,000. The nonprofit sector's share of paid employment with religion included then rises from 7.2 percent to 7.5 percent, and with volunteers, from 10.1 percent to 11.0 percent of the nonagricultural workforce.

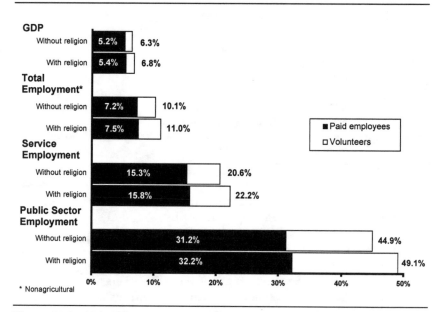

Figure 10.1 Nonprofits in Australia, with and without volunteers and religion, 1995, as a % of . . .

2. One of the larger nonprofit sectors

The size of the Australian nonprofit sector, measured in terms of paid employment, is larger than the international average and on a par with that in other developed countries.

- **Above the international average.** As Figure 10.2 shows, the relative size of the nonprofit sector, as measured by employment, varies greatly among countries, from a high of 12.6 percent of total nonagricultural employment in the Netherlands to a low of less than 1 percent of total employment in Mexico. The overall 22-country average, however, was 4.8 percent. This means that Australia, at 7.2 percent, is well above the global average.
- **Same as the other developed countries average.** Not only is it well above the 22-country average, but also nonprofit employment in Australia is marginally higher than the average for other developed countries. Thus, as shown in Figure 10.3, full-time equivalent employment in nonprofit organizations in Australia, at 7.2 percent of total employment, is just ahead of the average both for non-European developed countries (i.e., Australia, Israel, Japan, and the U.S.) of 6.9 percent and

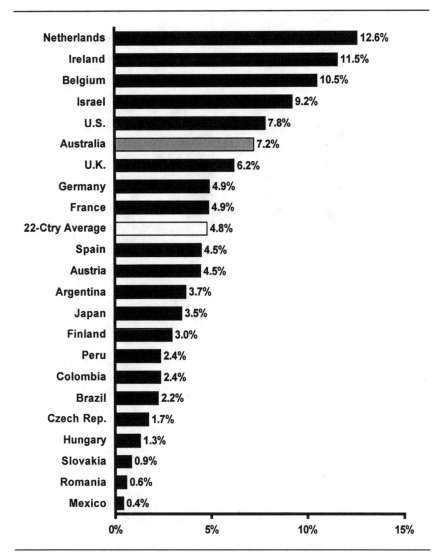

Figure 10.2   Nonprofit share of total employment, by country, 1995

for Western European countries of 7.0 percent. However, those averages conceal considerable variation, ranging, as was shown in Figure 10.2, from 12.6 percent for the Netherlands to 3.5 percent for Japan. Australia's ratio of nonprofit employment to total employment is higher than that in the United Kingdom and Germany, but marginally

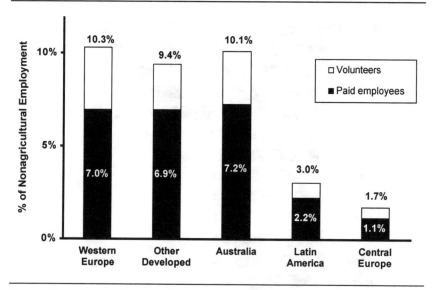

Figure 10.3   Nonprofit share of employment, with and without volunteers, Australia and four regions, 1995

lower than that in the United States and markedly lower than that in Ireland or Israel.

- **Position similar with volunteers.** When volunteers are added, nonprofit organizations account for 10.1 percent of total employment in Australia, on a par with that in Western Europe and other developed countries (see Figure 10.3).

3. A rich history of nonprofit activity

The relatively large size of the nonprofit sector in Australia is a product of the history of such institutions in this country. This history includes:[5]

- Government policy from almost the time of European settlement that encouraged the provision of social services and hospital care by private charitable organizations supported by government grants. It was within this policy tradition that a large increase in government funding in the 1970s and 1980s produced a proliferation of new community-based social service organizations, the most recent period of marked nonprofit growth.
- Sectarianism, or conflict between Catholic and Protestant churches, which divided Australians from the 1870s to the 1960s and prompted

the building of a separate Catholic school system and a proliferation of church-sponsored health and social service nonprofits.

- A benign climate, relatively high wages, and, from the late 19th century, a five-and-a-half-day work week which encouraged the growth of a vast array of sport and recreation organizations. In the 19th century this growth was further prompted by a strong social movement that encouraged the participation of young men in organized sports as a way of building character.

- A tradition of working class self-help imported from Britain that generated many types of mutual assistance organizations such as friendly societies, building societies, trade unions, and credit unions. The first two have since declined to almost nonexistence, while in the past decade trade union membership has also begun to decline markedly.

- A highly developed economy and high levels of education that have created a strong set of business and professional associations.

- Since 1901, a federal system of government built on six separate Australian colonies, and later, the territories, which meant that for every profession, trade, or cause, there are up to nine independent organizations.

4. Human services dominate

As is the case in other developed countries, human services—education, social services and health—dominate the nonprofit scene in Australia.

- **Almost two-thirds of nonprofit employment is in the three industries that constitute human services.** Of all the types of nonprofit activity, the one that accounts for the largest share of nonprofit employment in Australia is education. As shown in Figure 10.4, nearly one-quarter, or 23.3 percent, of all nonprofit employment in Australia is in the education field. This reflects in part the historical conflict between Catholicism and Protestantism that resulted in a large number of Catholic schools. Social services (20.1 percent) and health (18.6 percent) closely follow education. The share of nonprofit employment in the health field is considerably lower, however, than the developed country average (25.9 percent), though it is closer to the Western European average (21.9 percent). This reflects the growth of a public health system in Australia.

- **Significant shares of nonprofit employment in the culture and development fields.** The next largest fields of nonprofit activity are culture and recreation (16.4 percent), which includes sports and social clubs, and development and housing (10.8 percent). In both of these fields, nonprofit employment shares in Australia are higher than the average for developed countries generally (9.5 percent and 5.7 percent, respectively).

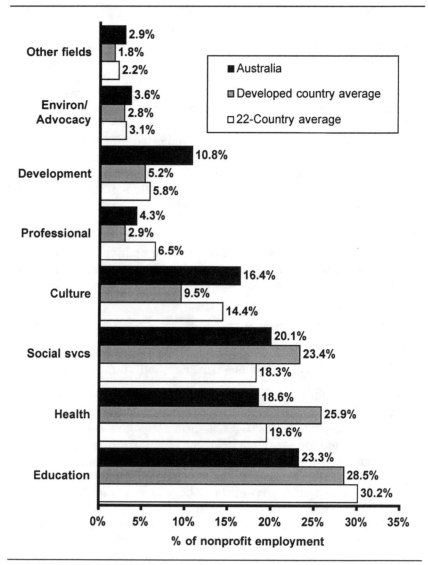

Figure 10.4   Composition of the nonprofit sector, Australia, developed countries, and 22-country average, 1995

- **Pattern shifts with volunteers.** This pattern changes when volunteer inputs are factored in. In particular, as shown in Figure 10.5, with volunteers included, the social services share of nonprofit employment in Australia increases from 20.1 percent to 23.6 percent and becomes the

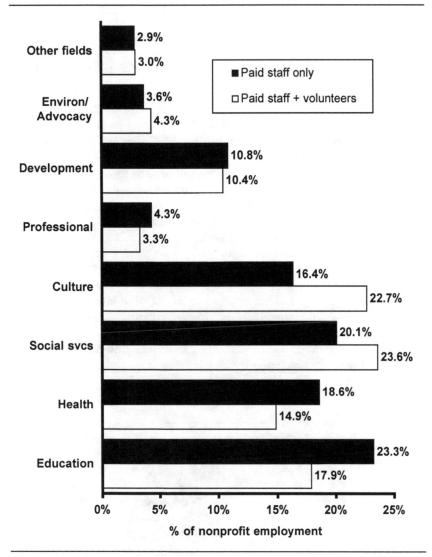

Figure 10.5 Share of nonprofit employment in Australia, with and without volunteers, by field, 1995

largest field of activity. The culture and recreation field also records a substantial increase (16.4 percent to 22.7 percent) to become the second largest field, reflecting the high level of volunteering for sports organizations.

5. Most revenue from fees, not philanthropy or public sector

Unlike the Western European countries, but like the U.S. and Japan, the Australian nonprofit sector receives the bulk of its revenue not from private philanthropy or the public sector but from fees and charges. In particular:

- **Fee income dominant.** The clearly dominant source of income of nonprofit organizations in Australia is fees and charges for the services that these organizations provide. As reflected in Figure 10.6, this source accounts for nearly two-thirds, or 62.5 percent, of all nonprofit revenue in Australia.
- **Smaller but significant share from the public sector.** Almost a third (31.1 percent) of nonprofit sector revenue comes from the public sector.
- **Very limited support from philanthropy.** By contrast, private philanthropy provides a very small share of total revenues. Thus, as Figure 10.6 shows, private philanthropy—from individuals, corporations, and foundations combined—accounts for 6.4 percent of nonprofit income in Australia.
- **Revenue structure with volunteers.** This pattern of nonprofit revenue changes significantly when volunteers are factored into the picture. In fact, as shown in Figure 10.7, the private philanthropy share increases from 6.4 percent to 23.4 percent. Fees are still the dominant revenue source, however, providing just over half of total nonprofit revenues.
- **Deviation from developed country pattern.** This pattern of nonprofit revenue in Australia differs considerably from the average for the de-

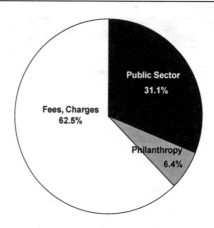

Figure 10.6   Sources of nonprofit revenue in Australia, 1995

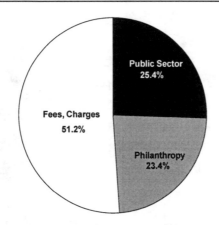

Figure 10.7   Sources of nonprofit revenue in Australia, with volunteers, 1995

veloped countries covered in the Johns Hopkins project. As shown in Figure 10.8, the nonprofit sectors in these thirteen developed countries rely, on average, for more than half (51.6 percent) of their revenues on public sector payments as compared to 31.1 percent in Australia. By contrast, fees and charges constitute a smaller 40.9 percent of income in these countries vs. 62.5 percent in Australia. The pattern of nonprofit finance in Australia thus resembles that in the U.S., where fees and charges also account for the largest share of nonprofit revenue (57 percent), rather than that in Western Europe, where public sector payments are the most important source.

- **Variations by subsector.** Even this does not do full justice to the complexities of nonprofit finance in Australia, however, because important differences exist in the finances of nonprofit organizations by subsector. In fact, when considering the revenue sources, three quite distinct patterns of nonprofit finance are evident among Australian nonprofits, as shown in Figure 10.9:

Most fields are fee-dominant. Fee income is the predominant source of income for six fields of nonprofit action in Australia: culture and recreation (91.5 percent), professional (90.5 percent), civic and advocacy (65.7 percent), development and housing (57.9 percent), health (52 percent), and the environment (45.2 percent). This is understandable enough in the case of cultural organizations (which includes sports associations and social clubs), where fee charges for attendance and membership dues are the primary source of income. It is also under-

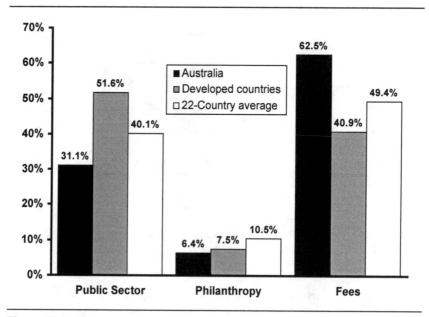

Figure 10.8   Sources of nonprofit cash revenue, Australia, developed countries, and 22-country average, 1995

standable in the case of professional and trade associations and civic and advocacy groups, where dues from members are also a major source of revenue. Similarly, many development and housing associations depend on membership fees or on the sale of their services for their income, as do environmental groups. The nonprofit health sector includes a large number of private hospitals that depend entirely on fee income, though public sector payments are also quite significant.

Significant public sector role in financing the education and social services fields. Public sector payments play the dominant role in two fields of nonprofit action, education and social services, though fee income is also quite important in both.

Philanthropy is dominant in only one field. Philanthropy is the dominant source of revenue for only international aid organizations, where it provides 70 percent of income. This would increase to two fields if religion (which receives 84 percent of its revenue from philanthropy) were added. Philanthropic intermediaries receive equal amounts of their income (37.5 percent) from private giving and fees and charges, most of the latter in the form of investment earnings.

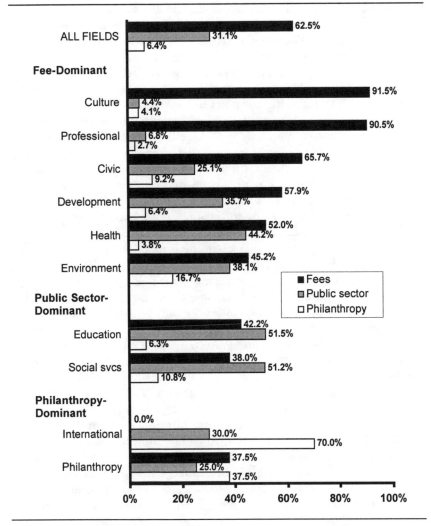

Figure 10.9   Sources of nonprofit cash revenue in Australia, by field, 1995

CONCLUSIONS AND IMPLICATIONS

Although the nonprofit sector emerges from the evidence presented here as both an important and a rather complex set of institutions in Australian society, it has never been less secure. This is a consequence of several developments.

- In public perception and discourse, Australia's organized world is divided into business and government. The recent dominance in public policy discussions of neo-liberal ideas has thus de-emphasized the role of government and emphasized the importance of business. Meanwhile, there is no recognition of a nonprofit sector; rather, there are distinct groups of diverse organizations in various industries that are not seen as constituting a distinct sector and making a unique contribution to society. As a result, their importance is underrecognized.
- There is a decline in public involvement in nonprofit organizations. Volunteering has declined over the past fifteen years; moreover, membership has also declined in most of the mass membership organizations such as churches, service clubs, trade unions, political parties, and youth groups. In others there is a shift from small to large organizations. People are seeking to reconfigure their relationship to nonprofit organizations as consumers rather than as members or active supporters. In so doing, they erase the distinction between nonprofit and for-profit.
- For-profit organizations are entering many fields previously occupied exclusively by nonprofits and, in some cases, displacing them. This has happened in the finance and insurance industry, and it is beginning to happen for social and sporting clubs. In health, the contribution of nonprofit hospitals is declining. And, in social services, for-profits are successfully competing for nonprofits in an increasing number of areas.
- In many fields, government policy changes have withdrawn or reduced any special privileges for nonprofits. Over the past decade, in fields such as social services, what had previously been a loose partnership between government and nonprofit organizations has been replaced by government-encouraged competition for government contracts among nonprofits and between nonprofits and for-profits, treating both forms of organizations alike. Changes in taxation legislation have removed almost all of the special treatment of mutual organizations and are slowly reducing some of the other special advantages of nonprofits.

At the same time, there are areas of limited growth, such as church groups working with the disadvantaged, self-help organizations in the health field, and advocacy organizations in the environment and human rights fields. However, the trends noted above seem more powerful as of this writing.

The nonprofit sector, therefore, faces serious challenges if it is to forge a renewed and relevant role for itself in the new millennium:

- Leaders in the various parts of the nonprofit sector will need to work together, both to learn from each other and to claim a distinct and important place for the nonprofit sector in debates about Australia's future. This will require, *inter alia,* establishing mutually respectful relationships with the government and business sectors.

* Nonprofit organizations will need to work out ways to reinvigorate their memberships and reengage with volunteers. To do this, they will need to respond to the changes in values, aspirations, and availability of free time of an increasingly diverse population.

* Nonprofit organizations need to explore new ways of raising the operating revenue and capital they need to pursue their missions. This should include increased donations from members of the public; by comparison with comparable countries, Australians are not generous to the nonprofit sector.

* Nonprofits will need to gain wider public respect and acknowledgment. To this end they will need to be more clearly and proactively accountable to the public and to forego the belief that filling out returns to government departments adequately meets their accountability obligations.

ENDNOTES

1. Mark Lyons and Susan Hocking of the Australian Nonprofit Data Project served as local associates to the Johns Hopkins Comparative Nonprofit Sector project. They were assisted by Charlotte Fabiansson and Miriam Wiggers de Vries and by a number of staff from the Australian Bureau of Statistics, especially Russell Rogers, Paul Sullivan, and Ross Upson. They were also aided by a local advisory committee which drew leaders from almost every field in which the nonprofit sector has a significant presence, as well as government officials from several departments with a strong interest in the nonprofit sector. These are listed in Appendix D.

2. The definitions and approaches used in the Johns Hopkins project were developed collaboratively with the cooperation of the Australian researchers and researchers in other countries and were designed to be applicable to Australia along with other project countries. For a full description of the Johns Hopkins project definition of the nonprofit sector and the types of organizations included, see Appendix A. For a full list of the other countries included, see Chapter 1 above and Lester M. Salamon and Helmut K. Anheier, *The Emerging Sector Revisited: A Summary, Revised Estimates* (Baltimore, MD: The Johns Hopkins Center for Civil Society Studies, 1999).

3. Lester M. Salamon (ed) *The International Guide to Nonprofit Law* (New York: John Wiley & Sons, 1997).

4. Technically, the more precise comparison is between nonprofit contribution to value added and gross domestic product. For the nonprofit sector, value added in economic terms essentially equals the sum of wages and the imputed value of volunteer time. On this basis, the nonprofit sector in Australia accounted for 3.9 percent of total value added.

5. For more detail see Mark Lyons, "Defining the Nonprofit Sector: Australia," *The Johns Hopkins Comparative Nonprofit Sector Project Working Paper Series,* No. 30. Baltimore: The Johns Hopkins Institute for Policy Studies, 1998.

CHAPTER 11

Israel: An Overview of Major Economic Parameters[1]

Benjamin Gidron, Hagai Katz, Helmut K. Anheier, and Lester M. Salamon

BACKGROUND

Like the state of Israel itself, the Israeli third or nonprofit sector is still relatively young.[2] However, third sector organizations played a central role in the formation of the country's basic social and economic policies even before the state was created. In the years that ensued, nonprofit organizations continued to provide services and contribute in other ways, sometimes acting as instruments of social change, but within the context of a state-centered, European-style "welfare state." Starting in the mid-1970s, however, the third sector in Israel began to grow dramatically in size—from hundreds of organizations to tens of thousands—and in range of activities. These changes can be attributed to the major social and economic changes in the country following the Six-Day and Yom Kippur wars as well as the more recent influx of immigrants following the collapse of Communism in Russia and Central Europe. In the process, the Israeli nonprofit sector has gained significantly in stature and importance.

Despite this, little has been known about this set of institutions in solid empirical terms. Although data on nonprofit organizations in Israel do exist, they are scattered among many public agencies, and no linkages have

Global Civil Society: Dimensions of the Nonprofit Sector by Lester M. Salamon, Helmut K. Anheier, Regina List, Stefan Toepler, S. Wojciech Sokolowski and Associates. Baltimore, MD: Johns Hopkins Center for Civil Society Studies, 1999.

existed to provide a systematic, comprehensive, and accessible picture of the sector. This has left policy-makers and sector leaders alike in the dark about this increasingly important component of Israeli life.

To correct this, a research team at the Israeli Center for Third-sector Research of the Ben-Gurion University of the Negev in Beer Sheva, Israel, joined with the Johns Hopkins Comparative Nonprofit Sector Project to develop the first systematic, comparative picture of Israeli third sector realities.[3] The resulting project thus offered ample opportunities both to capture local Israeli circumstances and peculiarities and to compare and contrast them to those in other countries both in the developed world and elsewhere in a systematic way.[4]

The present chapter reports on just one set of findings from this work, those relating to the size, structure, and financing of the nonprofit sector in Israel. Subsequent publications will fill in the historical, legal, and policy context of this sector and also examine the impact that this set of institutions is having. The data reported here draw heavily on official surveys of nonprofit institutions conducted by the National Accounts Department of the Israeli Central Bureau of Statistics (CBS) as well as other information. Unless otherwise noted, financial data are reported in U.S. dollars at the 1995 average exchange rate. (For a more complete statement of the sources of data, see Appendix C. For a more complete statement of the types of organizations included, see Chapter 1 and Appendix A.)

PRINCIPAL FINDINGS

Israel's third sector was a key player in building the institutional infrastructure of Israeli society. It maintains vital roles in providing services and in representing the population's many and varied interests (Gidron and Katz, 1998). Aside from its social and political importance, moreover, the nonprofit sector turns out to be a major economic force in Israel, accounting for very significant shares of national expenditures and employment. Israel's third sector is also a dynamic entity that continues to grow and change. More specifically, six major findings emerge from this analysis:

1. A major economic force

- **An $11 billion industry.** The economic importance of the third sector is readily apparent from an examination of its expenditures. Total third sector expenditures for 1995 exceeded $11 billion, or 33 billion New Israeli Shekels (NIS), representing 12.6 percent of the GDP.[5]
- **A major employer.** The third sector had a full-time equivalent (FTE) salaried workforce of approximately 145,000 in 1995.[6] This figure rep-

resents 9.2 percent of the country's total nonagricultural employment, close to 18 percent of total service employment, and the equivalent of 29 percent of the government workforce at all levels (see Table 11.1).

- **Third sector employees outnumber business sector employees in many industries.** In fact, employment in the Israeli nonprofit sector exceeds total employment in a number of industrial sectors. Thus, using head-count as opposed to FTE employment numbers, the Labor Force Surveys of the Central Bureau of Statistics (1995) show that the nonprofit sector employs almost three times as many people as the financial services industry (banking and insurance), and about half as many people as work in all of mining and manufacturing (see Figure 11.1).

- **Inclusion of volunteers increases the size of the sector.** With volunteers included, the full-time equivalent employment in the Israeli third sector rises by about 15 percent, to almost 177,000 full-time equivalent positions, representing 11 percent of total nonagricultural employment.

- **Religion.** The inclusion of nonprofit religious worship organizations adds another 1,770 paid employees and 1,144 full-time equivalent volunteers to the size of the Israeli nonprofit sector. With religion included, nonprofit paid employment in Israel therefore rises only 0.1 percent to 9.3 percent of total paid employment and to 11.1 percent of total paid plus volunteer employment. Because of the multifaceted nature of Judaism, Israel does not have a clear separation between religion and state, and certain religiously oriented activities, such as religious courts, whether Jewish, Muslim, or Christian, take place within public sector institutions (Gidron and Katz, 1998). In addition, individuals filling certain local and national religious functions are employees of the local or national government. Thus, only 30 percent of all religious employment is in the nonprofit sector. The true economic impact of religion on the nonprofit sector in Israel lies more in

Table 11.1   The nonprofit sector in Israel, 1995

$11 billion in expenditures
 — 12.6 percent of GDP

145,000 paid employees
 — 9.2 percent of total nonagricultural employment
 — 17.7 percent of total service employment
 — 29.0 percent of public employment

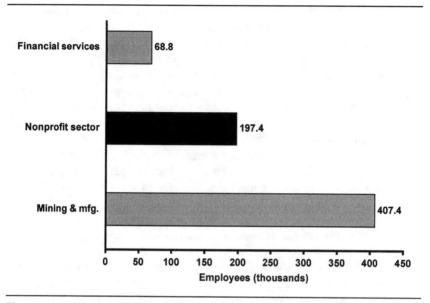

Figure 11.1   Nonprofit employment in Israel in context, 1995

religiously affiliated service provision, especially in education, than in strictly religious worship activities.

2. One of the largest nonprofit sectors in the world

The Israeli nonprofit sector is large not only in relation to the Israeli economy, but also compared to its counterparts in other countries.

- **Above the international average in employment.** As Figure 11.2 shows, the nonprofit share of total employment varies greatly among the 22 countries covered in the Johns Hopkins project, from 12.6 percent of total nonagricultural employment in the Netherlands to 0.4 percent in Mexico. The overall average was close to 5 percent. The Israeli third sector, with an employment share of 9.2 percent, thus lies well above the international average and ranks fourth among the countries studied, behind the Netherlands, Ireland, and Belgium, but ahead of the United States.
- **Above most other developed countries.** Not only is the third sector share of total nonagricultural employment in Israel almost twice the 22-country average, but it also exceeds the averages of both Western Europe and other developed countries (i.e., Australia, Japan, and the United States in addition to Israel). Thus, at 9.2 percent, Israel's non-

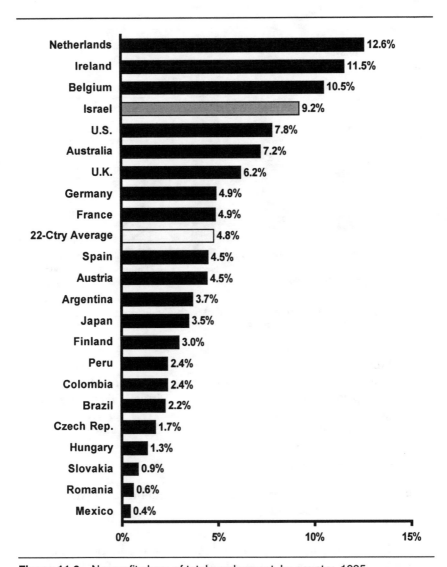

Figure 11.2 Nonprofit share of total employment, by country, 1995

profit share of total employment is about two percentage points above the average for Western European and other developed countries, which in turn greatly exceed the regional averages in Latin America and Central Europe (see Figure 11.3).

- **Margin narrows with volunteers.** Adding full-time equivalent volunteer labor to paid employment somewhat narrows the gap between Israel

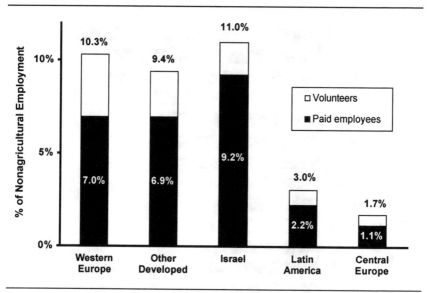

Figure 11.3   Nonprofit share of employment, with and without volunteers, Israel and four regions, 1995

and the other countries, however, indicating that the volunteer rate is comparatively low in Israel. However, at 11 percent, the nonprofit share of paid and volunteer employment in Israel still exceeds the averages in both the other developed countries (9.4 percent) and Western Europe (10.3 percent).

3. Education dominance

Similar to other developed countries, welfare and human services clearly dominate the third sector in Israel.

- **Education dominates sector employment.** By far the dominant element in the Israeli nonprofit sector, at least so far as employment is concerned, is the education component. As reflected in Figure 11.4, this one field by itself accounts for half of all nonprofit employment in Israel. This is significantly higher than the 22-country average and the average for the developed countries, though there is a similar education dominance in a number of countries in Latin America and Europe (e.g., Belgium and Ireland) where religious education—in these cases related to the Catholic Church—is prominent. In Israel, of course, it is Jewish ultra-orthodox education that is mostly responsible, but the fundamental pattern is quite similar. Additionally, other facets of educa-

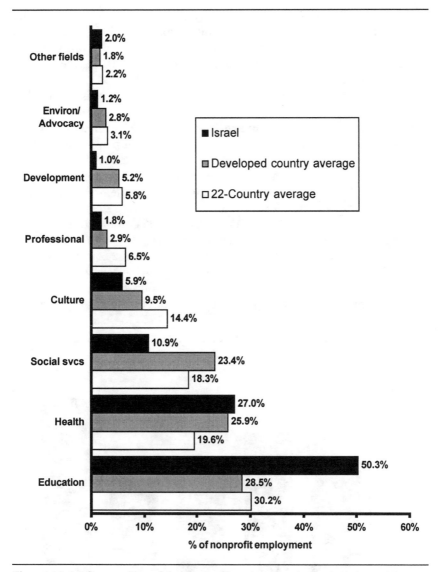

Figure 11.4 Composition of the nonprofit sector, Israel, developed countries, and 22-country average, 1995

tion, namely, higher education, vocational education, and adult education are also typically provided by third sector organizations.

- **Substantial presence in health.** If education is the major field of nonprofit activity in Israel, health is the second. As Figure 11.4 shows, 27 percent of total nonprofit employment in Israel is in the health field, substantially above the 22-country average though on a par with the other developed countries, including Japan and the United States, where nonprofit involvement in the health field is also pronounced. For the most part, this is due to the large "sick funds" in Israel, which also operate health care delivery systems. In fact, 44 percent of all health employment in Israel is in the nonprofit sector, as reflected in Figure 11.5.

- **More limited shares of nonprofit activity in social services, culture, and professional activity.** If education and health play larger roles in the Israeli nonprofit sector than they do elsewhere, social services, culture and recreation, and professional activity play smaller ones. Thus the social service share of total nonprofit employment in Israel is less than half of the developed country average (11 percent vs. 23 percent) and also considerably below the full 22-country average of 18 percent (see Figure 11.4). In culture and recreation the situation is quite similar, with the Israeli share well below the 22-country average.

Given the overall size of the Israeli nonprofit sector, these percentages are still consistent with a substantial nonprofit presence. Thus, for example, nonprofit organizations account for nearly 30 percent of

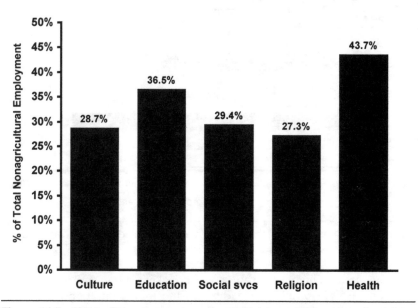

Figure 11.5   Nonprofit employment as share of total employment in selected service fields in Israel, 1995

all social service and cultural and recreation employment in the country (see Figure 11.5). Nevertheless, it remains the case that the substantial nonprofit presence in social services found in much of Western Europe is far less in evidence in Israel.

- **Pattern remains constant with volunteers.** Factoring volunteer labor into the picture does not fundamentally alter this overall pattern either. As shown in Figure 11.6, with volunteers included, education still accounts for the single largest share of total nonprofit employment (41 percent). However, its dominance is less pronounced than when paid employment alone is considered. Indeed, a considerable amount of volunteer labor flows into the social services field, increasing this field's share from 11 percent of paid nonprofit employment to 16

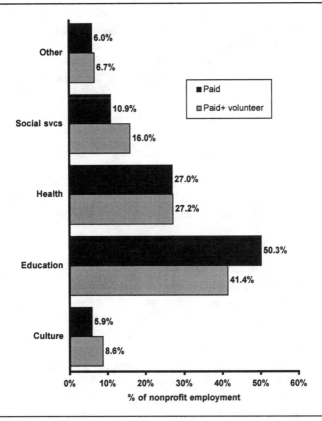

Figure 11.6   Paid and paid plus volunteer employment as share of total nonprofit employment in selected fields in Israel, 1995

percent of paid and volunteer employment. Culture and recreation also disproportionately benefits from volunteer input, which boosts its share from 6 percent to close to 9 percent, while the shares of health and other fields essentially remain constant.

- **Distribution of organizations vs. employees.** A somewhat different picture of the composition of the Israeli third sector emerges, however, when the focus is on the number of organizations in each field rather than the number of employees. Such an analysis better reflects the pluralistic nature of the Israeli population and its varied interests—the issues around which it chooses to organize—and therefore more closely approximates the "civil society" concept of the third sector. When the number of establishments is the focus, education still dominates, with 29 percent of the total, but the remaining categories are more evenly divided.[7] Thus, culture and recreation, religion, and welfare (social services plus health) each account for 15 percent of the establishments, and philanthropy for 10 percent (see Figure 11.7). In general, aside from health, these fields contain mostly small organizations that account for relatively small shares of total employment and expenditures. The health field is very different: although it comprises only 3 percent of the total number of establishments in the sector, it accounts for nine times that proportion of the employees.

4. A rich and complex history

That the nonprofit sector has achieved the scale that it has and takes the form that it does in Israel is a product of the rich and complex history the sector has had in this country. Key features of this history include the following:

- Heavy reliance on private nonprofit (mostly Zionist) organizations to provide practically all health, education, welfare, and cultural services to the Jewish population residing in what was then the Palestine Mandate area prior to the establishment of the state of Israel in 1948. The resulting organizations thus gained an important foothold and organizational base that survived the transition to statehood, particularly in the fields of health and education.
- A strong commitment to public support for basic welfare services—health, education, and social services—that reflected a social philosophy similar to the one that fostered the social democratic movements in Europe in the late 19th and early 20th centuries.
- The decision of the relatively new Israeli government in the 1950s to rely on the pre-existing "sick funds," particularly the one associated

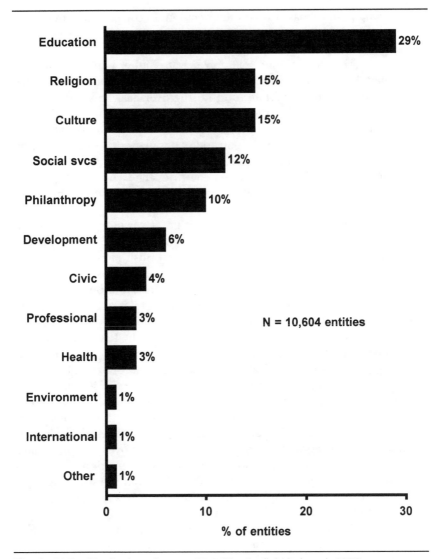

Figure 11.7 Distribution of nonprofit entities by field in Israel, 1995

with the General Federation of Labor, to provide primary health-care services to the Israeli population rather than establish a wholly government-operated national health-care system. The close association between the General Federation of Labor and the Labor government during those years and the need for the young government to maintain a strong political base explain this decision. In the process, however, it established a strong pattern of government-nonprofit cooperation in the health field.

- The decision to maintain a largely private higher education system, though heavily subsidized by public funding, in order to ensure academic freedom and facilitate fund raising overseas. This was coupled with an agreement between the ultra-orthodox political parties and *Mapai* (the Israeli Labor Party) in 1953, when the State Education Act was passed, allowing the ultra-orthodox population to establish an independent educational system very similar to the independent religious educational systems in other countries. The agreements pertaining to ultra-orthodox education have expanded considerably in recent years.

- The decision of the first government of the newly independent Israeli state under Prime Minister David Ben-Gurion to continue the arrangement that was in place during the British Mandate and leave matters important to the religious population, such as the laws regulating personal matters (e.g., marriage, divorce, and burials), to religious authorities sanctioned by the state. Similar accommodations were made with the Muslim and Christian populations as well. Within Israel, however, this created a situation whereby Jewish Orthodoxy gained a monopoly in the interpretation of Jewish law. As the religious population gained political strength, it was able to expand its influence and secure, for example, government support for its educational institutions, many of them nonprofit organizations. Indeed, for a whole variety of social and cultural reasons, the Jewish religious population is very active in initiating nonprofit organizations. More than 40 percent of all nonprofit organizations in Israel over the years have been initiated by this population; however, only a fraction of these receive ongoing public support. This is particularly interesting considering that the Jewish religious population comprises less than 20 percent of the total Israeli population.

- The development in more recent years of special interest and advocacy groups, attesting to Israel's character as a civil society. These diverse organizations reflect issues of concern to different groups of citizens motivated to join together in establishing an organization. Nonprofits registered in this period reflect varied (and sometimes peculiar) interests, including, for example, the Israel Association of Motor Model Fans, the Association of Victims of the Carmel Tunnels, and the Israeli Organization of Nail Technicians. In addition, the nature and structure of Israel's third sector in the early 1990s is also clearly influenced by economic (wage agreements, privatization), legal (new laws), and demographic (immigration) processes.

5. Most revenue from public funding, not philanthropy or earned income

Reflecting this history, the Israeli nonprofit sector receives most of its revenue from the central government and local authorities, and less from philanthropy and earned income (e.g., fees and charges).

- **Public funds dominate.** As shown in Figure 11.8, public funds—in the form of grants and contracts—account for nearly two-thirds (64 percent) of third sector financing in Israel. Earned income (the sale of services, membership fees, and investment income) accounts for 26 percent of sector financing. Donations from all sources—foreign and domestic—account for only 10 percent of support.
- **Revenue structure with volunteers.** The nonprofit revenue structure in Israel changes somewhat when volunteers are factored into the picture. As shown in Figure 11.9, with volunteers included, private philanthropy boosts its share substantially from 10 percent to 17 percent. Even so, however, public sector support, while decreasing from 64 percent to 59 percent, remains the overwhelmingly dominant revenue source, while the fees and charges share declines only marginally, from 26 percent to 24 percent.

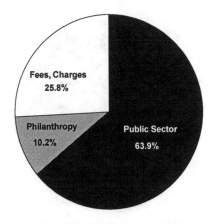

Figure 11.8   Sources of nonprofit revenue in Israel, 1995

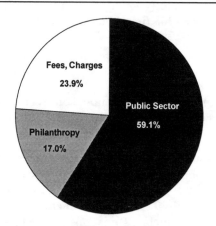

Figure 11.9   Sources of nonprofit revenue in Israel, with volunteers, 1995

- **Revenue structure with religion.** This overall pattern of nonprofit finance does not change further when account is taken of religious institutions, such as synagogues and churches. With religion included in addition to volunteers, the philanthropic share of total nonprofit revenue in Israel remains about 17 percent (see Figure 11.10).
- **Domestic and international private support.** Of the total private philanthropic support to the Israeli nonprofit sector, roughly half comes

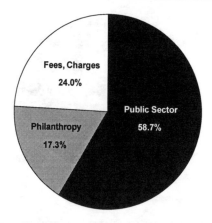

Figure 11.10   Sources of nonprofit revenue in Israel, with volunteers and religious worship, 1995

from overseas sources (Central Bureau of Statistics, 1996). The remainder, however, comes from Israeli domestic sources. Individuals and private households provided close to 14 percent of total donations, an estimated NIS 436 million in donations as of 1997 (Gidron, 1997). This is a higher rate of domestic giving than has previously been assumed, though it hardly dominates the revenue structure of the Israeli nonprofit sector.

- **Funding pattern differs from other developed countries.** The pattern of third sector finance in Israel differs in important ways from that in other developed countries as well as from the 22-country average (see Figure 11.11). More specifically, the share of public sector support in Israel is substantially above the average of developed countries in general (64 percent in Israel vs. 52 percent) and exceeds by far the 22-country average of 40 percent. By the same token, fee income plays a significantly less pivotal role in Israel than in other developed countries (26 percent in Israel vs. 41 percent) and globally (49 percent). The philanthropy share in Israel, on the other hand, is essentially on a par with the global average (10.2 percent in Israel vs. 10.5 percent) and slightly above the developed countries average (7.5 percent). The

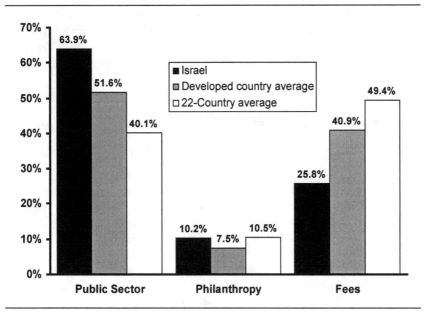

Figure 11.11   Sources of nonprofit cash revenue, Israel, developed countries, and 22-country average, 1995

structure of Israeli third sector finance thus most closely resembles that evident in Western Europe (see Chapter 1), with its heavy emphasis on state financing of nonprofit activity. This very likely reflects the heavy influence of Western European social democratic thinking on the early founders of the Israeli state coupled with the special history of the "sick funds" and the influence of the ultra-conservative religious community, particularly in the education sphere. Together, these factors have led to an active state presence in Israel that is nevertheless implemented in a number of crucial spheres by contracting with external, mostly nonprofit, agencies, thus blurring the boundaries between the third and the public sectors (see Gidron and Katz, 1998).

- **Public funding not the dominant revenue source in most subsectors.** While public funding accounts for the lion's share of total nonprofit income in Israel, it does not dominate the funding picture in all fields. To the contrary, such support is dominant in only three of the ten fields of nonprofit activity studied: health, education, and culture and recreation (see Figure 11.12). However, these three fields account for almost 90 percent of total third sector employment and revenue.

    In two other areas of nonprofit activity, the environment and professional and labor associations, fee income is clearly the dominant source; while in two others, civic and advocacy and international activity, the dominant source of revenue is philanthropy. In the remaining three areas of nonprofit activity (social services, housing and development, and philanthropy) the revenue is almost equally distributed among the three sources, with earned income in the lead over both public support and private giving.

6. Change between 1991 and 1995

Not only is the Israeli nonprofit sector large, but also it has been quite dynamic.

- **Continuing growth.** The Israeli third sector grew substantially in the early 1990s, though a bit more slowly than it had in the 1980s (Central Bureau of Statistics, 1996; Gidron, 1997). In particular, the number of active organizations rose nearly 50 percent from 8,562 in 1991 to 12,125 in 1995, an average annual increase of 11 percent. Employment in the sector also rose substantially, by approximately 15 percent over this same period, adding some 19,000 full-time positions. This was just slightly behind the overall employment growth in the Israeli economy, which was buoyed by the influx of Eastern European and Russian immigrants. The nonprofit share of total nonagricultural em-

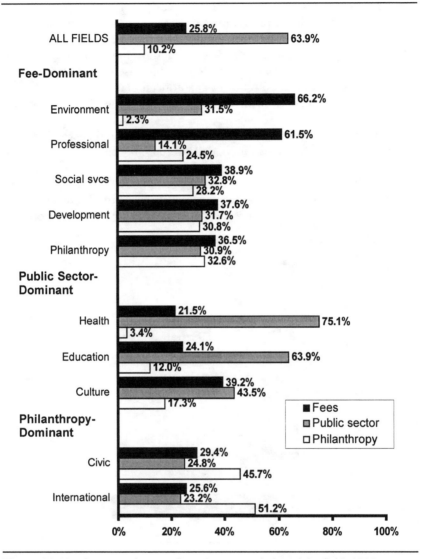

Figure 11.12 Sources of nonprofit cash revenue in Israel, by field, 1995

ployment thus decreased slightly from 10.7 percent to 9.3 percent during this period. At the same time, however, third sector expenditures as a share of GDP increased between 1991 and 1995 from 12.2 percent to 12.7 percent, partly due to significant wage raises for professionals in education, health, and social services.

- **Education the main source of third sector growth.** Most (80 percent) of the increase in employment that occurred in the Israeli nonprofit sector between 1991 and 1995 took place in the education field. In the process, education went from 40 percent of nonprofit employment to 50 percent, as Figure 11.13 reveals. This increase can be attributed to the expansion of the ultra-orthodox educational system and of existing higher education institutions, as well as the development of new colleges.
- **Employment gains in the environment, culture and recreation, and health.** Employment also increased substantially among environmental organizations, in culture and recreation, and in health. While the growth in the environment field was prompted by recent increases in public awareness of this issue, the rise in the culture and recreation field likely reflected the greater cultural diversity resulting from the

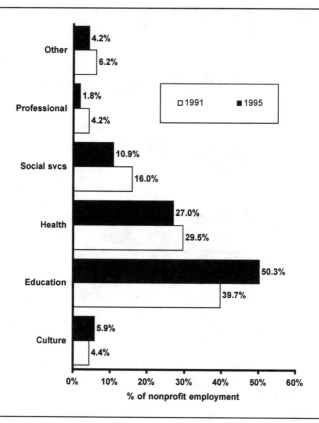

Figure 11.13   Nonprofit employment in selected field as shares of total nonprofit employment, Israel, 1991, 1995

large influx of immigrants from the former Soviet Union and a redefinition of some previously religious activities as cultural activities in order to meet new criteria for public funding established during this period. The health increases, while substantial, still lagged behind the overall growth of the sector so that the health share of the total declined somewhat.

- **Job losses in social services and professional associations and unions.** In the remaining fields of third sector activity, employment declined between 1991 and 1995. This may be related to the trend, particularly in social service organizations, to substitute contracting out of personnel services for hiring regular employees. In addition, recent changes and cutbacks in the General Federation of Labor, the *Histadrut,* led to decreased employment among trade associations. Taken together, therefore, these changes have led to a further concentration of the nonprofit sector in education.
- **Growth fueled largely by public payments.** That the Israeli third sector has continued to grow substantially in recent years is due in no small part to the continued expansion of public sector support. In fact, as Figure 11.14 shows, public financing grew from about half of total

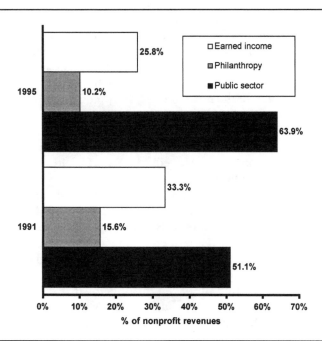

Figure 11.14   Sources of nonprofit revenue in Israel, 1991, 1995

nonprofit revenues in 1991 to almost two-thirds in 1995. New wage agreements with professionals in health and education played a substantial part in this increase. Earned income, on the other hand, did not keep pace, declining from one-third to about one-quarter of total revenues in the same period, while the philanthropy share declined from more than 15 percent to 10 percent. The relative decline in fee income distinguishes Israel from many other countries, where a commercialization trend is evident within the nonprofit sector. Apparently, growing government support has insulated the Israeli nonprofit sector from some of these commercialization pressures, at least in the fields where such support has been available. In the three fields where government support has declined, however, (culture and recreation, social services, and housing and community development), either private giving has increased enough to sustain continued growth (e.g., in culture and recreation) or growth has slowed (social services and housing and community development).

CONCLUSIONS

The Israeli nonprofit sector thus emerges from the data assembled here as one of the largest in the world in relative terms, accounting for 9.2 percent of Israel's nonagricultural employment. These findings contradict a common perception that the growth of the modern welfare state is antagonistic to nonprofit organizations. The case of Israel, like that of Belgium and the Netherlands (see Chapters 2 and 7), shows that antagonism is by no means necessary. To the contrary, the growth of the welfare state can *promote* the expansion of the nonprofit sector by mobilizing public funds to finance third sector services. This certainly has been the pattern in Israel, where a long tradition of close cooperation between the state and the nonprofit sector has made such arrangements easy to establish and sustain, particularly in certain fields, such as education and health, where the nonprofit sector enjoys significant political support.

The Israeli nonprofit sector grew from 1991 to 1995, although more slowly than in the 1980s, and more slowly than the economy as a whole during this period. This growth reflects in part the continued expansion of public sector support in the fields of education and health and in part the growing diversity of Israel's population and the proliferation of social concerns that has accompanied the slow normalization of public life.

This report uses a definition of the third sector that differs somewhat from that used by the Central Bureau of Statistics (CBS) or the one commonly perceived by the public. The CBS's definition of the "sector of nonprofit institutions" does not include many of the sector's smaller organizations; conversely, the public's concept of "civil society" excludes the very large organizations that shape, as has been seen, the size and the nature of the sector. The current analysis of Israel's third sector leads to a view more similar to the CBS concept, in which a few large organizations dominate the sector's economy. Future, more detailed analyses of other aspects of the sector may present a picture of the sector closer to the "civil society" concept.

A comparison of Israel's third sector with those of other nations makes clear, moreover, that Israel is quite similar to a number of European welfare states that embody a model of close cooperation between the third sector and the public sector in the provision of welfare services (Salamon and Anheier, 1999). This is evidenced in the relatively large size of the Israeli nonprofit sector, its high rate of public sector funding, and its focus on education and health.

Other dimensions researched in the context of this project, including the historical, legal, and policy frameworks, as well as the broader impact of the sector, will shed further light on these aspects and serve to complete the picture of the sector presented here. Along with the data reported here, they will further enhance understanding of Israel's third sector and provide insight for developing policies regarding its role in society.

REFERENCES

Ben-Ami I., "Government Involvement in the Arts in Israel—Some Structural and Policy Characteristics." *The Journal of Arts Management, Law and Society*, 26:3 (1996), 195–219.

Borzaga C. and Santuary A., *Social Enterprises and New Employment in Europe.* Trentino: CGM-Consorzio Nazionale della Cooperazione Sociale, 1998.

Central Bureau of Statistics, "Survey of Income and Expenditures of Nonprofit Institutions 1980–1981." Supplement to the *Monthly Bulletin of Statistics*, 12, December (1985) [Hebrew].

Central Bureau of Statistics, "Survey of Income and Expenditures of Nonprofit Institutions 1982– 1983." Supplement to the *Monthly Bulletin of Statistics*, 4, April (1988) [Hebrew].

Central Bureau of Statistics, *Labor Force Surveys, 1995.* Jerusalem: The Central Bureau of Statistics, Publication 1057, 1997.

Central Bureau of Statistics, *National Accounts of Israel, 1950–1995.* Jerusalem: The Central Bureau of Statistics, Publication 1042, 1997.

Central Bureau of Statistics, *Non Profit Institutions in Israel, 1991.* Jerusalem: The Central Bureau of Statistics, Publication 1016, 1996.

Central Bureau of Statistics, *Statistical Abstract of Israel, 1995.* Jerusalem: The Central Bureau of Statistics, 1996.

Central Bureau of Statistics, *Survey of Income and Expenditures of Nonprofit Institutions, 1980–1996.* Jerusalem: The Central Bureau of Statistics, Publication 1077, 1998.

Gidron B., "The Evolution of Israel's Third Sector: The Role of Predominant Ideology." *Voluntas*, 8:1 (1997): 11–38.

Gidron B., *Patterns of Giving and Volunteering of the Israeli Public: Interim Findings.* Beer Sheva: Ben-Gurion University of the Negev, Israeli Center for Third Sector Research, 1997 [Hebrew].

Gidron B. and Katz H., *Defining the Nonprofit Sector: Israel.* Working Papers of the Johns Hopkins Comparative Nonprofit Sector Project, no. 26, Salamon L.M. and Anheier H.K. (Eds.) Baltimore: The Johns Hopkins University, The Johns Hopkins Institute for Policy Studies, 1998.

James E., "The Nonprofit Sector in Comparative Perspective." In Powell, W.W. (Ed), *The Nonprofit Sector: A Research Handbook.* New Haven: Yale University Press, 1987.

Kramer R., "Is the Sector Concept Obsolete?" *Inside ISTR,* 3:1 (1995): 6–7.

Salamon L.M., "The Rise of the Nonprofit Sector." *Foreign Affairs,* 74:3 (1994).

Salamon L.M. and Anheier H.K. et al., *The Emerging Sector Revisited: A Summary, Revised Estimates.* Baltimore: The Johns Hopkins Center for Civil Society Studies, 1999.

Salamon L.M. and Anheier H.K., "In Search of the Nonprofit Sector I: The Question of Definitions." *Voluntas* 3:2 (1992): 125–152.

Salamon L.M. and Anheier H.K., "In Search of the Nonprofit Sector II: The Question of Classifications." *Voluntas* 3:3 (1992): 267–309.

Salamon L.M. and Anheier H.K., *Defining the Nonprofit Sector: A Cross-National Analysis.* Manchester: Manchester University Press, 1997.

Weisbrod B.A., *To Profit or not to Profit.* Cambridge: Cambridge University Press, 1998.

ENDNOTES

1. This chapter is based on a slightly different report published as "The Israeli Nonprofit Sector: An Overview of Major Economic Parameters" in June 1999 by the Israeli Center for Third-sector Research (ICTR), Ben-Gurion University of the Negev, Beer Sheva, Israel. The original report contains additional information of particular interest to Israeli readers and can be obtained by contacting ICTR at ictr@bgumail.bgu.ac.il.

2. The terms "third sector" and "nonprofit sector" will be used interchangeably throughout the chapter.

3. The work in Israel was coordinated by Prof. Benjamin Gidron of the Israeli Center for Third-sector Research at Ben-Gurion University, who served as local associate to this project, assisted by a team drawn from various research institutes in the country. The team was aided, in turn, by a local advisory committee made up of prominent government, academic, and business leaders (see Appendix D for a list of committee members). The Johns Hopkins project was directed by Lester M. Salamon and Helmut K. Anheier.

4. The definitions and approaches used in the project were developed collaboratively with the cooperation of the Israeli researchers and researchers in other countries and were designed to be applicable to Israel and the other project countries. For a full description of this definition and the types of organizations included, see Appendix A. For a full list of the other countries included, see Chapter 1 above and Lester M. Salamon and Helmut K. Anheier, *The Emerging Sector Revisited: A Summary, Revised Estimates* (Baltimore, MD: The Johns Hopkins Center for Civil Society Studies, 1999).

5. Technically, the more precise comparison is between nonprofit contribution to "value added" and gross domestic product. For the nonprofit sector, "value added" in economic terms essentially equals the sum of wages and the imputed value of volunteer time. On this basis, the nonprofit sector in Israel accounts for 7.3 percent of GDP—still a quite significant amount.

6. Since third sector organizations, particularly small and medium-sized organizations, frequently employ many part-time workers, a headcount of nonprofit employment would yield a significantly higher number of employees.

7. The basis for this analysis are some 12,500 economically active organizations that submit financial reports to the Department of Non-Profit and Public Institutions of the Income Tax Commission.

CHAPTER 12

Japan

Naoto Yamauchi, Hiroko Shimizu, S. Wojciech Sokolowski, and Lester M. Salamon

BACKGROUND

The Japanese nonprofit sector employs more workers than any other country covered in this volume, except the United States, and more than 15 times the number of workers employed in the Israeli nonprofit sector. However, when considered in the context of the entire national economy, Japan's nonprofit sector is among the smallest of the developed countries, and attracts relatively low levels of private giving and volunteering. At work are a number of factors, such as restrictive legislation and government bureaucracy, that have caused an "under-utilization" of the nonprofit potential in Japan. Events in the second half of the 1990s, including the growth of citizen-based grassroots organizations and the enactment of new facilitative legislation, hold promise for unleashing this untapped potential.

Beginning in 1990, before these events began to unfold, a Japanese research team affiliated with the first phase of the Johns Hopkins Comparative Nonprofit Sector Project initiated one of the first efforts to assess Japan's nonprofit sector in a systematic, comparative way.[1] The findings reported in this chapter are the result of a second phase of the Johns Hopkins project carried out in order to update the Phase I work and to extend the inquiry to

Global Civil Society: Dimensions of the Nonprofit Sector by Lester M. Salamon, Helmut K. Anheier, Regina List, Stefan Toepler, S. Wojciech Sokolowski and Associates. Baltimore, MD: Johns Hopkins Center for Civil Society Studies, 1999.

explore the contributions the Japanese nonprofit sector is making. This second phase in Japan is being conducted by a research team based at the Non-profit Organization (NPO) Research Forum of Japan.[2]

The present chapter reports on just one set of findings from this project, those relating to the size and structure of the Japanese nonprofit sector in 1995 and the changes the sector experienced between 1990 and 1995. Subsequent publications will fill in the historical, legal, and policy context of this sector and also examine the impact that this set of institutions is having. In Japan, the principal data sources used were the Survey on Private Nonprofit Institutions (*Minkan-hieiri-dantai jittaichosa*) and the Basic Survey on Civic Activity Organizations (*Shimin-katsudo-dantai kihonchosa*) conducted by the Japanese Government Economic Planning Agency. Unless otherwise noted, financial data are reported in U.S. dollars at the 1995 average exchange rate. (For a more complete statement of the sources of data, see Appendix C. For a more complete statement of the types of organizations included, see Chapter 1 and Appendix A.)

PRINCIPAL FINDINGS

Six major findings emerge from this work on the scope, structure, financing, and role of the nonprofit sector in Japan:

1. A substantial economic force

In the first place, aside from its social and political importance, the non-profit sector is a significant economic force in Japan, accounting for significant shares of national expenditures and employment.

More specifically:

- **A $214 billion industry.** Even excluding its religious worship component, the nonprofit sector in Japan had operating expenditures of nearly $214 billion in 1995, a considerable 4.5 percent of the country's gross domestic product.[3]
- **A major employer.** Behind these expenditures is a sizable workforce that includes the equivalent of 2.1 million full-time equivalent (FTE) paid workers. This represents 3.5 percent of all nonagricultural workers in the country, nearly 14 percent of service employees, and the equivalent of the total number of all federal, provincial, and municipal government workers (see Table 12.1).
- **More employees than in the largest private firm.** The Japanese non-profit sector engages at least 28 times more employees than the country's largest private corporation and nearly 7 times more than the

Table 12.1   The nonprofit sector in Japan, 1995

$ 213.6 billion in expenditures
    — 4.5 percent of GDP

2.1 million paid employees
    — 3.5 percent of total nonagricultural employment
    — 13.7 percent of total service employment
    — 39.8 percent of public employment

largest five firms combined. Thus, compared to the 2.1 million paid
workers employed in Japan's nonprofit organizations, Japan's largest
private corporation, Hitachi, Ltd., employs 77,000 workers, and the
top five firms employ approximately 318,000 (see Figure 12.1).

- **Volunteer inputs.** Even this does not capture the full scope of the nonprofit sector in Japan, for this sector also attracts a considerable
amount of *volunteer effort.* Indeed, an estimated 21.4 percent of Japanese citizens report contributing their time to nonprofit organizations.
This translates into another 700,000 FTE employees, which increases

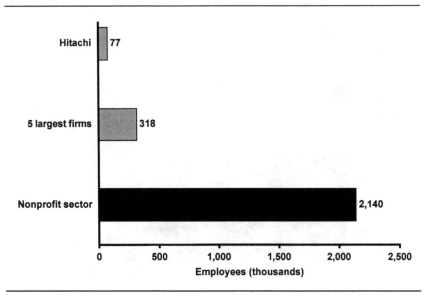

Figure 12.1   Employment in nonprofits vs. largest firms in Japan, 1995

the total number of FTE employees of nonprofit organizations in Japan to 2.8 million, or 4.6 percent of total employment in the country (see Figure 12.2).

- **Religion.** The inclusion of religious worship would boost these totals by another 148,000 paid employees and 155,000 FTE volunteers. With religious worship included, nonprofit paid employment therefore rises from 3.5 percent to 3.7 percent of total paid employment; factoring in volunteers, this figure increases to 5.1 percent. Religion also generates operating expenditures of some $23 billion, thus bringing total expenditures to over $236 billion, the equivalent of 5 percent of GDP excluding volunteers.

2. One of the largest nonprofit sectors among the 22 project countries

In terms of the number of people employed, Japan's nonprofit sector is clearly one of the largest in the world. However, in relation to the size of the national economy, the nonprofit sector in Japan falls behind that of most other developed, industrialized countries.

- **The second largest nonprofit sector.** At 2.1 million FTE workers, the Japanese nonprofit sector employs more people than that of any of

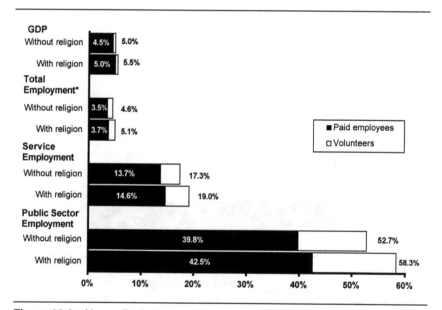

Figure 12.2   Nonprofits in Japan, with and without volunteers and religion, 1995, as a % of . . .

the other 21 project countries except the United States (8.6 million FTE employees). The country with the next largest nonprofit sector, Germany, has a considerably smaller sector (1.4 million FTE workers).

- **Below the international average.** Though large in absolute size, the Japanese nonprofit sector is still quite small in relation to the overall Japanese economy. As Figure 12.3 shows, the relative size of the nonprofit sector varies greatly among the countries studied, ranging from a

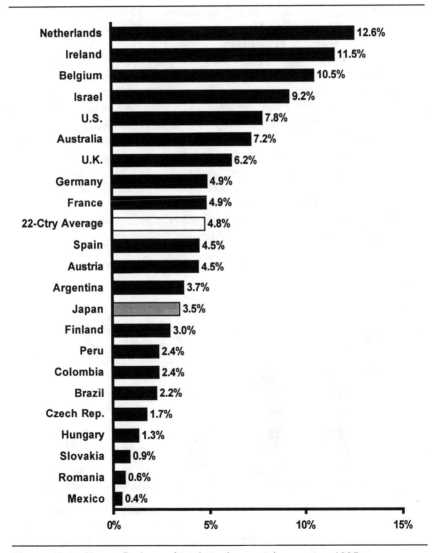

Figure 12.3 Nonprofit share of total employment, by country, 1995

high of 12.6 percent of total nonagricultural employment in the Netherlands to a low of less than 1 percent of total employment in Mexico. The overall 22-country average, however, is 4.8 percent. This means that, excluding religious worship, Japan's nonprofit sector falls below the global average, comprising 3.5 percent of total employment.

- **Below the developed countries average.** As shown in Figure 12.4, the relative share of employment in the Japanese nonprofit sector is about half that of the Western European (7.0 percent) and other developed countries (6.9 percent) averages. However, the level of employment still exceeds that in all Eastern European and most Latin American countries, as well as Finland.

- **Margin of difference widens with volunteers.** The margin of difference between the relative size of the Japanese nonprofit sector and that of other developed countries widens when volunteers are added. Thus, with volunteer time figured in, nonprofit organizations account for only 4.6 percent of total employment in Japan, whereas comparable figures for other developed countries are more than twice as large (see Figure 12.4). If Japan were to utilize the number of volunteers that is proportional to the size of its national economy and comparable to the number in other developed countries (on average about 3.1 percent of the nonagricultural employment), Japan would engage 1.9 million FTE volunteers, nearly 3 times as many as it does now. This is Japan's untapped "nonprofit potential."

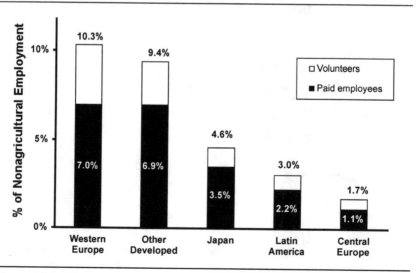

Figure 12.4   Nonprofit share of employment in Japan and four regions, 1995

3. A bifurcated nonprofit sector

While the overall size of the Japanese nonprofit sector is fairly large, as indicated by the data presented here, it consists of two different types of organizations. The first set of organizations are legally well-defined (based on the civil code) and well-recognized nonprofit corporations, such as public benefit corporations, medical corporations, private school corporations, and social welfare corporations. The central and local governments have had strong discretionary power over these organizations and have encouraged their growth. The second set of organizations is basically grassroots groups that engage in such activities as environmental protection, advocacy, community development, and international cooperation. Most of these grassroots organizations are small and their revenue structure is fairly fragile.

These nonprofit organizations have long been less visible in Japan than in most developed countries. Until the 1995 Kobe earthquake, Japanese nonprofit organizations operated in the shadow of the state. With little explicit public support, they scarcely recognized themselves as belonging to a coherent "sector." Moreover, existing legal provisions erected a seemingly insurmountable wall between formally incorporated nonprofit organizations and the sizable assortment of citizen groups that have emerged over the past decade or more at the community level in Japan. These citizen groups were cultivated over the last several years in response to the growing frustrations of citizens over environmental and social issues, among other problems; they sought to rectify the limitations that prevented citizen action in Japan's increasingly pluralistic—though still bureaucratically dominated—society by providing opportunities for civic engagement. In Japan, where a sharp divide has long existed between citizens and large incorporated nonprofit institutions, a divide now exists between these incorporated nonprofits and the growing number of informal citizen groups, in large part because these small organizations do not have access to official legal status and the important privileges that legal recognition carries with it.

4. Health dominance

Reflecting this fact, health care clearly dominates the nonprofit scene in Japan, similar to that in the United States and the Netherlands, but unlike the other project countries.

- **Over 47 percent of nonprofit employment in health.** Nonprofit employment in most Western European and Latin American countries is concentrated in either social services or education, while Eastern Europe's nonprofit sector is clearly dominated by culture and sports activities. In contrast, of all the areas of nonprofit activity, the field that accounts for the largest share of nonprofit employment in Japan is health care. As shown in Figure 12.5, 47.1 percent of all nonprofit employment in Japan is concentrated in the health care field. This is comparable to only two other countries in the sample: the United States

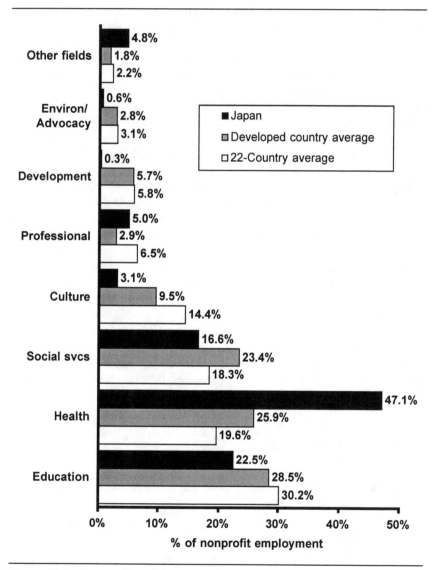

Figure 12.5   Composition of the nonprofit sector, Japan, developed countries, and 22-country average, 1995

(46.3 percent of nonprofit employment) and the Netherlands (41.8 percent). In the case of Japan, this heavy concentration of health care-related employment reflects the fact that the nonprofit sector is the major provider of health services in Japan. Indeed, over 70 percent of all health care employees are employed within the nonprofit sector. Consequently, health care dwarfs all other fields of activity in the Japanese nonprofit sector.

- **Sizable nonprofit presence in education and social services.** Another sizable portion of total nonprofit employment in Japan is concentrated in the fields of education and social services, which together account for 39 percent of all nonprofit employment, slightly below the developed country averages. Included here are many of Japan's higher education institutions as well as a number of large social service agencies operating with government sanction and recognition. The three social welfare fields—health care, education, and social services—thus jointly account for 86 percent of nonprofit sector employment in Japan, a much higher concentration than the 22-country average (68 percent).

- **Relatively smaller shares of nonprofit employment in other fields.** Compared to the overall 22-country average, other fields of activity absorb a significantly smaller share of nonprofit employment in Japan. This is particularly true of the economic development and culture fields, as well as the combined fields of environmental protection and advocacy, in which Japan is far below the developed-country and 22-country averages (Figure 12.5). Thus, while the development and housing field absorbs, on average, 5.8 percent of nonprofit employment in the 22 countries studied, less than 1 percent of nonprofit employees in Japan are engaged in this field. A similar disparity holds in the field of culture and recreation where the 22-country average of 14.4 percent is nearly five times the Japanese level of only 3.1. In the case of development and housing, the relatively minor involvement of nonprofits is very likely the result of the active role that the central and local governments have played in community development activities, thereby leaving little opportunity for private nonprofit development activities. In the case of culture, the meager support received from the public sector appears to be a major factor. More generally, however, it is the sheer difficulty of establishing and operating a nonprofit organization in these non-welfare service fields that reduces their weight in the composition of Japan's nonprofit sector.

- **Pattern remains steady with volunteers.** This pattern remains essentially the same when volunteer work is considered. In particular, as shown in Figure 12.6, with volunteers included, the prominence of health care in overall nonprofit employment in Japan decreases somewhat, yet

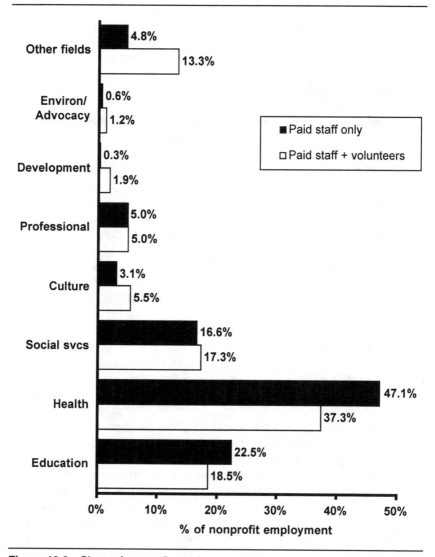

Figure 12.6   Share of nonprofit employment in Japan, with and without volunteers, by field, 1995

remains the single dominant field. Employment in the field of economic development increases six-fold when factoring in volunteer work; however, because of the small size of this field, this increase does not alter the overall picture of employment distribution across the fields of activity in Japan. Culture gains a somewhat larger share of employment when volunteers are added, increasing from 3.1 percent to 5.5 percent. However, the impact of volunteering on that field's share is considerably smaller than in other developed countries, especially in Western Europe. In France and Germany, for example, volunteers nearly triple culture's share of nonprofit employment. This reflects, in part, the fact that volunteering does not play as pronounced a role in Japan as it does in other developed countries since it was not as well-organized a component of Japanese social life prior to the recent Kobe earthquake.

5. Most revenue from service fees and public sector payments, not philanthropy

Consistent with the country's statist approach to the economy in general, as well as pivotal legislative changes introduced after World War II to stimulate the nongovernmental sector, Japan's nonprofit sector receives the bulk of its revenue not from private philanthropy but from service fees (52 percent) and public sector payments (45 percent).

- **Service fee income dominant.** Fees and other private payments for services account for more than half (52.1 percent) of all nonprofit sector revenues in Japan, as reflected in Figure 12.7. Public sector payments are comparable, amounting to 45.2 percent of the sector's revenue inflow.
- **Limited support from philanthropy.** By contrast, private philanthropy provides a minuscule share of total revenues. Thus, as Figure 12.7 also shows, private philanthropy—from individuals, corporations, and

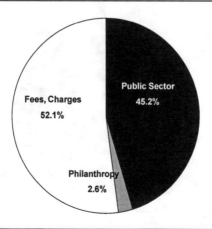

Figure 12.7   Sources of nonprofit revenue in Japan, 1995

foundations combined-accounts for only 2.6 percent of nonprofit income in Japan.

- **Revenue structure with volunteers.** This pattern changes only slightly
  when the value of volunteer input is added to private philanthropic
  contributions. As shown in Figure 12.8, the private philanthropy share
  of total income increases from 2.6 percent to 10.7 percent with volunteers included, but it is still substantially smaller than revenues gathered from the public sector and private service fees. This is due largely
  to the fact that, as previously noted, volunteering plays a relatively minor role in Japan's nonprofit sector.
- **Revenue structure with religion.** When religious worship institutions
  such as churches, shrines, and temples are taken into account, the
  philanthropic share of total nonprofit revenue in Japan rises from 2.6
  percent to 3.6 percent. Such religious institutions account for approximately 10 percent of the total revenue of Japan's nonprofit sector.
  With volunteers included as well, the private giving share rises to 12.3
  percent, as shown in Figure 12.9.
- **Similar to global average and developed countries.** The pattern of
  nonprofit finance evident in Japan is not significantly different from
  the 22-country average, or from the developed countries' average.
  Thus, as shown in Figure 12.10, while fees and charges represent the
  dominant source of nonprofit financial support in the 22-country average, its dominance is somewhat more pronounced in Japan (52.1
  percent of total revenue as compared to 49.4 percent overall). Public

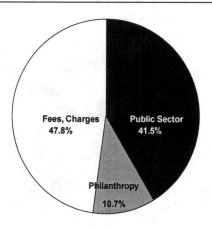

Figure 12.8   Sources of nonprofit revenue in Japan, with volunteers, 1995

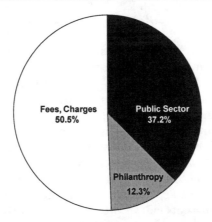

Figure 12.9   Sources of nonprofit revenue in Japan, with volunteers and religious worship, 1995

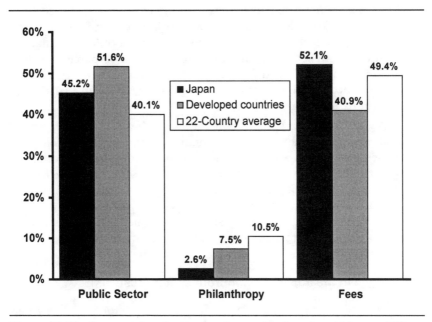

Figure 12.10   Sources of cash revenue, Japan, developed countries, and 22-country average, 1995

sector payments also comprise a slightly larger share of nonprofit income in Japan than the 22-country average (45.2 percent vs. 40.1 percent overall), though they constitute a slightly lower share in Japan than in the developed countries generally (51.6 percent). The sharpest disparity, however, is in the share of nonprofit revenue that comes from philanthropy, which is only 2.6 percent in Japan as compared with 10.5 percent in all project countries and 7.5 percent in the developed countries.

The structure of nonprofit finance evident in Japan reflects the long tradition of statism in this society and the cultural norms stressing cooperation and consensus over individualism. Nonprofit organizations consequently have emerged within the ambit of a clearly dominant state bureaucracy and allied corporate sector rather than as the product of grassroots citizen pressures. One of the interesting questions for the future is how extensively nonprofits will be able to go beyond these relatively narrow confines for nonprofit action.

• **Variations by field.** The general picture of Japanese nonprofit revenue masks some differences, however, among the different types of agencies. In fact, two distinct patterns of nonprofit finance are evident among Japanese nonprofits, as shown in Figure 12.11.

Fee-dominant fields. Fee income is the dominant source of income in eight of the ten fields of nonprofit activity in Japan. Professional organizations, labor unions, and business associations represent the most fee-dependent set of organizations, deriving over 99 percent of their income from dues and fees. Two other fields that rely heavily on earned income are education and culture, which receive 80–85 percent of their funding from fees.

Public sector-dominant fields. In the two remaining fields, health and social services, the Japanese government plays the dominant role in financing nonprofit action. This is consistent with Japan's tradition of government support in these areas of service, especially in the field of health. Under the Japanese comprehensive and compulsory health insurance system, a substantial part of the cost of medical service is paid by the government, though the services are actually delivered by large, private nonprofit hospital corporations.

6. Changes in the Japanese nonprofit sector (1990–95)

Between 1990 and 1995, the Japanese nonprofit sector grew by 27 percent, adding 451,000 new FTE jobs to the Japanese economy. The sector's growth exceeds that of total nonagricultural employment growth during

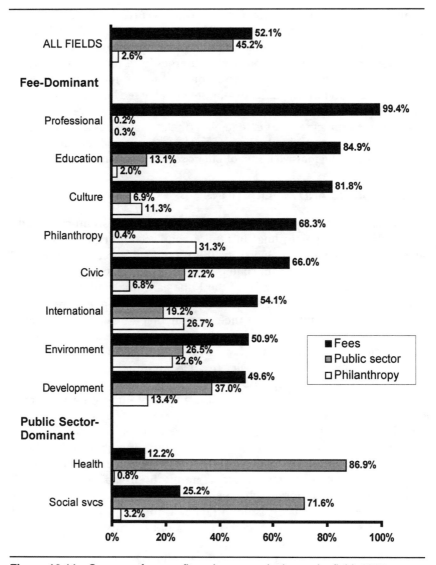

Figure 12.11 Sources of nonprofit cash revenue in Japan, by field, 1995

the same period by a ratio of 2:1. However, the expansion of the nonprofit sector was not as fast as that of the service industry as a whole. As a result, the nonprofit sector's share of service employment actually shrank from 8.6 percent in 1990 to 6.8 percent in 1995.

Another interesting shift in this time period occurred in the sector's revenue structure. Total inflation-adjusted revenue grew by over $23 billion, of which nearly 98 percent came from public sector payments. This trend toward etatization of the nonprofit sector diverges from that toward marketization, i.e., growing reliance on fee income, observed in the U.S., France, and Germany. In fact, the inflation-adjusted level of fee income in Japan actually shrank between 1990 and 1995. At the same time, the level of support from private giving grew 22 percent. Nevertheless, since this income source accounts for only a miniscule share of total nonprofit revenue, this growth was dwarfed by the massive influx of public sector payments.

CONCLUSIONS AND IMPLICATIONS

The Japanese nonprofit sector stands today at an important crossroads. Though containing many huge institutions and accounting for a considerable range of human service activity, this set of institutions long operated in the shadow of a dominant state bureaucracy and enjoyed only limited grassroots support. In the wake of the Kobe earthquake of 1995 and the subsequent Russian oil tanker disaster in the Sea of Japan—events that demonstrated the limitations of the governmental bureaucracy and galvanized the Japanese voluntary spirit—the winds of change are clearly blowing in Japan. A new "NPO law" (Law to Promote Specific Nonprofit Activities), passed by the Japanese Diet in 1998, significantly simplified the process of obtaining nonprofit legal status for unincorporated groups. "Civil society" (*shimin shakai*) has become a topic of interest for the Japanese media and has penetrated public discourse. Moreover, a growing number of academics and researchers have discovered the nonprofit sector and have begun to build knowledge about its contours and possibilities. Politicians, bureaucrats, and even the general public are becoming increasingly more interested in the potential roles of nonprofits in Japanese society.

All of this poses important challenges but also important opportunities for Japanese nonprofits. At issue in Japan, as in many of the developed countries, is not simply the *existence* of nonprofit organizations but rather more fundamental questions: for what purpose and *under what terms* should nonprofits exist? Important questions are thus being raised about the character of the nonprofit organizations that exist and about the values they should be called on to serve.

As these issues are debated, the Japanese nonprofit sector, like those in the other developed countries covered in this volume, faces the challenge of cultivating and maintaining the citizen base that has begun to expand over the last decade. As part of this effort, nonprofit organizations in Japan, both the more formal "corporations" and the grassroots groups, will face the challenge of moving toward greater openness in disclosing their activities to the general public. This will help to ensure their accountability and defend the sector's worth.

The expansion of both private giving and volunteering will also be important for the future of Japan's nonprofit sector. As has been shown in this chapter, Japan has low levels of private giving and volunteering in comparison with other developed countries. The aging population in Japan may represent a large reservoir of potential volunteers and donations that remain yet "untapped" for the expansion of the philanthropic share of nonprofit operations. However, in order to tap this potential reservoir, the tax system must be drastically reformed to reward charitable donations and volunteering more generously.

These and other changes are very much "in the wind" in Japan. The next few years will determine whether they settle down to earth.

ENDNOTES

1. For some of these Phase I results published in English, see Tadashi Yamamoto, *The Nonprofit Sector in Japan* (Manchester, U.K.: Manchester University Press, 1998); Takayoshi Amenomori, "Japan," in Lester M. Salamon and Helmut K. Anheier, eds., *Defining the Nonprofit Sector: A Cross-national Analysis* (Manchester, U.K.: Manchester University Press, 1997); and the chapter on Japan in Lester M. Salamon, *The International Guide to Nonprofit Law* (New York: John Wiley & Sons, 1997).

2. Naoto Yamauchi and Masaaki Homma, both members of the NPO Research Forum of Japan and professors at Osaka University, served as local associates for the project in this second phase. In developing the estimates presented in this chapter, they were assisted by Takafumi Tanaka of Tokyo Gakugei University and Hiroko Shimizu of the Osaka School of International Public Policy at Osaka University. Additional assistance has been provided by Atsuko Hattori and Satoko Maekawa (along with Hiroko Shimizu) in the giving and volunteering survey; James O'Leary and Reiko Asano in the legal and policy analyses; and Masayuki Deguchi, Reiko Asano, Susumu Furutachi, Yuko Hattori, Kenjiro Hirayama, Makoto Iwata, Tomoyuki Kafuku, and Yoshihiro Mishima in the impact analysis. The Johns Hopkins project is directed by Lester M. Salamon and Helmut K. Anheier.

3. Technically, the more precise comparison is between nonprofit contribution to "value added" and gross domestic product. For the nonprofit sector, "value added" in economic terms essentially equals the sum of wages and the imputed value of volunteer time. On this basis, the nonprofit sector in Japan accounted for 2.7 percent of total value added.

CHAPTER 13

The United States

S. Wojciech Sokolowski and Lester M. Salamon

BACKGROUND

Traditionally, the United States has been considered the seedbed of nonprofit activity. Alexis de Tocqueville, a keen 19th century observer of American institutional life, aptly considered voluntary associations to be a uniquely democratic response to solving social problems in a society characterized by extensive equality. Indeed, the early implementation of democratic forms of governance in the U.S. created ample room for social movements and civic initiatives that coalesced into voluntary associations. Even with the ascent of the New Deal and Keynesian economic policies, deep-seated American misgivings about excessive governmental power limited the scope of government social protections and left ample room for a sizable private nonprofit sector. Today, the nonprofit sector accounts for half of the U.S. colleges and hospitals, nearly two-thirds of all social service agencies, most civic associations, and almost all symphony orchestras.[1] Yet, as has been shown in previous chapters, the U.S. does not have the world's largest nonprofit sector.

Although the U.S. nonprofit sector is now well-documented and studied, the absence of comparable data from other countries made it very difficult

Global Civil Society: Dimensions of the Nonprofit Sector by Lester M. Salamon, Helmut K. Anheier, Regina List, Stefan Toepler, S. Wojciech Sokolowski and Associates. Baltimore, MD: Johns Hopkins Center for Civil Society Studies, 1999.

to place the U.S. sector in an international context. An initial effort in this regard began in 1990 with the first phase of the Johns Hopkins Comparative Nonprofit Sector Project. For this second phase effort, focusing on the nonprofit sector in 1995, the research drew heavily on estimates developed by Murray Weitzmann and Virginia Hodgkinson of the Independent Sector, based largely on U.S. Bureau of Economic Statistics and U.S. Census Bureau data. Those data are reported here with relatively minor adjustments and are supplemented by other information drawn from surveys of service industries carried out by the Bureau of the Census and other sources as reported in Lester Salamon's *America's Nonprofit Sector: A Primer.* (For a more complete statement of the sources consulted to compile the data reported here, see Appendix C.)

PRINCIPAL FINDINGS

Six major findings emerge from this work on the scope, structure, financing, and role of the U.S. nonprofit sector.[2]

1. A major economic force

In the first place, aside from its social and political importance, the nonprofit sector turns out to be a significant economic force in the U.S., accounting for significant shares of national expenditures and employment. More specifically:

- **A $500 billion industry.** Even excluding its religious worship component, the nonprofit sector in the U.S. had operating expenditures of $502 billion in 1995, or 6.9 percent of the country's gross domestic product, a quite significant amount.[3]
- **A major employer.** Behind these expenditures lies an important workforce that includes nearly 8.6 million full-time equivalent (FTE) paid workers. This represents 7.8 percent of all nonagricultural workers in the country, 16.5 percent of service employment, and the equivalent of nearly half as many people as work for government at all levels: federal, state, and local (see Table 13.1).
- **More employees than in the largest private firms.** Put somewhat differently, nonprofit employment in the U.S. outdistances the employment in the largest private business in the country, and does so by a ratio of twelve-to-one. Thus, as shown in Figure 13.1, compared to the 8.6 million paid workers in U.S. nonprofit organizations, the largest U.S. private corporation, General Motors, employed only 711,000 workers as of 1995. Indeed, the U.S. nonprofit sector employs as many workers as the fifty largest

Table 13.1   The nonprofit sector in the U.S., 1995

$ 502.0 billion in expenditures
— 6.9 percent of GDP

8.6 million paid employees
— 7.8 percent of total nonagricultural employment
— 16.5 percent of total service employment
— 46.7 percent of public employment

companies in the country, including such giants as Wal-Mart (over half a million employees), Pepsico (423,000), Ford Motor Company (322,000), AT&T (over 300,000), IBM (256,000), and General Electric (222,000).

- **Outdistances many industries.** Indeed, more people work in the nonprofit sector in the U.S. than in many entire industries in the country. Thus, as shown in Figure 13.2, nonprofit employment in the U.S. exceeds that in the three largest manufacturing industries combined (machinery manufacturing, manufacturing of transportation equipment, and manufacture of food products). In fact, nonprofit employment is also larger than the employment in the business services and finance, real estate, and insurance industries.

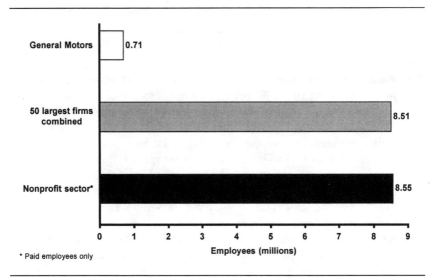

* Paid employees only

Figure 13.1   Employment in nonprofits vs. largest firms in the U.S., 1995

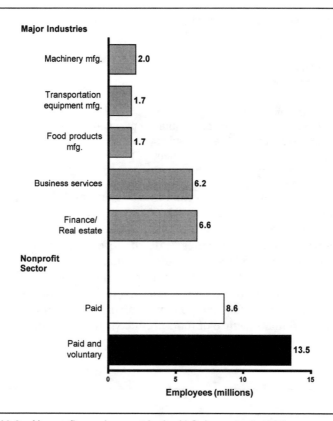

Figure 13.2   Nonprofit employment in the U.S. in context, 1995

- **Volunteer inputs.** Even this does not capture the full scope of the non-profit sector in the U.S., for this sector also attracts a considerable amount of *volunteer effort.* Indeed, an estimated 49 percent of the U.S. population reports contributing their time to nonprofit organizations. This translates into another 5 million FTE employees, which boosts the total number of FTE employees of nonprofit organizations in the U.S. to 13.5 million, or nearly 12 percent of total employment in the country (see Figure 13.3). With the voluntary FTE workers included, the nonprofit sector is the second largest non-government industry in the U.S., surpassed only by retail trade.
- **Religion.** The inclusion of religion, moreover, would boost these to-tals by another 1 million paid employees and 2.3 million full-time equivalent volunteers. As shown in Figure 13.3, with religion included, nonprofit paid employment therefore rises from 7.8 percent to 8.8

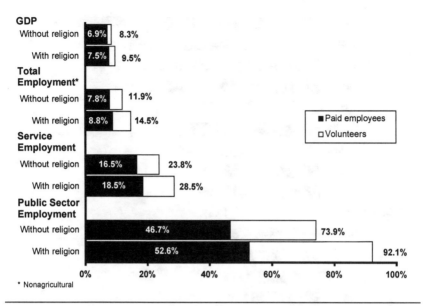

Figure 13.3 Nonprofits in the U.S., with and without volunteers and religion, 1995, as a % of . . .

percent of total employment and paid plus volunteer employment from 11.9 percent to 14.5 percent. Religion also boosts operating expenditures by $45.6 billion, thus bringing total expenditures to $548 billion, the equivalent of 7.5 percent of gross domestic product.

2. One of the largest, but not *the* largest nonprofit sector in the world

Despite its considerable scale, the U.S., contrary to public perceptions, does not have the largest nonprofit sector in the world when the size of the nation's economy is taken into account.

- **Considerably above the international average, but not the largest.** As Figure 13.4 shows, the relative size of the nonprofit sector varies greatly among countries, from a high of 12.6 percent of total nonagricultural employment in the Netherlands to a low of less than 1 percent of total employment in Mexico. The overall 22-country average, however, was close to 5 percent. This means that the U.S., at 7.8 percent without religious worship, lies substantially above the global average. However, it falls below three Western European countries—the

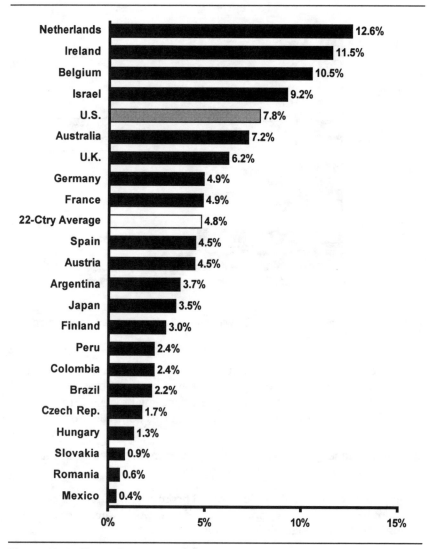

Figure 13.4 Nonprofit share of total employment by country, 1995

Netherlands (12.6 percent), Ireland (11.5 percent), and Belgium (10.5 percent), as well as Israel (9.2 percent).

- **Slightly above developed country averages.** The relative size of the U.S. nonprofit sector is not only larger than the overall 22-country average, but also it is above the average of the nine Western European countries (7.0 percent) and that of the four other developed countries which include Australia, Israel, Japan and the U.S. (6.9 percent), as shown in Figure 13.5.

- **Margin widens with volunteers.** This margin widens considerably when volunteers are added. Thus, with volunteer time included, nonprofit organizations account for 11.9 percent of total employment in the U.S., which exceeds the Western European average of 10.3 percent and the other developed countries' average of 9.4 percent (see Figure 13.5). The widening of this gap is due to a significantly greater volunteer input in the U.S. (equivalent to 4 percent of nonagricultural employment) than exists in any other developed country except the Netherlands (6.1 percent), France (4.7 percent) and the U.K. (4.4 percent).

3. A rich history of nonprofit activity[4]

That the nonprofit sector is highly developed in the U.S. is a product of the peculiar culture and history of this country and the special niche that nonprofit institutions have consequently come to fill. Key features of this history include the following:

- A strongly individualistic cultural ethos that has produced deep-seated antagonism to concentrated power, whether political or economic.

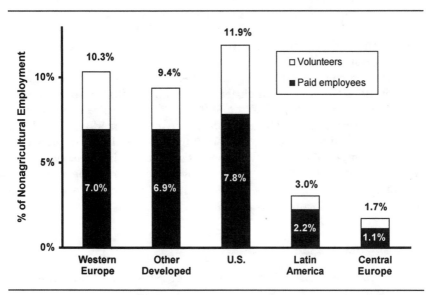

Figure 13.5   Nonprofit share of employment, with and without volunteers, U.S. and four regions, 1995

This has made Americans reluctant to rely too heavily on government to cope with social and economic problems, thus leaving such significant problems to be tackled through private voluntary effort.

- Strong economic interests that have reinforced this cultural ethos in order to avoid government interference with business and to escape taxation beyond what was considered absolutely necessary. This has contributed to an "ideology of voluntarism" that has made support of voluntary approaches to social problem-solving an important political issue and ideological symbol. In addition, until relatively recently, it has made the development of nonprofit institutions and the solving of social problems heavily dependent on the availability of voluntary, private support.

- A frontier history in which society developed before government, thus establishing a pattern of group action to provide for common needs rather than a pattern of turning to governmental authorities.

- A history of concern for religious freedom and the avoidance of government interference with religious worship, which created a secure arena for private action for the common good outside the sphere of the state. Many early nonprofit institutions in such fields as health, education, and social services began as affiliates of these religious institutions.

- A diverse population fueled by successive streams of immigrants who brought with them their own cultural norms and community institutions, which helped foster numerous nonprofit social groups in the New World.

- A generally facilitative legal structure for the formation and operation of private, nonprofit organizations.

- A strong commitment to freedom of expression, and hence to the institutions through which citizens could join together to petition government and otherwise work to improve their collective well-being.

- A resulting pattern of social problem-solving that made it difficult for government to extend its reach without engaging the aid of private institutions, both nonprofit and for-profit. When social protections were extended in the 1960s, therefore, government turned heavily to private nonprofit institutions for help, thereby subsidizing an extensive expansion of nonprofit activity.

4. Health dominance

The structure of the U.S. nonprofit sector reflects this set of historical circumstances.

- **Over 46 percent of nonprofit employment in health.** In the first place, the major institutions in the American nonprofit sector are heavily concentrated in the fields of health, higher education, and high culture. Of these, health care is clearly the largest in terms of expenditures and employment. Thus, as Figure 13.6 shows, almost half (46 percent) of all nonprofit employment in the U.S. is in the health field. This is more than twice as high as the global average of 19.6 percent and almost

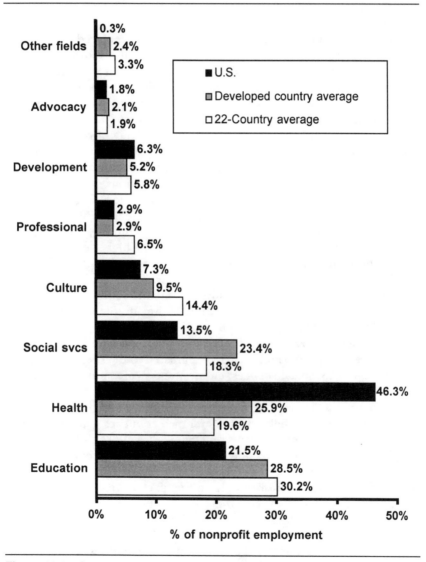

Figure 13.6   Composition of the nonprofit sector, U.S., other developed countries, and 22-country average, 1995

double the developed country average of 25.9 percent. This reflects the fact that the U.S. resisted the development of a government-operated health care delivery system. When a system of public health insurance for the elderly was finally adopted in the mid-1960s, therefore, the major beneficiaries were private, nonprofit hospitals, which constituted over half of the hospitals in the country.

- **Considerable nonprofit presence in higher education.** While health clearly dominates the nonprofit employment picture in the United States, substantial numbers of people are also employed in nonprofit education institutions. In fact, as Figure 13.6 also shows, one out of every five nonprofit employees in the United States works in the educational field. This is proportionally well below the all-country average and also falls below the developed country average. The principal reason for this is that the tradition of separation of church and state in the U.S. has limited the growth of public funding of religiously affiliated education institutions in this country, particularly at the elementary and secondary levels. Ninety percent of elementary and secondary education in the U.S. is thus in public institutions operated by local governments, unlike the situation in many Western European countries, where a tradition of state support of religiously affiliated elementary and secondary education is evident. By contrast, however, nonprofit institutions are firmly entrenched at the higher education level in the United States. Many such institutions evolved from religious backgrounds, but most are secular today. Together they constitute some of the most prestigious universities in the country (e.g., Harvard University, Princeton University, Yale University, Stanford University, and Johns Hopkins University).

- **Relatively smaller shares of nonprofit employment in social services, culture, and professional activity.** Compared to the overall 22-country average, U.S. social services, culture, and professional associations (which also include labor unions) absorb a smaller share of nonprofit employment. Thus, while a quarter of all nonprofit employment is in the social services field in the developed countries generally, in the U.S. this figure is only 13.5 percent. Similarly, culture and professional associations account for only 7.3 and 2.9 percent of employment in the U.S. nonprofit sector compared to 14.4 and 6.5 percent of nonprofit employment, respectively, in the 22 countries. One reason for this, of course, is the sheer size of the health component of the nonprofit sector, which makes other portions appear smaller by comparison. Also at work, however, has been the more limited public support for both social services and culture and the generally weak position of labor unions (though not business and professional organizations) in American society.

- **Pattern shifts with volunteers.** This pattern changes significantly when volunteer inputs are factored in. In particular, as shown in Figure 13.7, with volunteers included, health considerably looses its salience, even though it is still the dominant field. Another significantly affected field is advocacy, whose share of nonprofit employment

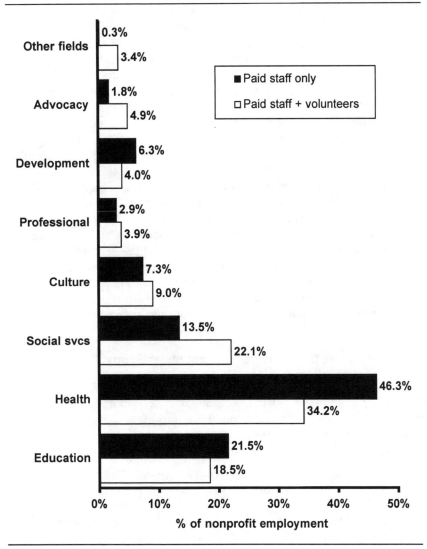

Figure 13.7   Share of nonprofit employment in the U.S., with and without volunteers, by field, 1995

increases almost three-fold from under 2 percent to nearly 5 percent. Social services also gains a substantial share (22 percent with volunteers), although that gain is not as dramatic as in the case of advocacy.

The low volunteering rates in health are explained by the professionalization of health care that leaves very little room for amateurs. For every FTE health care volunteer working in 1995, there were six professionals. By contrast, nearly three times as many FTE volunteers worked for advocacy organizations as professionals. This is consistent with the tradition of voluntary agencies serving as a platform for political mobilization. Finally, as is the case in most of the countries covered in this volume, social service organizations in the U.S. absorb a significant share (more than one-third) of all volunteering. These volunteers more than double the amount of human resources devoted to providing social services.

- **Religion.** The overall structure of the American nonprofit sector does not change fundamentally with the inclusion of religious worship organizations (churches, synagogues, mosques). To be sure, such organizations account for larger shares of nonprofit employment and volunteering than in the other countries studied. Thus, as Figure 13.8 shows, such religious organizations constitute over 11 percent of nonprofit paid employment and over 30 percent of full-time equivalent volunteering in the U.S. nonprofit sector compared to 3.5 percent and 11 percent, respectively, in Western Europe and 5.5 percent and 18 percent, respectively, in the other developed countries. Even with religious organizations included, however, health, education, and social services remain the dominant fields of nonprofit activity, together accounting for nearly three-fourths of total nonprofit sector employment.

5. Most revenue from service fees, not philanthropy

Contrary to public perceptions and political rhetoric, private philanthropy is not the major source of revenue of American nonprofit organizations. In fact, it is not even the second most important source. Rather, most nonprofit revenue comes from service fees and public sector payments.

- **Service fee dominant.** The dominant source of income of the nonprofit sector in the U.S. is service fee revenue. This source accounts for over $320 billion, or 56.6 percent of all U.S. nonprofit revenue (see Figure 13.9).
- **Public sector support.** The second most important revenue source for American nonprofit organizations is the public sector. Public sector support accounted as of 1995 for 30.5 percent of all nonprofit

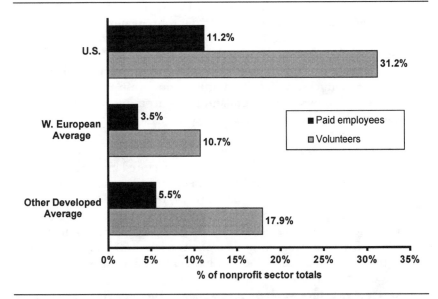

Figure 13.8   Employment and volunteering in nonprofit religious worship
organizations as share of total nonprofit employment and
volunteering, U.S., W. Europe, and other developed countries,
1995

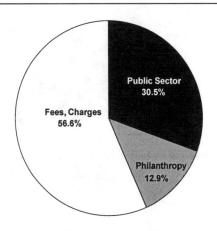

Figure 13.9   Sources of nonprofit revenue in the U.S., 1995

revenues. This reflects the widespread partnership that developed between government at all levels and nonprofit organizations during the Great Society era of the 1960s, when government social welfare spending expanded greatly.

- **Limited support from philanthropy.** By contrast, private philanthropy provides a much smaller share of total nonprofit revenue. Thus, as Figure 13.9 shows, private philanthropy—from individuals, corporations, and foundations combined—accounts for only 12.9 percent of nonprofit income in the U.S.
- **Revenue structure with volunteers.** This pattern of nonprofit revenue changes dramatically when volunteers are factored into the picture. In fact, as shown in Figure 13.10, the share of private philanthropy doubles from 12.9 percent to 26.9 percent, thereby becoming slightly greater than public sector payments (25.6 percent), but still considerably below service fees (47.4 percent). This fact testifies to the importance of volunteering in the operations of the U.S. nonprofit sector. As these data show, the value of volunteering is at least as significant as that of monetary gifts.
- **Revenue structure with religious worship.** The overall pattern of nonprofit finance in the U.S. changes even further when account is taken of religious worship institutions, such as churches and synagogues. Such religious worship institutions account for approximately $65 billion, or 10 percent of the total revenue of the U.S. nonprofit sector. Most of these monies (nearly 95 percent) come from private giving. With religion included, therefore, the philanthropic share of total

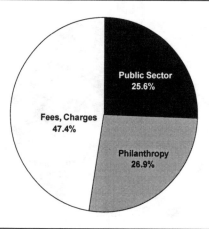

Figure 13.10   Sources of nonprofit revenue in the U.S., with volunteers, 1995

nonprofit revenue in the U.S. rises from 12.9 percent to 21 percent. With volunteers included as well, the private giving share rises to 37 percent (see Figure 13.11).

- **Deviation from the all-country and developed country patterns.** The revenue structure of the U.S. nonprofit sector thus differs considerably from the global average and all 13 other developed countries. As Figure 13.12 shows, the role of public sector payments is considerably lower in the U.S. than in the developed countries generally (30.5 percent vs. 51.6 percent) or in all 22 countries (40.1 percent). In fact, the level of public support for the nonprofit sector in the U.S. is the lowest among all developed countries, and falls behind even some Eastern European nations such as the Czech Republic or Romania.

By contrast, the share of nonprofit income coming from fees and charges is considerably higher in the U.S. than it is in the developed countries generally or the 22-country average (56.6 percent vs. 40.9 percent and 49.4 percent, respectively).

Similarly, though smaller than might be expected given the rhetoric of American philanthropy, private giving comprises a larger share of nonprofit revenue in the U.S. than it does, on average, in all 22 of the countries examined or in just the developed countries (12.9 percent vs. 10.5 percent and 7.5 percent, respectively). At the same time, however, private philanthropy still plays a smaller part in the financing of nonprofit action in the U.S. than it does in a number of other countries, including several in Central Europe.

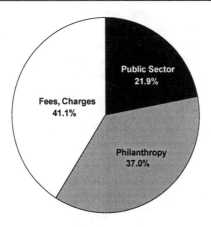

Figure 13.11 Sources of nonprofit revenue in the U.S., with volunteers and religious worship, 1995

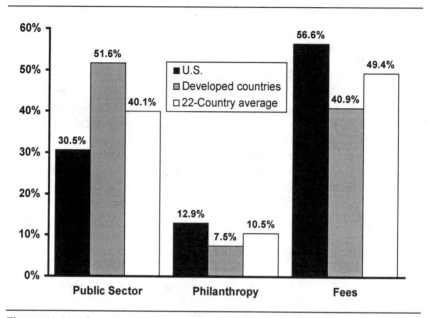

Figure 13.12   Sources of nonprofit cash revenue, U.S., developed countries, and 22-country average, 1995

Clearly, the partnerships between government and the nonprofit sector that have developed in Western Europe have failed to develop as fully in the United States. Although private giving has helped the sector to sustain itself in this context, it hardly has provided sufficient support. Instead, nonprofit organizations have turned extensively to the market for support, charging fees for their services and often collecting substantial amounts of revenue in the process.

• **Variations by subsector.** This overall picture of nonprofit finance does not apply across the board, however. Rather, important differences exist in the revenue structure of nonprofit organizations by field of activity. In fact, two quite distinct patterns of nonprofit finance are evident among the U.S. nonprofits, as shown in Figure 13.13.

Fee-dominant fields. Fee income is the dominant source of income in seven of the eight fields of nonprofit action for which data were gathered. The field most heavily dependent on this revenue source is work-related organizations (professional associations and labor unions) which derive most of their revenues from membership dues. This is followed by philanthropy, which receives no significant public sector payments, and derives most of its revenues from investment income. In three fields, the structure of revenue is somewhat more balanced. This

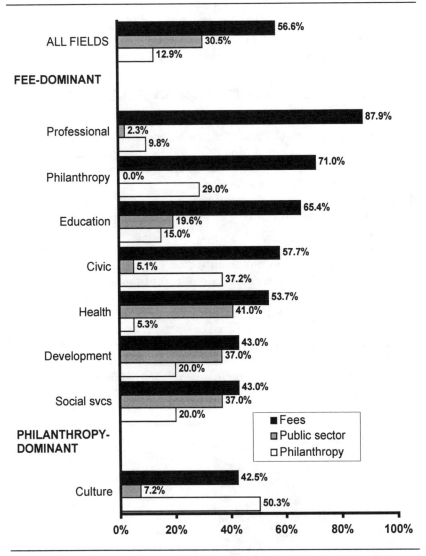

Figure 13.13 Sources of nonprofit cash revenue in the U.S., by field, 1995

includes health, where extensive fee income is partly balanced by substantial public sector support; and also development and social services, where significant philanthropic support is present as well.

Private philanthropy-dominant fields. While private philanthropy is far from being the dominant source of nonprofit income in the U.S.

overall, it turns out to be the dominant source of income in at least one field—the field of culture. This reflects the lack of political support for "high culture" in the U.S. and the resulting dependence of cultural institutions on the support of wealthy patrons.

6. Change in the U.S. nonprofit sector (1990–1995)

Between 1990 and 1995 the nonprofit sector in the U.S. grew by 20 percent, exceeding the growth rate of the entire economy by a ratio of almost 3:1 (the overall growth rate during this period was about 8 percent). However, that growth rate was pretty much in line with employment growth in the service sector, which grew faster than the rest of the economy. Since the nonprofit sector is, for the most part, a sub-component of the service sector, its rate of growth can be explained by the growing prominence of services in the U.S. economy.

A more interesting shift in this period of time occurred in the revenue structure of the American nonprofit sector. Of the total growth in nonprofit revenues during this period, 26 percent came from public sector payments, 12 percent from philanthropy, and 62 percent from service fees (Figure 13.14). In other words, service fees contributed disproportionately to the growth of the sector compared to what its share of total revenue at the start of the period would have suggested. This pattern is similar to that observed in other developed countries, particularly France and Germany (see Chapters 4 and 5), though there such fees started from a considerably smaller base.

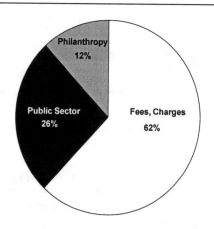

Figure 13.14   Shares of nonprofit revenue growth, by source, U.S., 1990–1995

CONCLUSIONS AND IMPLICATIONS

The nonprofit sector thus emerges from the evidence presented here as both a sizable and a rather complex set of institutions in U.S. society. Not only does this set of institutions serve important human needs and embody important national values stressing individual initiative in the solution of public problems, it also constitutes a major, and growing, economic force and is a significant contributor to political as well as social life.

At the same time, the U.S. nonprofit sector is experiencing important changes that are opening new opportunities while also exposing the sector to significant dangers.[5] On the positive side of the ledger, a number of demographic developments such as the aging of the population, the transformation of the role of women, and continued changes in family structure are boosting demand for the kinds of services that nonprofit organizations traditionally have provided—such as day care, elderly care, health care, and other human services. In addition, the sector has benefited from increased visibility and professionalization in recent decades as a product of expanded research, the establishment of a number of sector-wide infrastructure organizations, and the emergence of a number of nonprofit management training programs. At the same time, there is considerable evidence of continued reinvigoration of the grassroots base of this sector as new social movements have emerged in fields as diverse as environmental protection, poverty alleviation, and expansion of the rights of women. Finally, the considerable economic growth that the U.S. has experienced over the past two decades has produced fortunes that, potentially at least, could propel charitable giving upward; and this is taking place at a time when corporations are coming to appreciate as well the strategic value of community investments.

On the other side of the ledger, however, American nonprofits have been facing a considerable fiscal squeeze as a consequence of reductions in government support triggered by a conservative backlash against the Great Society legislation of the 1960s. While organizations have responded to this situation by expanding their reliance on fee-for-service income, this has had the unfortunate result of demonstrating the income-generating potential of many of these fields, enticing for-profit competitors to move more heavily into them. In some areas, such as home health, in fact, for-profits have displaced nonprofits as the predominant providers. Indeed, because of their superior access to capital, for-profits are poised to challenge nonprofit organizations across a broad front, especially given the increased questioning of nonprofit effectiveness that seems to be under way and the shift of social welfare policy toward job readiness and employability rather than general human development as its principal goal. All of this is forcing nonprofit organizations to become more market-oriented in their operations, but at the price of posing questions about the legitimacy of the special tax and other privileges that they enjoy.

What this suggests is that the survival and prosperity of nonprofit institutions is not only at issue in the developing regions of Africa, Asia, and Latin America and the transition societies of Central and Eastern Europe. Despite the considerable scale of these institutions, indeed perhaps *because* of their considerable scale, the future of these institutions is very much in question in mature market economies as well. Certainly in the United States, where a somewhat naïve myth of voluntarism has long enveloped the nonprofit sector, recent years have witnessed a steady broadening of the gap between what nonprofit organizations have had to do to prosper and grow and what popular mythologies have expected them to do to retain public support. The result has been a virtual crisis of legitimacy for America's nonprofit sector that has manifested itself in declining public confidence, increased demands for accountability, challenges to tax-exempt status, questioning of the sector's advocacy role, and considerable unease about a range of pay and perquisite issues.

Those committed to the retention of a sphere of social action outside the market and the state therefore cannot afford to take the survival of this set of institutions for granted, even in the United States where commitment to this type of institution is an integral part of national traditions. Certainly, there is a need to re-examine the role and character of these institutions regularly in the light of new circumstances and needs. It is hoped that the kind of information developed in this report, and in the project of which it is a part, can contribute usefully to this purpose.

ENDNOTES

1. Lester M. Salamon, *America's Nonprofit Sector: A Primer.* 2nd edition. (New York: The Foundation Center, 1999).

2. The structural-operational definition of the nonprofit sector used by the Johns Hopkins project is considerably broader than that commonly accepted in the U.S. Beyond the 501(c)(3) and 501(c)(4) organizations that are generally considered to be nonprofits, the project's definition includes work-related organizations (unions and professional associations), political organizations, and certain types of member-serving associations. For a summary of that defintion, see Chapter 1 above and Appendix A.

3. Technically, the more precise comparison is between nonprofit contribution to "value added" and gross domestic product. For the nonprofit sector, "value added" in economic terms essentially equals the sum of wages and the imputed value of volunteer time. On this basis, the nonprofit sector in the U.S. accounted for 4.5 percent of total value added.

4. For more information on the history of the U.S. nonprofit sector, see Peter Dobkin Hall, "A Historical Overview of the Private Nonprofit Sector," in Walter Powell (ed.) *The Nonprofit Sector: A Research Handbook* (New Haven: Yale University Press, 1987), pp. 3–26; Lester M. Sala-

mon, *America's Nonprofit Sector: A Primer,* 2nd ed. (New York: The Foundation Center, 1999); and Lester M. Salamon, *Partners in Public Service: Government-Nonprofit Relations in the Modern Welfare State* (Baltimore: The Johns Hopkins University Press, 1995).

5. This section draws heavily on Lester M. Salamon, *America's Nonprofit Sector: A Primer* (New York: The Foundation Center, 1999), Chapter 12, pp. 161–180.

PART 4

Central and Eastern Europe

The rebirth of civil society, of organized political and social life outside the boundaries of the party-state, played a major role in the revolutions of 1989 that brought about the collapse of Communist dictatorships throughout Central and Eastern Europe. Not surprisingly, therefore, one of the signal developments of the past decade in this region has been the re-emergence of nonprofit organizations in many different spheres.

Important as this development has been, however, it has not been without its strains. As a consequence, the nonprofit sector in Central and Eastern Europe has not developed as fully, or as quickly, as many assumed, and remains uneven from place to place. What is more, this sector has taken a particular form in this region reflecting at once the particular legal framework within which it has developed and the heritage of the recent past. In particular, culture and recreation organizations, many of which were tolerated and even encouraged during the Communist period, play a much larger part in the structure of the nonprofit sector in most of Central and Eastern Europe than they do in Western Europe. On the other hand, social welfare organizations, which are heavily supported by state subsidies in Western Europe, play a much smaller part to the east, where the Western European practice of extensive government support to nonprofit service providers in the field of social welfare is far less apparent. Whether this disparity will persist or prove to be another temporary transition phenomenon is difficult to foresee at this time. But that it imparts a special flavor to the Central European nonprofit scene is certain.

283

CHAPTER 14

The Czech Republic

Pavol Frič, Rochdi Goulli, Stefan Toepler, and
Lester M. Salamon

BACKGROUND

As in other countries in Central and Eastern Europe, civil society and the
nonprofit sector in the Czech Republic saw a tremendous upsurge after
1989, when the Communist Party's monopoly of power was abolished.
While the Czech nonprofit sector appears, on balance, perhaps less visible
than its counterparts in other Central European countries, it has reached a
comparatively high level of development. This is so despite the skepticism
of the former neo-liberal government of Prime Minister Václav Klaus about
the necessity of a nonprofit sector. Fortunately, however, civil society also
had a high-level proponent in President Václav Havel. Largely due to
Havel's influence, civil society in the Czech Republic is increasingly thought
of in positive terms as a set of citizens' activities that counterbalance state
bureaucracy and state centralism.[1]

The work reported here was designed to bring the Czech civil society
sector into empirical focus for the first time. The work was carried out by a
Czech research team at the Institute of Sociological Studies in the Faculty
of Social Sciences of the Charles University in Prague as part of a collaborative international inquiry, the Johns Hopkins Comparative Nonprofit

Global Civil Society: Dimensions of the Nonprofit Sector by Lester M. Salamon, Helmut K.
Anheier, Regina List, Stefan Toepler, S. Wojciech Sokolowski and Associates. Baltimore, MD: Johns Hopkins Center for Civil Society Studies, 1999.

Sector Project.[2] It thus offered ample opportunities both to capture local Czech circumstances and peculiarities and to compare and contrast them to those in other countries both in Central and Eastern Europe and elsewhere in a systematic way.[3] The result is a comprehensive empirical overview of the Czech nonprofit sector and a systematic comparison of Czech nonprofit realities to those elsewhere in Central and Eastern Europe and the rest of the world.

The present chapter reports on just one set of findings from this project, those relating to the size and structure of the nonprofit sector in the Czech Republic and elsewhere. Subsequent publications will fill in the historical, legal, and policy context of this sector. The data reported here draw heavily on the annual sets of national accounts, employment data, and selective censuses of households conducted by *Český statistický úřad—ČSÚ* (Czech Statistical Office), and numerous additional sources of statistical information. Unless otherwise noted, financial data are reported in U.S. dollars at the 1995 average exchange rate. (For a more complete statement of the sources of data, see Appendix C. For a more complete statement of the types of organizations included, see Chapter 1 and Appendix A.)

PRINCIPAL FINDINGS

Five major findings emerge from this work on the scope, structure, financing, and role of the nonprofit sector in the Czech Republic:

1. A sizable economic force

In the first place, aside from its social and political importance, the nonprofit sector turns out to be a modest but growing economic force in the Czech Republic.

More specifically:

- **An $800 million industry.** Even excluding its religion component, the nonprofit sector in the Czech Republic had operating expenditures of $800 million in 1995, or 1.6 percent of the country's gross domestic product, a substantial amount for a sector that essentially has had only six years to develop more or less freely (see Table 14.1).[4]
- **An important employer.** Behind these expenditures lies a sizable workforce that already includes the equivalent of 74,200 full-time equivalent paid workers. This represents 1.7 percent of all nonagricultural workers in the country, 3.4 percent of service employment, and the equivalent of 6 percent of the government employment at all levels—central, provincial, and municipal.

Table 14.1 The nonprofit sector in the Czech Republic, 1995

$ 803.6 million in expenditures
— 1.6 percent of GDP

74,200 paid employees
— 1.7 percent of total nonagricultural employment
— 3.4 percent of total service employment
— 5.9 percent of public employment

- **More employees than in the largest private firm.** Put somewhat differently, nonprofit employment in the Czech Republic easily outdistances the employment in the largest private business in the country, and does so by a ratio of approximately 3:1. Thus, compared to the 74,200 paid workers in the Czech Republic's nonprofit organizations, the largest Czech private corporations, *Škoda Automobilová* or Chemapol Group, each employ between 20,000 and 30,000 workers.
- **Outdistances some industries.** Indeed, more people now work in the nonprofit sector in the Czech Republic than in some entire industries in the country. As shown in Figure 14.1, nonprofit employment in the Czech Republic outdistances employment in the country's petrochemical and printing industries. In addition, employment in the nonprofit sector in the Czech Republic is essentially on a par with the employment in food manufacturing and textiles, and equals almost three-quarters of the employment in transportation.
- **Volunteer inputs.** Even this does not capture the full scope of the nonprofit sector in the Czech Republic, for this sector also attracts a considerable amount of *volunteer* effort. Indeed, an estimated 10 percent of the Czech population reports contributing their time to nonprofit organizations. This translates into another 40,900 full-time equivalent employees, which boosts the total number of full-time equivalent workers at nonprofit organizations in the Czech Republic to 115,000, or 2.7 percent of total employment in the country (see Figure 14.2).
- **Religion.** The inclusion of religion, moreover, would boost the totals to 78,200 paid employees and 45,400 full-time equivalent volunteers. With religion included, nonprofit paid employment therefore rises to 1.8 percent of the total and paid plus volunteer employment to 2.9 percent. Religion also boosts operating expenditures to a total $860 million. Including religion and volunteering would thus bring total

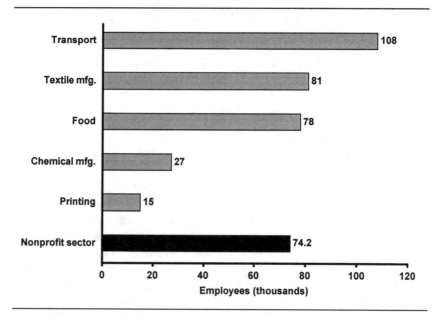

Figure 14.1   Nonprofit employment in the Czech Republic in context, 1995

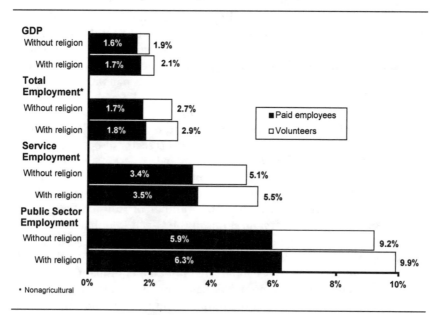

Figure 14.2   Nonprofits in the Czech Republic, with and without volunteers and religion, 1995, as a % of . . .

expenditures to close to $1.1 billion—the equivalent of 2.1 percent of the gross domestic product (see Figure 14.2).

2. One of the largest nonprofit sectors in Central Europe

Not only is the Czech nonprofit sector relatively sizable in relation to the Czech economy, but also it is large relative to its counterparts elsewhere in Central and Eastern Europe, though it still falls behind the level in Western European countries.

- **Below the international average.** As Figure 14.3 shows, the relative size of the nonprofit sector varies greatly among countries, from a high of 12.6 percent of total nonagricultural employment in the Netherlands to a low of 0.4 percent of total employment in Mexico. The overall 22-country average, however, is close to 5 percent. This means that the Czech Republic, at 1.7 percent without religion, falls below the global average, which is not surprising given the hostility toward such organizations during the Communist era that ended only six years prior to the date reported on here.
- **Considerably above the Central European average.** While it falls below the 22-country average, nonprofit employment as a share of total employment is still higher in the Czech Republic than it is elsewhere in Central Europe. Thus, as shown in Figure 14.4, full-time equivalent employment in nonprofit organizations in the Czech Republic, at 1.7 percent of total employment, is proportionally 65 percent greater than the Central European average of 1.1 percent. Indeed, of the other Central European countries covered by this project, only Hungary comes close to the Czech Republic in the scale of nonprofit employment.
- **Margin widens with volunteers.** This margin widens, moreover, when volunteers are added. Thus, with volunteer time included, nonprofit organizations account for 2.7 percent of total employment in the Czech Republic, which is a full percentage point above the regional average of 1.7 percent (see Figure 14.4).

3. A rich, but also troubled history of nonprofit activity in the Czech Republic

That the Czech nonprofit sector is comparatively highly developed in the region is very likely a product of the rich, but also troubled, history that such institutions have had in this country.[5] This history includes:

- The early origins of philanthropy and the nonprofit sector were tied to Christianity with the first foundations appearing as early as the 13th

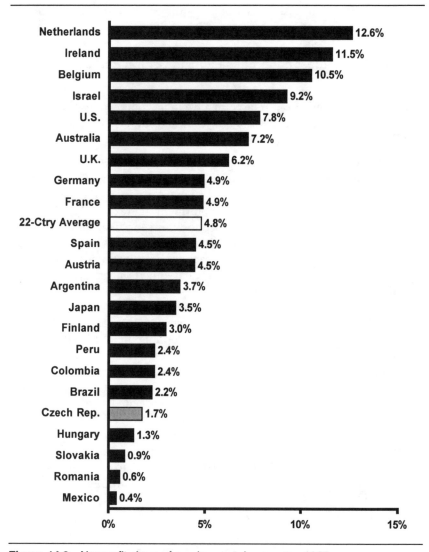

Figure 14.3   Nonprofit share of employment, by country, 1995

century. The leading role of the Catholic Church was reduced, however, by the Reform Church movement in the early 15th century and the growing role of urban communities.

- The forced re-Catholicization of the country after 1621 under the House of Habsburg restored the position of the Catholic Church,

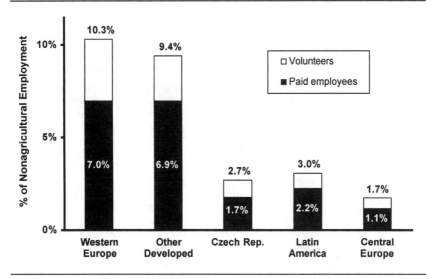

Figure 14.4   Nonprofit share of employment, with and without volunteers, Czech Republic and four regions, 1995

which clearly dominated such fields as education. The Church's prominence, however, was broken again in the second half of the 18th century. In this period of Enlightened Absolutism, the Church came under state surveillance, and education and charitable activities were taken over by the state.

- The period of the so-called National Revival beginning around 1830 brought a substantial blossoming of societies and foundations, especially those with patriotic, cultural, and women's educational goals.
- The collapse of the Habsburg Empire and the creation of the Czechoslovak Republic in 1918 brought a new surge of societies, associations, and foundations with educational, cultural, charitable, health, or social purposes that were formed on an ethnic, religious, or above all civic, basis. Statistical research in the 1930s registered 5,130 societies, and the nonprofit sector accounted for about 26 percent of total social care expenditures. With the German occupation in 1939, civic activities were banned, however.
- After World War II, activities of associations were renewed, but only for a short time: the Communist coup of 1948 interrupted their development. From 1951 onwards, church activities were limited to worship and education, whereas health and social care came under direct state control. All permitted socio-political activities were consolidated

within the National Front, an umbrella for political organizations, trade unions and so-called voluntary social organizations. Membership in these organizations was often formal, but was considered an expression of loyalty to the state. Statistical data from 1972 reflect the full extent of the organization of state-controlled public life: In a country with a population of 14.5 million, individuals held a total of 19 million memberships in the organizations that comprised the National Front.

- The political opening toward the end of the 1960s briefly reawakened the real interest of citizens in public affairs, but this was once again banned following the military invasion by the Warsaw Pact countries in 1968. Some political activists survived as dissidents. Only after 1980, however, were the environmental movement and some educational and scientific activities tolerated.

- A number of current organizations began their activities informally in the late 1980s. The activity of civic initiatives culminated in the revolution of 1989. In 1990, Act No. 83 on the Association of Citizens, regulating the activities of civic associations, was passed and new organizations finally were allowed to develop again independent of the state.

4. Culture and recreation dominance

Similar to other Central European countries, but unlike the all-country average, culture and recreation clearly dominates the nonprofit scene in the Czech Republic.

- **Thirty-one percent of nonprofit employment in the culture and recreation field.** Of all the types of nonprofit activity, the one that accounts for the largest share of nonprofit employment in the Czech Republic is culture and recreation. As shown in Figure 14.5, 31 percent of all nonprofit employment in the Czech Republic is in this field, mostly in sports and hobby clubs. This is comparable to the Central European average of 35 percent, but it greatly exceeds the 22-country average of 14 percent. This situation reflects the long tradition of culture and sports clubs in the Czech Republic and in other Central European countries and the fact that these activities were tolerated, and often encouraged, under the Communist regime.

- **Relatively smaller shares of nonprofit employment in the welfare fields of education, health, and social services.** Compared to the overall 22-country average, core welfare services in the fields of education, health, and social services absorb a smaller share of nonprofit employment in the Czech Republic. Thus, while these fields absorb more than two-thirds of nonprofit employment on average, they account for

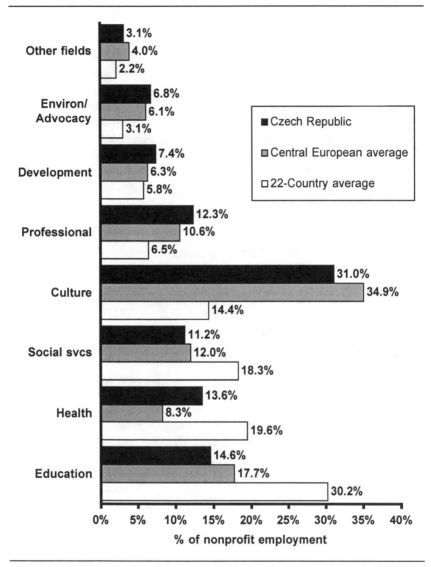

Figure 14.5   Composition of the nonprofit sector, Czech Republic, Central
Europe, and 22-country average, 1995

39 percent of all nonprofit employment in the Czech Republic, of
which 15 percent is in education, 14 percent in health care, and 11
percent in social services. This reflects the state dominance of these
critical welfare functions during the Communist era.

- **Sizable nonprofit presence in professional associations.** Another sizable portion of total nonprofit employment in the Czech Republic is in the professional associations and unions field. This field accounts for 12 percent of Czech nonprofit employment, which is almost twice the 22-country average of 6.5 percent and even slightly greater than the Central and Eastern European average of 11 percent. This very likely reflects the heritage of the Communist period, which established a more definitive state role in encouraging (and controlling) trade unions as well as a broad range of professional groupings.
- **Significant nonprofit development and advocacy employment.** Compared to the employment in nonprofit culture and recreation, education, health, social welfare, and professional organizations, the share of Czech nonprofit employment in the development field and in the related fields of advocacy and environmental protection is considerably smaller. Altogether, these fields absorb 14 percent of all nonprofit employment in this country. However, this greatly exceeds the 22-country average of 9 percent, perhaps reflecting the civic activities that produced the Czech Republic's "velvet revolution" of 1989. An additional 3 percent of nonprofit employees fall into other categories, including philanthropy and international activities.
- **Pattern shifts with volunteers.** This pattern is intensified when volunteer inputs are factored in. In particular, as shown in Figure 14.6, with volunteers included, the culture and recreation share of nonprofit employment increases from 31 percent to 36 percent; and the combined development, advocacy, and environment share rises from 14 percent to 16 percent. Clearly, these activities attract considerable popular support in the Czech Republic. For example, culture accounts for 28.7 percent and development and environment/advocacy account for 26 percent of the total memberships in the Czech nonprofit sector (6.7 million members).

5. Most revenue from fees, not philanthropy or public sector

Consistent with its composition and similar to other countries in the region, the Czech Republic's nonprofit sector receives the bulk of its revenue not from private philanthropy or the public sector, but from fees and charges. In particular:

- **Fee income dominant.** The overwhelmingly dominant source of income of nonprofit organizations in the Czech Republic is fees and charges for the services that these organizations provide. As reflected in Figure 14.7, this source alone accounts for nearly half, or 47 percent, of all nonprofit revenue in the Czech Republic.

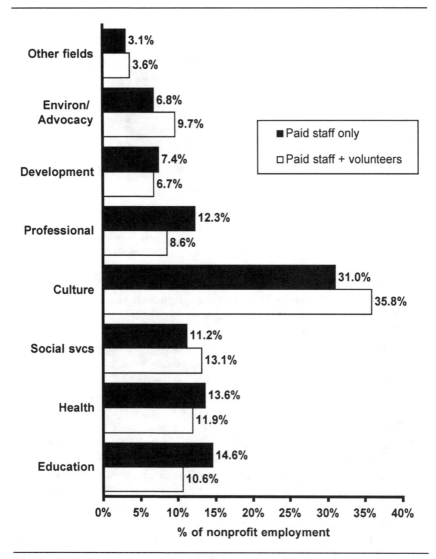

Figure 14.6 Share of nonprofit employment in the Czech Republic, with and without volunteers, by field, 1995

- **Substantial public sector support.** Public sector payments account for another 39.4 percent of Czech nonprofit revenue, which is a relatively high share both for Central Europe and for much of the rest of the world. Interestingly, the centralized Communist-era state funding system for voluntary organizations was largely left intact after 1989. While

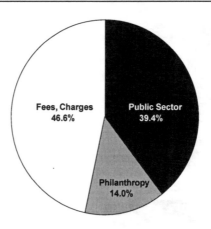

Figure 14.7   Sources of nonprofit revenue in the Czech Republic, 1995

the system is frequently criticized for being inadequate and inconsistent with the new realities of the sector, it nevertheless has contributed to relatively substantial levels of state support over the past years.

- **Considerable support from philanthropy.** By contrast, private philanthropy provides a much smaller, though still notable, share of total revenues. Thus, as Figure 14.7 shows, private philanthropy—from individuals, corporations, and foundations combined—accounts for 14 percent of nonprofit income in the Czech Republic, which is higher than the 22-country average of 11 percent, but significantly below the Central and Eastern European average of close to 21 percent.
- **Revenue structure with volunteers.** This pattern of nonprofit revenue changes significantly when volunteers are factored into the picture. In fact, as shown in Figure 14.8, the share of private philanthropy increases substantially from 14 percent to 30 percent. Public sector support decreases somewhat from 39 percent to slightly less than one-third. The proportion of fee support declines from 47 percent to 38 percent, though it still remains the dominant revenue source.
- **Revenue structure with religion.** The overall pattern of nonprofit finance in the Czech Republic changes only slightly when account is taken of religious institutions, such as churches and synagogues. Such religious institutions account for approximately 6.8 percent of the total revenue of the Czech nonprofit sector. With religion included, therefore, the philanthropic share of total nonprofit revenue in the Czech Republic rises from 14 percent to 15 percent. With volunteers included as well, the private giving share rises to 31 percent (see Figure 14.9).

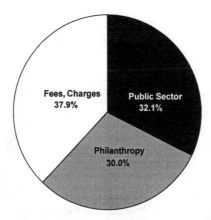

Figure 14.8 Sources of nonprofit revenue in the Czech Republic, with volunteers, 1995

- **Similar to other Central European countries.** The pattern of nonprofit finance evident in the Czech Republic is quite similar to that elsewhere in Central Europe. As shown in Figure 14.10, the nonprofit organizations in the other Central European countries included in this project (Hungary, Romania and Slovakia) derived the majority of their revenues from

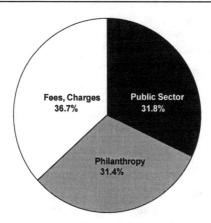

Figure 14.9 Sources of nonprofit revenue in the Czech Republic, with volunteers and religious worship, 1995

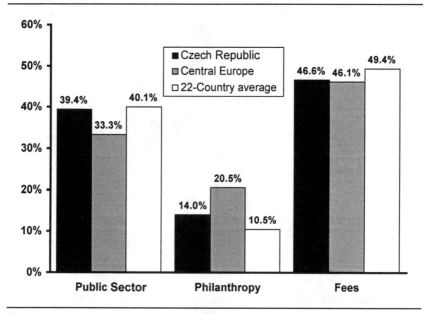

Figure 14.10   Sources of nonprofit cash revenue, the Czech Republic, Central Europe, and 22-country average, 1995

fees and charges. Thus, compared to the Czech Republic's 46.6 percent, the share of total nonprofit income coming from fees stood at 46.1 percent for all four Central European countries. The public sector and philanthropy shares of nonprofit revenue in the Czech Republic deviated slightly from the regional average, with the public sector share stronger in the Czech Republic than elsewhere in the region (39 percent vs. 33 percent on average) and philanthropy somewhat weaker (14 percent vs. 20.5 percent).

- **Similar to the global average.** While the revenue structure of the Czech nonprofit sector is generally similar to that elsewhere in Central Europe, it also mirrors that evident elsewhere in the world. Thus, as Figure 14.10 shows, while fees and charges are the dominant element in the financial base of the nonprofit sector globally, its dominance is only a little more pronounced than it is in the Czech Republic (49 percent of total revenue compared to 47 percent). Similarly, public sector payments comprise essentially the same share of nonprofit income in these other countries on average (40 percent vs. 39 percent in the Czech Republic). Quite clearly, it would seem that the Czech Republic is approaching a pattern of cooperation between nonprofit organizations and the state that is similar to that in these other countries.[6]

- **Variations by subsector.** Even this does not do full justice to the complexities of nonprofit finance in the Czech Republic, however. This is so because important differences exist in the finances of nonprofit organizations by subsector. In fact, three quite distinct patterns of nonprofit finance are evident among Czech nonprofits, as shown in Figure 14.11:

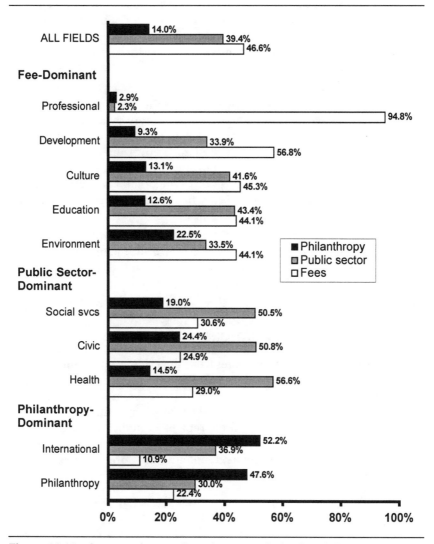

Figure 14.11   Sources of nonprofit cash revenue in the Czech Republic, by field, 1995

Fee-dominant fields. Fee income is the dominant source of income in five fields of nonprofit action for which data were gathered (professional associations, development, culture and recreation, education, and the environment). The fee dominance is most strongly pronounced in the cases of professional associations and development and housing, where membership dues or rental income are the primary sources of income. But fee income is also the single largest revenue source of nonprofit cultural and educational establishments, as well as environmental organizations. In education, however, fees barely edge out public support as the largest source (44 percent vs. 43 percent), and government support, at 42 percent, is also not far behind fee income with 45 percent in the cultural arena.

Public sector-dominant fields. In three fields, health, civic, and social services, government plays the dominant role in financing nonprofit action in the Czech Republic, accounting for more than half of total revenue in each field. To a certain degree, this may be due to counterpart, or matching, contributions of the Czech government, which are required by agreements with the European Union's PHARE program, and other international public grants. The dominant source of public payments in the civic and advocacy field is mandatory budgetary payments of the state to political organizations.

Private philanthropy-dominant fields. While private philanthropy is far from being the dominant source of nonprofit income in the Czech Republic overall, it turns out to be the dominant source of income in international activities and in the philanthropy field, which would naturally be expected to be supported chiefly by private giving.

CONCLUSIONS AND IMPLICATIONS

The nonprofit sector thus emerges from the evidence presented here as both a growing and rather complex set of institutions in Czech society. Not only does this set of institutions serve important human needs, it also constitutes a growing economic force and is a significant contributor to political as well as social life. However, there remain a number of current trends and key challenges that will need to be addressed to ensure the further development of the sector into the next millennium. More specifically, these trends and challenges include:

- **The prospect of consolidation.** While the nonprofit sector in the Czech Republic is still going through a period of expansion, the latest data suggest that the growth rate of nonprofit organizations is beginning to slow down, and that a phase of market saturation for the services provided by these organizations is approaching. This means that in the short run a more intensive consolidation within the nonprofit sector may take place that will separate those that will survive from those that will have to dissolve. The outcome of this trend will be heavily influenced by the overall economic conditions, the further development of the legislative framework, and the political climate. In principle, this consolidation could lead to improvements in the overall position of the sector, as decreases in quantity might result in increases in quality. The present state of affairs, however, raises doubts about whether this will actually be the case.

- **Legal regulation.** The legislative framework for the nonprofit sector is as yet incomplete, is sometimes unnecessarily complicated, and does not provide sufficient protection against the misuse of the nonprofit status. While, on the one hand, the current regulatory system makes it difficult for nonprofits to operate freely, on the other hand, it is not strict enough to overcome the existing negative image and create a climate of trust. The incomplete character of the regulation governing nonprofit organizations has led to some confusion about the actual differences between various types of organizations. For example, in the recent past, foundations had been able to carry out the same activities as civic associations, and civic associations performed tasks that the law intended public benefit corporations to undertake. Judging from their activities, these organizational forms have been virtually indistinguishable. In this sense, the relatively new Act on Foundations and Funds has been one step toward clarifying the respective roles and characteristics of different legal forms. In general, creating a new and comprehensive legal framework has been the main area of cooperation between the nonprofit sector and the state.

- **Nonprofit finance.** The system of state financing that was taken over from the Communist era still lacks a clear plan for the development of the nonprofit sector and suffers from excessive centralism. It gives the impression of a long-term provisional arrangement waiting for a definite solution that has yet to materialize. On the other hand, there is little doubt that state support will continue to be of central importance to the nonprofit sector. The present system of state financing of nonprofit organizations, however, fosters an atmosphere of uncertainty and has a tendency to keep alive those organizations that "know the ropes," but not necessarily those that provide the highest quality services. Foreign sources of finances for nonprofit organizations are beginning to diminish rapidly, which, especially in the area of human rights, could give rise to major problems. Because the general public often fails to reconcile profit-generating activities with nonprofit status, the economic activities of nonprofit organizations remain their most controversial income source; however, final regulatory guidelines for such activities are still lacking. More optimism for the future lies in sponsorships as another important source of nonprofit revenues. Current developments do not suggest that the amount of corporate support is rising markedly, but a cultivation of corporations is taking place and leading to a more effective use of these resources.

In sum, the development of the nonprofit sector as outlined above suggests that any consolidation pressures that are likely to take shape in the near future will have some benefits, but will also cause substantial problems. In addition, even though the number of nonprofit organizations is presently increasing, fatigue is beginning to show in the activities of many of them, as a result both of uncertainties generated by the current legal and fiscal environments and of over-exertion of nonprofits in trying to meet their own objectives. Many organizations work on a voluntary basis and cannot afford to pay a professional workforce. The possibility of professionalizing the staff of nonprofit organizations will play a decisive role not only in the oncoming process of consolidation, but also in further shaping the nonprofit sector in Czech society.

While the challenges remain substantial, the interest that the recently elected new government is beginning to show in the nonprofit sector gives rise to new hopes. In particular, the Social Democratic Party, which is now one of the ruling parties, not only exhibits a positive attitude towards the nonprofit sector, but Social Democrats also recently initiated several practical steps to improve the sector's position in society. The most important is a government effort to complete the legal framework for the nonprofit sector and to unfreeze funds that were dedicated to nonprofit purposes by former governments. Another positive change is the cooperation between the new government and nonprofit organizations in the process of preparing the Czech Republic for the administration and distribution of regional financial support from the European Union. This process will have strong positive consequences for the financial resources and regional integration of nonprofit organizations in this country.[7]

ENDNOTES

1. See P. Frič, H. Šilhánová, R. Goulli, L. Deverová and P. Pajas, *The Nonprofit Sector in the Czech Republic. The Socio-Political Context.* European Studies Center of the Institute for East-West Studies, Prague 1996.

2. The work in the Czech Republic was coordinated by Martin Potůček, Director of the Institute of Sociological Studies, Charles University, and Pavol Frič, who served as local associates to this project. Assisting them were Rochdi Goulli and five other researchers, including

student assistants Leila Goulliová and Olga Vyskočilová. The team was aided, in turn, by a local advisory committee made up of seven prominent philanthropic, academic, and business leaders (see Appendix D for a list of committee members). The Johns Hopkins project was directed by Lester M. Salamon and Helmut K. Anheier, and the Central and Eastern European portion of the work overseen by Stefan Toepler.

3. The definitions and approaches used in the project were developed collaboratively with the cooperation of the Czech researchers and researchers in other countries and were designed to be applicable to the Czech Republic and the other project countries. For a full description of this definition and the types of organizations included, see Appendix A. For a full list of the other countries included, see Chapter 1 above and Lester M. Salamon and Helmut K. Anheier, *The Emerging Sector Revisited: A Summary, Revised Estimates* (Baltimore, MD: The Johns Hopkins Center for Civil Society Studies, 1999).

4. Technically, the more precise comparison is between nonprofit contribution to "value added" and gross domestic product. For the nonprofit sector, "value added" in economic terms essentially equals the sum of wages and the imputed value of volunteer time. On this basis, the nonprofit sector in the Czech Republic accounted for 1.1 percent of total value added.

5. See P. Frič, L. Deverová, P. Pajas, and H. Šilhánová, "Defining the Nonprofit Sector: The Czech Republic." *Working Papers of The Johns Hopkins Comparative Nonprofit Sector Project*, No 27. Baltimore, MD: Johns Hopkins Center for Civil Society Studies, 1998.

6. R. Goulli, "Veřejná politika a transformace vládního a nevládního neziskového sektoru—problémy financování" (The Public Economy and the Transformation of Government and the Non-Governmental Nonprofit Sector: Problems of Funding). In *Centrální politické rozhodování v ČR.* 1. díl. Institut sociologických studií FSV UK, Praha 1998.

7. P. Frič, *Aktivity a potřeby neziskových organizací v ČR* (Activities and Needs of Nonprofit Organizations in the Czech Republic). Agnes—ICN, Praha 1998.

In Memoriam

Ágnes Vajda

As this volume went to press, the tragic news reached us that Ágnes Vajda, one of our Hungarian Associates, had succumbed to a long and severe illness. Ágnes was an outstanding researcher and a wonderful colleague. We will sorely miss her.

CHAPTER 15

Hungary

István Sebestény, Éva Kuti, Stefan Toepler, and
Lester M. Salamon

BACKGROUND

Like the Czech Republic, Hungary boasts one of the better developed nonprofit sectors in Central and Eastern Europe. The government posture towards the sector generally has been benign during the early 1990s, contributing to sustained development of the sector even after the original euphoria of the immediate post-1989 period began to subside. In fact, data collected through this project in Hungary over time show both strong economic growth and the beginning of changes in the composition and revenue structure of the Hungarian nonprofit sector between the early and mid-1990s.[1]

The work presented here was carried out by a Hungarian research team hosted by the Civitalis Research Association as part of a collaborative international inquiry, the Johns Hopkins Comparative Nonprofit Sector Project.[2] It thus offers an opportunity both to examine local Hungarian circumstances and peculiarities and to compare and contrast them to those in other countries both in Central and Eastern Europe and elsewhere in a systematic way.[3]

The present chapter reports on just one set of findings from this project, those relating to the size of the nonprofit sector in Hungary and elsewhere.

Global Civil Society: Dimensions of the Nonprofit Sector by Lester M. Salamon, Helmut K. Anheier, Regina List, Stefan Toepler, S. Wojciech Sokolowski and Associates. Baltimore, MD: Johns Hopkins Center for Civil Society Studies, 1999.

Subsequent publications will fill in the historical, legal, and policy context of this sector and also examine the impact that this set of institutions is having in Hungarian society. The data reported here draw heavily on the official survey of nonprofit organizations conducted annually by the Voluntary Sector Statistics unit of the Hungarian Central Statistical Office, with which local associates István Sebestény and Éva Kuti are affiliated. Unless otherwise noted, financial data are reported in U.S. dollars at the 1995 average exchange rate. (For a more complete statement of the sources of data, see Appendix C. For a more complete statement of the types of organizations included, see Chapter 1 and Appendix A.)

PRINCIPAL FINDINGS

Six major findings emerge from this work on the scope, structure, financing, and role of the nonprofit sector in Hungary:

1. A sizable economic force

In the first place, aside from its social and political importance, the nonprofit sector turns out to be a significant economic force in Hungary, accounting for sizable shares of national expenditures and employment. More specifically:

- **A $1.2 billion industry.** In 1995, the nonprofit sector in Hungary had operating expenditures of US$1.2 billion (HUF155 billion), or 2.8 percent of the country's gross domestic product, a quite significant amount.[4]
- **An important employer.** Behind these expenditures lies an important workforce that includes the equivalent of 45,000 full-time equivalent paid workers. This represents 1.3 percent of all nonagricultural workers in the country, 2.2 percent of service employment, and the equivalent of 4.6 percent of the public sector workforce at all levels—national and municipal (see Table 15.1).
- **More employees than in the largest private firm.** Put somewhat differently, nonprofit employment in Hungary easily outdistances the employment in the largest private business in the country, and does so by a ratio of 4:1. Thus, compared to the 45,000 paid workers in Hungary's nonprofit organizations, Hungary's largest private corporation, Dunaferr Groups, employs only 11,000 workers (see Figure 15.1). What is more, nonprofit employment also compares favorably with the workforce in large public enterprises: While smaller than the Hungarian Railways Co. Ltd. (59,000 employees), the nonprofit sector em-

Table 15.1 The nonprofit sector in Hungary, 1995

$1.2 billion in expenditures
— 2.8 percent of GDP

45,000 paid employees
— 1.3 percent of total nonagricultural employment
— 2.2 percent of service employment
— 4.6 percent of public sector employment

ploys slightly more people than the second largest public enterprise, Hungarian Post Office Co. Ltd. with 44,000 employees.

• **Outdistances some industries.** Indeed, more people work in the non-profit sector in Hungary than in some entire industries in the country. Nonprofit employment in Hungary outdistances employment in the country's mining and quarrying industry and, within the manufacturing sector, the employment in the non-metallic mineral production and furniture industries.

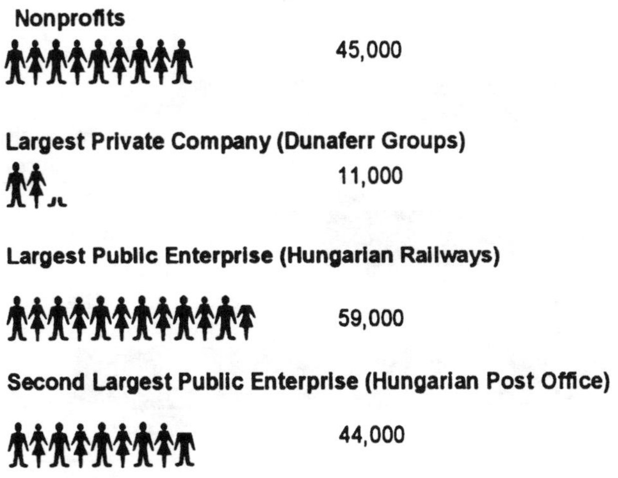

Nonprofits

45,000

Largest Private Company (Dunaferr Groups)

11,000

Largest Public Enterprise (Hungarian Railways)

59,000

Second Largest Public Enterprise (Hungarian Post Office)

44,000

Figure 15.1 Employment in nonprofits vs. largest private and public firms in Hungary, 1995

- **Volunteer inputs.** Even this does not capture the full scope of the non-profit sector in Hungary, for this sector also attracts a considerable amount of *volunteer effort*. The volunteer labor contributed by the Hungarian population translates into at least another 10,000 full-time equivalent employees, which boosts the total number of full-time equivalent employees of nonprofit organizations in Hungary to close to 55,000, or 1.6 percent of total nonagricultural employment in the country[5] (see Figure 15.2).

2. One of the larger nonprofit sectors in Central and Eastern Europe

Not only is the Hungarian nonprofit sector fairly sizable in relation to the Hungarian economy, but it is also large relative to its counterparts in the other Central and Eastern European countries that were included in this study, though it falls significantly below the level in Western European countries.

- **Below the international average.** As Figure 15.3 shows, the relative size of the nonprofit sector varies greatly among countries, from a high of 12.6 percent of total nonagricultural employment in the Netherlands

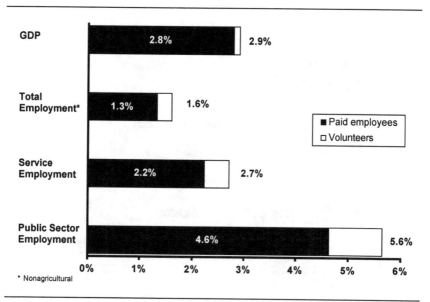

Figure 15.2   Nonprofits in Hungary, with and without volunteers, 1995, as a % of . . .

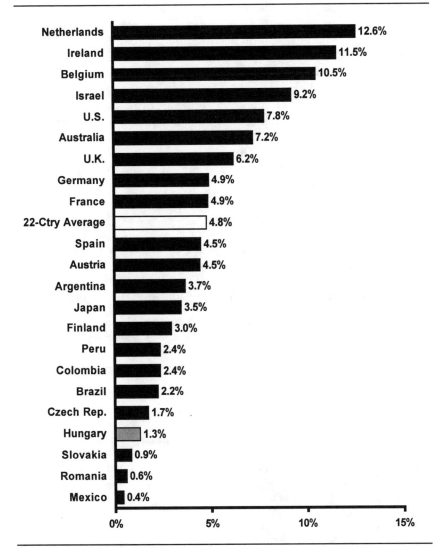

Figure 15.3 Nonprofit share of total employment, by country, 1995

to a low of 0.4 percent of total employment in Mexico. The overall 22-country average is close to 5 percent. This means that Hungary, at 1.3 percent, is well below the global average. However, it still clearly exceeds Mexico and two of its Central and Eastern European counterparts (Romania and Slovakia).

- **Above the Central and Eastern European average.** While it falls below the 22-country average, however, nonprofit employment as a share of total employment is still higher in Hungary than it is elsewhere in Central and Eastern Europe. Thus, as shown in Figure 15.4, full-time equivalent employment in nonprofit organizations in Hungary, at 1.3 percent of total employment, is proportionally nearly 20 percent greater than the Central and Eastern European average of 1.1 percent. The overall development of the Hungarian nonprofit sector has thus outpaced that of most of its Central and Eastern European counterparts, even though the Hungarian nonprofit sector is still smaller than the sector in Latin America, the other developing region included in this study.

3. A rich history of nonprofit activity

That the nonprofit sector is already relatively well developed in Hungary less than a decade after the fall of the Communist regime there in 1989 is very likely a product of the rich history that such institutions have had in this country despite the Communist interlude of 40 years.[6] This history includes:

- A strong tradition of "oppositional" voluntary movements, resulting from the historical role voluntary associations played in the fight for

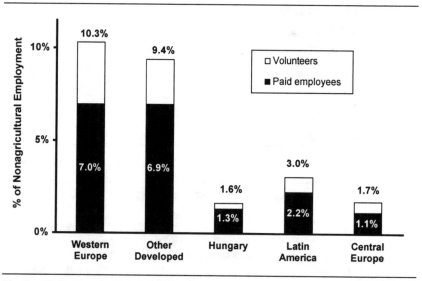

Figure 15.4   Nonprofit share of employment, with and without volunteers, Hungary and four regions, 1995

Hungarian political, economic, and cultural independence and for the preservation of national identity;

- The long-standing claim of voluntary organizations, as representatives of civil society and based on their "pioneer" role in the development of welfare services, to the right to influence and control social and economic policy and the use of public properties and government funds;
- An extensive system of cooperative partnerships between local governments and private foundations and supporters co-financing a variety of public welfare institutions that emerged in the first half of the 19th century and remained in force until the Second World War;
- The growth of the voluntary sector in the cultural and political arena beginning in the latter half of the 19th century after Hungary gained substantial autonomy from the Habsburg Empire;
- The partial toleration of certain types of cultural groupings and social organizations under the Communist regime, some of which developed into substitutes for political parties in the 1980s;
- A generally benign, though not always fully supportive, posture of the post-1989 governments; and
- A historically based flexibility of institutional choice in a survival-oriented society resulting in the mushrooming of nonprofit organizations aiming to find appropriate answers to the challenges of the transition period.

4. Culture and recreation dominance

Similar to other Central and Eastern European countries, but unlike the all-country average, culture and recreation organizations clearly dominate the nonprofit scene in Hungary, at least in terms of employment and command of resources.

- **Nearly 40 percent of nonprofit employment in culture and recreation.** Of all the types of nonprofit activity, the one that accounts for the largest share of nonprofit employment in Hungary is culture and recreation. As shown in Figure 15.5, 38 percent of all nonprofit employment in Hungary is in the culture and recreation field. (This share amounted to 64 percent in 1990.) This is even above the Central and Eastern European average of slightly less than 34 percent, but it greatly exceeds the 22-country average of 14 percent. This situation very likely reflects the heritage of the previous regime, as culture and recreation were among the few fields of social activity that were tolerated and even encouraged by the Communist state. Accordingly,

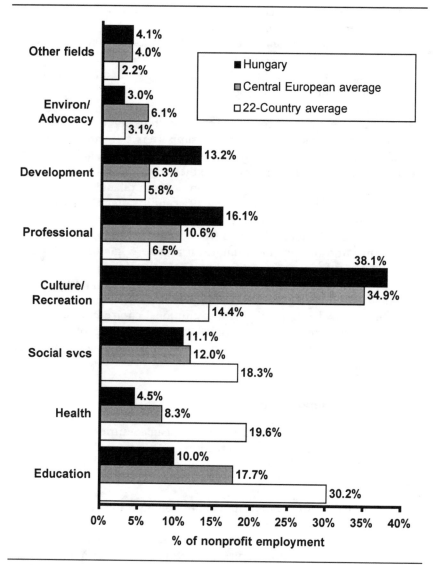

Figure 15.5   Composition of the nonprofit sector, Hungary, Central Europe, and
22-country average, 1995

nonprofit organizations established before 1990 account for about
two-thirds of the employment in culture and recreation, although they
represent only one-third the number of organizations. Nevertheless,
there are significant differences within this large culture and recreation group: the 'old' nonprofit organizations account for only 12 per-

cent of the employment in the culture subfield, but 75 and 84 percent, respectively, in the subfields of sports and recreation. These figures suggest that the culture subfield is dominated by newer organizations. Newly created nonprofits are also more numerous in sports and recreation, but they have not developed the economic weight of their counterparts established either in the state socialist period or even much before.

- **Sizable nonprofit presence in professional associations and unions.** Another sizable portion of total nonprofit employment in Hungary is in professional associations and unions. This field accounts for 16 percent of total nonprofit employment, which brings Hungary considerably above the 22-country average of 6 percent and even well above the Central European countries as a whole (10 percent). Similar to the culture and recreation field, the relative prevalence of professional associations and unions in Hungary and Central and Eastern Europe at large is another remnant of the previous Communist regime, where these institutions were party-controlled and as such strongly encouraged. Membership in professional groups and unions often also served as a prerequisite for preferential treatment, economic advancement, and even access to higher education. Nonetheless, the heritage of the state socialist period seems to be much weaker in the field of professional associations and unions than in sports and recreation. The share of the organizations created before 1990 is only 17 percent, and they account for only about 40 percent of the employees. Understandably enough, a great many new advocacy organizations, unions, and professional groups have emerged during the transition period that began in 1989, and they have significantly challenged the position of the old organizations.

- **Relatively smaller shares of nonprofit employment in the core welfare areas of health, social services, and education.** Compared to the overall 22-country average, education, health, and social services absorb only a relatively small share of nonprofit employment in Hungary. Thus, while these three fields absorb more than two-thirds of nonprofit employment on average, they account for only one-fourth of nonprofit employment in Hungary. This very likely reflects the chronic shortage of resources available to potential nonprofit entrepreneurs and also the greater willingness of Hungarians, and other Eastern and Central Europeans in general, to continue to rely on the state to provide these services. By the same token, it also reflects the greater reluctance of governments in this region to share core welfare responsibilities with the emerging nonprofit sector.

- **Strong nonprofit employment in housing and community development.** Compared to the employment in nonprofit social welfare, education, and health organizations, the share of Hungarian nonprofit employment in the development field is quite substantial. This field accounts for 13 percent of all nonprofit employees in Hungary, making it the third largest field of nonprofit employment after culture and recreation and professional associations and unions. What is more, the Hungarian employment share in this field is almost twice the global average. By contrast, the related fields of advocacy and environmental protection do not absorb much employment in Hungary. In fact, the 3 percent share in Hungary is on a par with the international average, but quite below the level of other Central and Eastern European countries. An additional 4 percent of nonprofit employees fall into other categories, including philanthropy and international activities.

- **Pattern remains constant with volunteers.** This pattern remains the same when volunteer inputs are factored in. In particular, as shown in Figure 15.6, with volunteers included, the shares of total paid and volunteer employment hardly change. In some fields, including culture and recreation, education, development, and professional associations and unions, the combined employment share drops slightly; while it gains some ground in social services and civic and advocacy.

An important ambiguity is thus evident in the structure of the nonprofit sector in Hungary, as it is in other Central and Eastern European countries. Indeed, the data show that the post-Communist nonprofit sector in this country still owes parts of its structure to the legacies of the previous regime. This is apparent in the relatively strong position of both culture and recreation and professional associations and unions in the employment base of the Hungarian nonprofit sector. Both fields constituted the realm of the allowed, and even encouraged, social organizations under Communism. Firmly controlled by party and state, membership was only formally voluntary, as many social and economic privileges were typically dependent on membership in such organizations. Altogether, these two fields account for more than half of total nonprofit employment—by far outdistancing employment in the new, post-Communist areas of nonprofit activity and civil society. The other striking implication of these data is that five years after the fall of the Berlin wall, the Hungarian nonprofit sector, as well as its other Central and Eastern European counterparts, while developing considerable strength, still has quite a way to go before it reaches the scale of similar institutions in Western Europe.

5. Most revenue from private fees, not philanthropy or the public sector

Consistent with the dominance of culture and recreation as well as professional associations and unions, typically fee-dependent fields, the Hun-

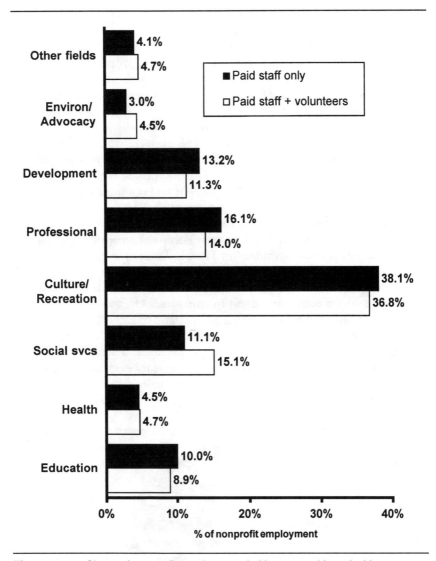

Figure 15.6 Share of nonprofit employment in Hungary, with and without volunteers, by field, 1995

garian nonprofit sector receives the bulk of its revenue not from private philanthropy or the government, but from private fees and charges. In particular:

- **Fee income dominant.** The overwhelmingly dominant source of income of nonprofit organizations in Hungary is private fees and charges. As reflected in Figure 15.7, this source alone accounts for more than half, or 55 percent, of all nonprofit revenue in Hungary.

- **Limited support from philanthropy and government.** By contrast, private philanthropy and government payments provide much smaller shares of total revenue. Thus, as Figure 15.7 shows, private philanthropy—from individuals, corporations, and foundations combined—accounts for 18 percent of nonprofit income in Hungary, while public sector payments account for 27 percent.

- **Revenue structure with volunteers.** This pattern of nonprofit revenue does not change significantly when volunteers are factored into the picture. In fact, as shown in Figure 15.8, public sector revenue declines from 27.1 percent to 26.2 percent and the private philanthropy proportion increases from 18.4 percent to 21.1 percent, but fee income still remains the largest revenue source.

- **Similar to other Central and Eastern European countries.** The pattern of nonprofit finance evident in Hungary is comparable to that elsewhere in Central and Eastern Europe. Thus, as shown in Figure 15.9, like Hungary, the nonprofit organizations in the Central and Eastern European countries included in this project derive on average the largest share of their revenues from fees and charges. Thus, compared to Hungary's 55 percent, the share of total nonprofit income coming from fees stands at 46 percent for the region as a whole. The philanthropy share of nonprofit revenue in Hungary deviates slightly from the regional average, with philanthropic income somewhat weaker in Hungary than elsewhere in the region (18 percent vs. 21 percent on av-

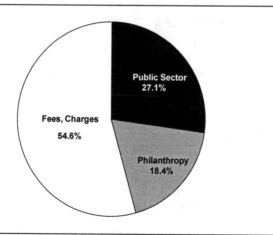

Figure 15.7 Sources of nonprofit revenue in Hungary, 1995

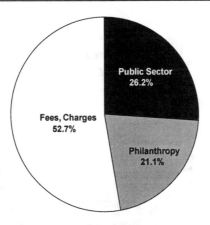

Figure 15.8 Sources of nonprofit revenue in Hungary, with volunteers, 1995

erage). Public sector payments as well are below the regional average (27 percent vs. 33 percent).

- **Deviation from the global average.** While the revenue structure of the Hungarian nonprofit sector generally mirrors that elsewhere in Central and Eastern Europe, it differs considerably from that evident elsewhere in the world. Thus, as Figure 15.9 also shows, while fees and charges are the dominant element in the financial base of the nonprofit sector globally, their dominance is still somewhat less pronounced than it is in Hungary (49 percent of total revenue compared to 55 percent). By contrast, public sector payments comprise a considerably larger share of nonprofit income in these other countries on average (40 percent vs. 27 percent in Hungary). On the other hand, the share of philanthropic income in Hungary, like in the region in general, is proportionally about 60 percent *greater* than the corresponding share of private giving in nonprofit revenue globally (18 percent vs. 11 percent). Quite clearly, a different pattern of cooperation has taken shape between nonprofit organizations and the state in these other countries. Although the government posture towards the sector is generally positive, the Hungarian nonprofit sector evidently has not yet established a full-fledged cooperative partnership with the state. Indeed, the sector has not taken over the provision of a significant part of state-financed welfare services, which would result in significantly higher public support, as is the case in Western Europe.
- **Variations by subsector.** Even this does not do full justice to the complexities of nonprofit finance in Hungary, however. This is so because

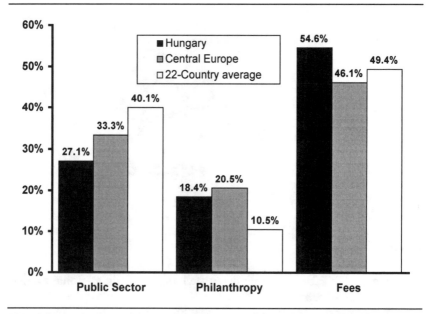

Figure 15.9   Sources of nonprofit cash revenue, Hungary, Central Europe, and 22-country average, 1995

important differences exist in the finances of nonprofit organizations by subsector. In fact, three quite distinct patterns of nonprofit finance are evident among Hungarian nonprofits, as shown in Figure 15.10:

Fee-dominant fields. Fee income is the dominant source of income in six of the fields of nonprofit action for which data were gathered. Professional organizations and unions, with 89 percent of their revenue from private fees, are essentially financed by membership dues and other earned income. In the environmental field, fees account for more than two-thirds of total income, which is explained by the fact that many environmental organizations provide pollution abatement and other environmental services, and also conduct feasibility studies for for-profit firms and public authorities. In culture and recreation and education, fees account for slightly more than half of total revenue, and in the development and housing and philanthropy fields for slightly less than half.

Public sector-dominant fields. In three other fields, government plays the dominant role in financing nonprofit action in Hungary. More specifically, public sector payments account for two-thirds of the revenue of organizations working internationally, and 55 percent in the case of

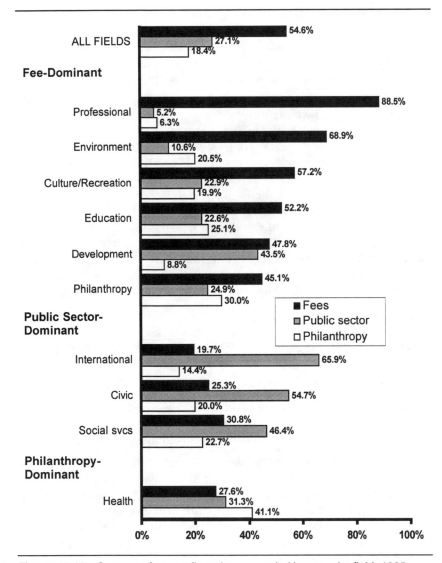

Figure 15.10 Sources of nonprofit cash revenue in Hungary, by field, 1995

civic and advocacy organizations. The nonprofit organizations in these fields that can firmly rely on government funds include Roma and other minority organizations, the Helsinki Committee, the international peace movement, organizations preparing for European integration, and sister city associations. In addition, there are some very large public foundations dealing with ethnic and minority problems that are generously supported by the state, as well. In social services, government support stands at nearly half of all revenues, or 46 percent. This is a significant development reflecting a new pattern of contracting out by government of important welfare services.

Philanthropy-dominant field. The only field of nonprofit activity in Hungary where private philanthropy provides the relatively largest share of revenue (though not the majority) is the health area. Private donations account for 41 percent of total revenue in this field, compared to 31 percent from public sector payments and 28 percent from private fees and charges. Since health is typically financed primarily by either fees or third-party payments from public health insurance funds worldwide, the Hungarian case is somewhat of an anomaly. The most likely explanation for this finding is that nonprofit health organizations have been especially active in the first years of transition in establishing foundations to raise private funds for public hospitals or special treatment of individuals or certain groups, while the development of service-providing nonprofit organizations in this field has been slower.

6. Change in the Hungarian nonprofit sector from 1990 to 1995

Not only does the Hungarian nonprofit sector represent a substantial economic force, it is also a significantly growing force. Indeed, the growth that has occurred between 1990 and 1995 has proved beyond any doubt that the nonprofit sector in Hungary is ever more firmly taking its place on the social, political, and economic map of this country. More specifically:

- **Strong economic growth.** Between 1990 and 1995, employment in the Hungarian nonprofit sector grew by 37 percent, adding the full-time equivalent of more than 12,000 new jobs to the 1990 employment base of slightly less than 33,000 full-time equivalent employees. In addition, adjusted for inflation, the operating expenditures of the sector doubled in this five-year period from HUF26 billion in 1990 to more than HUF52 billion in 1995.
- **Change in the composition.** While employment actually declined in the fields of culture and recreation and social services by 18 percent and 7 percent, respectively, it grew very substantially in all other fields. More specifically, employment grew by a factor of 7 in education, 17 in philanthropic intermediaries, 27 in health, and 112 in development and housing. Thus in the first half of the 1990s, the nonprofit sector in Hungary made significant progress towards establishing a stronger

presence in a much more varied range of fields than in the immediate aftermath of the revolution of 1989.

- **Change in the revenue base.** In the 1990 to 1995 period, the revenue composition of the Hungarian nonprofit sector also underwent change, although the overall revenue structure remained stable. Perhaps most significantly, public sector payments increased from 23 percent of total revenue in 1990 to 27 percent of a larger total in 1995. The shares of both private philanthropy and fees and charges, by contrast, decreased proportionally.

CONCLUSIONS AND IMPLICATIONS

The nonprofit sector thus emerges from the evidence presented here as an already important and complex set of institutions in Hungarian society. Not only does this set of institutions serve important human needs, it also constitutes a growing economic force and is a significant contributor to political and social life. To a certain extent, the Hungarian nonprofit sector is still marked by its pre-1989 heritage; but the newer parts of the sector are gaining ground, and the sector has begun to move into core service areas such as education, social care, health, and community development and housing. At the same time, however, this sector remains a fragile organism in Hungarian society and a number of problems remain. More specifically, these problem areas include:

- **The problem of legal and economic regulation.** The present regulation of the Hungarian nonprofit sector is a complicated set of particular and more or less contradictory laws and government decrees developed by different legislative and governmental bodies. Occasionally, the recommendations of the Supreme Court and the practices developed by individual county courts have more influence on the registration and tax treatment of nonprofits than the written law itself. Although a new nonprofit law was intended to resolve the inconsistency problems, it has in fact aggravated them and created new internal tensions within the regulatory framework and also within the nonprofit sector. This lack of consistent and comprehensive regulation is both dangerous and harmful. A correct, carefully thought out, generally known and accepted regulatory framework, as well as clear accounting rules and strict tax inspection would be prerequisites for solving other problems of the nonprofit sector.
- **Financial vulnerability.** The relatively low level of economic development together with the problems of the transition period have created an economic environment that makes Hungarian nonprofit organizations

financially fragile. The obvious dynamism and viability of the sector as a whole does not automatically translate into sustainability at the level of individual organizations. On the contrary, most nonprofit organizations suffer from financial uncertainty and from the lack of organizational maturity. In order to reform the welfare system and open the door for nonprofit service providers, the system of funding should also be reformed. For whoever is the service provider, one of the most important sources of financing public services is obviously the state budget. State support through grants, contracts, subsidies, statutory and fee-for-service payments, and/or indirect tax advantages is crucial for the development of the Hungarian nonprofit sector. The government is, however, rather ambivalent on this issue. While it welcomes nonprofit service providers and occasionally supports them, it still has not decided on a long-term strategy for developing a new welfare mix and an appropriate system of financing. Currently, the practice tends to be chaotic and contradictory. The tax system has been under "reconstruction" for several years, and the rules are changing continuously. Thus, tax advantages have not become a source of support on which voluntary organizations can firmly rely. As far as direct state support is concerned, the situation is not much clearer or better. Although the Anglo-Saxon so-called "arm's length" principle and the Western European subsidiarity principle are "imported" concepts and not rooted in the Hungarian political culture, they represent an attractive element of a recently developed vocabulary that perfectly fits the ideology, but not always the behavioral patterns and the everyday practice, of the government.

• **The problem of effectiveness and legitimacy.** In close connection with these economic difficulties, nonprofit organizations also face serious employment and efficiency problems. For lack of sufficient and stable funding, many nonprofits find it difficult to hire well-trained employees. The growth of nonprofit employment cannot keep pace with the general development of the sector. Consequently, the need for professionalization, for significantly improved management, and for proper accounting has remained an important challenge for the Hungarian nonprofit sector at large. These problems of effectiveness are in sharp contrast with the general rhetoric, the claim that the nonprofit sector is legitimated by its service provision role and the relatively high efficiency of these services. The frequently repeated, but poorly documented, statements about high effectiveness are thus not confirmed by everyday experience. Indeed, a great many nonprofit organizations are not able to fulfill their mission for lack of sufficient income, well-trained staff, and satisfactory infrastructure. Under these circumstances, solemn testimonies reflecting wishful thinking are likely to result in a legitimacy crisis.

- **Accountability problems and trustworthiness.** As a reaction to the strong government control under state socialism, Hungarian nonprofit organizations are extremely anxious regarding their independence and reluctant to disclose any financial or management information. However, this general insistence on secrecy creates a climate that is advantageous only for those organizations that misuse the nonprofit form, infringe professional and ethical norms or operate as tax shelters. The misbehavior of a small number of nonprofits can severely undermine the reputation of the nonprofit sector as a whole, and lost trustworthiness may significantly decrease donors' willingness to support voluntary initiatives. To build a mechanism of state scrutiny that could guarantee accountability and to develop self-regulatory schemes and ethical codes that would push nonprofit organizations toward more transparency are among the most urgent tasks to be undertaken.
- **Weak sectoral identity and insufficient cooperation within the sector.** An institutional field can gain collective identity if its members tend to move in concert. The lack of such coordinated movements is one of the most difficult problems in the Hungarian voluntary sector. The different roles nonprofit organizations play create some "natural" divisions between them. Advocacy groups frequently resent the pragmatism and opportunism of service-providers, while the latter think that their own activities are much more important and useful than the ones other nonprofits are engaged in. Recreation clubs and membership organizations feel neglected and discriminated against. There are tensions and conflicts between the old-fashioned, formerly government-controlled voluntary associations and the new institutions of civil society, between small and large organizations, and also between the heads of government-funded, foreign-funded, and grassroots organizations. Very few activists within smaller organizations seem to understand that their organizations belong to a sector and their problems probably can be solved only in cooperation with their counterparts. Developing identity and sector-wide cooperation is clearly a challenge that should be met in the very short run, because a nonprofit community divided by rivalry will not be able to represent civil society and cope with fiscal, economic, and legitimacy problems.

Recently, important headway has been made on many of these challenges, as it increasingly has become clear that civil society and the broad range of nongovernmental organizations in operation in Hungary have become an essential factor in the post-Communist evolution of society as well as in Hungary's ability to cope with the dynamics of the transition processes. Nevertheless, much remains to be done to enhance the maturation of the sector, increase its sustainability, and put it even more firmly on the social, economic, and political map of this country.

ENDNOTES

1. The results of the earlier phase of this work were reported in Éva Kuti, *The Nonprofit Sector in Hungary*, Vol. 2 of the Johns Hopkins Nonprofit Sector Series. Manchester, U.K.: Manchester University Press, 1996.

2. The work in Hungary was coordinated by Local Associates István Sebestény, Éva Kuti, and Ágnes Vajda. The team was aided, in turn, by a local advisory committee made up of eight prominent local leaders and researchers (see Appendix D for a list of committee members). The Johns Hopkins project was directed by Lester M. Salamon and Helmut K. Anheier and the Central and Eastern European portion of the work overseen by Stefan Toepler.

3. The definitions and approaches used in the project were developed collaboratively with the cooperation of the Hungarian researchers and researchers in other countries and were designed to be applicable to Hungary and the other project countries. For a full description of this definition and the types of organizations included, see Appendix A. For a full list of the other countries included, see Chapter 1 above and Lester M. Salamon and Helmut K. Anheier, *The Emerging Sector Revisited: A Summary, Revised Estimates* (Baltimore, MD: The Johns Hopkins Center for Civil Society Studies, 1999).

4. Technically, the more precise comparison is between nonprofit contribution to "value added" and gross domestic product. For the nonprofit sector, "value added" in economic terms essentially equals the sum of wages and the imputed value of volunteer time. On this basis, the nonprofit sector in Hungary accounted for 0.9 percent of total value added.

5. In Hungary, volunteering information was derived from an organizational, not a population, survey. The extent of volunteering, as reported here, is therefore likely to underestimate the total volunteering that is taking place in this country, since it covers only the volunteering for registered and surveyed organizations.

6. For further details, see Kuti, É., "Hungary," in Lester M. Salamon and Helmut K. Anheier, *Defining the Nonprofit Sector: A Cross-national Analysis*. Manchester, U.K.: Manchester University Press, 1997; and Kuti, É., *The Nonprofit Sector in Hungary*. Manchester, U.K.: Manchester University Press, 1996.

CHAPTER 16

Poland: A Partial View

Ewa Leś, Sławomir Nałęcz, Jan Jakub Wygnański,
Stefan Toepler, and Lester M. Salamon

BACKGROUND

When the independent trade union movement *Solidarność* (Solidarity) was born in the Polish city of Gdansk in 1980, it was perhaps among the earliest and most visible indications that the course of history in the entire region of Central and Eastern Europe was beginning to change. More specifically, the emergence of *Solidarność* signaled a new stage of civil society development across the region and was thus a harbinger of the processes that eventually led to the fall of the Berlin wall, the overthrow of the communist regimes, and the reunification of Europe. With political and economic freedoms re-instituted in Poland and the other former Soviet bloc countries a decade later, civil society and the nonprofit sector soon gained even firmer ground in Polish society, as this chapter will indicate.

The work presented here was carried out by a Polish research team at the KLON/JAWOR Database on NGOs (nongovernmental organizations) as part of a collaborative international inquiry, the Johns Hopkins Comparative Nonprofit Sector Project.[1] It thus offers ample opportunities both to capture local Polish circumstances and peculiarities and to compare and contrast them to those in other countries both in Central and Eastern

Global Civil Society: Dimensions of the Nonprofit Sector by Lester M. Salamon, Helmut K. Anheier, Regina List, Stefan Toepler, S. Wojciech Sokolowski and Associates. Baltimore, MD: Johns Hopkins Center for Civil Society Studies, 1999.

Europe and elsewhere in a systematic way.[2] However, work in Poland began at a later stage than in other project countries, and a more complete set of data was not yet ready for release as this volume went to press.

The present chapter thus reports on just one limited set of findings from this project, those relating to the size of the nonprofit sector in Poland and elsewhere. Importantly, the findings presented here are preliminary and remain subject to substantial revision and re-evaluation pending further research and analysis. Subsequent publications will go beyond this first cut, provide a broader empirical picture, fill in the historical, legal, and policy context of this sector, and also examine the impact that this set of institutions is having in Polish society. The data reported here draw heavily on the 1997 census of nonprofit organizations and the 1997 employment survey both of which were carried out by GUS, the Polish Central Statistical Office. Additional research work, including a giving and volunteering survey and supplementary oganizational survey conducted by the project team, will supplement and further extend these initial data. Unless otherwise noted, financial data are reported in U.S. dollars at the 1997 average exchange rate. (For a more complete statement of the types of organizations included, see Chapter 1 and Appendix A. For more detail on the methodology used, see Appendix C.)

PRELIMINARY FINDINGS

Keeping in mind the above caveat regarding the preliminary nature of the data, three initial findings emerge on the scope of the nonprofit sector in Poland:

1. A minor but growing economic force

In the first place, while its social and political impact has been substantial, the nonprofit sector remains a relatively modest economic force in Poland.

More specifically:

- **A modest employer.** Excluding religion, the Polish nonprofit sector employs nearly 91,000 full-time equivalent paid workers, which is a small but significant workforce. This figure represents 1 percent of nonagricultural paid employment in the country, 2.8 percent of service employment, and the equivalent of 1.9 percent of the government workforce at all levels (see Table 16.1).
- **More employees than in the largest private firm.** Although small, nonprofit employment in Poland still easily outdistances the employment

Table 16.1 The nonprofit sector in Poland, initial estimates, 1997

90,987 full-time equivalent paid employees
— 1.0 percent of total nonagricultural employment
— 2.8 percent of total service employment
— 1.9 percent of public employment

in the largest private business in the country, and does so by a ratio of 6:1. Thus, compared to the 98,387 paid workers (head count) in Polish nonprofit organizations, Poland's largest private corporation, Daewoo-FSO Ltd., employs only 15,797 workers (see Figure 16.1). Moreover, nonprofit employment in Poland exceeds the combined employment of the 14 largest private companies. On the other hand, employment in Polish NGOs is lower than it is in the largest state-owned enterprise, *PKP* (Polish Rail), with 243,472 workers, though it is on a par with the second largest public enterprise, *Poczta Polska* (the Polish Mail Service), with 98,000 workers.

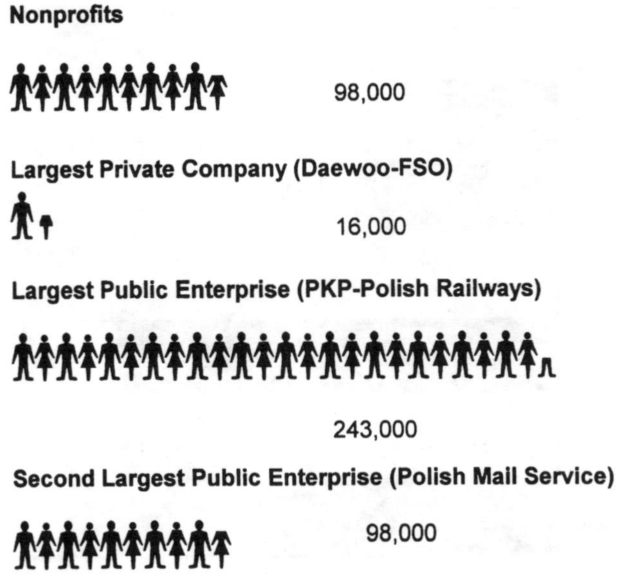

Nonprofits

98,000

Largest Private Company (Daewoo-FSO)

16,000

Largest Public Enterprise (PKP-Polish Railways)

243,000

Second Largest Public Enterprise (Polish Mail Service)

98,000

Figure 16.1 Employment (headcount) in nonprofits vs. largest private and public firms in Poland, 1997

- **On a par with several industries.** Compared to other industries, the size of the Polish nonprofit sector remains rather modest according to these initial estimates. Nevertheless, nonprofit employment in Poland is essentially on a par with the printing industry and outdistances a number of smaller industries, including the air transport, fishing, computer, research and development, forestry, and insurance industries.
- **Volunteer inputs.** A picture of the Polish nonprofit sector would not be complete without considering volunteering, for this sector attracts a considerable amount of *volunteer effort*. Indeed, an estimated 16 percent of the adult population reports contributing their time to nonprofit organizations. (If volunteering for religious institutions were included, this figure would increase to 25 percent.) Without religion, this translates into another 20,473 full-time equivalent employees, which boosts the total number of full-time equivalent employees of nonprofit organizations in Poland to 111,460, or 1.2 percent of total employment in the country (see Figure 16.2).
- **Religion.** The inclusion of religion, moreover, would boost these totals by another 27,564 paid employees and 8,381 full-time equivalent volunteers. With religion included, nonprofit employment therefore rises to 1.3 percent of total paid employment and to 1.5 percent of to-

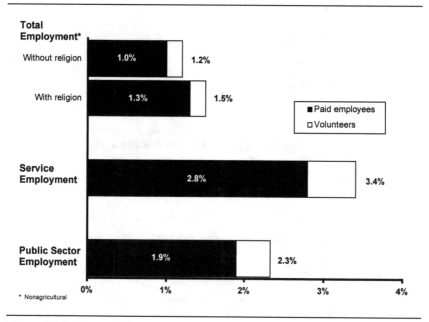

Figure 16.2   Nonprofit employment in Poland in context, 1997

tal paid and volunteer employment. The influence of religion on the Polish nonprofit sector, however, extends even further. Indeed, Catholic Church-affiliated service providers account for approximately one-third of nonprofit employment without religion.

The Polish nonprofit sector in the 1990s thus emerges from these preliminary findings as a modest, but still significant economic force both in terms of employment and volunteer input. This is so despite severe limitations, such as an unfavorable ideological environment, legal and financial restrictions, and socio-economic barriers that prevented citizens from active involvement in public initiatives for half a century (1947–1989).

2. A mid-sized nonprofit sector for Central Europe

Although the Polish nonprofit sector is still fairly small in relation to the overall Polish economy and to its counterparts in Western Europe, it is close to the level of other Central European countries.

- **Considerably below the international average.** As Figure 16.3 shows, the relative size of the nonprofit sector varies greatly among countries, from a high of 12.6 percent of total nonagricultural employment in the Netherlands to a low of 0.4 percent of total employment in Mexico. The overall 22-country average (calculated without these initial Polish data), however, was close to 5 percent. This means that Poland, with 1 percent without religion, falls considerably below the global average.
- **Almost on par with the Central and Eastern European average.** While it falls below the 22-country average, nonprofit employment as a share of total employment in Poland occupies a middle position among the Central and Eastern European countries studied. Thus, as shown in Figure 16.4, full-time equivalent employment in Polish nonprofit organizations, with 1 percent of total employment, is only slightly below the 1.1 percent average of the other four Central and Eastern European countries (the Czech Republic, Hungary, Romania, and Slovakia). Indeed, as a share of total employment, nonprofit employment in Poland exceeds that in two of the Central and Eastern European countries covered in this project—Romania (0.6 percent) and Slovakia (0.9 percent).
- **Margin widens with volunteers.** The margin between Poland and the other Central and Eastern European countries widens, however, when volunteers are added. Thus, with volunteer time included, nonprofit organizations account for 1.2 percent of total employment in Poland, but 1.7 percent on average in the other four Central and Eastern European countries (see Figure 16.4).

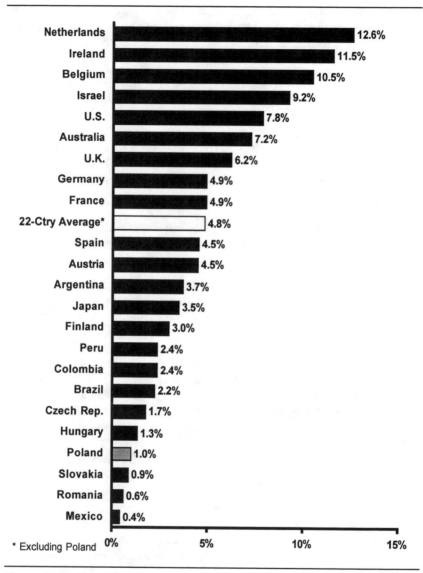

Figure 16.3   Nonprofit share of total employment, by country, 1995

3. A rich and complex history of nonprofit activity

That the Polish nonprofit sector has reached a substantial degree of de-velopment during the period since 1989 and despite the severe restrictions it faced under communism is, in no small part, a result of the long, rich

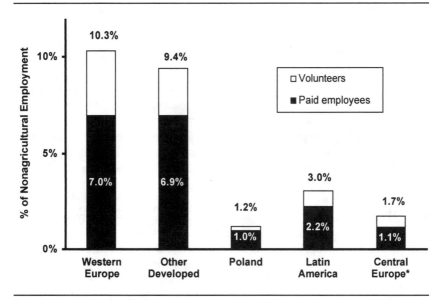

Figure 16.4 Nonprofit share of employment, with and without volunteers, in Poland and four regions, 1995

and, at times, complicated history that citizens' initiatives have experienced in this country over the past 1,000 years. In other words, Poland's current nonprofit sector is as much the result of cultural and institutional experiences accumulated during many centuries as it is the product of the deterioration of the Communist welfare state and the political breakthrough of 1989.

More specifically, from the Middle Ages to the end of the 18th century, when Poland lost its sovereignty, two key traditions shaped the evolution of voluntary activity in this country: first, religious charity and philanthropy fostered by the Catholic Church; and second, a more secular welfare tradition marked by interventions and contributions of the aristocracy and the municipalities beginning in the late 14th century. Both traditions remained intact during the following period of partition from 1795 to 1918. However, with Poland divided among, and ruled by, the neighboring empires, a new ethos of independence and patriotic inspiration developed that became crucial in bolstering national identity and the organization of Polish society against, and in spite of, the hegemonic rule of the foreign powers.

Significantly, the independence movement in the 19th century was cultivated and housed by the Roman Catholic Church as well as secular nonprofit organizations and thus emerged closely interdependent with the prior traditions. This pattern, moreover, would continue to hold throughout the most critical times of Polish history in the 20th century, including the Nazi occupation during World War II and the Communist takeover thereafter. Not surprisingly, it forcefully re-emerged in the late 1970s, giving birth to the Solidarity trade union movement in 1980–81. The remarkable renaissance of nonprofit organizations in Poland after 1989 would not have been possible without the joint effort of the religious and secular formal and informal networks rooted in the Christian tradition, the humane inspirations of the Enlightenment period, and the ethos of independence. In all of this, the Roman Catholic Church played a crucial role. In many ways, the fact that about one-third of paid nonprofit employment is in church-related organizations today can be seen as the result and legacy of the Church's influence dating back to the 11th century.

That the nonprofit sector in Poland has not developed even further since 1989 is due to a variety of factors. After 1989, pressures from below—spontaneous, grassroots initiatives—made the most crucial contributions to building the institutional capacity of the Polish nonprofit sector. However, attempts to establish a larger scale nonprofit service delivery infrastructure that would necessitate a greater employment base remained hindered by the continued monopolistic position of the state in fields such as social services, education, and health care. Moreover, insofar as strategies for de-monopolizing the public welfare sphere were discussed throughout the 1990s, the decision-makers favored commercial privatization over what might be termed "socialization," that is, the transfer of welfare service delivery into the nonprofit sector.

The further growth of the sector therefore depends to a large part on whether the state will show a greater willingness to transfer parts of its public welfare programs to nonprofit providers and provide a more enabling environment for citizens' activities. At the same time, it is worth noting that the relatively modest share of nonprofit employment must also be seen against the background of the larger privatization context: The private business sector so far only accounts for about half of the total Polish economy. Thus, while the Polish nonprofit sector may seem small compared to its Western counterparts, a similar point could be made about the whole private economy in this country.

CONCLUSIONS AND IMPLICATIONS

The nonprofit sector thus emerges from the evidence presented here as a sizable set of institutions in Polish society. The remarkable upsurge in the formation of citizens' organizations in Poland after 1989 is without question one of the most salient outcomes of the transition. By the same token, it is also an expression of the intensity of the pent-up demand for public participation that existed in Polish society between 1947 and 1989 and the willingness of citizens to take active part in the process of establishing a new political, economic, and social order after the breakthrough of 1989.

However, the renaissance of the nonprofit sector in this country turned out to be a complex process, as the still limited economic position of the sector after almost a decade of transition clearly indicates. On the one hand, further analysis will show that the scope and structure of the Polish nonprofit sector in the 1990s still reflect the limitations and the priorities that the Communist regime designed for citizens' activities. On the other hand, the current development level of the sector also shows the unexpectedly slow pace of the institutionalization of nonprofit organizations as service providers and guardians of the public interest.

To some degree, this is due to the ambiguous policies towards this set of institutions pursued by the various political coalitions in power after 1989. To be sure, at the most fundamental level, there was a firm consensus among all political elite that voluntary organizations are an indispensable element of a democratic system. This consensus was enshrined in those parts of the general legal framework that guarantee the principles that underpin nonprofit organizations, especially the freedom of expression and the freedom of association. After these general principles were put in place, however, there was considerably less eagerness on the part of subsequent governments to establish a sound legal and financial basis for nonprofit organizations to deliver public services and advocate for public causes.

The evolution of the Polish nonprofit sector since 1989 thus did not proceed without paradoxes and, in many ways, remains unfinished. Among the most striking paradoxes is that the government continues to overlook these organizations as meaningful social partners in service delivery and in formulating public policy agendas despite the Solidarity trade union movement's crucial role in the rebirth of parliamentary democracy and the market economy in Poland. Also under-recognized is the inherent capacity of the sector to complement and enhance government service provision. In addition to the often highly unpredictable and at times chaotic government policies towards the sector that seem to seriously endanger the role of nonprofits in society, other crucial external and internal challenges include:

- **Privatization, as opposed to "socialization," of the public welfare system.** While the importance of the nonprofit sector for democratic development, as previously noted, is recognized in general terms, its role as a full-fledged *partner* of both central and local governments in service delivery has not yet been fully embraced by the political elite. Indeed, in the neo-liberal strategy adopted by the Polish government to reconstruct the state welfare system and reduce state assistance, priority has been given to the "privatization" of the welfare system through market and quasi-market institutions at the expense of a "socialization" of state welfare through greater involvement of the nonprofit sector.

- **Fostering legitimacy through self-regulation.** Although the development and enforcement of codes of conduct, accountability, and administrative standards are of critical importance, in reality, the impact of such rules is not yet strong enough to discourage misconduct and dishonest practices firmly.

- **Capacity building and sustainability.** Over the first few years after 1989, Polish nonprofit organizations developed some 300 networks and umbrella groups at both the local and national level. The Forum of Non-Governmental Initiatives, the Union of Catholic Associations and Movements, and the Union of Social Service Non-Profit Organizations are the most prominent examples of such national umbrella organizations. Despite this substantial sectoral infrastructure, however, most nonprofit organizations in Poland still do not identify themselves as part of a separate "third sector," and have not perceived the need for self-organization, which is one of the key issues in establishing financial sustainability for the sector. In Poland, as in other countries of Central and Eastern Europe, it is thus crucially important to continue to develop training programs and capacity-building efforts to enhance the professionalization of nonprofit organizations. In addition, constant efforts are needed to promote and strengthen voluntary activity as well as to build meaningful relationships with the corporate sector.

Taken together, these external and internal challenges can potentially severely impede the nonprofit sector's ability to address social issues, meet human needs, and prevent the social marginalization of minority groups as well as the fragmentation of Polish society. The lack of resources has slowed the efforts of nonprofit organizations to mitigate rapidly growing social and economic inequalities and, more generally, to bridge the gap between the profound pressures society is confronted with and the shrinking role of the public sector. It is hoped that the kind of data generated within this project will help overcome these hurdles and finally allow Polish society to fully tap into the potentials of the nonprofit sector in this period of major social and economic change.

ENDNOTES

1. The work in Poland is coordinated by Local Associates Ewa Leś (University of Warsaw) and Jan Jakub Wygnański (KLON/JAWOR), who were assisted by Sławomir Nałęcz at KLON/JAWOR. The team was aided, in turn, by a local advisory committee made up of 14 prominent academics, government and parliament officials, and nonprofit leaders (see Ap-

pendix D for a list of committee members). The Johns Hopkins project was directed by Lester M. Salamon and Helmut K. Anheier and the Central and Eastern European portion of the work overseen by Stefan Toepler.

2. The definitions and approaches used in the project were developed collaboratively with the cooperation of the Polish researchers and researchers in other countries and were designed to be applicable to Poland and the other project countries. For a full description of this definition and the types of organizations included, see Appendix A. For a full list of the other countries included, see Chapter 1 above and Lester M. Salamon and Helmut K. Anheier, *The Emerging Sector Revisited: A Summary, Revised Estimates* (Baltimore, MD: The Johns Hopkins Center for Civil Society Studies, 1999).

CHAPTER 17

Romania

Daniel Saulean, Dan Stancu, Carmen Epure,
Stefan Constantinescu, Simona Luca, Adrian Baboi Stroe,
Oana Tiganescu, Bogdan Berianu, Stefan Toepler, and
Lester M. Salamon

BACKGROUND

Remaining largely a rural and economically less developed society far into the 20th century, the Eastern European country of Romania endured a particularly oppressive and stringent dictatorship during the Communist era. After the fall of the Ceauşescu regime in 1989, civil society reemerged vigorously, but remained hampered economically by a lack of domestic resources and an outdated and insufficient legal framework. The Romanian nonprofit sector thus has not yet been able to fully reach the level of its Central European counterparts.

The findings presented here are the product of work carried out by a Romanian research team hosted by the Civil Society Development Foundation (CSDF) in Bucharest, as part of the Johns Hopkins Comparative Nonprofit Sector Project.[1] It thus offered ample opportunities both to capture local Romanian circumstances and peculiarities and to compare and contrast them to those in other countries both in Central and Eastern Europe and elsewhere in a systematic way.[2]

The present chapter reports on just one set of findings from this project, those relating to the size of the nonprofit sector in Romania and elsewhere.

Global Civil Society: Dimensions of the Nonprofit Sector by Lester M. Salamon, Helmut K. Anheier, Regina List, Stefan Toepler, S. Wojciech Sokolowski and Associates. Baltimore, MD: Johns Hopkins Center for Civil Society Studies, 1999.

Subsequent publications will fill in the historical, legal, and policy context of this sector and also examine the impact that this set of institutions is having. The data reported here draw heavily on a National Nongovernmental Organization (NGO) Census conducted by the Civil Society Development Foundation, surveying the known universe of Romanian nonprofit organizations. Unless otherwise noted, financial data are reported in U.S. dollars at the 1995 average exchange rate. (For a more complete statement of the sources of data, see Appendix C. For a more complete statement of the types of organizations included, see Chapter 1 and Appendix A.)

PRINCIPAL FINDINGS

Five major findings emerge from this work on the scope, structure, financing, and role of the nonprofit sector in Romania:

1. A still-developing economic force

In the first place, aside from its social and political importance, the nonprofit sector turns out to be a small but developing economic force in Romania. More specifically:

- **A $90 million industry.** In 1995, the nonprofit sector in Romania had operating expenditures of $90.3 million (ROL183 billion), or 0.3 percent of the country's gross domestic product, a quite modest amount though impressive in light of the constraints that limited the development of these organizations until quite recently.[3]
- **An important employer.** Behind these expenditures lies a workforce that includes the equivalent of 37,000 full-time equivalent paid workers. This represents 0.6 percent of all nonagricultural workers in the country, 1.2 percent of service employment, and the equivalent of almost one percent of the workforce of government at all levels— national and local (see Table 17.1).
- **More employees than in the largest private firm.** Significantly, even in its relatively embryonic form, nonprofit employment in Romania outdistances the employment in the largest private business in the country, and does so by about 30 percent. Thus, compared to the 37,000 paid workers in Romania's nonprofit organizations, Romania's largest private company, Dacia S.A.—a manufacturer of machinery, equipment, and furniture—employs only 29,000 workers (see Figure 17.1).
- **Outdistances some industries.** Indeed, as many people work in the nonprofit sector in Romania as in some entire branches of industry within the country. Thus, nonprofit employment in Romania matches, or even outdistances, employment in industries such as tobacco; paper

Table 17.1   The nonprofit sector in Romania, 1995

$ 90.3 million in expenditures
— 0.3 percent of GDP

37,353 paid employees
— 0.6 percent of total nonagricultural employment
— 1.2 percent of total service employment
— 0.9 percent of public employment

and cardboard manufacturing; crude oil processing; coal and nuclear fuel treatment; chemical and synthetic fiber manufacturing; radio, TV, and communication equipment; medical, precision, and optical equipment; and water collection, treatment, and distribution.

- **Volunteer inputs.** This does not capture the full scope of the nonprofit sector in Romania, however, for the sector also attracts a considerable amount of *volunteer effort*. Indeed, according to representative national surveys on philanthropic behavior undertaken by CSDF in association with the Center for Urban and Regional Sociology in Bucharest, this volunteer effort translates into another 46,000 full-time equivalent employees, which more than doubles the total number of full-time equivalent employees of nonprofit organizations in Romania to close to 84,000 or 1.3 percent of total nonagricultural employment in the country[4] (see Figure 17.2).

2. The smallest nonprofit sector in Eastern and Central Europe

Not only is the Romanian nonprofit sector still fairly small in relation to the Romanian economy, but it is also small relative to its counterparts elsewhere around the world. So far, it has even lagged somewhat behind the

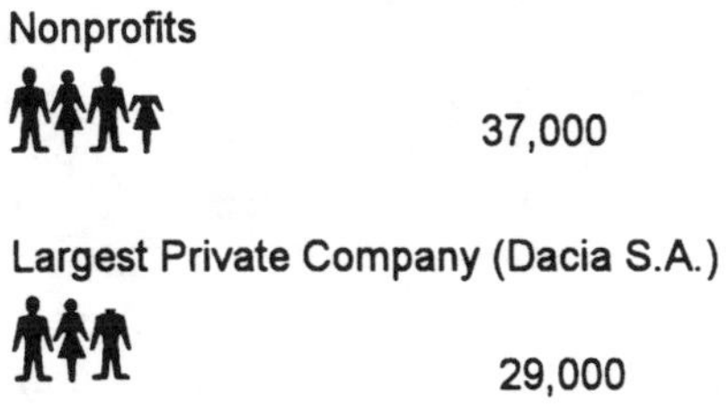

Nonprofits

37,000

Largest Private Company (Dacia S.A.)

29,000

Figure 17.1   Employment in nonprofits vs. largest private firm in Romania, 1995

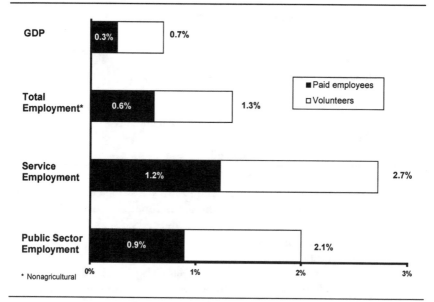

Figure 17.2   Nonprofits in Romania, with and without volunteers, 1995, as a % of . . .

level in the other Eastern and Central European countries included in this study.

- **Significantly below the international average.** As Figure 17.3 shows, the relative size of the nonprofit sector varies greatly among countries, from a high of 12.6 percent of total nonagricultural employment in the Netherlands to a low of 0.4 percent of total employment in Mexico. The overall 22-country average is close to 5 percent. At 0.6 percent, employment in the Romanian nonprofit sector is one of the lowest of all the countries studied. However, it is somewhat higher than in Mexico and is not much below the Slovakian share.
- **Lagging behind the Eastern and Central European average.** In addition to falling significantly below the 22-country average, the nonprofit share of total employment in Romania is also considerably lower than it is elsewhere in Eastern and Central Europe. Thus, as shown in Figure 17.4, full-time equivalent employment in nonprofit organizations in Romania, at 0.6 percent of total employment, is only slightly more than half of the Eastern and Central European average of 1.1 percent. This appears to be, in part, a reflection of the fact that the overall development of the Romanian economy has not kept pace with that of its Central European counterparts.

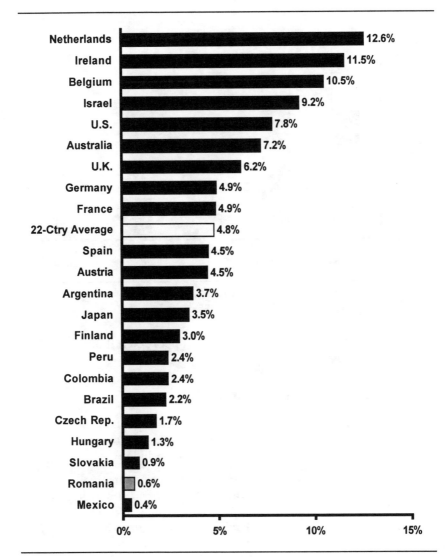

Figure 17.3   Nonprofit share of total employment, by country, 1995

- **Margin narrows with volunteers.** This margin narrows considerably, however, when volunteers are added. Thus, with volunteer time included, nonprofit organizations account for 1.3 percent of total employment in Romania, which is considerably closer to the regional average of 1.7 percent (see Figure 17.4). What this suggests is that Romanian

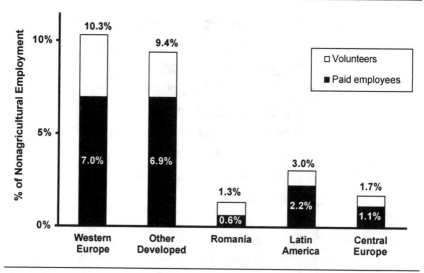

Figure 17.4   Nonprofit share of employment, with and without volunteers, Romania and four regions, 1995

nonprofits enjoy considerable popular support even though they lack economic resources.

3. A troubled history of nonprofit activity

That the nonprofit sector is relatively underdeveloped in Romania is very likely a product of the troubled history of this country and its philanthropic and nonprofit institutions.[5] This history includes:

- The precarious geopolitical position that Romania maintained essentially until the 20th century, which left the territories with predominantly Romanian populations politically divided and ruled from the outside in the shifting power balances of the neighboring Austro-Hungarian, Ottoman, and Russian empires;
- The traditionally rural and atomistic organization of Romanian society and economy that hindered the modernization of the Romanian territories until late in the 19th century;
- The prevalence of the Orthodox Church, which, unlike the Catholic Church in Western and Central Europe, failed to foster the notion of charity and the responsibility of individuals to take on a significant role in social affairs;
- The late unification of all predominantly Romanian territories, which occurred only after the First World War. The development of a

nascent democracy and civil society during the inter-war period ended soon again with the abolition of parliamentary pluralism in 1938, military rule during World War II, and the subsequent Communist takeover; and

- The extreme economic policies and political suppression of the totalitarian Communist regime under Nicolae Ceaușescu, which left the country resource-poor and with a severely shattered economic and social structure after the revolution of 1989.

4. Culture and recreation dominance

Similar to other Eastern and Central European countries, but unlike the all-country average, the culture and recreation field clearly dominates the nonprofit scene in Romania.

- **Thirty-four percent of nonprofit employment in culture and recreation.** Of all the types of nonprofit activity, the one that accounts for the largest share of nonprofit employment in Romania is culture and recreation. As shown in Figure 17.5, 34 percent of all nonprofit employment in Romania is concentrated in the culture and recreation field. This is almost exactly on par with the Eastern and Central European average of 35 percent, but greatly exceeds the 22-country average of 14 percent. This situation very likely reflects aspects of the heritage of the previous regime, as culture and recreation were among the few fields of social activity tolerated and even encouraged by the Communist state.
- **Sizable nonprofit presence in social services.** Another sizable portion of total nonprofit employment in Romania is in the social service field. Altogether, this field accounts for one-fifth, or 21 percent, of total nonprofit employment, which puts Romania slightly ahead of the 22-country average of 18 percent, and also represents a much stronger presence than in Central and Eastern Europe on average (12 percent). This very likely reflects, in part, the extraordinary social needs of groups, such as orphans and the elderly, burdened by the extreme economic distress and hardship caused by Romania's slow and hesitant progress towards economic restructuring and political liberalization. As a result, important segments of the Romanian NGO scene have emerged in an attempt to offer an appropriate response to these urgent social needs.
- **Relatively smaller shares of nonprofit employment in education and health, and in professional associations.** Compared to the overall 22-country average, education and health absorb a smaller share of nonprofit employment in Romania. Thus, while these two fields absorb al-

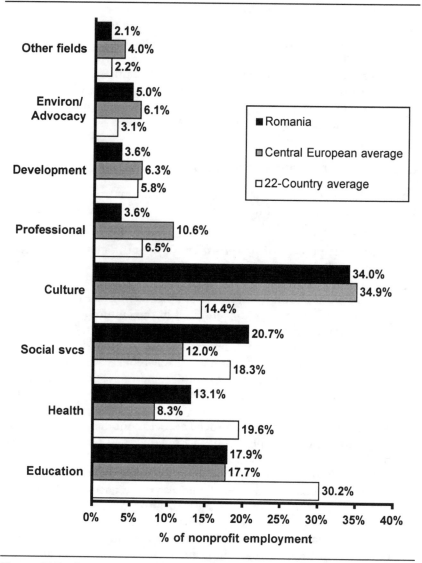

Figure 17.5 Composition of the nonprofit sector, Romania, Central Europe, and 22-country average, 1995

most half of nonprofit employment on average within the 22 project countries, they account for only 31 percent of nonprofit employment in Romania. This very likely reflects the continued position of dominance that the state has maintained in these two crucial service areas. Romania also shows a relatively small share of employment in professional associations (comprising 3.6 percent of total nonprofit employment), which stands in contrast to the regional pattern in which professional associations and unions typically constitute a relative stronghold of nonprofit activity. This stronghold typically exists because, like cultural and recreational organizations, professional associations were historically tolerated, and even encouraged, by the Communist regime. While trade unions and professional associations do have relatively high membership rates in Romania, employment in these organizations nevertheless remains relatively small. This is mostly due to a chronic deficiency of resources that all organizations in this field suffer and the absence of any material support from the state. In addition, unions, for the most part only present in large state-owned corporations, typically work to maintain their position and status within the context of their individual enterprises. These unions focus primarily on solving concrete work-related problems for which dedicated and professional staff is less needed.

- **Average share of nonprofit development and advocacy employment.** Compared to the nonprofit employment in the fields of culture and recreation, social welfare, education, and health, the share of Romanian nonprofit employment in the development field and in the related fields of advocacy and environmental protection is considerably smaller. Altogether, these fields absorb close to 9 percent of all nonprofit employment in the country, essentially on par with the 22-country average of 8.9 percent, but considerably less than the Central European average of 12 percent. An additional 2 percent of nonprofit employees fall into other categories, including philanthropy and international activities.
- **Pattern shifts with volunteers.** This pattern changes considerably when volunteer inputs are factored in. In particular, as shown in Figure 17.6, with volunteers included, the social services share of total nonprofit employment rises dramatically, from one-fifth to almost one-third of the total. In fact, the social services field attracts close to 42 percent of all volunteering in this country. Again this is a reflection of the extreme social and humanitarian needs that arose as a result of Romania's economic and political transition and the evident willingness of Romanian citizens to pitch in voluntarily to help. The two other fields that disproportionately benefit from volunteer labor are the environment, which boosts its share of employment from less than 1 percent to slightly more than 2 percent, and international activities, which goes from 1 percent to 4 percent.

An important ambiguity is thus evident in the structure of the nonprofit sector in Romania that is in some respects similar to that in other Eastern and Central European countries. This is apparent in the relatively strong position of the culture and recreation field in the employment base of the

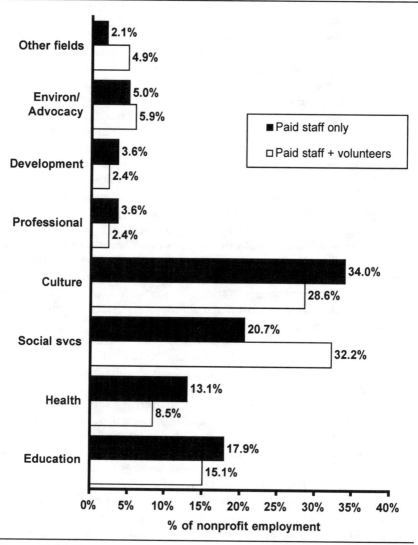

Figure 17.6   Share of nonprofit employment in Romania, with and without
volunteers, by field, 1995

Romanian nonprofit sector. Culture and recreation represent a larger
share of nonprofit employment in Romania than in the combined fields of
education and health—two of the core constituents of nonprofit activity
throughout the world. This is a reflection of the fact that cultural, sports,
and hobby activities were among the only social activities tolerated, and

even supported, by the Communist regime. In contrast to the Central European countries studied in this project, however, professional associations and unions—remnants of the Communist era that play an important role in the composition of Eastern and Central European nonprofit sectors—constitute only a relatively small part of nonprofit employment in Romania. This special characteristic of the Romanian nonprofit sector must be understood in the context of the extreme brutality and oppressiveness of the Ceauşescu regime, which left Romanians even more distrusting of social institutions than the citizens of other countries in the region.

The harshness of Communist totalitarianism in Romania—aiming at the near total destruction of the traditional social and economic bases of Romanian society—also led to the economic collapse and severe pauperization of Romania after 1989. With an economy in deep recession and state social welfare expenditures, in real terms, falling considerably behind the pre-1989 levels, a domestic resource base to sustain the nascent, re-emerging civil society was essentially lacking. This, in turn, helps to explain why the Romanian nonprofit sector did not reach the same level of development as its Central European counterparts.

5. Most revenue from international public sector sources, not philanthropy or fees

It is not surprising that the Romanian nonprofit sector receives the bulk of its revenue not from private philanthropy, the Romanian government, or even private fees or payments, but from international public sector sources. In particular:

- **International public sector income dominant.** The dominant source of income of nonprofit organizations in Romania is provided by international government sources, including the European Union, the United States, and a broad range of other mostly Western European countries. As reflected in Figure 17.7, total public sector support alone accounts for almost half (45 percent), of all nonprofit revenue in Romania. The share of domestic public sector payments, however, is less than 7 percent, a mere fraction of the assistance provided by international governments.
- **Limited support from philanthropy and fees.** By contrast, both private philanthropy and fee income provide much smaller shares of total revenue. Thus, as Figure 17.7 shows, private philanthropy—from individuals, corporations, and foundations combined—accounts for 26.5 percent of nonprofit income in Romania, while fees account for 28.5 percent.
- **Total international support accounts for more than half of revenue.** A significant share of the private philanthropy received by Romanian

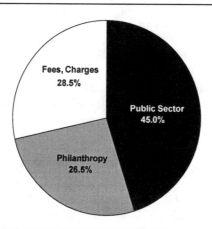

Figure 17.7   Sources of nonprofit revenue in Romania, 1995

nonprofits comes from international funders, as well, including the Soros Foundation and other private foundations outside of Romania. Including this private international aid, over half of Romanian nonprofit income comes from foreign sources.

- **Revenue structure with volunteers.** This pattern of nonprofit revenue changes dramatically, however, when volunteers are factored into the picture. In fact, as shown in Figure 17.8, with volunteers included, private philanthropy increases from slightly more than one-quarter (26.5

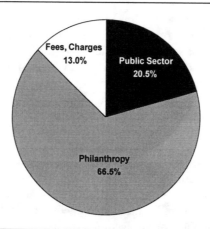

Figure 17.8   Sources of nonprofit revenue in Romania, with volunteers, 1995

percent) of Romanian nonprofit income to two-thirds (66.5 percent), thereby clearly overtaking both fee income, which drops from 28.5 percent to 13 percent, as well as public sector support, which decreases from almost half (45 percent) to only one-fifth of total revenue. This again reflects the considerable voluntary energy that has been tapped by the Romanian nonprofit sector.

- **Different from other Eastern and Central European countries.** The pattern of nonprofit finance evident in Romania differs significantly from that elsewhere in Eastern and Central Europe. Thus, as shown in Figure 17.9, unlike Romania, the nonprofit organizations in the Central European project countries (the Czech Republic, Hungary, and Slovakia) derived the largest share of their revenue from fees. Thus, compared to Romania's 29 percent, the share of total nonprofit income coming from fees stood at 46 percent for the Eastern and Central European countries on average. The public sector and private philanthropy shares of nonprofit revenue in Romania also deviate from the regional average, with both types of income comprising higher shares in Romania than elsewhere in the region (private philanthropy constitutes 27 percent in Romania vs. 21 percent on average

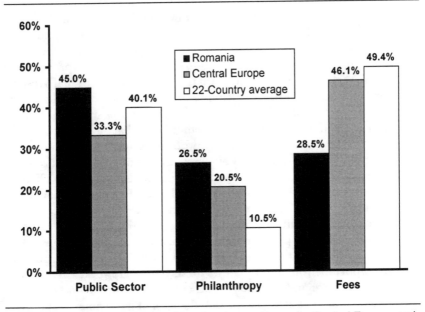

Figure 17.9 Sources of nonprofit cash revenue, Romania, Central Europe, and 22-country average, 1995

in Central Europe; and public sector support constitutes 45 percent in Romania vs. 33 percent on average in Central Europe). Clearly, the deviation of the Romanian revenue profile from the regional pattern results from the extreme scarcity of domestic resources and the concomitant disproportionately strong share of international public and private support.

- **Deviation from the global average.** Not only does the revenue structure of the Romanian nonprofit sector generally differ from that elsewhere in Eastern and Central Europe, but it also differs considerably from that evident elsewhere in the world. Thus, as Figure 17.9 also shows, while fees and charges are the dominant element in the financial base of the nonprofit sector globally, their importance is considerably less pronounced in Romania (49 percent of total revenue on average in the 22 project countries compared to 29 percent in Romania). By contrast, the share of private philanthropy in Romania is more than twice the global average (27 percent in Romania vs. 11 percent globally); and the share of public sector payments is also notably higher. As noted before, this deviation from the global average largely reflects the resource poverty within Romania and the presence of foreign support.

- **Variations by subsector.** This overall pattern of nonprofit finance operates in almost all fields in Romania, as shown in Figure 17.10:

  Public sector-dominant field. In all but two fields (professional associations and development), government sources play the dominant role in financing nonprofit action in Romania. Again, this is a reflection of the significant role that international public support—provided by multilateral agencies as well as a large number of individual Western countries—plays in the financing of the nonprofit sector in Romania. Substantial assistance flows into core welfare services such as health, social care, and education, as well as other fields that have gained importance in the Eastern and Central European context. In the case of the philanthropy field, the nearly 50 percent share of government revenue is a result of the fact that Western governments occasionally channel their assistance through local intermediaries. In the base year, 1995, before the establishment of the Civil Society Development Foundation, for example, significant funds provided by the European Union's PHARE assistance program were distributed by the International Management Foundation in Bucharest. Fees and private philanthropy play an important role among all of these fields. However, in only two fields—culture and recreation, and civic and advocacy—do these two revenue sources begin to approach the level of government support.

  Fee-dominant field. Fee income is the dominant source of income in one of the fields of nonprofit action for which data were gathered. Pri-

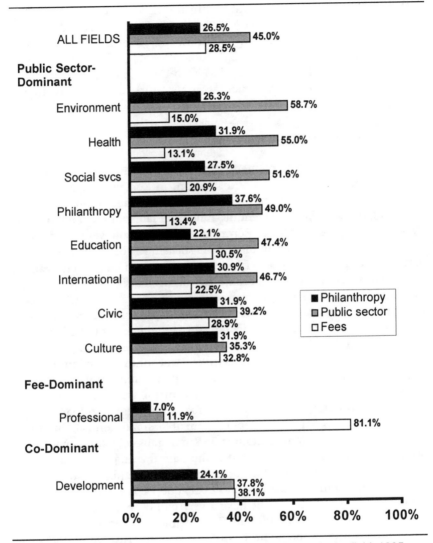

Figure 17.10 Sources of nonprofit cash revenue in Romania, by field, 1995

vate fees constitute 81 percent of total revenue within professional organizations and unions; these fees essentially consist of membership dues and other earned income.

Co-dominant field. In the development and housing field, fee income is very substantial, but essentially on par with public sector payments. These two revenue sources, fee income and government income, are thus essentially co-dominant within the development and housing field. The nearly equal share of these two sources of revenue is very likely a reflection of the distinct financing patterns of the two main subgroups. While housing tends to be dominated by (rental) fee income, the development arena has been one of the prime targets for some international government assistance programs, such as the European Union's PHARE Program.

CONCLUSIONS AND IMPLICATIONS

The nonprofit sector that emerges from the evidence presented here is an important and complex set of institutions in Romanian society. At the same time, this sector remains an extremely fragile organism in Romania, struggling to meet the overwhelming humanitarian, cultural, environmental, and development needs of Romanian society without yet having a firm domestic support structure in place. The social and economic destruction that the Ceauşescu regime left behind greatly diminished the state's ability to fulfill its social welfare responsibilities; comprehensive government policies aimed at fostering a partnership with the nonprofit sector did not take shape in the years after 1989. Moreover, even the legal framework has remained both outdated and insufficient. In fact, the Law of 1924, enacted during the brief democratic interlude of the inter-war period, still constitutes the legal base for nonprofit activities and voluntary action. In addition, the infiltration of Romanian society by the Communist state and especially its brutal secret police, Securitate, left major scars on the psyche of the Romanian population. Thus, many social institutions still face a high degree of public mistrust and skepticism, or at least indifference. In this respect, the relatively high willingness of Romanians to volunteer for nonprofit organizations is a good sign. On the other hand, population surveys on the associative and philanthropic behavior of Romanians also show that only one-third of the population have a very good opinion of nonprofit organizations, whereas 8 percent have a very bad opinion and 58 percent have no opinion or are indifferent. Thus, while the Romanian nonprofit sector has made outstanding progress in gaining the trust of the Romanian public, a lot of work still lies ahead.

To correct these problems, a number of steps seem appropriate:

- **Resource development.** Perhaps the overriding need in Romania at present is to create a sustainable domestic financial base for the sector to combat its weak economic capacity, lead the sector beyond its current state of vulnerability, and ultimately reduce its dependence on international assistance. The key challenges lie in fostering closer relationships with the public sector both nationally and locally, increasing domestic government support, and developing comprehensive government policies in this respect. Moreover, this will also require significant improvements in the fiscal incentives currently provided to further stimulate individual giving, business support, and the development of institutional philanthropy locally.

- **Reforming the legal framework.** Another key challenge is the need for a substantial reform and modernization of the general legal framework for the sector. The Law of 1924 is not only outdated, it also contains elements directly contrary to the current needs of the sector; for example, it considers donations to be an exceptional (rather than proper and necessary) source of financing.
- **Fostering legitimacy.** The persistent ambiguity of the Romanian nonprofit sector is due, in large part, to the legitimacy problems the sector continues to face. For better or worse, the early evolution of the sector in the immediate aftermath of the fall of Communism produced a limited, but highly publicized, number of scams, scandals, and other questionable transactions relating to the transformation of the assets of formerly government or party agencies and social organizations in Romania as well as in other countries in the region. In combination with the lingering popular indifference to, if not mistrust of, nonprofit organizations and other types of societal institutions, this has posed a significant legitimacy challenge. To overcome this, a significant investment in public education will be needed along with the development of effective codes of conduct by nonprofit organizations themselves.
- **Capacity building.** A final conclusion that emerges from the data presented here concerns the time frame required for building a truly viable and self-sustaining nonprofit sector in Romania. As was shown here, despite some considerable growth, five years after the fall of Communism, the Romanian nonprofit sector remained a pale reflection of its counterparts elsewhere in the world, even compared to Central Europe. To grow and nurture a sustainable nonprofit sector obviously takes more than a few years of investment. Accordingly, it is crucial to continue to expand training and capacity building efforts at significant levels in the foreseeable future. So, too, it seems pertinent to continue efforts to nurture an institutional infrastructure for this sector in Romania, to facilitate training efforts and information sharing, and to provide a unified voice vis-a-vis the government, especially at the national level.

Recently, important headway has been made on many of these challenges, as it increasingly has become clear that the civic movement and the broad range of nongovernmental organizations in Romania have become an essential factor in the post-Communist evolution of society as well as in Romania's ability to cope with the dynamics of the complex transition processes. With the election of both a new government in 1996 and a former NGO leader as the country's president, the initial "cold" period in the government/nonprofit relations has come to an end. Nevertheless, much remains to be done to enhance the growing maturation of the sector, increase its sustainability, and put it more firmly on the social, economic, and political map of this country.

ENDNOTES

1. The work in Romania was coordinated first by Dan Stancu and then Daniel Saulean of the Civil Society Development Foundation in Bucharest, who served as successive local associates over the three-year period of the project. Assisting them were Carmen Epure, Stefan Constantinescu, Simona Luca, Adrian Baboi, Oana Tiganescu, and Bogdan Berianu. The team was aided, in turn, by a local advisory committee made up of seven prominent local scholars and experts (see Appendix D for a list of committee members). The Johns Hopkins project was directed by Lester M. Salamon and Helmut K. Anheier and the Central and Eastern European portion of the work was overseen by Stefan Toepler.

2. The definitions and approaches used in the project were developed collaboratively with the cooperation of the Romanian researchers as well as researchers in other countries and were designed to be applicable to Romania and the other project countries. For a full description of this definition and the types of organizations included, see Appendix A. For a full list of the other countries included, see Chapter 1 above and Lester M. Salamon and Helmut K. Anheier, *The Emerging Sector Revisited: A Summary, Revised Estimates* (Baltimore, MD: The Johns Hopkins Center for Civil Society Studies, 1999).

3. Technically, the more precise comparison is between nonprofit contribution to "value added" and gross domestic product. For the nonprofit sector, "value added" in economic terms essentially equals the sum of wages and the imputed value of volunteer time. On this basis, the nonprofit sector in Romania accounted for 0.6 percent of total value added, an actually larger amount.

4. For further details, see *Romanians' Philanthropic and Associative Behavior*. Results of a national opinion survey conducted by the Center for Urban and Regional Sociology on behalf of the Civil Society Development Foundation. Bucharest: CSDF, 1997.

5. For further details, see Daniel Saulean and Carmen Epure, "Defining the Nonprofit Sector: Romania," *Working Papers of the Johns Hopkins Comparative Nonprofit Sector Project*, No. 32 (Baltimore, MD: Johns Hopkins Center for Civil Society Studies, 1998), pp. 2–10; and Maria Bucur, "Philanthropy, Nationalism and the Growth of Civil Society in Romania," *Working Papers of the Johns Hopkins Comparative Nonprofit Sector Project*, No. 31 (Baltimore, MD: Johns Hopkins Center for Civil Society Studies, 1998).

CHAPTER 18

Slovakia

Helena Woleková, Alexandra Petrášová, Stefan Toepler, and Lester M. Salamon

BACKGROUND

Like Romania, the Slovak nonprofit sector appears to be somewhat less developed in economic terms than its Central European neighbors of Hungary and the Czech Republic. In large part, this is due to the attempts of post-Communist governments to preserve centralized state control, which essentially kept the Slovak nonprofit sector out of the provision of crucial welfare services even more so than in other countries in the region. This does not mean, however, that the Slovak nonprofit sector lacks vitality. To the contrary, Slovakia's nonprofit organizations have developed into a flexible, unified, creditable, and highly effective mechanism of citizen education and participation that has made substantial contributions to democratic development in this country.

The work presented here was carried out by a Slovak research team hosted by the Social Policy Analysis Center (S.P.A.C.E.) Foundation as part of the Johns Hopkins Comparative Nonprofit Sector Project.[1] It thus offered ample opportunities both to capture local Slovak circumstances and peculiarities and to compare and contrast them to those in other countries both in Central and Eastern Europe and elsewhere in a systematic way.[2]

Global Civil Society: Dimensions of the Nonprofit Sector by Lester M. Salamon, Helmut K. Anheier, Regina List, Stefan Toepler, S. Wojciech Sokolowski and Associates. Baltimore, MD: Johns Hopkins Center for Civil Society Studies, 1999.

The present chapter reports on just one set of findings from this project, those relating to the size of the nonprofit sector in Slovakia and elsewhere. Subsequent publications will fill in the historical, legal, and policy context of this sector and also examine the impact that this set of institutions is having in Slovak society. The data reported here draw heavily on an official survey of nonprofit organizations conducted by the Statistical Office of the Slovak Republic in 1996. The survey was designed in close cooperation between the Statistical Office and the project team. Unless otherwise noted, financial data for Slovakia are reported in U.S. dollars at the 1996 average exchange rate. (For a more complete statement of the sources of data, see Appendix C. For a more complete statement of the types of organizations included, see Chapter 1 and Appendix A.)

PRINCIPAL FINDINGS

Four major findings emerge from this work on the scope, structure, financing, and role of the nonprofit sector in Slovakia:

1. A modest economic force

In the first place, aside from its social and political importance, the nonprofit sector turns out to be a significant economic force in Slovakia, though still accounting for relatively modest shares of national expenditures and employment. More specifically:

- **A $247 million industry.** Even excluding its religion component, the nonprofit sector in Slovakia had operating expenditures of $247 million (7.6 billion Slovak crowns) in 1996, or 1.3 percent of the country's gross domestic product, a modest, but still significant amount.[3]
- **An important employer.** Behind these expenditures lies a sizable workforce that includes more than 16,000 full-time equivalent paid workers. This represents 0.9 percent of all nonagricultural workers in the country, 1.4 percent of service employment, and the equivalent of 2 percent of the government workforce at all levels—federal, provincial, and municipal (see Table 18.1).
- **Matches employment in largest private firm.** Put somewhat differently, nonprofit employment in Slovakia is essentially on a par with employment in the largest private business in the country, the East Slovak Iron Foundry VSZ in Košice.
- **Outdistances some industries.** Indeed, as many people work in the nonprofit sector in Slovakia as in some entire industries in the country. Thus, as shown in Figure 18.1, nonprofit employment in Slovakia

Table 18.1   The nonprofit sector in Slovakia, 1996

$ 247.1 million in expenditures
— 1.3 percent of GDP

16,200 paid employees
— 0.9 percent of total nonagricultural employment
— 1.4 percent of total service employment
— 2.0 percent of public employment

---

outdistances employment in industries such as printing and hotels and restaurants. Moreover, nonprofit employment is not far behind the employment level in the Slovak mining, textiles, and chemical manufacturing industries.

- **Volunteer inputs.** Even this does not capture the full scope of the non-profit sector in Slovakia, for this sector also attracts a considerable amount of *volunteer effort*. Indeed, this translates into at least another 7,000 full-time equivalent employees, which boosts the total number

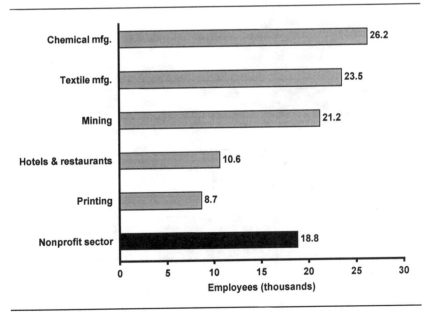

Figure 18.1   Nonprofit employment (head count) in Slovakia in context, 1996

of full-time equivalent employees of nonprofit organizations in Slovakia to 23,000 or 1.2 percent of total employment in the country (see Figure 18.2).

- **Religion.** The inclusion of religion, moreover, would add to these totals another 2,700 paid employees. With religion included, nonprofit paid employment therefore rises slightly to 1 percent of the total and paid plus volunteer employment to 1.4 percent. Religion also increases operating expenditures by approximately $19 million (590 million crowns), thus bringing total expenditures to close to $266 million (8.2 billion crowns), the equivalent of 1.4 percent of GDP without the imputed value of volunteer time, and 1.5 percent with volunteer time.

2. One of the smaller nonprofit sectors in Central and Eastern Europe

While it is beginning to take its place as a serious component of the Slovak economy, the Slovak nonprofit sector is small relative to its counterparts elsewhere in the world, and even lags a little behind the level in other Central European countries.

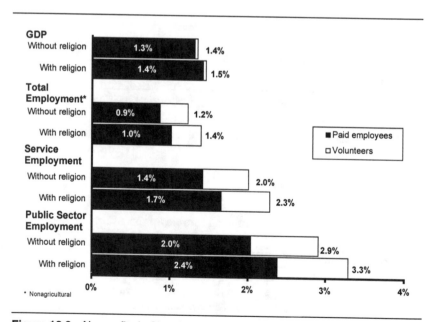

Figure 18.2   Nonprofits in Slovakia, with and without volunteers, 1996, as a % of . . .

- **Significantly below the international average.** As Figure 18.3 shows, the relative size of the nonprofit sector varies greatly among countries, from a high of 12.6 percent of total nonagricultural employment in the Netherlands to a low of 0.4 percent of total employment in Mexico. The overall 22-country average, however, is close to 5 percent.

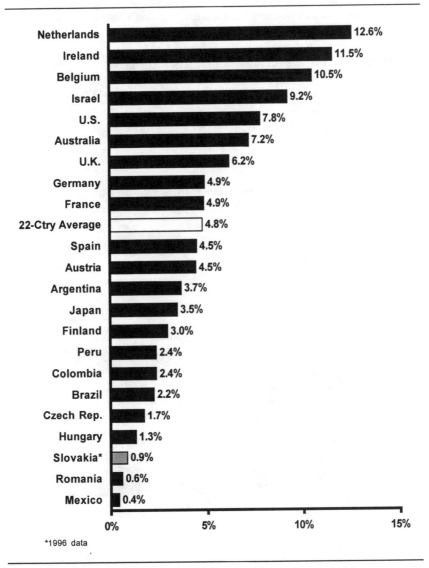

Netherlands	12.6%
Ireland	11.5%
Belgium	10.5%
Israel	9.2%
U.S.	7.8%
Australia	7.2%
U.K.	6.2%
Germany	4.9%
France	4.9%
22-Ctry Average	4.8%
Spain	4.5%
Austria	4.5%
Argentina	3.7%
Japan	3.5%
Finland	3.0%
Peru	2.4%
Colombia	2.4%
Brazil	2.2%
Czech Rep.	1.7%
Hungary	1.3%
Slovakia*	0.9%
Romania	0.6%
Mexico	0.4%

*1996 data

Figure 18.3   Nonprofit share of total employment, by country, 1995

This means that Slovakia, at 0.9 percent, falls significantly below the global average.

• **Just under the Central and Eastern European average.** In addition to falling significantly below the 22-country average, nonprofit employment as a share of total employment also falls below the level elsewhere in Central and Eastern Europe. Thus, as shown in Figure 18.4, full-time equivalent employment in nonprofit organizations in Slovakia, at 0.9 percent of total employment, is just below the Central and Eastern European average of 1.1 percent.

• **Margin widens slightly with volunteers.** This margin widens slightly, moreover, when volunteers are added. Thus, with volunteer time included, nonprofit organizations account for 1.2 percent of total employment in Slovakia, which is 30 percent below the regional average of 1.7 percent (see Figure 18.4).

3. Culture and recreation dominance

Similar to other Central and Eastern European countries, but unlike the all-country average, culture and recreation clearly dominate the nonprofit scene in Slovakia.

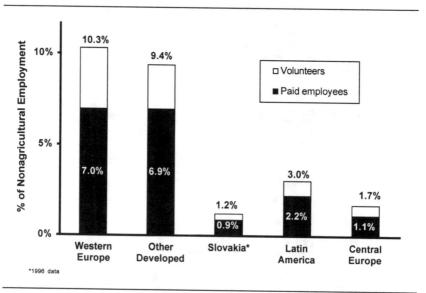

Figure 18.4   Nonprofit share of employment, with and without volunteers, Slovakia and four regions, 1995

- **Close to 37 percent of nonprofit employment in culture and recreation.** Of all the types of nonprofit activity, the one that accounts for the largest share of nonprofit employment in Slovakia is culture and recreation. As shown in Figure 18.5, 37 percent of all nonprofit employment

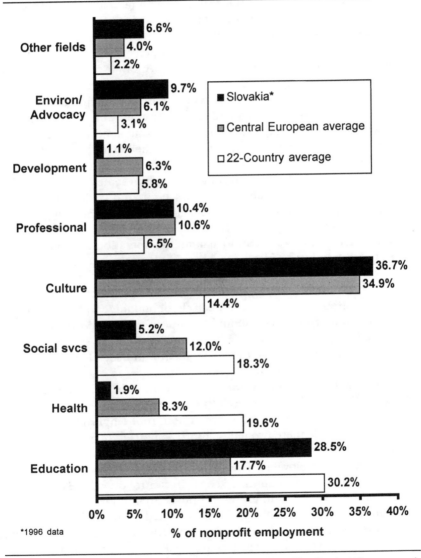

Figure 18.5 Composition of the nonprofit sector, Slovakia, Central Europe, and 22-country average, 1995

in Slovakia is in the culture and recreation field. This is comparable to the Central and Eastern European average of 35 percent, but it greatly exceeds the 22-country average of 14 percent. This situation very likely reflects the heritage of the previous regime, as culture and recreation were among the few fields of social activity that were tolerated and even encouraged by the Communist state. The same holds true for professional associations and unions, which also account for a comparatively larger share of nonprofit employment in Slovakia than the international average (10 percent in Slovakia vs. 7 percent internationally).

- **Sizable nonprofit presence in education.** Another sizable portion of total nonprofit employment in Slovakia is in the education field. This field accounts for almost 29 percent of all nonprofit employment, most of which is in primary and secondary education. The education share of nonprofit employment in Slovakia thus almost reaches the international average and is significantly higher than in other Central and Eastern European countries. This suggests that nonprofits were relatively successful in establishing footholds in some parts of the education field—most notably grammar schools and trade academies—after the private provision of core welfare services (including education) became legally possible in 1990. Both the Catholic and the Protestant Churches began to assume the operation of some former state schools; but private nonprofit schools also resulted significantly from teacher initiatives driven by the desire to use and explore new and alternative teaching methods. For the most part, these private schools are housed in state-owned school buildings and are financed by the state. However, it should be kept in mind that the education share is high primarily in relative terms and would be smaller if other nonprofit service areas, especially health and social services, were more developed in Slovakia.

- **Very small shares of nonprofit employment in health and social services.** Compared to the overall 22-country average, health and social services absorb a very small share of nonprofit employment in Slovakia. Thus, while these two fields absorb 38 percent of global nonprofit employment on average, they account for only 7 percent of nonprofit employment in Slovakia. This very likely reflects the determination of the post-1989 governments to keep firm control over these two crucial welfare fields. Accordingly, all hospitals in Slovakia are state-owned with the exception of three church-affiliated hospitals. What is more, in the peculiar health care privatization environment in this country, all private health care providers are legally defined as commercial organizations, meaning that even the three church hospitals are technically for-profit rather than nonprofit institutions. The nonprofit sector thus essentially has been left outside the health care privatization process that has taken place in ambulatory services, pharmacies, and health spas. In the social service field, no privatization has taken place whatsoever, as the state continues to provide the same services as before 1990. New kinds of social services provided by nonprofit organizations remain at best on the fringe of the Slovak welfare system.

- **Relatively strong nonprofit civic and advocacy employment.** The related fields of advocacy and environmental protection emerge as the fourth largest arena of nonprofit activity in Slovakia, after culture and recreation, education, and professional associations and unions. These fields absorb close to 10 percent of all nonprofit employment in the country, which is about three times as much as the 22-country average of 3 percent, testifying to the pronounced advocacy orientation of the Slovak nonprofit sector. By contrast, development and housing, with 1 percent of employment, represents a mere fraction of both the international average of 6 percent and the Central and Eastern European average of 6.3 percent. An additional 7 percent of nonprofit employees fall into other categories, including international activities and philanthropy.

In sum, the structure of the Slovak nonprofit sector can best be understood as being influenced by three crucial factors:

- The heritage of the previous regime, which tolerated social activity in the field of culture and recreation and actively promoted membership in the professional organizations and unions that were formerly controlled by the Communist party. After 1990, however, these organizations shed Communist control and adopted new, democratic structures. In addition, a number of new professional organizations and unions have emerged.
- Over its 40-year rule, the Communist regime in Slovakia essentially eliminated basic human rights and democratic institutions, and exerted tremendous control over the educational system. After 1990, a large number of independent civil initiatives came into being to advocate individual rights and to promote leisure activities or environmental protection. At the same time, these organizations became one of the main mechanisms for citizens to gain information and learn about democratic behavior. The activities of these new initiatives proved very important as new, post-1990 governments showed the tendencies to continue some practices of the previous regime. This was especially the case with the Mečiar government, which after 1995 increasingly began to show disregard for the law. The relatively high share of environmental and civic and advocacy employment in Slovakia (close to

10 percent of total nonprofit employment) is therefore a direct result of this crucial role that civic organizations have played in the post-Communist development of this country.

- The process of transforming the national economy into a market system that began in the former Czechoslovakia after 1990 and continued after the separation into the independent Czech and Slovak Republics in 1993 led to the creation of a private business sector in addition to the state sector. This privatization process, however, did not include a consistent government posture that would have accepted a role for the nonprofit sector in the transformation of the formerly state-run welfare system (i.e., education, health, and social services). Because the government has not changed its position and the reform process in this area is very slow, the role of the Slovakian nonprofit sector remains even more limited than elsewhere in Central and Eastern Europe, particularly in the provision of health and social services.

4. Most revenue from fees and charges, not philanthropy or the government

Consistent with its culture and recreation orientation, the Slovak nonprofit sector receives the bulk of its revenue not from private philanthropy or the government, but from fees and charges. In particular:

- **Fee income dominant.** The overwhelmingly dominant source of income of nonprofit organizations in Slovakia is fees and charges for services that these organizations provide. As reflected in Figure 18.6, this source alone accounts for more than half, or 55 percent, of all nonprofit revenue in Slovakia.
- **Limited support from philanthropy and public sector payments.** In contrast, private philanthropy and public sector payments provide much smaller shares of total revenues. Thus, as Figure 18.6 shows, private philanthropy—from individuals, corporations, and foundations combined—accounts for 23 percent of nonprofit income in Slovakia, while public sector support accounts for 22 percent.
- **Revenue structure with volunteers.** This pattern of nonprofit revenue hardly changes when volunteers are factored into the picture. In fact, as shown in Figure 18.7, private philanthropy increases only slightly from 23 percent to 25 percent with volunteers included, while fees and charges still account for more than half of total revenue. What is more, adding religion would not further change the picture.
- **Similar to other Central and Eastern European countries.** The pattern of nonprofit finance evident in Slovakia is generally comparable to that elsewhere in Central and Eastern Europe. In particular, as shown

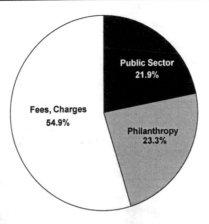

Figure 18.6   Sources of nonprofit revenue in Slovakia, 1996

in Figure 18.8, the nonprofit organizations in the Central and Eastern European countries included in this project also derived on average the largest share of their revenues from fees and charges, though the share was slightly less than Slovakia's (46 percent vs. 55 percent in Slovakia). The philanthropy share of nonprofit revenue in Slovakia basically matched the regional average (23 percent in Slovakia vs. 21 percent on average in Central Europe). Government support, however, was somewhat weaker in Slovakia (22 percent vs. 33 percent in Central and Eastern Europe generally).

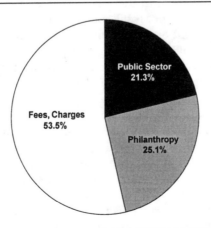

Figure 18.7   Sources of nonprofit revenue in Slovakia, with volunteers, 1996

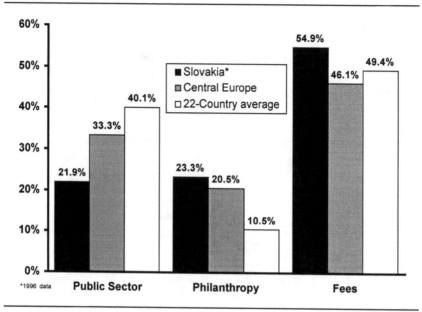

Figure 18.8   Sources of nonprofit cash revenue, Slovakia, Central Europe, and 22-country average, 1995

- **Deviation from the global average.** While the revenue structure of the Slovak nonprofit sector generally mirrors that elsewhere in Central and Eastern Europe, it differs considerably from that evident elsewhere in the world. Thus, as Figure 18.8 also shows, while fees and charges are the dominant element in the financial base of the nonprofit sector globally, their dominance is still somewhat less pronounced than it is in Slovakia (55 percent of total revenue in Slovakia compared to 49 percent globally). Similarly, the philanthropic share of nonprofit income in Slovakia, as in the region in general, accounts for more than twice the global average (23 percent in Slovakia vs. 11 percent globally). In contrast, public sector payments comprise a considerably larger share of nonprofit income in these other countries on average (40 percent vs. 22 percent in Slovakia). Quite clearly, a different pattern of cooperation has taken shape between nonprofit organizations and the state in these other countries. Evidently, the Slovak nonprofit sector has not yet established a firm cooperative partnership with the state. While this is true to a degree for all Central and Eastern European countries, the reluctance of past governments to grant the nonprofit sector a role in the welfare services arena has stood in the way of further developing such partnerships in Slovakia.

- **Variations by subsector.** Even this does not do full justice to the complexities of nonprofit finance in Slovakia, however. This is so because important differences exist in the finances of nonprofit organizations by field. In fact, three quite distinct patterns of nonprofit finance are evident among Slovak nonprofits, as shown in Figure 18.9:

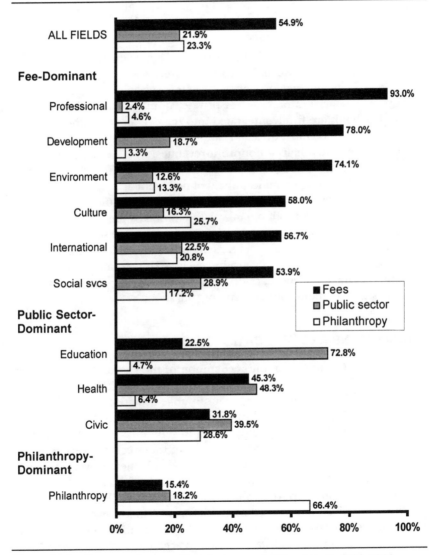

Figure 18.9 Sources of nonprofit cash revenue in Slovakia, by field, 1996

Fee-dominant fields. Fee income is the dominant source of income in six fields of nonprofit activity for which data were gathered, accounting for more than 90 percent of revenues in professional associations and unions, around three-quarters of total revenue in the development and housing and environmental fields, and more than half of all revenues in culture and recreation, international activities, and social services.

One private philanthropy-dominant field. Private giving turns out to be the dominant source of income in only one field of nonprofit activity, i.e., philanthropic intermediaries.

Public sector-dominant fields. In three Slovakian nonprofit fields (education, health, and civic and advocacy) government plays the dominant role in financing. In education, government subsidies account for almost three-quarters (73 percent) of private, nonprofit school income, as such schools are firmly integrated into the overall educational finance system of this country. In health care, public sector payments account for slightly less than half of nonprofit revenues, with fees and charges, at 45 percent, accounting for most of the remainder. As noted before, however, health is not a significant field of nonprofit activity. Essentially, the Red Cross, which is partially supported by the state, is the only significant health-related nonprofit organization in Slovakia. Finally, at close to 40 percent, government support is also the single largest source of revenue for civic, legal service, and political organizations, which, in part, reflects state subsidies for minority groups, such as Hungarian and Roma civic and cultural associations, associations for people with disabilities, youth and student unions, and women's organizations.

CONCLUSIONS AND IMPLICATIONS

The end of Communism, the recognition of the Declaration of Human Rights, and the break-up of Czechoslovakia in the early 1990s provided significant impulses for the development of public activities in Slovakia, especially in advocacy, public education, the development of new democratic institutions and independent media, and a variety of community initiatives. Although post-Communist governments, like the Mečiar government, attempted to keep society under firm state control, they proved unable to hamper this development. To the contrary, civic activities became the most important force in support of democracy in Slovakia. However, the state kept its centralized dominance in crucial service fields and did not leave room for the nonprofit sector to develop a strong position in the delivery of human services. In fact, the state refused to accept emerging nonprofit organizations as partners, although the many volunteers and specialists—

some of whom had left their jobs in similar state organizations—were working hard to develop innovative projects and to offer new kinds of services.

Because of these two trends, the Slovak nonprofit sector emerged with little support and cooperation from the government, but proved to be very flexible, united, and able to mobilize very quickly. This flexibility, unity, and mobilization potential was most clearly demonstrated in the nationwide "Third Sector SOS" campaign in 1996 that mobilized against a discriminatory foundation law proposed by the government. The nonprofit sector potential was further demonstrated in 1998 with the "OK '98" public campaign for an independent and fair election, which aimed to inform and mobilize especially young, first-time voters.

As a result of both of these highly effective campaigns and also the day-to-day civic activities undertaken by and on behalf of citizens, the nonprofit sector has become very popular and positively valued in Slovakia. Moreover, in contrast to the experience of the nonprofit sector in some other countries in the region, the development of the Slovak nonprofit sector was not marked by any scandals concerning the privatization of assets or other dubious financial transactions. The transformation of formerly socialist "public or social organizations" into democratically led associations and unions took place without any attempt at profiteering or any significant public controversies.

At present, the nonprofit sector in Slovakia is continuing to build, diversify, and decentralize its infrastructure. Supportive infrastructures are not only being formed for the whole sector, but also for the different professional and volunteer activities that the sector encompasses. One of the most important voluntary groups in this respect is the "Gremium of the 3rd Sector," which represents sectoral interests with the government administration, the parliament, and other partners. Currently, the Gremium is coordinating activities on such crucial issues as decentralizing political power, promoting the integration of Slovakia into the European Union, and improving the transparency of public decision-making.

In sum, while the role of the Slovak nonprofit sector remains limited in the provision of welfare services, nonprofit organizations in this country are very alive in advocating the rights of citizens and in supporting democracy. With the credibility and legitimacy that the sector has gained in this country and with the continuing build-up of infrastructure, it seems most likely that Slovakia's nonprofit organizations will be able to maintain their special role in the democratic transformation in the future.

ENDNOTES

1. The work in Slovakia was coordinated by Helena Woleková of the S.P.A.C.E. Foundation, who served as local associate to this project. Assisting her were Alexandra Petrášová of the

Statistical Office of the Slovak Republic, Martin Bútora of the Institute for Public Issues, Gabriela Dudekova of the Historical Institute of the Slovak Academy of Sciences, and the legal expert Ján Hrubala. The team was aided, in turn, by a local advisory committee made up of five prominent local leaders and researchers (see Appendix D for a list of committee members). The Johns Hopkins project was directed by Lester M. Salamon and Helmut K. Anheier, and the Central and Eastern European portion of the work was overseen by Stefan Toepler.

2. The definitions and approaches used in the project were developed collaboratively with the cooperation of the Slovak researchers and researchers in other countries and were designed to be applicable to Slovakia and the other project countries. For a full description of this definition and the types of organizations included, see Appendix A. For a full list of the other countries included, see Chapter 1 above and Lester M. Salamon and Helmut K. Anheier, *The Emerging Sector Revisited: A Summary, Revised Estimates* (Baltimore, MD: The Johns Hopkins Center for Civil Society Studies, 1999).

3. Technically, the more precise comparison is between nonprofit contribution to "value added" and gross domestic product. For the nonprofit sector, "value added" in economic terms essentially equals the sum of wages and the imputed value of volunteer time. On this basis, the nonprofit sector in Slovakia accounted for 0.5 percent of total value added.

PART 5

Latin America

Civil society has had an especially rich history in Latin America, stretching back to the pre-Hispanic principle of Andean reciprocity and other indigenous traditions, and amplified by the charitable and educational institutions affiliated with the Catholic Church during the colonial and post-independence periods.

In recent decades, however, this sector has been significantly reinvigorated by the emergence of liberation theology and by a new *associativism* that has empowered new strata of society and encouraged a broad process of democratization. The result is a rich assortment of institutional types—still dominated in terms of overall economic weight by religiously affiliated schools and hospitals, but also including more autonomous community-based groups, human rights agencies, and nongovermental development organizations of various types. All of these organizations occupy the space between the market and the state, yet are only beginning to recognize themselves as parts of a single social and economic sector.

CHAPTER 19

Argentina

Mario Roitter, Regina List, and Lester M. Salamon

BACKGROUND

The presence of private nonprofit organizations in Argentina, as in most of the Latin American countries, can be traced back to the colonial period, when the Catholic Church and its adherents created the first charity hospitals and orphanages. Many of these more traditional organizations have persisted through the end of the 20th century, and over time new forms of organizations dedicated to the public good or to the well-being of their members have emerged in response to political, economic, cultural, and social changes and needs.

However, the concept that these different types of organizations, e.g., hospitals, universities, sports clubs, school "cooperators," neighborhood associations, and human rights organizations, constitute an identifiable sector is relatively recent, and only partially accepted. Indeed, only in the last decade has something that could be called a "third," "voluntary," or "nonprofit" sector come to be publicly recognized and become an object of serious academic research. Not surprisingly, therefore, several obstacles remain in the way of achieving the full visibility and strengthening of the Argentine nonprofit sector: (a) the scarcity of quantitative information on

Global Civil Society: Dimensions of the Nonprofit Sector by Lester M. Salamon, Helmut K. Anheier, Regina List, Stefan Toepler, S. Wojciech Sokolowski and Associates. Baltimore, MD: Johns Hopkins Center for Civil Society Studies, 1999.

the sector as a whole; (b) the overlap and heterogeneity of both the terms and the legal norms applying to the different types of organizations; and (c) the limited number of studies delving into the structure and development of the sector that take into account the specific historical, cultural, and political features of Argentina.

It is for this reason that the work reported on here is so important. This work was carried out by an Argentine research team at the *Centro de Estudios de Estado y Sociedad* (CEDES) as part of the Johns Hopkins Comparative Nonprofit Sector Project.[1] It thus offered ample opportunities both to capture local Argentine circumstances and peculiarities and to compare and contrast them to those in other countries both in Latin America and elsewhere in a systematic way.[2] The result is the first comprehensive empirical overview of the Argentine nonprofit sector and the first systematic comparison of Argentine nonprofit realities to those elsewhere in Latin America and the rest of the world.

The present chapter reports on just one set of findings from this project, those relating to the size and structure of the nonprofit sector in Argentina and elsewhere. Subsequent publications will fill in the historical, legal, and policy context of this sector and also examine the impact that this set of institutions is having. The data reported here draw heavily on the 1994 National Economic Census conducted by *Instituto Nacional de Estadística y Censos* (INDEC-the National Bureau of Statistics and Census). In addition, the project team supplemented this with other government reports and with a special population survey designed to fill in the more informal parts of the "third sector" in Argentina. Unless otherwise noted, financial data are reported in U.S. dollars at the 1995 average exchange rate. (For a more complete statement of the sources of data, see Appendix C. For a more complete statement of the types of organizations included, see Chapter 1 and Appendix A.)

PRINCIPAL FINDINGS

Five major findings emerge from this work on the scope, structure, financing, and role of the nonprofit sector in Argentina:

1. A major economic force

The nonprofit sector turns out to be a significant economic force in Argentina, accounting for considerable shares of national expenditures and employment. More specifically:

- **A $12 billion industry.** Even excluding its religion component, the nonprofit sector in Argentina had operating expenditures of $12 bil-

lion (about 12 billion Argentine pesos) in 1995, or 4.7 percent of the
country's gross domestic product, a quite significant amount.[3]

- **A major employer.** Behind these expenditures lies a sizable workforce
  that includes the equivalent of 395,000 full-time equivalent paid workers. This represents 3.7 percent of all nonagricultural workers in the
  country, 9.4 percent of service employment, and the equivalent of
  nearly one-third as many people as work for government at all levels—
  federal, provincial, and municipal (see Table 19.1).
- **More employees than in the largest private firms.** Put somewhat differently, nonprofit employment in Argentina easily outdistances the
  employment in the largest private businesses in the country. Thus,
  compared to the 395,000 paid workers in Argentina's nonprofit organizations, Argentina's 100 largest private corporations together employ approximately 280,000 workers (see Figure 19.1).
- **Volunteer inputs.** Even this does not capture the full scope of the nonprofit sector in Argentina, for this sector also attracts a considerable
  amount of *volunteer effort.* Indeed, an estimated 20 percent of the

---

Table 19.1   The nonprofit sector in Argentina, 1995

$12.0 billion in expenditures
— 4.7 percent of GDP

395,000 paid employees
— 3.7 percent of total nonagricultural employment
— 9.4 percent of total service employment
— 30.9 percent of public sector employment

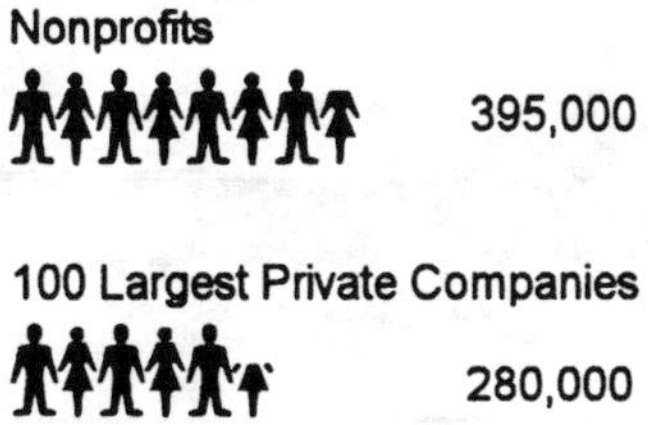

Nonprofits
395,000

100 Largest Private Companies
280,000

Figure 19.1   Employment in nonprofits vs. largest private firms in Argentina,
1995

Argentine population reports contributing their time to nonprofit organizations. This translates into another 264,000 FTE employees,
which boosts the total number of FTE employees of nonprofit organizations in Argentina to 659,000, or 6 percent of total nonagricultural
employment in the country (see Figure 19.2).

- **Religion.** The inclusion of religion, moreover, would boost these totals
by another 68,899 paid employees and 127,000 full-time equivalent volunteers. As also shown in Figure 19.2, with religion included, nonprofit
paid employment therefore rises to 4.4 percent of the total and paid
plus volunteer employment to 7.7 percent. Religion also boosts operating expenditures by $1.2 billion, thus bringing total expenditures to
$13.2 billion, the equivalent of 5.1 percent of gross domestic product.

2. One of the largest nonprofit sectors in Latin America

While the Argentine nonprofit sector is fairly sizable in relation to the Argentine economy, it is clearly large relative to its counterparts elsewhere in
Latin America, though still below the level in Western European countries.

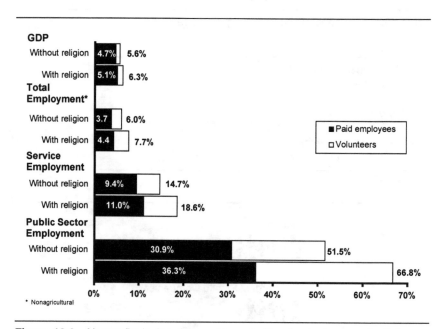

Figure 19.2   Nonprofits in Argentina, with and without volunteers and religion,
1995, as a % of . . .

- **Slightly below the international average.** As Figure 19.3 shows, the relative size of the nonprofit sector varies greatly among countries, from a high of 12.6 percent of total nonagricultural employment in the Netherlands to a low of less than 1 percent of total employment in

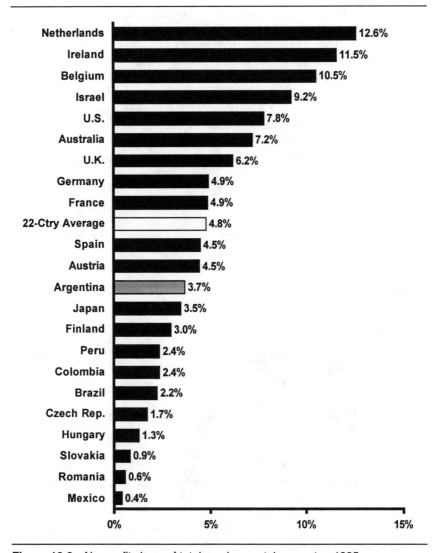

Netherlands	12.6%
Ireland	11.5%
Belgium	10.5%
Israel	9.2%
U.S.	7.8%
Australia	7.2%
U.K.	6.2%
Germany	4.9%
France	4.9%
22-Ctry Average	4.8%
Spain	4.5%
Austria	4.5%
Argentina	3.7%
Japan	3.5%
Finland	3.0%
Peru	2.4%
Colombia	2.4%
Brazil	2.2%
Czech Rep.	1.7%
Hungary	1.3%
Slovakia	0.9%
Romania	0.6%
Mexico	0.4%

Figure 19.3 Nonprofit share of total employment, by country, 1995

Mexico. The overall 22-country average, however, was close to 5 percent. This means that Argentina, at 3.7 percent without religion, falls somewhat below the global average. However, it still exceeds Japan and Finland and comes close to some of the Western European countries, such as France (4.9 percent) and Spain (4.5 percent).

- **Considerably above the Latin American and Central European averages.** Although it falls below the 22-country average, however, nonprofit employment as a share of total employment is still considerably higher in Argentina than it is elsewhere in Latin America and also higher than it is in Central Europe. Thus, as shown in Figure 19.4, FTE employment in nonprofit organizations in Argentina, at 3.7 percent of total employment, is proportionally 60 percent greater than the Latin American average of 2.2 percent. Indeed, none of the other Latin American countries covered by this project comes close to Argentina in the scale of its nonprofit employment. And Argentina is even farther above the Central European average of 1.1 percent.
- **Margin widens with volunteers.** This margin widens, moreover, when volunteers are added. Thus, with volunteer time included, nonprofit organizations account for 6.0 percent of total employment in Ar-

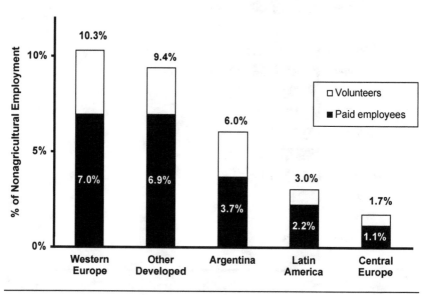

Figure 19.4   Nonprofit share of employment in Argentina and in four regions, 1995

gentina, which is twice as much as the Latin American regional average of 3.0 percent (see Figure 19.4).

3. A rich history of nonprofit activity

That the nonprofit sector is relatively highly developed in Argentina is a product of the rich history that such institutions have had in this country and the country's current transition process. This history includes:[4]

- The extensive array of Catholic Church-inspired organizations created to found monasteries, take care of cemeteries, and assist the poor in colonial times;
- The secular organizations such as the *Sociedad de Beneficencia* (Society of Beneficence) created by groups of high society women under the general tutelage of the governmental authorities with the secularization of Argentine society following independence and during the early 19th century;
- The sizable number of mutual benefit organizations, social and sport clubs, schools, and libraries created by the massive waves of immigrants that arrived in Argentina in the late 19th and early 20th centuries, and the subsequent transformation of many of these organizations into labor unions and social welfare institutions in the early part of the 20th century;
- The further institutionalization of civil society organizations during the Peronist period following World War II and their greater integration into the state system, with the formation of *obras sociales* (workers' mutual insurance organizations linked mainly to trade unions) and of the *unidades básicas* (basic units) that formed the social base of the Peronist movement in local neighborhoods throughout the country;
- The numerous research centers and foundations created by scientists and intellectuals forced to leave the public universities during the late 1960s and 1970s, a period marked by political instability and military dictatorships;
- The human rights organizations that emerged during the last military dictatorship (1976–1983) demanding state action against human rights violations. These organizations played a central role in the democratic transition in the 1980s.

4. Education dominance

Similar to other Latin American countries, education clearly dominates the nonprofit scene in Argentina.

- **Over 40 percent of nonprofit employment in education.** Of all the types of nonprofit activity, the one that accounts for the largest share of nonprofit employment in Argentina is education, mostly primary and secondary education. As shown in Figure 19.5, 41.2 percent of all

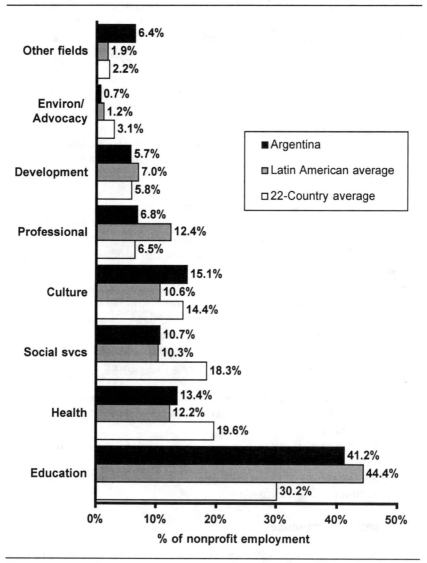

Figure 19.5   Composition of the nonprofit sector, Argentina, Latin America, and 22-country average, 1995

nonprofit employment in Argentina is in the education field. This is comparable to the Latin American average of 44.4 percent, but it greatly exceeds the 22-country average of 30.2 percent. This situation very likely reflects the long tradition of Catholic elementary and secondary schooling in Argentina and elsewhere in Latin America.

- **Relatively smaller shares of nonprofit employment in health and social services.** Compared to the overall 22-country average, health and social services absorb a smaller share of nonprofit employment in Argentina. Thus, while these two fields absorb nearly 37.9 percent of nonprofit employment on average, they account for only 24.1 percent of nonprofit employment in Argentina. This difference reflects the state's intervention in the provision of health and social services over time. Nevertheless, the Argentine nonprofit sector has a long tradition in the delivery of health care in particular, and even today has a sizable presence in this field, represented most prominently by the nonprofit hospitals, mutual associations, medical foundations, and *obras sociales,* i.e., the mutual associations created at the end of the 19th century that have emerged as pivotal elements in the Argentine health care and social welfare systems.
- **Sizable nonprofit presence in professions and social life.** Another sizable portion of total nonprofit employment in Argentina is in the culture and recreation field and in the professions. Altogether, these two fields account for 21.9 percent of all nonprofit employment, of which 15.1 percent is in social and recreational activity and almost 7 percent in professional associations and unions. This reflects, in part, the prominence of community-based sports programs in Argentine society. In addition, Argentina has long had a strong union movement and professional middle class, both of which have created significant organizational bases.
- **Limited nonprofit development and advocacy employment.** Compared to the employment in nonprofit education, social welfare, sports and professional organizations, the share of Argentine nonprofit employment in the development field and in the related fields of advocacy and environmental protection is considerably smaller. Altogether, these fields absorb 6.4 percent of all nonprofit employment in the country, slightly less than the 22-country average of 8.9 percent. An additional 6.4 percent of nonprofit employees fall into other categories, including philanthropy, international, and "other."
- **Pattern shifts with volunteers.** This pattern changes considerably when volunteer inputs are factored in. In particular, as shown in Figure 19.6, with volunteers included, the development share of nonprofit employment jumps from 5.7 percent to 15.7 percent and the combined civic and advocacy and environment share increases from less than 1 percent

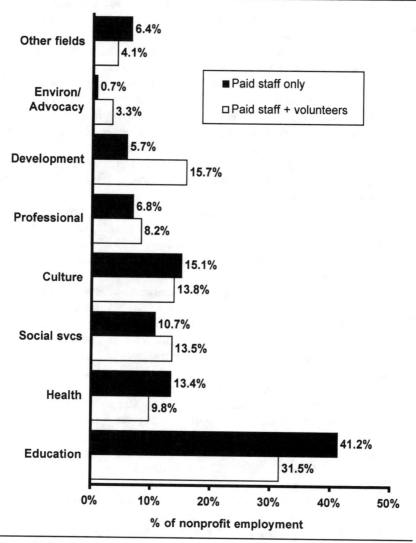

Figure 19.6   Share of nonprofit employment in Argentina, with and without volunteers, by field, 1995

to 3.3 percent. Similarly, the share of nonprofit employment absorbed in the social services field also swells, from 10.7 percent without volunteers included to 13.5 percent with volunteers. While education still dominates the Argentine nonprofit sector's activities with volunteers counted in, its dominance is nowhere near as extensive thanks to the ability of development, advocacy, and social service organizations to attract volunteers.

5. Most revenue from fees, not philanthropy or public sector

The Argentine nonprofit sector receives the bulk of its revenue not from private philanthropy but from fees and charges, and does so to an even greater extent than do nonprofit organizations in most other countries outside of Latin America. In particular:

- **Fee income dominant.** The overwhelmingly dominant source of income of nonprofit organizations in Argentina is fees and charges for the services that these organizations provide. As reflected in Figure 19.7, this source alone accounts for nearly three-quarters, or 73.1 percent, of all nonprofit revenue in Argentina.[5]
- **Limited support from philanthropy and the public sector.** In contrast, private philanthropy and the public sector provide much smaller shares of total revenues. Thus, as Figure 19.7 shows, private philanthropy—from individuals, corporations, and foundations combined—accounts for only 7.5 percent of nonprofit income in Argentina, while public sector payments, including compulsory payments to the *obras sociales* which are used to finance health and related social welfare benefits, account for 19.5 percent.
- **Revenue structure with volunteers.** This pattern of nonprofit revenue changes significantly when volunteers are factored into the picture. In

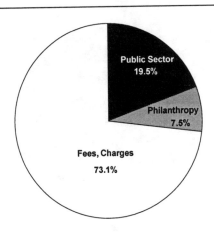

Figure 19.7   Sources of nonprofit revenue in Argentina, 1995

fact, as shown in Figure 19.8, private philanthropy increases substantially, from 7.5 percent to 23.0 percent. It thus overtakes public sector support, whose proportion declines from 19.5 percent to 16.2 percent. Even with volunteers included, however, fees remain the dominant revenue source.

- **Revenue structure with religion.** The overall pattern of nonprofit finance in Argentina changes dramatically when account is taken of religious institutions, such as churches and synagogues. Such religious institutions account for approximately 12 percent of the total revenue of the Argentine nonprofit sector, almost all of it from private giving. With religion included, therefore, the philanthropic share of total nonprofit revenue in Argentina rises from 7.5 percent to 18.6 percent. With volunteers included as well, the private giving share rises to 33.4 percent (see Figure 19.9).

- **Similar to other Latin American countries.** The pattern of nonprofit finance evident in Argentina is quite similar to that elsewhere in Latin America. Thus, as shown in Figure 19.10, like Argentina, the nonprofit organizations in the other Latin American countries included in this project (Brazil, Colombia, Mexico, and Peru) also derived the overwhelming majority of their revenues from fees and charges. Thus, compared to Argentina's 73.1 percent, the share of total nonprofit income coming from fees stood at 74.0 percent for all five Latin American countries. The public sector and philanthropic shares of nonprofit revenue in Argentina deviated slightly from the regional average, with public sector support stronger in Argentina than else-

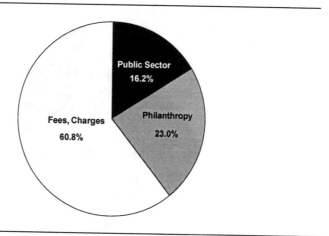

Figure 19.8   Sources of nonprofit revenue in Argentina, with volunteers, 1995

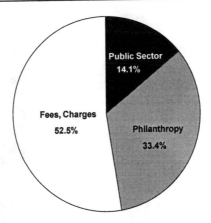

Figure 19.9   Sources of nonprofit revenue in Argentina, with volunteers and religious worship, 1995

where in the region (19.5 percent vs. 15.5 percent on average) and private giving somewhat weaker (7.5 percent vs. 10.4 percent).

- **Deviation from the global average.** While the revenue structure of the Argentine nonprofit sector generally mirrors that elsewhere in Latin America, it differs considerably from that evident elsewhere in the world, and particularly in the more developed countries. Thus, as Figure 19.10 also shows, while fees and charges are the dominant element in the financial base of the nonprofit sector globally, this dominance is considerably less pronounced than it is in Argentina (49.4 percent of total revenue compared to 73.1 percent in Argentina). By contrast, public sector payments comprise a considerably larger share of nonprofit income in these other countries on average (40.1 percent vs. 19.5 percent in Argentina). Quite clearly, a different pattern of cooperation has taken shape between nonprofit organizations and the state in these other countries. This is markedly so in Western Europe, where public sector payments comprise on average well over half of nonprofit revenues. Evidently, the long history of adversarial relations between the state and nonprofit groups in Argentina has yielded a very different pattern of nonprofit finance, one that is far more dependent on charitable contributions and private fees.

- **Variations by subsector.** Even this does not do full justice to the complexities of nonprofit finance in Argentina, however. This is so because important differences exist in the finances of nonprofit organizations by field of activity. In fact, three quite distinct patterns of

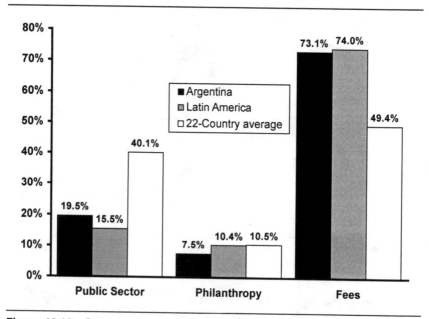

Figure 19.10   Sources of nonprofit cash revenue, Argentina, Latin America, and 22-country average, 1995

nonprofit finance are evident among Argentine nonprofits, as shown in Figure 19.11:

Fee-dominant fields. Fee income is the dominant source of income in seven fields of nonprofit action for which data were gathered. This is understandable enough in the cases of business and professional, as well as social and cultural, associations where membership dues are the primary source of income. But fee income also plays the dominant role in financing nonprofit health and educational establishments, as well as social service, environment, and development organizations, in Argentina. In the cases of health and education, this reliance on fees reflects in part the dominance of public sector entities in direct service provision in these fields and the relatively limited amount of state subsidies for nonprofit providers, which derive approximately one-quarter of their income from public sector sources, well below the 22-country average. However, public sector support for primary and secondary education is stronger, accounting for nearly one-third of the revenue for this subfield. In the case of social services, environment, and development, the prominence of private fees reflects the fact that these are organized as associations or mutual help groups that collect

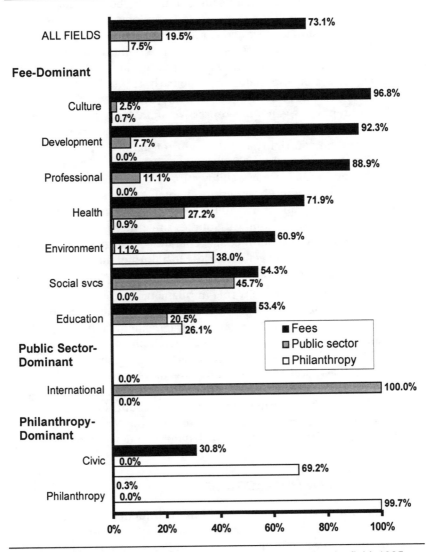

Figure 19.11 Sources of nonprofit cash revenue in Argentina, by field, 1995

membership fees, though in the case of social services, public sector payments are also significant.

Private philanthropy-dominant fields. While private philanthropy is far from the dominant source of nonprofit income in Argentina overall, it turns out to be the dominant source of income both for foundations, which would naturally be expected to be supported chiefly by private philanthropy, and for civic and advocacy organizations. These latter organizations represent, in a sense, the more political side of the nonprofit sector, which has been quite important in the development of Argentine society especially since the early 1980s. As a general rule, such organizations lacked access to domestic public sector support in the context of a generally repressive state from the latter 1950s through the early 1980s. Indeed, they have functioned as mechanisms to defend human rights and the rights of the disadvantaged against state power, and, in the 1990s, have come to take the lead in anti-corruption and public accountability efforts. They have therefore been forced to rely extensively on private charitable support, mostly from international foundations during the years of authoritarian rule, but increasingly also from domestic sources since then. In addition, they have had to devise other income-generating strategies, including the sale of their services, to generate close to a third of their revenue.

Public sector-dominant field. In only one field (international) does government play the dominant role in financing nonprofit action in Argentina. For the most part, this consists of the Argentine government's counterpart contributions required by agreements with international agencies such as UNICEF and the UN Development Programme.

While not the dominant source of income, the public sector is still a considerable source of nonprofit revenue in some fields: social services, where it accounts for 46 percent of the total; health, where it accounts for 27.2 percent; and education, where it accounts for 21 percent. In the case of social services, this largely results, however, from the mandatory social welfare payments channeled through the *obras sociales*.

CONCLUSIONS AND IMPLICATIONS

The nonprofit sector thus emerges from the evidence presented here as both a sizable and a rather complex set of institutions in Argentine society. Not only does this set of institutions serve important human needs, it also constitutes a major, and apparently growing, economic force and is a significant contributor to political as well as social life.

At the same time, this sector is a somewhat fragile organism in Argentina, undergoing significant changes as the nation itself is in the midst of structural transformation, with results for both that are still quite uncertain. Until very recently, nonprofit organizations were hardly distinguishable as an identifiable sector in Argentine society, in large part because the borders between the public and private spheres of action were never clear. A history of clientelism kept some of the more traditional service-oriented and neighborhood-based organizations subservient to state institutions or to powerful economic elites. At the same time, numerous associations and mutual help groups emerged in the late 19th and early 20th centuries quite independent of government intervention or notice. At the beginning of the 1970s, however, new types of nonprofit institutions emerged, among them those known popularly as "nongovernmental organizations" (NGOs). These NGOs, generally formed by professionals, have gained a reputation for their commitment to establishing a sphere of citizen action independent of the authoritarian state and serving as a rallying point for human rights, for civil control over governmental actions, and for the political and economic empowerment of the poor. These newer institutions, like their more traditional counterparts, remain vulnerable at the present time, however, in the wake of an ongoing realignment of the roles of the state, the market and the civil society sectors. These nonprofit organizations generally lack a secure revenue base, face enormous management challenges, and operate in a legal environment that is far too complex and ambiguous.

To correct these problems, a number of steps seem appropriate:

- **Making "sector" a reality.** In the first place, serious steps are needed to bridge the divide that exists between the various components of the Argentine nonprofit sector and foster a common understanding of a "sector" sharing common interests and needs. The emergence of the concept of "civil society" has been useful in this regard, but more dialogue and interaction will be required. What is more, it will be necessary to increase the visibility of this set of organizations with the general public, with political leaders, and with the business community.
- **Capacity building.** One way to foster a sense of a distinctive nonprofit sector in Argentina is to invest in the capacity of this sector through improved training and strengthening of infrastructure organizations. Although considerable effort has been put into training nonprofit personnel in Argentina, indigenous capacity to provide such training, and indigenous infrastructure organizations, have been lacking until recently. Building these capabilities thus seems a high priority. Equally important is further encouraging indigenous philanthropic institutions to buttress the financial base of the sector. In short, Argentina is ripe for a major nonprofit sector capacity-building campaign to bring its civil society sector more fully into a position to operate with partners in government and the business sector.

- **Regularizing partnerships with government and business.** The relationship between the nonprofit sector and the state has long been complicated in Argentina. Many early nonprofit institutions were fostered by the state, while the Peronist and later regimes integrated other nonprofit institutions, such as the *obras sociales*, into state social welfare systems. During the thirty years between the fall of the Perón government and the re-establishment of democracy, however, relations between government and at least one portion of the nonprofit sector, the NGOs, deteriorated badly, as NGOs formed specifically to challenge authoritarian rule and protect civil and human rights that the regime was infringing.

  Despite these strains, an important priority for the future is to build a firmer foundation for broader cooperation between these two sectors. Such cooperation will be crucial for the long-term financial viability of the nonprofit sector, but it must be based on a reasonable degree of autonomy for the nonprofit partners. Critical to this is the creation of stable institutional settings for public-private cooperation and of contractual guarantees and mechanisms of public accountability and transparency regarding the management and distribution of funds.

- **Making room in the public space.** One way to foster a greater partnership between nonprofit organizations and the state is to ensure nonprofit organizations a more secure place at the table in the so-called "public space" that has recently opened in Argentina. Clearly, advances have been made in bringing nonprofit organizations into the process of public policy formulation and implementation in Argentina, but much has yet to be done.

- **Reforming the legal and tax framework.** The legal framework for nonprofit organizations in Argentina mainly consists of the general provisions of the civil code. However, they are insufficient considering the complex reality and dynamics of the sector. Thus, a set of ad hoc rules has been developed by national and local public agencies. This complicated and sometimes overlapping framework creates difficulties for the accountability of the organizations, the visibility of the sector as a whole, and the possibility of obtaining empirical data.

- **Building the philanthropic base.** Also important to the future development of the nonprofit sector in Argentina will be the building of a more secure fiscal base, particularly for the civic, advocacy, development, and environmental organizations that have played such an important part in the development of a new type of nonprofit presence in Argentine society. Given the pressures likely to persist on government budgets, this will require building up the base of indigenous philanthropic support through encouragement of private giving within Argentine society and fostering foundations and other institutional mechanisms of private philanthropy.

Important changes are underway in Argentine society at the present time as memories of military rule subside and the economy responds to the strictures of economic adjustment. In this climate, new opportunities exist to regularize not only economic life, but political and social life as well. Among the more hopeful developments signaling such regularization is the emergence of a definable "nonprofit sector," a set of institutions outside the market and the state through which citizens can join together to pursue a wide variety of social, political, and economic objectives. Such institutions have a long and distinguished history in Argentina, yet their recent evolution still constitutes an important new beginning. From the evidence presented here, it is clear that this set of institutions already plays a more important economic role in Argentina than it does in most other Latin American countries. The evidence presented here should help lay the groundwork for the improved position that this set of organizations rightfully deserves.

ENDNOTES

1. The work in Argentina was coordinated by Mario Roitter of CEDES, who acted as local associate to the project. Assisting him were Andrea Campetella, Inés González Bombal, Candelaria Garay, and Daniel Gropper. The team was aided, in turn, by a local advisory committee made up of 11 prominent philanthropic, government, academic, and business leaders (see Appendix D for a list of committee members). The Johns Hopkins project was directed by Lester M. Salamon and Helmut K. Anheier and the Latin American portion of the work overseen by Regina List.

2. The definitions and approaches used in the project were developed collaboratively with the cooperation of the Argentine researchers and researchers in other countries and were designed to be applicable to Argentina and the other project countries. For a full description of this definition and the types of organizations included, see Appendix A. For a full list of the other countries included, see Chapter 1 above and Lester M. Salamon and Helmut K. Anheier, *The Emerging Sector Revisited: A Summary, Revised Estimates* (Baltimore, MD: The Johns Hopkins Center for Civil Society Studies, 1999).

3. Technically, the more precise comparison is between nonprofit contribution to "value added" and gross domestic product. For the nonprofit sector, "value added" in economic terms essentially equals the sum of wages and the imputed value of volunteer time. On this basis, the nonprofit sector in Argentina accounted for 3.2 percent of total value added, still a quite significant amount.

4. For further details on these developments, see Andrea Campetella, Inés González Bombal, and Mario Roitter, "Defining the Nonprofit Sector: Argentina," *Working Papers of the Johns Hopkins Comparative Nonprofit Sector Project*, no. 33. Edited by Lester M. Salamon and Helmut K. Anheier. (Baltimore, MD: The Johns Hopkins Institute for Policy Studies, 1998), pp. 2–8.

5. This figure would be even higher if the revenues received by the *obras sociales* were treated as fees. These revenues are collected from workers by a set of institutions known as

obras sociales, which are akin to mutual societies, and then used to finance health care and other social services for the contributors. However, contributions to these funds are required by law. Therefore, the contributions are quite similar to tax payments since they are mandated by governmental authorities. They have been categorized therefore as public sector payments.

Chapter 20

Brazil

Leilah Landim, Neide Beres, Regina List, and
Lester M. Salamon

BACKGROUND

In Brazil as in Argentina, the "third sector issue" is currently a topic of major debate in political forums, the press, and academia. Although nonprofit and charitable organizations have long been a part of Brazilian society, they have become a focal point of discussion only over the past two decades, especially in relation to the country's transition from military dictatorship to democracy, the re-alignment of the borders between state, market, and civil society, and the struggle to combat persistent inequality and poverty. This is the case not only for the recently emerged nongovernmental organizations (NGOs), but also for the more traditional charitable organizations linked to the Catholic Church. What becomes clear in this chapter is the importance of the nonprofit sector in the Brazilian economy, as well as society.

During the first phase of the Johns Hopkins Comparative Nonprofit Sector Project, an intensive review of the historical, legal, and policy background of Brazil's nonprofit sector was undertaken, but resources did not permit an in-depth economic analysis. Now, the project's second phase has focused on the sector's economic role in Brazil as well as its impact on

Global Civil Society: Dimensions of the Nonprofit Sector by Lester M. Salamon, Helmut K. Anheier, Regina List, Stefan Toepler, S. Wojciech Sokolowski and Associates. Baltimore, MD: Johns Hopkins Center for Civil Society Studies, 1999.

society. This chapter reports on the economics of the Brazilian nonprofit sector, in particular, its size as measured by expenditures and employment, the value of volunteer input, the relative economic importance of the nonprofit sector in various "industries," and its finances. Future publications will present results from the other aspects of the project.

The second phase of work was carried out by a Brazilian research team based at the *Instituto Superior de Estudos da Religião* (ISER-Higher Institute for Studies of Religion),[1] in collaboration with the Johns Hopkins Comparative Nonprofit Sector Project. The principal data source used for these estimates was the 1991 nationwide Population Census, conducted by the Brazilian Institute of Geography and Statistics (IBGE), and a 1995 microcensus. The resulting data were complemented with, and tested against, information from a variety of other sources, including surveys conducted by ministries, other government agencies, and umbrella groups in selected fields of activity such as environment and civic/advocacy organizations. (For a more complete statement of the sources consulted to compile the data reported here, see Appendix C.)

PRINCIPAL FINDINGS

Five major findings emerge from this work on the scope, structure, financing, and role of the nonprofit sector in Brazil:

1. A sizable and growing economic force

In the first place, aside from its social and political importance, the nonprofit sector turns out to be a growing economic force in Brazil, accounting for important shares of national expenditures and employment. More specifically:

- **A $10.6 billion industry.** The nonprofit sector in Brazil had operating expenditures of $10.6 billion in 1995, or the equivalent of 1.5 percent of the country's gross domestic product.[2]
- **A major and growing employer.** Behind these expenditures lies a sizable workforce that includes approximately 1 million full-time equivalent (FTE) paid workers. This represents 2.2 percent of all nonagricultural workers in the country, 7.8 percent of service employment, and the equivalent of 19.4 percent of the people who work for government at all levels—federal, state, and municipal (see Table 20.1). Estimates also indicate that 340,000 FTE jobs were created in the Brazilian nonprofit sector between 1991 and 1995, an increase of 44 percent. This means that employment in Brazil's nonprofit sector grew more than

Table 20.1 The nonprofit sector in Brazil, 1995

$10.6 billion in expenditures
— 1.5 percent of GDP

1.0 million paid employees
— 2.2 percent of total nonagricultural employment
— 7.8 percent of total service employment
— 19.4 percent of public sector employment

twice as fast as employment in the nation's overall economy, which experienced only 20 percent growth.

- **More employees than in the largest private firm.** Put somewhat differently, nonprofit employment in Brazil easily outdistances the employment in the largest private business in the country, and does so by a factor of 16. Thus, compared to the 1 million paid workers in Brazil's nonprofit organizations, Brazil's largest private corporation, Bradesco, employs only 62,450 workers (see Figure 20.1).

- **Volunteer inputs.** Even this does not capture the full scope of the nonprofit sector in Brazil, for the sector also attracts a considerable amount of *volunteer effort*. Indeed, an estimated 16 percent of the Brazilian population reports contributing their time to nonprofit organizations. This translates into another 139,216 full-time equivalent employees, which boosts the total number of full-time equivalent employees of nonprofit organizations in Brazil to nearly 1.2 million, or 2.5 percent of total employment in the country (see Figure 20.2).

- **Religion.** The inclusion of religion, moreover, would boost these totals by another 93,837 paid employees and 195,882 FTE volunteers.

Nonprofits

 1,000,000

Largest private firm (Bradesco)

62,450

Figure 20.1 Employment in nonprofits vs. largest firm in Brazil, 1995

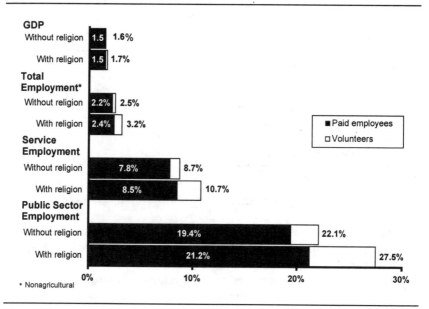

Figure 20.2   Nonprofits in Brazil, with and without volunteers and religion, 1995, as a % of . . .

With religion included, nonprofit paid employment therefore rises to 2.4 percent of the total, and paid plus volunteer employment to 3.2 percent (see Figure 20.2). Religion also increases operating expenditures by $470 million, thus bringing total expenditures to $11.1 billion, the equivalent of 1.5 percent of gross domestic product.

2. Comparable to the Latin American average

The Brazilian nonprofit sector, though modest in relation to the Brazilian economy, is on a par with the Latin American average, but it is below the level of all developed countries.

- **Below the international average.** As Figure 20.3 shows, the relative size of the nonprofit sector varies greatly among countries, from 12.6 percent of total nonagricultural employment in the Netherlands to less than 1 percent of total employment in Mexico. The overall average for the 22 countries in which data were assembled through this project, however, was 4.8 percent. This means that Brazil, at 2.2 percent without religion, falls well below the global average.
- **At the Latin American average.** While it is lower than the 22-country average, however, nonprofit employment in Brazil as a share of total

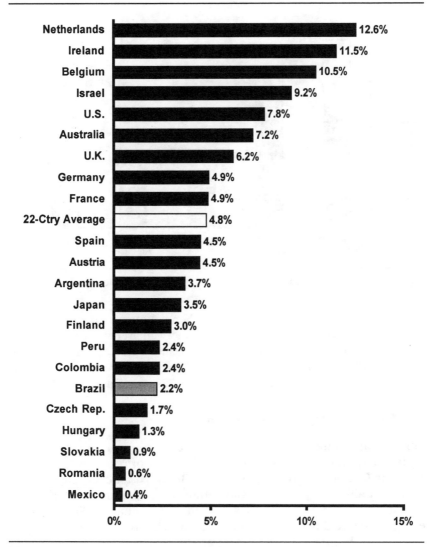

Figure 20.3 Nonprofit share of total employment, by country, 1995

employment falls right at the Latin American average (2.2 percent), as shown in Figure 20.4. Still, the absolute size of the Brazilian nonprofit sector is the largest in Latin America, employing more FTE workers than in the other four Latin American countries combined, and more than most European countries. This is not surprising given the size of the Brazilian population and economy.

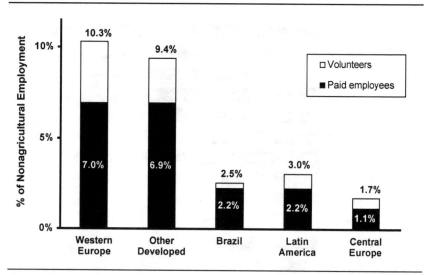

Figure 20.4   Nonprofit share of employment in Brazil and in four regions, 1995

- **Position changes with volunteers.** When volunteers are added, a gap opens between Brazil and the Latin American average. Thus, with volunteer time included, nonprofit organizations account for 2.5 percent of total employment in Brazil, below the regional average of 3 percent (see Figure 20.4), and less than half the 22-country average.

3. A limited history of nonprofit activity

The relatively modest size of the nonprofit sector in Brazil can best be understood against the backdrop of the history of relations among the state, the Catholic Church, and society in Brazil. Historically, the state has been centralizing, patrimonial, and authoritarian, playing a major role in molding Brazil's political, social, and economic institutions. Furthermore, except in selected periods, the Catholic Church has been a strong ally of the state in shaping this society. This produced a weak civil society, which has been maturing and growing more vigorously only in the last 20 or 30 years. Highlights of this history are described below:[3]

- During almost four centuries, all organizations that were established in Brazil for social welfare, health, education, and leisure existed under the aegis of the Catholic Church, which was backed by the Portuguese crown under the *padroado* system in which the Church subordinated itself to the state. Many religious orders and countless brotherhoods and fraternities were created for worship as well as leisure, socializing, and access to social services. These latter groups were supported for the most part by their members and enjoyed relative autonomy since the small and segmented group of clergymen were spread throughout the huge territory and could not exert much control. Most notably, the *Irmandades da Misericórdia* (Brotherhoods of Mercy) were responsible for the first hospitals and are still among the leaders of nonprofit initiatives in Brazilian society.

- There was no significant movement of secular voluntary associations until the end of the 19th century when mutual societies proliferated and the first trade unions emerged. Mutual benefit societies provided their members medical and pharmaceutical care as well as assistance in cases of unemployment, disability, or death. To the extent that such societies attracted workers, they became more politicized and class-oriented, adding to the growing numbers of trade unions. As the trade union movement radicalized, it was repressed by the state. At the same time, professional associations, linked to the consolidating middle class, were established.

- During the 1930s and the government of Getulio Vargas (1930–45), industrialization took hold as the state intervened extensively in Brazil's society and economy. Unions and social welfare services were controlled both politically and administratively by the state, and the state expanded direct provision of education, culture, and health services. Nevertheless, this social security structure, which granted benefits only to those linked to productive activities, excluded the majority of the population. It coexisted with a parallel structure through which the state collaborated with civil society organizations by granting exemptions, tax incentives, and funding. Indeed, there was a clear pact between the state and the Catholic Church, which had established a widespread network of nonprofit schools, hospitals, and other charitable agencies. Other religious organizations such as the Kardecist spiritists and some Protestants, as well as a small number of secular nonprofit organizations, also engaged in partnership with the state in the provision of health, education, and social services.

- Following the military coup of 1964 and in the midst of processes of modernization, social diversification, and urbanization, Brazilian society gradually reorganized itself through the multiplication of associations that were mostly independent of, or opposed to, the state. At this time, the Catholic Church took a stand against the military regime and played an important role in the development of secular movements of workers, laborers, professionals, and residents of poor neighborhoods that created a vast new field of "associativism." In this new wave, Brazil's

NGOs—a collection of nonrepresentational organizations combining idealism and professionalism—had a prominent position.

- More recently many civil organizations have been growing in number, diversifying, and focusing on constructing civil society and promoting citizenship. They include women's, anti-racist, environmental, indigenous people's defense, civil rights, advocacy, and consumer protection organizations. They developed and diversified as part of Brazil's modernization process and espoused the causes of autonomy and democratic participation. In addition, a new and growing corporate philanthropy movement emerged in the last ten years. New interactions and partnerships among different civil society organizations (old and new) have become possible, as have new forms of collaboration between nonprofit organizations and government agencies, not only for the provision of services, but also for formulating, implementing, and overseeing public policy.

4. Education dominance

Despite the recent proliferation of new agencies, education dominates the nonprofit scene in Brazil as it does in Argentina and the other Latin American countries.

- **More than one-third of nonprofit employment in education.** Of all the types of nonprofit activity, the one that accounts for the largest share of nonprofit employment in Brazil is education. As shown in Figure 20.5, more than one-third, or 36.9 percent, of all nonprofit employment in Brazil is in the education field. This is less than the Latin American average of 44.4 percent, but higher than the 22-country average of 30.2 percent. The weight of education in the Brazilian nonprofit sector reflects the long tradition of Catholic and other religious elementary and secondary schooling in Brazil and elsewhere in Latin America, as well as a national law that requires private higher education establishments to take the nonprofit form.

- **Above the Latin American average in the health, culture and recreation, and social services fields.** The shares of nonprofit employment in health (17.8 percent), culture and recreation (17.0 percent), and social services (16.4 percent) in Brazil are nearer to the 22-country averages for these fields than to the Latin American averages. In the cases of health and social services, this reflects the long history of Catholic Church involvement in these fields, as exemplified by the hospitals and social service agencies of the *Irmandades da Misericórdia* (Brotherhoods of Mercy). It also reflects the work of organizations more recently es-

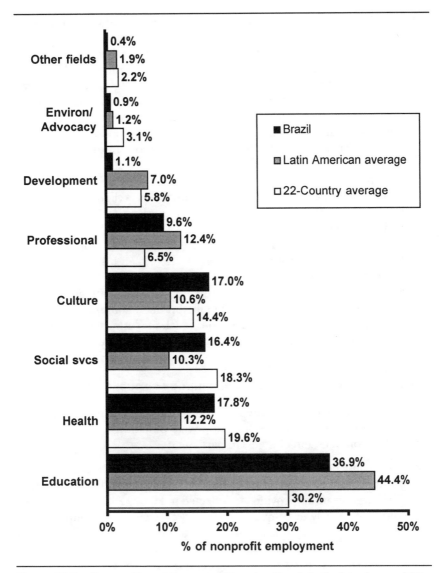

Figure 20.5 Composition of the nonprofit sector, Brazil, Latin America, and 22-country average, 1995

tablished by other religious groups such as Kardecist spiritism and by immigrants such as the Lebanese and Israelis. Notably, in the culture and recreation field, sports organizations account for 95 percent of employment.

- **Sizable share of employment in professional associations and unions.**
  Professional and trade associations and unions account for 9.6 percent of nonprofit employment in Brazil. This is smaller than the Latin
  American average of 12.4 percent, but larger than the overall 22-coun-
  try average of 6.5 percent. In the mid-1970s, during the authoritarian
  period, unions and professional organizations expanded vigorously,
  assuming political opposition roles in the struggle for democracy.
  Since then, these associations have become important actors in public
  policy debates. The relatively strong presence of professional associations and unions in Brazil's nonprofit sector reflects these recent
  movements.
- **Pattern shifts with volunteers.** This pattern changes slightly when volunteer inputs are factored in. The change is most significant in the fields of
  social services and development. As shown in Figure 20.6, with volunteers included, the social services share of nonprofit employment in
  Brazil jumps from 16.4 percent to 19.2 percent, and the development
  share nearly triples from 1.1 percent to 3.0 percent. Social services,
  which attracted an estimated 40 percent of FTE volunteers, thus becomes the second largest field within the Brazilian nonprofit sector once
  volunteers are factored in. Education, which also attracted a significant
  share of volunteers (21.3 percent), remains predominant, however.

5. Most revenue from fees, not philanthropy or public sector

Like its Latin American counterparts, the Brazilian nonprofit sector receives the bulk of its revenue not from private philanthropy or the public
sector, but from fees and charges. In particular:

- **Fee income dominant.** The clearly dominant source of income of nonprofit organizations in Brazil is fees and charges for the services that
  these organizations provide. As reflected in Figure 20.7, this source accounts for nearly three-quarters, or 73.8 percent, of all nonprofit revenue in Brazil, a significant part of it in the form of fees for services
  provided by hospitals and other health care facilities.
- **Limited support from philanthropy and the public sector.** In contrast,
  private philanthropy and the public sector provide much smaller shares
  of total revenues. Thus, as Figure 20.7 shows, private philanthropy—
  from individuals, corporations, and foundations combined—accounts
  for 10.7 percent of nonprofit income in Brazil, while public sector payments account for 15.5 percent.
- **Revenue structure with volunteers.** This pattern of nonprofit revenue
  changes measurably when volunteers are factored into the picture. In
  fact, as shown in Figure 20.8, the private philanthropy share increases

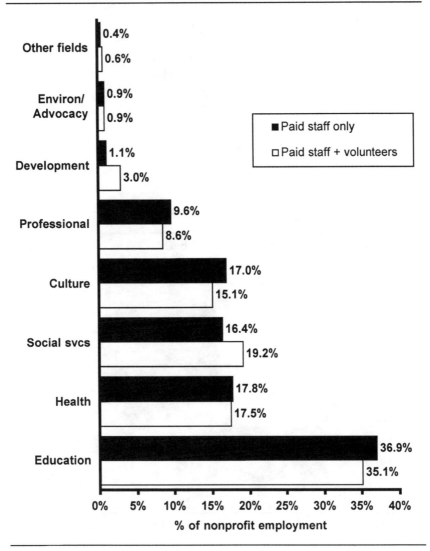

Figure 20.6   Share of nonprofit employment in Brazil, with and without volunteers, by field, 1995

from 10.7 percent to 16.3 percent, thereby overtaking public sector support, whose proportion declines from 15.5 percent to 14.5 percent. Still, fees remain the clearly dominant revenue source.

- **Revenue structure with religion.** The overall pattern of nonprofit finance in Brazil changes dramatically when account is taken of

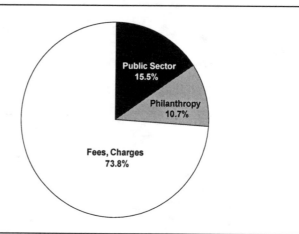

Figure 20.7   Sources of nonprofit revenue in Brazil, 1995

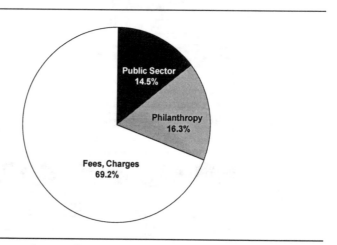

Figure 20.8   Sources of nonprofit revenue in Brazil, with volunteers, 1995

religious congregations such as churches and synagogues. With religion included, the philanthropic share of total nonprofit revenue in Brazil rises from 10.7 percent to 17.0 percent. With volunteers included as well, the private giving share rises to 26.1 percent (see Figure 20.9).

• **Similar to other Latin American countries.** The pattern of nonprofit finance evident in Brazil is quite similar to that elsewhere in Latin

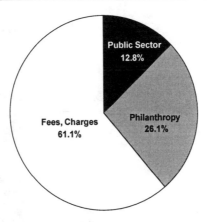

Figure 20.9   Sources of nonprofit revenue in Brazil, with volunteers and religious worship, 1995

America. Thus, as shown in Figure 20.10, like Brazil, the nonprofit organizations in the Latin American countries included in this project also derived the majority of their revenues from fees and charges. In fact, the share of total nonprofit income coming from fees stood at 74.0 percent for all five Latin American countries, on a par with the Brazilian figure of 73.8 percent. The public sector and philanthropic shares of nonprofit revenue in Brazil were also equivalent to the regional average, with public sector support in Brazil equal to the regional average of 15.5 percent and private giving slightly above (10.7 percent vs. 10.4 percent).

- **Deviation from the global average.** While the revenue structure of the Brazilian nonprofit sector mirrors that in Latin America generally, it differs considerably from that evident elsewhere in the world. Thus, as Figure 20.10 also shows, although the dominant element in the financial base of the nonprofit sector globally is fees and charges, this dominance is considerably less pronounced than it is in Brazil (49.4 percent of total revenue compared to 73.8 percent in Brazil). In contrast, public sector payments comprise a considerably larger share of nonprofit income in all the countries on average (40.1 percent vs. 15.5 percent in Brazil). Quite clearly, a different pattern of cooperation has taken shape between nonprofit organizations and the state in other parts of the world. This is markedly so in Western Europe, where public sector payments comprise on average well over half of

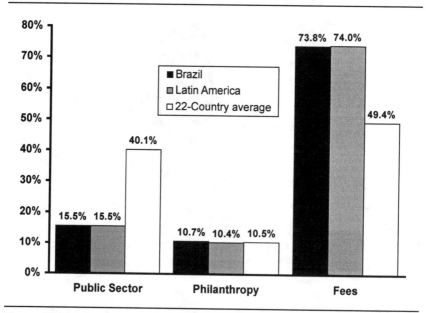

Figure 20.10   Sources of nonprofit cash revenue in Brazil, Latin America, and 22-country average, 1995

nonprofit revenues. Evidently, the public sector's relative disinterest in the work of nonprofit institutions in Brazil has yielded a very different pattern of nonprofit finance, one that is far more dependent on private fees, charitable donations, and volunteering.

- **Variations by subsector.** Even this does not do full justice to the complexities of nonprofit finance in Brazil, however. This is so because important differences exist in the finances of nonprofit organizations by subsector. In fact, three quite distinct patterns of nonprofit finance are evident among Brazilian nonprofits, as shown in Figure 20.11:

Fee-dominant fields. Fee income is the dominant source of income in six of the nine fields of nonprofit action for which data were gathered (professional, international, health, culture, education, and civic and advocacy). This is understandable enough in the case of professional associations and unions, as well as cultural and sports groups, where membership dues and fees for the services they provide are the primary sources of income. Perhaps surprisingly, this is also the case for international-oriented and civic and advocacy groups, which organize as membership associations. Furthermore, as might be expected, educational and health institutions receive fees for the services they provide, though they also receive payments from the public sector.

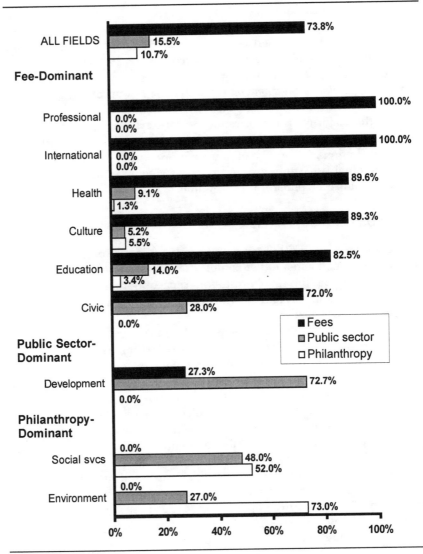

Figure 20.11   Sources of nonprofit cash revenue in Brazil, by field, 1995

Public sector-dominant field. Government plays the dominant role in financing nonprofit action in only one field—development and housing—for which it provides nearly three-quarters (72.7 percent) of cash revenues. Interestingly, when the value of volunteer time is added, private philanthropy becomes the primary source of income for the field.

While not the dominant source of income, moreover, the public sector is still a considerable source of nonprofit revenue in several additional fields: social services, where it accounts for 48 percent of the total; civic and advocacy, where it accounts for 28 percent; and environment, where it accounts for 27 percent.

- *Private philanthropy-dominant fields.* Brazilian nonprofit organizations in two fields—social services and environment—rely on private giving for the majority of their revenue. Social service agencies receive just over half of their income from private philanthropy, mainly individual contributions. In the case of nonprofit organizations working on environmental issues, however, corporate giving accounts for the larger share of private philanthropic revenue.

CONCLUSIONS AND IMPLICATIONS

The nonprofit sector thus emerges from the evidence presented here as both an important and a rather complex set of institutions in Brazilian society. Not only does this set of institutions serve important human needs, it also constitutes a major, and growing, economic force and is a significant contributor to political as well as social life.

This sector is currently undergoing significant changes—as in other parts of the world—and facing specific challenges related to the history of Brazilian society and to the ongoing re-alignment of the roles of the state, the market, and the civil society. The main topics debated in Brazilian society today include the role of nonprofit organizations in mobilizing material resources; their functions as agents for, extensions of, or substitutes for the state; their capacity to influence public policy; their effectiveness and their potential for alleviating poverty; and their contribution to democratization and the maintenance and manifestation of ethnic identity, indigenous culture, and "forgotten" values of altruism and social solidarity. These issues are wide-ranging, reflecting the very diversity of the Brazilian nonprofit sector. The resolution of these debates implies changes in the sector and its relationships with the state and society, and the outcomes are still quite uncertain.

To face these issues, a number of steps seem appropriate:

- **Building visibility and public awareness.** Serious steps are needed to bridge the divide that exists between the various components of the Brazilian nonprofit sector and to foster greater public awareness about the nature and roles of nonprofit organizations in this society. It will be necessary to increase the visibility of this set of organizations with the general public, with political leaders, and with the business community.
- **Capacity building.** One way to foster a sense of a distinctive nonprofit sector in Brazil and to bolster the effectiveness of nonprofit organiza-

tions is to invest in the capacity of this sector through improved training and strengthening of infrastructure organizations. Although considerable effort has been put into training nonprofit personnel in Brazil, local capacity to provide such training and infrastructure organizations has been lacking until recently. Building these capabilities thus seems a high priority.

- **Regularizing partnerships with government and business.** The relationship between the nonprofit sector and the state has long been problematic in Brazil. For some nonprofit organizations, their relationships of cooperation with the state have been marked by patron-client patterns and by corrupt practices such as the diversion of public funds into private hands. For another set of organizations, relations with the state have been marked by conflict arising from the successive authoritarian regimes and the strong movements for human and civil rights and democracy led by these organizations. Over the last two decades, however, there have been new efforts to foster more transparent policies for government collaboration and public oversight. Notable are the recent changes in legislation regarding the regulation of relations between the state and civic organizations. Thus, a priority for the future is to continue efforts to build a firmer foundation for cooperation between these two sectors that is based on a reasonable degree of autonomy for the nonprofit partners.

- **Making room in the public space.** One way to foster a greater partnership between nonprofit organizations and the state is to ensure nonprofit organizations a more secure place at the table in the so-called "public space" that has opened in Brazil. Clearly, advances have been made in bringing nonprofit organizations into the process of public policy formulation and implementation in Brazil, but much has yet to be done.

- **Building the philanthropic base.** Also important to the future development of the nonprofit sector in Brazil is building a more secure domestic fiscal base. This will require building up the base of indigenous philanthropic support through encouragement of private giving within Brazilian society and fostering foundations and other institutional mechanisms of private philanthropy.

Changes are under way in Brazilian society at the present time despite the vestiges of military rule that are still alive in civic culture and institutions and the impact of economic adjustment. In this climate, many opportunities and obstacles exist to regularizing not only economic life, but political and social life as well. In these processes, important and diversified roles are being played by the "nonprofit sector," the set of institutions outside the market and the state through which citizens can join together to pursue a wide variety of social, political, and economic objectives. The evidence presented here should help lay the groundwork for the improved position that this set of organizations needs if Brazil is to continue on its path toward greater economic and political stability, democracy, and a stronger civil society.

ENDNOTES

1. The work in Brazil was coordinated by Leilah Landim, who acted as local associate to the project. Assisting her in this second phase effort were Neide Beres and Maria Celi Scalon. The Johns Hopkins project was directed by Lester M. Salamon and Helmut K. Anheier and the Latin American portion of the work overseen by Regina List.

2. Technically, the more precise comparison is between nonprofit contribution to "value added" and gross domestic product. For the nonprofit sector, "value added" in economic terms essentially equals the sum of wages and the imputed value of volunteer time. On this basis, the nonprofit sector in Brazil accounted for just under 1 percent of total value added.

3. See Leilah Landim, "The nonprofit sector in Brazil," in Helmut K. Anheier and Lester M. Salamon, *The Nonprofit Sector in the Developing World*, Manchester: Manchester University Press, 1998. Also "Brazil," in Lester M. Salamon and Helmut K. Anheier (eds), *Defining the Nonprofit Sector: A Cross-national Analysis*, Manchester: Manchester University Press, 1997.

CHAPTER 21

Colombia:
A diverse nonprofit sector

Rodrigo Villar, Regina List, and Lester M. Salamon

BACKGROUND

The set of organizations considered to be part of the nonprofit sector in Colombia shares several characteristics with those in Argentina and Brazil. Among these similarities are the modest size of the nonprofit sector in terms of paid employment; the strong influence of the Catholic Church in the origins and later development of the sector; the role that the struggles between the Church, government, and various political parties have played in promoting or suppressing the evolution of different types of organizations; and the emergence of new, more autonomous nonprofit organizations in recent decades. What distinguishes the Colombian nonprofit sector are its apparent diversity, reflected in the relative balance of its composition, and the higher levels of private philanthropy on which its organizations rely.

This chapter presents an overview of research findings relating to the size, composition, and revenue structure of the nonprofit sector in Colombia as well as an initial effort to explain the above-mentioned similarities and differences. This work was carried out by a Colombian research team based at the *Confederación Colombiana de Organizaciones No-Gubernamentales*

Global Civil Society: Dimensions of the Nonprofit Sector by Lester M. Salamon, Helmut K. Anheier, Regina List, Stefan Toepler, S. Wojciech Sokolowski and Associates. Baltimore, MD: Johns Hopkins Center for Civil Society Studies, 1999.

(Colombian Confederation of Nongovernmental Organizations) as part of the Johns Hopkins Comparative Nonprofit Sector Project.[1] The data reported here were assembled on the basis of three main data sources: the 1990 National Economic Census, a 1990 survey of nonprofit entities conducted by Fundación Social, and tax data provided by DIAN, the national tax authority. (For a more complete statement of the sources of data, see Appendix C.) Unless otherwise noted, financial data are reported in U.S dollars at the 1995 average exchange rate.

The present chapter reports on just one set of findings from this project. Subsequent publications will fill in the historical, legal, and policy context of this sector and also examine the impact that this set of institutions is having.

PRINCIPAL FINDINGS

Five major findings emerge from this work on the scope, structure, financing, and role of the nonprofit sector in Colombia:

1. An economic force

In the first place, aside from its social and political importance, the nonprofit sector turns out to be an economic force in Colombia, accounting for important shares of national expenditures and employment. More specifically:

- **A $1.7 billion industry.** The nonprofit sector in Colombia had operating expenditures of more than $1.7 billion (1.57 trillion Colombian pesos) in 1995, or the equivalent of 2.1 percent of the country's gross domestic product, a quite significant amount.[2]
- **A major employer.** Behind these expenditures lies a sizable workforce that includes nearly 287,000 full-time equivalent (FTE) paid workers. This represents 2.4 percent of all nonagricultural workers in the country, 14.9 percent of service employment, and the equivalent of nearly one-third as many people as work for government at all levels—federal, departmental, and municipal (see Table 21.1).
- **Volunteer inputs.** Even this does not capture the full scope of the nonprofit sector in Colombia, for this sector also attracts a considerable amount of *volunteer effort*. Indeed, an estimated 48 percent of the Colombian population reports volunteering for some type of organization, governmental or nongovernmental. The time they contribute to nonprofit organizations translates into another 90,756 FTE employees, which boosts the total number of FTE employees of nonprofit organizations in Colombia to 377,617, or 3.1 percent of total employ-

Table 21.1   The nonprofit sector in Colombia, 1995

$ 1.7 billion in expenditures
— 2.1 percent of GDP

286,900 paid employees
— 2.4 percent of total nonagricultural employment
— 14.9 percent of total service employment
— 30.7 percent of public employment

ment in the country (see Figure 21.1). This number would undoubtedly be larger if churches and other places of religious worship were included, but such data were unavailable for Colombia.

2. One of the larger nonprofit sectors in Latin America

The Colombian nonprofit sector, while modest in relation to the Colombian economy, is larger than the Latin American average, though it still falls short of the level of developed countries.

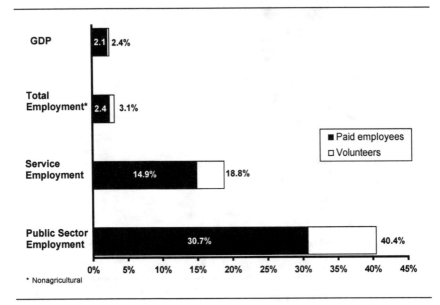

Figure 21.1   Nonprofit employment in Colombia, with and without volunteers, 1995, as a % of . . .

- **Half the international average.** As Figure 21.2 shows, the relative size of the nonprofit sector varies greatly among countries, from a high of 12.6 percent of total nonagricultural employment in the Netherlands to a low of less than 1 percent of total employment in Mexico. The overall 22-country average, however, was 4.8 percent. This means that

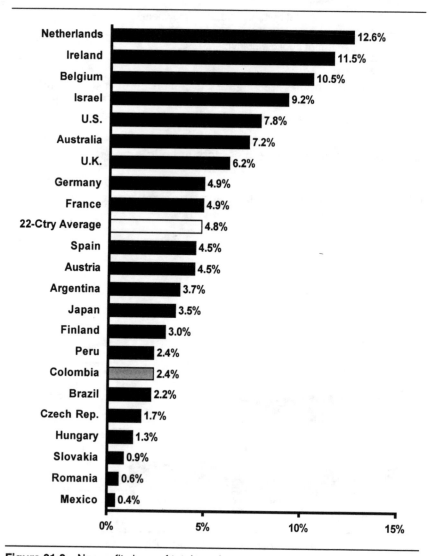

Figure 21.2 Nonprofit share of total employment, by country, 1995

the Colombian nonprofit sector's share of total employment, at 2.4 percent, falls well below the global average.

- **Slightly above the Latin American average.** While it falls below the 22-country average, however, nonprofit employment as a share of total employment in Colombia is still slightly above the Latin American average. Thus, as shown in Figure 21.3, FTE employment in nonprofit organizations in Colombia, at 2.4 percent of total employment, is just ahead of the Latin American average of 2.2 percent.
- **Maintains position with volunteers.** As noted above, when volunteers are included, nonprofit organizations account for 3.1 percent of total employment in Colombia. This is still just above the regional average of 3 percent (see Figure 21.3), but less than half the 22-country average of 6.9 percent.

3. A rich history of nonprofit activity

That the nonprofit sector is relatively well developed in Colombia is very likely a product of the rich history that such institutions have had in this country. As noted in the introduction to this chapter, the Catholic Church, government, and political parties have had significant influence in the sector's development. Highlights of this history include:[3]

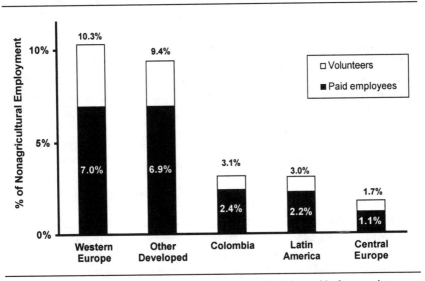

Figure 21.3   Nonprofit share of employment in Colombia and in four regions, 1995

- The extensive array of charitable organizations—schools, hospitals, orphanages, and hospices—administered by the Catholic Church at the behest of the Spanish Crown during the colonial period and supported by local government funds, private bequests, and *obras pías* (pious works), i.e., individual donations to the Church.
- The schools and associations in defense of Catholic education that were organized by the Catholic Church and that often blossomed especially during periods of liberal, secularist reforms that attempted to exert governmental control over education.
- *Juntas de Beneficencia* (Charity Boards) set up in the middle of the 19th century as a mechanism for government to secularize welfare aid and to exercise greater control over charitable organizations that were typically operated by private, mainly religious, agencies and funded heavily by public resources.
- Private charitable organizations outside the control of the *Juntas*. Among them is the Saint Vincent de Paul Society, which was founded in the mid-19th century with a variety of charitable purposes and was financed by a mix of private and public sector income. Other examples are the *Círculo de Obreros* (Workers' Circle) and *Caja Social de Ahorros* (Social Savings Bank), founded in the early 20th century by Father Campoamor to serve working-class needs.
- *Cajas de Compensación Familiar* (Family Compensation Funds), a type of social security system originally created by the National Industrialists Association in 1954 to distribute subsidies for workers' families. By 1957, the national government made employer payments to these nonprofit organizations mandatory.
- Organizations, such as the *Juntas de Acción Comunal* (Community Action Groups), *Consejos Verdes* (Green Councils), and *Hogares Infantiles de Bienestar Familiar* (Family Welfare Homes), spawned over the past decades by government programs designed to maximize scarce government financial support by harnessing the voluntary input of community members. The *Juntas* are currently the most widespread type of nonprofit organization in Colombia (more than 42,000 organizations), and membership is estimated to be 15 percent of the adult population.
- Nongovernmental organizations (NGOs) that emerged beginning in the 1960s spurred by the new social orientation of the Catholic Church, the discontent of the professional classes with the political left, and the loss of faith in the ability of traditional political parties and, therefore, governments to deal with pressing social problems. These NGOs are said to promote participation, democracy, and social development and operate in diverse fields, especially "modern" development topics such as environment, gender, human rights, and peace.

- Corporate foundations, many founded in the 1960s and 1970s to advance economic development, frequently via the promotion of microenterprises, as well as to address other environmental, educational, and social needs. Prominent examples include *Fundación Social* and *Fundación para la Educación Superior* (FES-Foundation for Higher Education) which established separate companies to generate resources to pursue their social missions. These foundations are often promoted by public and private international development agencies as philanthropic models for other countries.
- The trade and professional associations, as well as women's organizations, that overcame extreme political polarization in Colombia's society during the 20th century to promote their special interests, and in many instances, as noted above, to provide services to their members and other affiliates.

4. Balanced composition

Unlike the other Latin American countries and the 22-country overall picture, none of the fields of nonprofit activity clearly dominates the nonprofit scene in Colombia, reflecting the sector's broad diversity.

- **Over one-quarter of nonprofit employment in education.** Of all the types of nonprofit activity, the one that accounts for the largest share of nonprofit employment in Colombia is education. As shown in Figure 21.4, 26.1 percent of all nonprofit employment in Colombia is in the education field, approximately half in primary and secondary education and nearly half in higher education. The weight of higher education is due largely to a national law requiring that all private higher education institutions take the nonprofit form. Still, although education does absorb the largest share of employment in Colombia, it does not dominate the sector as it does in the rest of Latin America (an average of 44.4 percent) or in much of the rest of the countries studied (22-country average of 30.2 percent).
- **Smaller, but significant, shares of nonprofit employment in four other fields.** As noted above, Colombia's nonprofit sector is particularly remarkable because of its balanced composition. The share of nonprofit employment of each of the next four largest fields of activity ranges from 17.5 percent (health) on the high end to 13.1 percent (development) on the lower end, with professional associations (15.1 percent) and social services (14.6 percent) in between. In each of these fields, the share of nonprofit employment in Colombia is greater than the average share of all five Latin American countries. This demonstrates

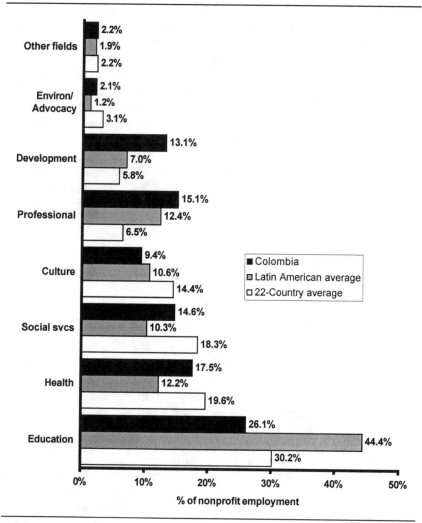

Figure 21.4   Composition of the nonprofit sector, Colombia, Latin America, and 22-country average, 1995

clearly that Colombia's nonprofit sector is more diverse than that elsewhere in Latin America.

- **Pattern shifts with volunteers.** When volunteer inputs are factored in, the composition of the nonprofit sector in Colombia changes notably, though it remains balanced overall. In particular, as shown in Figure 21.5, with volunteers included, the margin of difference among the

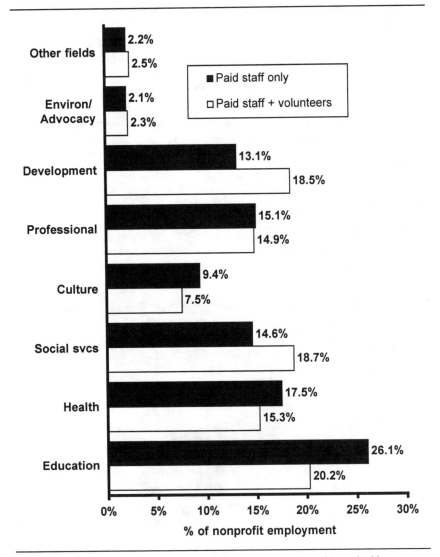

Figure 21.5   Share of nonprofit employment in Colombia, with and without volunteers, by field, 1995

top five fields of activity narrows. Even though education continues to absorb the largest share of employees in the sector, the social services share increases from 14.6 percent to 18.7 percent, and the development share of nonprofit employment rises from 13.1 percent to 18.5

percent when volunteers are included. This brings these two fields above health, whose share actually declines from 17.5 percent to 15.3 percent. This result is not so surprising given that nearly 32 percent of the FTE volunteers report devoting their energies to social service agencies, such as *Hogares,* and 36 percent are involved in development-related organizations, primarily community-based ones such as *Juntas de Acción Comunal.* In Colombia, volunteering takes place mainly in the context of mutual help and solidarity-type activities, i.e., poor neighbors helping each other, rather than as part of more traditional charity-oriented activities with the better-off helping those in need.

5. Most revenue from fees, not philanthropy or public sector

The Colombian nonprofit sector receives the bulk of its revenue not from private philanthropy or the public sector, but from fees and charges, and does so to an even greater extent than do nonprofit organizations in most other countries. In particular:

- **Fee income dominant.** The overwhelmingly dominant source of income of nonprofit organizations in Colombia is fees and charges for the services that these organizations provide. As reflected in Figure 21.6, this source alone accounts for 70.2 percent of all nonprofit revenue in Colombia.

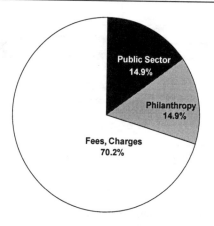

Figure 21.6   Sources of nonprofit revenue in Colombia, 1995

- **Limited support from philanthropy and the public sector.** In contrast, private philanthropy and the public sector provide much smaller shares of total revenues. Thus, as Figure 21.6 shows, private philanthropy—from individuals, corporations, and foundations combined—and public sector payments each account for 14.9 percent of nonprofit income in Colombia.
- **Revenue structure with volunteers.** This pattern of nonprofit revenue changes significantly when volunteers are factored into the picture. In fact, as shown in Figure 21.7, private philanthropy increases from 14.9 percent to 24.9 percent of total income with volunteers included, clearly surpassing public sector support, whose proportion declines slightly from 14.9 percent to 13.1 percent. Fees remain the dominant revenue source, however, accounting for nearly two-thirds of the total.
- **Similar to other Latin American countries.** The pattern of nonprofit finance evident in Colombia is quite similar to that exhibited in Latin America in general. Thus, as shown in Figure 21.8, the nonprofit organizations in the five Latin American countries on average derived the overwhelming majority of their revenues from fees and charges. Compared to Colombia's 70.2 percent, the share of total nonprofit income coming from fees stood at 74.0 percent for all five Latin American countries. While the public sector share of nonprofit revenue in Colombia roughly matched the regional average, private philanthropic support was found to be stronger in Colombia than in the region as a whole

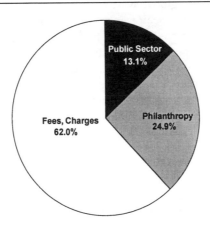

Figure 21.7   Sources of nonprofit revenue in Colombia, with volunteers, 1995

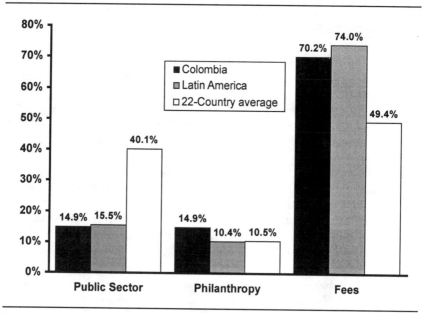

Figure 21.8   Sources of nonprofit cash revenue, Colombia, Latin America, and 22-country average, 1995

(14.9 percent vs. 10.4 percent on average), due at least in part to the significant support provided by corporations and corporate foundations.

- **Deviation from the global average.** While the revenue structure of the Colombian nonprofit sector generally mirrors that elsewhere in Latin America, it differs considerably from that evident elsewhere in the world. Thus, as Figure 21.8 also shows, while fees and charges are the dominant element in the financial base of the nonprofit sector globally, their dominance is considerably less pronounced than it is in Colombia (49.4 percent of total revenue compared to 70.2 percent in Colombia). By contrast, public sector payments comprise a considerably larger share of nonprofit income in these other countries on average (40.1 percent vs. 14.9 percent in Colombia), but private giving is weaker (10.5 percent vs. 14.9 percent in Colombia). Quite clearly, a different pattern of cooperation has taken shape between nonprofit organizations and the state in these other countries. In Colombia, government has most often played the role of promoter rather than funder. As noted previously, some of the most widespread nonprofit initiatives have been developed as a result of government-sponsored programs.

Still, the programs are designed to rely most heavily on volunteer labor input, not government financing.

- **Picture changes with volunteers.** As noted above, the makeup of the revenue stream in Colombia changes considerably when volunteers are added. So too does the position of the Colombian nonprofit sector in relation to the global averages. Thus, with volunteers added to private giving, philanthropy's share of total revenue in Colombia rises from 14.9 percent to 24.9 percent. The 22-country average, however, jumps from 10.5 percent without volunteers to 26.5 percent with them, leaving Colombia slightly behind the global average.

- **Variations by subsector.** Important differences exist in the finances of Colombia's nonprofit organizations depending on their main field of activity. In fact, three quite distinct patterns of nonprofit finance are evident among Colombian nonprofits, as shown in Figure 21.9:

Fee-dominant fields. Fees and charges are the dominant source of income in seven fields of nonprofit action for which data were gathered. This is understandable enough in the cases of business and professional associations, where membership dues are the primary source of income; culture and sports, where entrance fees are likely to be charged; and philanthropic intermediaries, where earnings on income are the major source of income. But fee income also plays the dominant role in financing nonprofit health, educational, social service, and civic and advocacy organizations. In the cases of health and social services, this reliance on fees reflects in part the clients' willingness to pay for services outside of what the public sector provides. Civic and advocacy activities are, like other association-based activities, funded in large part by membership fees.

Private philanthropy-dominant fields. While private philanthropy is far from the dominant source of nonprofit income in Colombia overall, it turns out to be the dominant source of income for environment, development, and international organizations. This reflects, in part, the interests of corporate philanthropy programs and corporate foundations in these newer fields, as opposed to the more traditional service-providing fields.

Public sector as major source. Public sector support is not the primary source of income in any of these fields; however, it is still considerable for several fields. These include the traditional social welfare fields of health, where public sector support (mainly social security payments) accounts for 25.7 percent of income; and social services, where it accounts for 19.6 percent. Public sector support is also remarkably strong

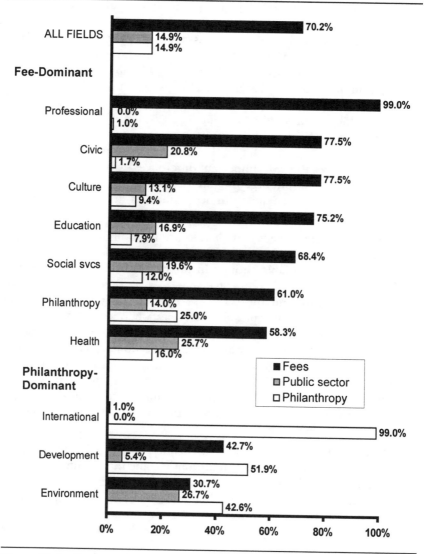

Figure 21.9   Sources of nonprofit cash revenue in Colombia, by field, 1995

in less traditional fields such as environment (26.7 percent of total revenue) and civic and advocacy (20.8 percent), in which agencies at various levels of government contract out services to nonprofit organizations. It is likely that the public sector share of nonprofit revenue will expand as the government moves toward less implementation and more oversight of social programs, and therefore a greater tendency to contract out service provision.

CONCLUSIONS AND IMPLICATIONS

Colombia's nonprofit sector as portrayed in this chapter is a complex and diverse set of institutions. Not only does this set of institutions serve important human needs, it also constitutes an important, and apparently growing, economic force and is a significant contributor to political as well as social life.

At the same time, this sector remains somewhat fragile in Colombia, undergoing significant changes with results that are still quite uncertain. Throughout Colombia's history, alongside the organizations that have emerged as a result of government-sponsored programs, there have been numerous examples of nonprofit organizations created quite independently of government and political parties. Since the 1960s, these relatively autonomous organizations, as well as the newer so-called nongovernmental organizations (NGOs), have expanded in number, scope, and influence. Over the same period, those organizations that were created in the shadow of the state have steadily gained and exerted their independence and political autonomy.

The new national Constitution adopted in 1991 lays out the institutional and legal conditions for the greater visibility and independence of nonprofit entities. It also facilitates their participation and active presence in public policy debate, in the provision of social services, and in the monitoring of governmental programs. At the same time, this opening presents a number of challenges for Colombian nonprofit organizations, government agencies, businesses, and the Colombian population:

- **Promoting an enabling environment.** One of the keys to a healthy and vigorous nonprofit sector in Colombia is the existence of a democratic and pluralistic environment in which diverse organizations can flourish. This requires an institutional framework that permits the participation of the sector's organizations in public deliberations and establishes clear "rules of the game."
- **Capacity building.** One way to foster a sense of a distinctive nonprofit sector in Colombia is to invest in the capacity of this sector through improved training and strengthening of infrastructure organizations, where it is needed. Although considerable effort has been put into training nonprofit personnel in Colombia, many organizations still lack the skills they need in both service provision and advocacy. Assessing the diverse levels of capability among the sector's organizations and strengthening the whole thus seem high priorities. Colombia is

ripe for a major nonprofit sector capacity-building campaign to prepare the country's civil society sector to further develop and maintain
its position as a partner with government and the business sector.

- **Regularizing partnerships with government.** The relationship between
  the nonprofit sector and the state has long been complicated in
  Colombia. Many nonprofit institutions have been created out of gov-
  ernment-initiated programs and some became the vehicles for clientelism, in which funding or support is exchanged for favors or votes.
  Recent regulations introduced with the new Constitution have re-
  shaped the working relations between government and nonprofit entities. The challenge now is to ensure that these changes do not ad-
  versely affect either the long-term financial viability of the nonprofit
  sector or the nonprofit partners' ability to maintain a reasonable degree of autonomy.
- **Making room in the public space.** One way to foster a greater partnership between nonprofit organizations and the state is to ensure nonprofit organizations a more secure place at the table in the so-called
  "public space." Clearly, advances have been made in bringing nonprofit organizations into the process of public policy formulation and
  implementation in Colombia, especially through the adoption of the
  1991 Constitution, but much has yet to be done.

Despite signals of revitalization among civil society organizations and
their increasingly active and autonomous presence in public affairs, the
space opened for them is challenged by limits to civic participation imposed
by continuing political violence. The social and institutional reconstruction
of Colombia requires the development of a legitimate public space in which
the diverse actors recognize and respect each other. In the face of the political violence Colombia faces at the end of the 20th century, this requires, at
the most basic level, the re-establishment of rules for peaceful co-existence
and guaranteed human rights. Further, it demands, on one hand, a decisive
effort toward continued democratization on the part of the government
and, on the other hand, overcoming the particularism of many civil society
organizations. Placing the common good as a general orientation for action
in the midst of a great diversity of interests is a great challenge faced by the
sector's organizations.

It is hoped that the work that has been done in this project can help
Colombia's nonprofit sector better identify and meet some of these challenges and make the most of the opportunities that now appear to be
opening. However incomplete, if the work reported here has contributed
to this, it will have served its purpose well.

ENDNOTES

1. The work in Colombia was coordinated by Rodrigo Villar, who acted as local associate for the project. Assisting Mr. Villar were Hernán Vargas and Victor Manuel Quintero in the economic aspects, Beatriz Castro in the analysis of the historical development of the sector, Alfonso Prada in the understanding of the legal background, and Manuel Rojas in the impact analysis. The team was aided, in turn, by a local advisory committee of six nonprofit sector leaders (see Appendix D for a list of committee members). The Johns Hopkins Project was directed by Dr. Lester M. Salamon and Dr. Helmut K. Anheier and the Latin American work overseen by Regina List.

2. Technically, the more precise comparison is between nonprofit contribution to "value added" and gross domestic product. For the nonprofit sector, "value added" in economic terms essentially equals the sum of wages and the imputed value of volunteer time. On this basis, the nonprofit sector in Colombia accounted for 1.5 percent of total value added.

3. For further details on these developments, see Rodrigo Villar, "Defining the Nonprofit Sector: Colombia," *Working Papers of the Johns Hopkins Comparative Nonprofit Sector Project*, No. 29, Baltimore: The Johns Hopkins Institute for Policy Studies, 1998.

CHAPTER 22

Mexico

Gustavo Verduzco, Regina List, and Lester M. Salamon

BACKGROUND

For most of the 20th century, the nonprofit sector in Mexico has played only a minor role in human service delivery and development work, areas which have been the domain of the state at least since the Mexican Revolution (1911–1921) and the 1926 creation of the *Partido Revolucionario Institucional* (PRI-Institutional Revolution Party). Furthermore, the single party state has not provided encouragement, much less room, for independent nonprofit organizations to flourish. This is not to say that the ideals and practice of "solidarity," mutual help, and the public good are not in evidence. Rather, they tend to be expressed or mobilized in either ad hoc efforts or groups that are not self-governed. Thus, although these activities and groupings may not fall within this project's concept[1] of "nonprofit organizations," they certainly hold potential for the future.

What is reported on here are the findings relating to the size, composition, and revenue structure of the set of organizations making up the nonprofit, or "third," sector in Mexico and its position in comparison with other countries in Latin America and the world. The work was carried out by a Mexican research team under the auspices of the *Centro Mexicano para la Filantropía*

Global Civil Society: Dimensions of the Nonprofit Sector by Lester M. Salamon, Helmut K. Anheier, Regina List, Stefan Toepler, S. Wojciech Sokolowski and Associates. Baltimore, MD: Johns Hopkins Center for Civil Society Studies, 1999.

(CEMEFI-Mexican Center for Philanthropy).[2] The principal data source used for these estimates was the 1993 National Economic Census, conducted by *Instituto Nacional de Estadística, Geografía e Informática* (INEGI-National Institute of Statistics, Geography and Information). Unless otherwise noted, financial data are reported in U.S. dollars at the 1995 average exchange rate. (For a more complete statement of the sources of data, see Appendix C.)

PRINCIPAL FINDINGS

Five major findings emerge from this work on the scope, structure, financing, and role of the nonprofit sector in Mexico:

1. An undeveloped force

In the first place, despite its growing social and political importance, the nonprofit sector turns out to be a less developed economic force in Mexico than might be expected, accounting for only modest shares of national expenditures and employment. More specifically:

- **A $1.3 billion industry.** The nonprofit sector in Mexico had operating expenditures of $1.3 billion in 1995 (8.8 billion Mexican pesos), or 0.5 percent of the country's gross domestic product, a quite modest amount.[3]
- **A modest employer.** Behind these expenditures lies a workforce that includes the equivalent of 93,809 full-time equivalent (FTE) paid workers. This represents 0.4 percent of all nonagricultural workers in the country, 1.2 percent of service employment, and the equivalent of 2.4 percent of the people who work for government at all levels—federal, state, and municipal (see Table 22.1).
- **Volunteer inputs.** This certainly does not capture the full scope of the nonprofit sector in Mexico, for this sector attracts a considerable amount of *volunteer effort* as well. Indeed, an estimated 10 percent of the Mexican population reports contributing their time to nonprofit organizations. This translates into a minimum of 47,000 additional FTE employees,[4] which increases the total number of FTE employees of nonprofit organizations in Mexico by more than 50 percent to 141,000, or 0.7 percent of total employment in the country (see Figure 22.1).

2. The smallest nonprofit sector in Latin America

Not only is the Mexican nonprofit sector small in relation to the overall Mexican economy, but also it is small relative to its counterparts elsewhere in Latin America and the rest of the world.

Table 22.1   The nonprofit sector in Mexico, 1995

$1.3 billion in expenditures
— 0.5 percent of GDP

93,809 paid employees
— 0.4 percent of total nonagricultural employment
— 1.2 percent of total service employment
— 2.4 percent of public sector employment

- **Significantly below the international average.** As Figure 22.2 shows, the relative size of the nonprofit sector varies greatly among countries. The overall 22-country average, however, was 4.8 percent. Not only was Mexico's nonprofit sector well below this average at 0.4 percent, it was in 1995 the smallest of the 22 countries studied.
- **Considerably below the Latin American average.** Nonprofit employment as a share of total employment is also considerably lower in Mexico than it is elsewhere in Latin America. Thus, as shown in Figure 22.3, FTE employment in nonprofit organizations in Mexico, at 0.4 percent of total employment, is less than one-fifth of the Latin American average of 2.2 percent.

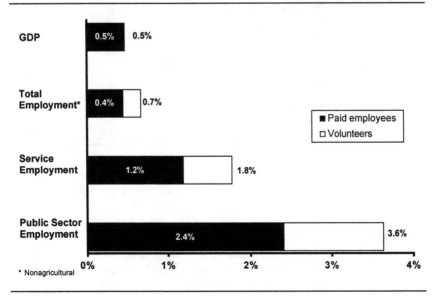

Figure 22.1   Nonprofits in Mexico, with and without volunteers, 1995,
as a % of . . .

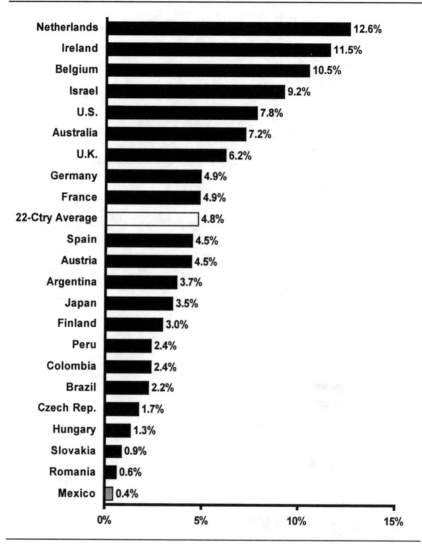

Figure 22.2   Nonprofit share of total employment by country, 1995

- **Margin narrows with volunteers.** This margin narrows slightly when volunteers are added. Thus, with volunteer time included, nonprofit organizations account for 0.7 percent of total employment in Mexico, just under one-fourth of the regional average of 3.0 percent (see Figure 22.3).

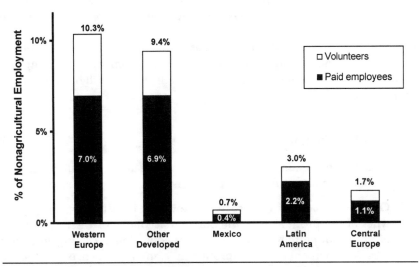

Figure 22.3   Nonprofit share of employment, with and without volunteers,
Mexico and four regions, 1995

3. A mixed history of nonprofit activity

Until the early 1900s, the development of the nonprofit sector in Mexico
was similar to that in other Latin American countries. In particular, the
strength and extension of the Catholic Church's influence during the colonial period led to the creation of numerous charitable service entities, including hospitals and schools. However, the development of autonomous
lay organizations was discouraged.

As happened in many other Latin American countries, struggles between the Catholic Church and the new state in Mexico followed independence from the colonial power in 1821. In the case of Mexico, the battles
resulted in the expropriation of Catholic Church property and the virtual
ruin of the existing nonprofit sector since neither the new government nor
the Catholic Church had resources to sustain it.

The Mexican Revolution (1911–1921) brought the state, and the *Partido
Revolucionario Institucional* (PRI-Institutional Revolution Party), to the fore-
front. During the 1940–1965 period, economic prosperity allowed the state
and the PRI to expand and exert firmer control over the provision of
basic human services, especially health and social services. Much like the
Catholic Church in colonial times, the post-revolutionary state and the PRI
discouraged the formation of autonomous and voluntary associations. As a

result, independent nonprofit organizations play very minor roles in social welfare service delivery as well as community and economic development efforts.

Since 1990, however, Mexico's increasing democratic openness has been creating a new and favorable ground for the development of the nonprofit sector. Nonetheless, the effects of these recent changes will be seen only in years to come.

4. Education dominance

Similar to other Latin American countries, but unlike the all-country average, education clearly dominates the nonprofit scene in Mexico.

- **Over 40 percent of nonprofit employment in education.** Of all the types of nonprofit activity, the one that accounts for the largest share of nonprofit employment in Mexico is education. As shown in Figure 22.4, 43.2 percent of all nonprofit employment in Mexico is in the education field. This is comparable to the Latin American average of 44.4 percent, but it greatly exceeds the 22-country average of 30.2 percent. This situation reflects the extent to which the nonprofit sector, although very small, has been an alternative for some Catholic anti-government groups in Mexico.

- **One-third of employment in professional and trade associations.** The next largest share of nonprofit employment in Mexico is in professional and trade associations, as well as unions. At 30.5 percent, this is five times the 22-country average (6.5 percent), and two-and-one-half times the Latin American average for the field. The prominence of these activities in Mexico is a remnant of the country's industrialization and economic boom period (1940–1965) during which numerous trade and professional organizations were created.

- **Smaller shares of nonprofit employment in health and social services.** Compared to the overall 22-country average, health and social services absorb a much smaller share of nonprofit employment in Mexico. Thus, while these two fields absorb 38 percent of nonprofit employment on average, they account for only 17 percent of nonprofit employment in Mexico. This reflects, in great part, the extensive governmental presence in the delivery of these services, especially since the creation of the PRI. Thus, there is little room left for non-state, non-party providers.

- **Some nonprofit presence in social life.** Another modest portion of total nonprofit employment in Mexico is in the culture and recreation field. This field accounts for 7.7 percent of all nonprofit employment in Mexico. This reflects, in part, the prominence in Mexican society of

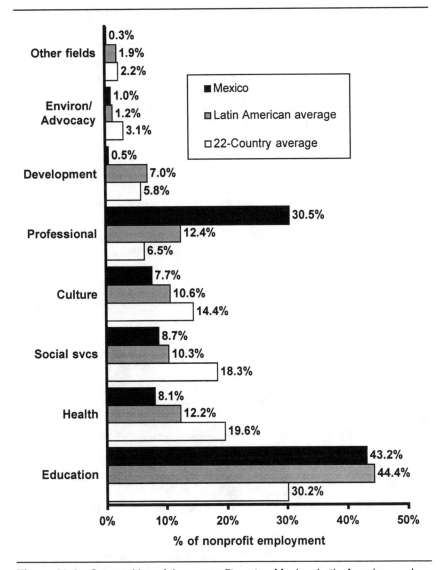

Figure 22.4   Composition of the nonprofit sector, Mexico, Latin America, and
22-country average, 1995

community-based sports programs, mainly sponsored by popularity-
seeking governments.

• **Limited nonprofit environment, development, and advocacy employment.** Compared to the employment in nonprofit education, social
welfare, and sports and professional organizations, the share of Mexi-

can nonprofit employment in the development field and in the related fields of advocacy and environmental protection is minuscule. Altogether, these fields absorb less than 1.5 percent of all nonprofit employment in the country, well below the 22-country average of 8.9 percent and even the Latin American average of 8.2 percent. In this case, as in health and social services, the post-revolutionary government has made its own efforts to control these activities.

- **Pattern shifts with volunteers.** This pattern changes considerably when volunteer inputs are factored in. In particular, as shown in Figure 22.5, with volunteers included, the development share of nonprofit employment more than doubles from 0.5 percent to 1.2 percent, and the combined civic and advocacy and environment share increases from 1 percent to 2.6 percent. Similarly, the share of nonprofit employment absorbed in the social service field also swells, from 8.7 percent without volunteers to over 16 percent with volunteers. Furthermore, education no longer dominates the Mexican nonprofit sector's activities with volunteers counted in. Instead, its share drops from 43.2 percent to 30.7 percent, while the share of professional and trade associations rises from 30.5 percent to 33.6 percent, just edging out education.

5. Most revenue from fees, not public sector or philanthropy

Consistent with the dominance of education and professional associations, and the long history of direct state provision of key services, the Mexican nonprofit sector receives the bulk of its revenue from fees and charges, and does so to even a greater extent than do nonprofit organizations in most other countries. In particular:

- **Fee income dominant.** The overwhelmingly dominant source of income of nonprofit organizations in Mexico is fees and charges for the services that these organizations provide. As reflected in Figure 22.6, this source alone accounts for 85.2 percent of all nonprofit revenue in Mexico.
- **Limited support from philanthropy and the public sector.** In contrast, private philanthropy and the public sector provide much smaller shares of total revenue. Thus, as Figure 22.6 shows, private philanthropy— from individuals, corporations, and foundations combined—accounts for only 6.3 percent of nonprofit income in Mexico, while public sector payments account for a mere 8.5 percent.
- **Revenue structure with volunteers.** This pattern of nonprofit revenue changes significantly when the imputed value of volunteers is factored

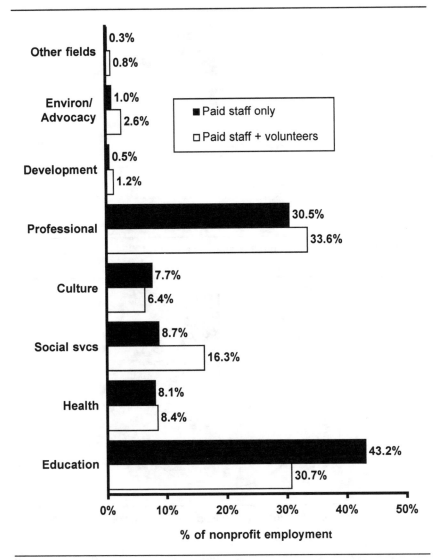

Figure 22.5 Share of nonprofit employment in Mexico, with and without volunteers, by field, 1995

into the picture. In fact, as shown in Figure 22.7, private philanthropy increases substantially from 6.3 percent to 17.9 percent, thereby over-taking public sector support, which declines from 8.5 percent to 7.5 percent. Fees, however, remain by far the dominant revenue source.

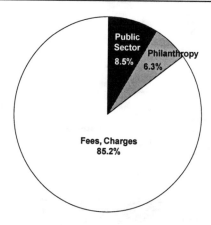

Figure 22.6   Sources of nonprofit revenue in Mexico, 1995

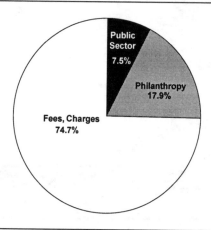

Figure 22.7   Sources of nonprofit revenue in Mexico, with volunteers, 1995

- **Similar to other Latin American countries.** The pattern of nonprofit finance evident in Mexico is similar to that elsewhere in Latin America. Thus, as shown in Figure 22.8, like Mexico, the nonprofit organizations in the other Latin American countries included in this project also derived the overwhelming majority of their revenues from fees and charges. Thus, compared to Mexico's 85.2 percent, the share of total nonprofit income coming from fees stood at 74.0 percent for all five Latin American countries. The public sector share of nonprofit rev-

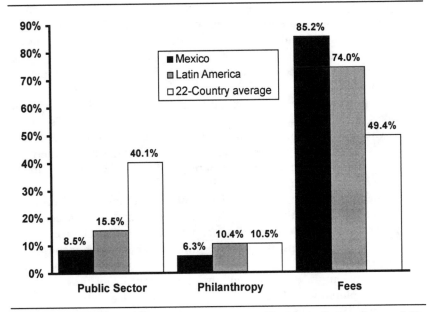

Figure 22.8 Sources of nonprofit cash revenue, Mexico, Latin America, and 22-country average, 1995

enue in Mexico deviated quite a bit from the regional average, however, with public sector support much weaker in Mexico than in the region as a whole (8.5 percent vs. 15.5 percent on average). The share of private giving was also smaller in Mexico than the average (6.3 percent vs. 10.4 percent). When volunteers are added, however, the private giving share in Mexico comes much closer to the Latin American average (17.9 percent vs. 19.2 percent).

- **Deviation from the global average.** While the revenue structure of the Mexican nonprofit sector generally mirrors that elsewhere in Latin America, it differs considerably from that evident elsewhere in the world, and particularly in the more developed countries. Thus, as Figure 22.8 also shows, while fees and charges are the dominant element in the financial base of the nonprofit sector globally, its dominance is considerably less pronounced than it is in Mexico (85.2 percent of total revenue in Mexico compared to 49.4 percent globally). In contrast, the public sector share of nonprofit income in these other countries averages nearly five times more than that in Mexico (40.1 percent vs. 8.5 percent in Mexico). Quite clearly, a different pattern of cooperation has taken shape between nonprofit organizations and the state in these other countries. This is markedly so in Western Europe, where public sector payments comprise on average well over half of nonprofit revenues. Evidently, the long history of adversarial relations between the state and nonprofit groups in Mexico has yielded a very different pattern of nonprofit finance, one that is far more dependent on private fees.

• **Variations by subsector.** As might be suspected given that fee income takes up an overwhelming share of the revenue stream of the sector as a whole in Mexico, it is also the dominant source of income for all fields of nonprofit activity. However, as shown in Figure 22.9, there are some differences in the finances of nonprofit organizations working in the various subsectors. For example, public sector support exceeds 10 percent in only two fields: professional associations and unions, and recreation and culture. This assistance frequently has been perceived as the government's means to generate support from such broad-based membership groups. By contrast, philanthropic giving accounts for one-quarter of the income of the newer types of nonprofit organizations working in the civic and advocacy, philanthropy, environment, and development fields.

Since 1995, the year for which these estimates were made, the funding situation has changed measurably. Experts in each of these fields report increased government support for all sorts of nonprofit organizations, including those that received none previously. In addition, new foundations have emerged to facilitate organized philanthropy and other forms of private involvement.

CONCLUSIONS AND IMPLICATIONS

The Mexican nonprofit sector thus emerges from the evidence presented here as a relatively minor contributor to the nation's economy. Its development as a set of autonomous organizations was stunted during Mexico's pre-revolution history by the struggles between the Catholic Church and the state and, during most of the 20th century, by the ruling PRI governments.

However, beginning in the 1980s and into the 1990s, the nonprofit sector has begun to flourish in Mexico outside the confines of both the Catholic Church and the state. The financial crises experienced during the last two decades of the 20th century and the economic reforms enacted to respond to them have resulted in a gradual retrenchment of the government from many social services and a dramatic increase in the need for such services. Nonprofit organizations have stepped up not only to fill these gaps and provide services, but also to demand a seat at the table

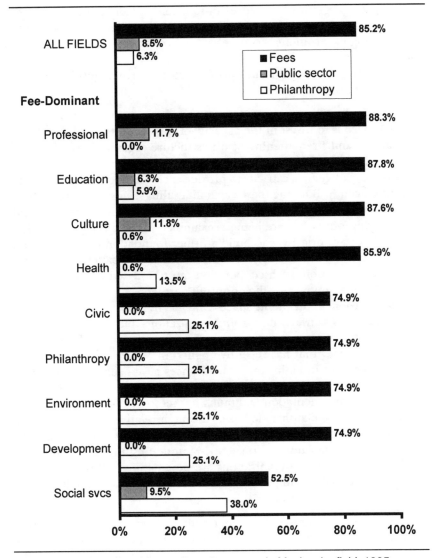

Figure 22.9 Sources of nonprofit cash revenue in Mexico, by field, 1995

where social policy and programs are made. At the same time, private businesses and philanthropists are beginning to establish foundations and other mechanisms to finance this emerging sector.

In the wake of widespread electoral fraud in the late 1980s, a number of efforts emerged to monitor the 1994 presidential election. Many of the resulting ad hoc groups have since consolidated to form permanent organizations that expanded their objectives to include promoting civic education, holding government accountable, and other activities beyond election monitoring.

To facilitate the Mexican nonprofit sector's further development, a number of steps seem appropriate:

- **Capacity building.** One way to foster an autonomous nonprofit sector in Mexico is to invest in the capacity of this sector through improved training and strengthening of infrastructure organizations. Although considerable effort has been put into training nonprofit personnel in Mexico, indigenous capacity to provide such training has been lacking until recently. Building these capabilities thus seems a high priority.
- **Building cooperation with government.** As the roles of the state and the nonprofit sector are being reexamined at the close of the 1990s, an important priority is to build a firmer foundation for cooperation between these two sectors. To avoid the historical patterns of government domination, such cooperation must be based on a reasonable degree of autonomy for the nonprofit partners.
- **Making room in the public space.** One means to foster more balanced partnerships between nonprofit organizations and the state is to ensure nonprofit organizations a more secure place in the so-called "public space" that has recently opened in Mexico. As in Colombia and elsewhere in Latin America, advances have been made in bringing nonprofit organizations into the process of public policy formulation and implementation, but much has yet to be done.
- **Building the philanthropic base.** Although relatively strong in some fields of activity, philanthropy is not yet a significant source of income for the Mexican nonprofit sector. Maintaining the autonomy that Mexico's nonprofit organizations are now gaining will require building up the base of indigenous philanthropic support through encouragement of private giving.

In light of recent events and current trends, it appears likely that Mexico's nonprofit sector will look very different at the turn of the century, making a more significant economic, as well as social and political, contribution to Mexican society than it did in 1995. It is hoped that the data and analysis presented here can serve not only to increase the visibility of the sector now but also to provide a benchmark for continued monitoring into the future.

ENDNOTES

1. For a more complete description of the project's structural-operational definition and the types of organizations included, see Chapter 1 and Appendix A.

2. The work in Mexico was coordinated by Gustavo Verduzco of *El Colegio de Mexico,* who acted as local associate to the project. Assisting him were Rosa María Fernández and María Gallo. The team was aided, in turn, by a local advisory committee (see Appendix D for a list of committee members). The Johns Hopkins project was directed by Lester M. Salamon and Helmut K. Anheier and the Latin American portion of the work overseen by Regina List.

3. Technically, the more precise comparison is between nonprofit contribution to "value added" and gross domestic product. For the nonprofit sector, "value added" in economic terms essentially equals the sum of wages and the imputed value of volunteer time. On this basis, the nonprofit sector in Mexico accounted for 0.3 percent of total value added.

4. Because the Mexican team was unable to conduct a population survey on giving and volunteering practices and used unpaid labor as a proxy, it is very likely that volunteering is underestimated.

CHAPTER 23

Peru

Cynthia Sanborn, Hanny Cueva, Felipe Portocarrero,
Regina List, and Lester M. Salamon

BACKGROUND

As in Mexico, the nonprofit sector in Peru can trace its roots at least partially to ancient traditions of solidarity and mutual self-help among civilizations that pre-dated the Spanish colonial enterprise. In Peru this is known today as "Andean reciprocity." This thread is woven throughout the history of the nonprofit, or third, sector in Peru and is evident in the diverse set of community-based associations that today make up the sector's core. Alongside these are the institutions affiliated with the Catholic Church that have provided charitable and other human services since the Spanish colonial period, as well as the nongovernmental organizations (NGOs) that have emerged more recently in search of alternative solutions to poverty, environmental degradation, and human rights abuses. Together, these organizations have the capacity to mobilize significant human resources.

This chapter reports on the size, composition, and finances of the nonprofit sector in Peru, and places these findings in comparative context with the other countries included in the Johns Hopkins Comparative Nonprofit Sector Project. Future publications will present in-depth analyses of the historical development of the sector, the legal, regulatory, and policy environ-

Global Civil Society: Dimensions of the Nonprofit Sector by Lester M. Salamon, Helmut K. Anheier, Regina List, Stefan Toepler, S. Wojciech Sokolowski and Associates. Baltimore, MD: Johns Hopkins Center for Civil Society Studies, 1999.

ment in which it operates, and the impact the sector has within Peruvian society.

The work was carried out by a Peruvian research team based at the *Centro de Investigación de la Universidad del Pacífico* (Research Center of the University of the Pacific).[1] To develop the estimates presented here, the Peruvian team relied mainly on major censuses and surveys conducted by ministries and other government agencies in the principal fields of activity such as health and education. The National Economic Census and a variety of private data sources were used to complement the principal sources. Unless otherwise noted, financial data are reported in U.S. dollars at the 1995 average exchange rate. (For a more complete statement of the sources of data, see Appendix C.)

PRINCIPAL FINDINGS

Through the above-mentioned combination of public and private sources, the Peruvian research team identified approximately 110,621 private nonprofit organizations in existence as of 1995, without including places of religious worship, cooperatives, unions, or political parties. Of this number, 64,905 are community-based organizations, 29,491 are sports and cultural organizations, and 14,346 are education institutions. Because many of these organizations do not keep or publish accounts or personnel lists, the estimates provided here on employment and operating expenditures cover only about 49,400 nonprofit organizations.[2]

Five major findings emerge from the work about this set of organizations in Peru:

1. An economic force

In the first place, aside from its social and political importance, the nonprofit sector turns out to be a significant economic force in Peru, accounting for greater shares of national expenditures and employment than had been commonly assumed. More specifically:

- **A $1.2 billion sector.** The nonprofit sector in Peru had operating expenditures of $1.2 billion (2.7 billion Peruvian soles) in 1995, or 2.0 percent of the country's gross domestic product.[3]
- **An important employer.** Behind these expenditures lies a sizable workforce that includes the equivalent of 126,988 full-time equivalent (FTE) paid workers.[4] This represents 2.4 percent of all nonagricultural workers in the country, 3.2 percent of service employment, and the equivalent of 16.5 percent of the people who work for government at

all levels—central, departmental, and municipal (see Table 23.1). Comparatively speaking, more people thus work in the nonprofit sector in Peru than in the country's most profitable private industries such as mining (around 40,000 workers) and fishing (around 60,000 workers). However, nonprofit employment is modest when compared to the microenterprises sector (around 4.5 million workers), which are as a group the nation's largest employers by far.

* **Volunteer inputs.** These data alone do not capture the full scope of the nonprofit sector in Peru, however, as this sector also attracts a considerable amount of *volunteer effort*. The 49,430 organizations covered in this study also employed around 26,400 FTE volunteers. This raises the total number of FTE employees in the sector to over 150,000, or nearly 3 percent of total employment in the country (see Figure 23.1).

Furthermore, other information gathered by the Peruvian team that is not directly comparable to the national-level data used above suggests that the actual number of volunteers in Peru's nonprofit sector is considerably greater. For example, according to a giving and volunteering survey conducted in 1998,[5] an estimated 31 percent of the Peruvian population reported contributing volunteer time to nonprofit organizations. If the total volunteer effort were projected on the basis of this survey, more than 165,000 FTE volunteer workers would be identified, boosting total paid and volunteer employment in the nonprofit sector to over 292,000, or 5.5 percent of total employment in the country.

2. On a par with other Latin American countries

The Peruvian nonprofit sector is thus comparable in size to that in other Latin American countries, but smaller than that of most developed countries.

* **Half the international average.** As Figure 23.2 shows, the relative size of the nonprofit sector varies greatly among countries, from a high of

---

Table 23.1 The nonprofit sector in Peru, 1995

$1.2 billion in expenditures
   — 2.0 percent of GDP

126,988 paid employees
   — 2.4 percent of total nonagricultural employment
   — 3.2 percent of total service employment
   — 16.5 percent of public sector employment

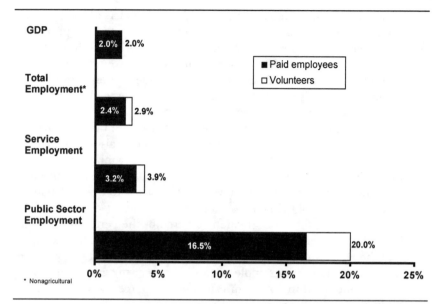

Figure 23.1   Nonprofits in Peru, with and without volunteers, 1995, as a % of . . .

12.6 percent of total nonagricultural employment in the Netherlands to a low of less than 1 percent of total employment in Mexico. The overall 22-country average, however, was 4.8 percent. This means that Peru, at 2.4 percent, falls well below the global average.

- **Comparable to the Latin American average.** While it is lower than the 22-country average, nonprofit employment in Peru as a share of total employment is comparable to or slightly above the Latin American average. Thus, as shown in Figure 23.3, FTE paid employment in nonprofit organizations in Peru, at 2.4 percent of total employment, is just above the Latin American average of 2.2 percent.

- **Position similar with volunteers.** When volunteers are added (using the more conservative estimate), nonprofit organizations account for 2.9 percent of total employment in Peru, similar to the Latin American regional average, but less than one-third the average for Western Europe or other developed countries (see Figure 23.3).

3. A rich history of nonprofit activity

The nature and scope of the nonprofit sector in Peru is associated with the country's ancient historical traditions, as well as with social and eco-

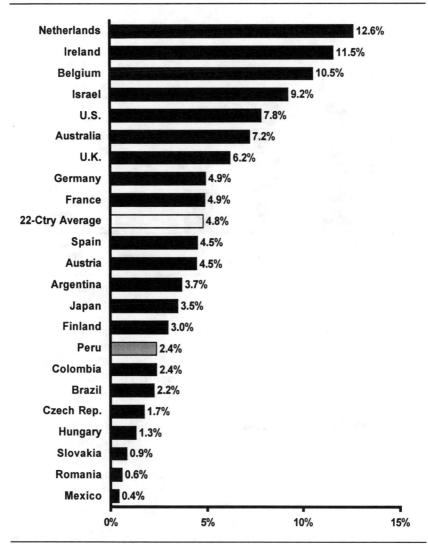

Figure 23.2   Nonprofit share of total employment, by country, 1995

nomic transformations experienced during the last half of the 20th century. This history includes:

- **Andean reciprocity.** The pre-Hispanic civilizations of the Andes resolved their problems of hunger and misery through a principle known today as "Andean reciprocity," creating an organizational

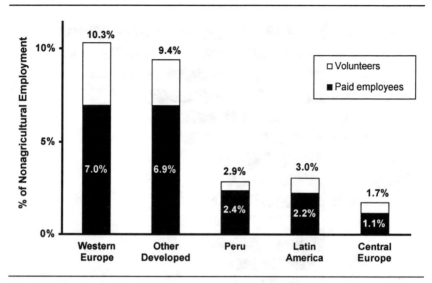

Figure 23.3   Nonprofit share of employment in Peru and in four regions, 1995

system that was able to articulate the production and distribution of goods among many inhabitants. This system was based on existing kinship ties among the diverse communities (or *ayllus*) that formed society and on the obligations that these groups had to turn over their excess production to the state to be redistributed among the neediest populations.

- **The Catholic Church and cultural sincretism.** With the Spanish invasion and conquest, the Catholic Church also arrived in the Andean region, and its primary mission was to convert the indigenous population. The collision between Western religion and existing civilizations produced a cultural sincretism that dramatically transformed this history. Hence, during the Viceroyalty of Peru, dozens of *cofradias* and *hermandades* (religious brotherhoods) appeared among all social strata, each under the protection of a distinct patron saint. Furthermore, during the colonial period the Catholic Church was in charge of the creation and administration of hospitals, asylums, schools, and other charitable works.
- **Mutual aid societies.** Once independence from Spain was achieved in the early 19th century, and after a period of enormous political turbulence from 1860 onward, numerous mutual aid societies began to emerge, promoted by artisans and workers whose main objective was to take care of their members in cases of illness, accident, or death.

- **Elite philanthropy.** Throughout the 19th century and the first half of the 20th, Peruvian upper classes developed philanthropic practices inspired by Christian charity and moral and philosophical considerations towards the needy. The elite also managed and financed, through donations and wills, the country's *Sociedades de Beneficencia* (Beneficent Societies), charitable organizations attending to the needs of the aged, orphans, and the indigent. Today this philanthropic spirit appears to be taken up, in a limited but increasing way, by new business elites through various forms of "corporate social responsibility" and through the formation of corporate foundations.
- **Urbanization and migration.** In the 1950s and 1960s, the accelerated urbanization of Peru's coastal cities and massive migration from the countryside to urban areas, particularly to the capital city of Lima, transferred to the cities the Andean highlands traditions of self-help and collective labor, as well as the cultural manifestations and kinship ties that are typical of the extended families of the countryside. All of these helped them to form support networks for the newly arrived and for those who decided to leave their places of origin to seek progress in the city. Decades later, in the face of the mounting economic crisis of the mid- and late 1980s, these networks would form the basis for new neighborhood defense organizations, *comedores populares* (community soup kitchens), and *comités de vaso de leche* ("Glass of Milk" committees).
- **New social movements.** During the last twenty years, Peru has experienced a process of formation and multiplication of new nonprofit organizations, characterized by their emphasis on autonomy from the state and by a more critical attitude towards traditional clientelist and paternalistic practices of both public authorities and private elites. These include dozens of New Left parties and movements, and hundreds of new trade unions and popular organizations, formed in the 1970s and early 1980s. They also include diverse grassroots social organizations formed largely by poor women, urban and rural self-defense committees (particularly those that formed to confront the threat of the Shining Path terrorists), and numerous NGOs formed by middle class professionals whose activities focus on the promotion of development, popular education, the defense of human rights and women's rights, and the protection of the environment.

4. Education dominance

Similar to other Latin American countries, education clearly dominates the nonprofit scene in Peru.

- **Nearly three-fourths of nonprofit employment in education.** Of all the types of nonprofit activity, the one that accounts for the largest share of nonprofit paid employment in Peru is education, mostly primary and secondary education. As shown in Figure 23.4, 74.5 percent of all

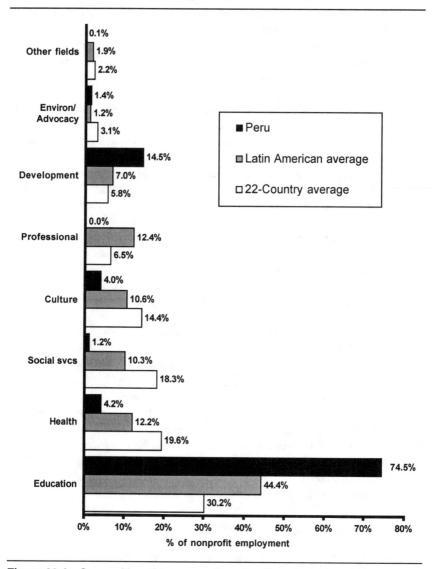

Figure 23.4   Composition of the nonprofit sector, Peru, Latin America, and 22-country average, 1995

paid nonprofit employment in Peru is in the education field.[6] Primary and secondary education alone accounts for nearly 48 percent of nonprofit employees, reflecting the historical role of the Catholic Church in these institutions. Furthermore, until 1995, national laws required private educational establishments to take the nonprofit legal form. The education share of nonprofit employment in Peru is well above the Latin American average of 44.4 percent and greatly exceeds the 22-country average of 30.2 percent.

- **Sizable share of employment in the development field.** The next largest field of nonprofit paid employment is development, which accounts for 14.5 percent of total nonprofit sector employment, double the Latin American average (7.0 percent) and more than twice the 22-country average (5.8 percent).[7] This field is heavily populated by the so-called nongovernmental organizations (NGOs) that provide support and training to community-based development efforts.
- **Much smaller shares of nonprofit employment in health and social services.** Compared to the overall 22-country average, health and social services absorb a miniscule share of paid nonprofit employment in Peru. Thus, while these two fields absorb 37.9 percent of nonprofit employment on average, they account for only 5.4 percent of nonprofit paid employment in Peru. In the case of health, this reflects, in part, the dominance of public sector hospitals and other health care facilities. For social services, the picture is altogether different, as shown below.
- **Important presence of social services when volunteers are included.** With volunteers added, the social services share of the official estimate of nonprofit employment in Peru jumps from 1.2 percent to 17.7 percent, as shown in Figure 23.5. The share rises slightly further to 18.3 percent with the "unofficial" projection of volunteer involvement. This result is not surprising given that the nonprofit organizations included in this field are community-based income support programs promoted by the government, such as *comedores populares* (soup kitchens) and *comités de vaso de leche* ("Glass of Milk" committees), that rely almost entirely on volunteer labor.
- **Volunteers also active in culture and recreation.** Although paid employment in nonprofit culture and recreation organizations is a scant 4.0 percent of total nonprofit employment (and just 3.4 percent with volunteers added), this may be a significant underestimation. Indeed, as shown in Figure 23.5, if projections from the above-mentioned giving and volunteering survey were used, the culture and recreation field would represent 15.7 percent of total paid and volunteer employment in the Peruvian nonprofit sector, greater than the field of development

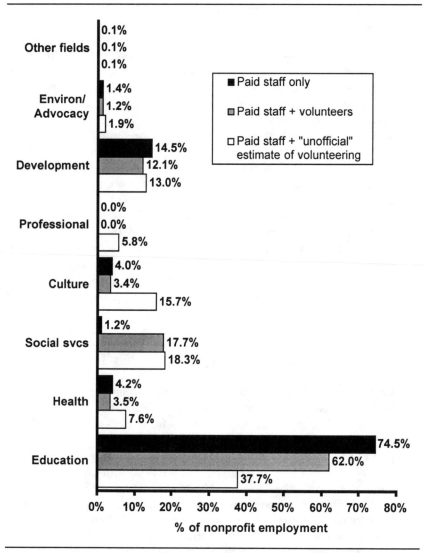

Figure 23.5   Share of nonprofit employment in Peru, with and without
volunteers, and with an "unofficial" estimate of volunteering, 1995

and only slightly less than social services. This reflects the presence of
community-based sports clubs and cultural associations.

In summary, the structure of the nonprofit sector in Peru, as in other
parts of Latin America, reflects a clear dominance of education in the employment base. However, it also demonstrates considerable heterogeneity

in the range of organizations and activities involved and in the contribution of volunteer efforts. The prominence of education, for example, reflects the historical role of the Catholic Church in providing primary and secondary education, especially to the nation's upper and middle classes, but in recent years there has also been a rapid increase in the number of private schools serving poorer students. The overall importance of the development field in these paid employment estimates, meanwhile, reflects the significant role of NGOs, which largely employ middle class professionals, but which are dedicated to providing support and training programs in low-income communities.

5. Most revenue from fees, not philanthropy or public sector

Like its Latin American counterparts, the Peruvian nonprofit sector receives the bulk of its revenue not from private philanthropy but from fees and charges. In particular:

- **Self-generated income dominant.** The majority of income of nonprofit organizations in Peru is self-generated, through fees and charges for the services that these organizations provide, as well as membership dues. As reflected in Figure 23.6, this source accounts for approximately two-thirds, or 67.8 percent, of all nonprofit revenue in Peru.
- **Limited support from philanthropy or the public sector.** In contrast, both private philanthropy and the public sector (domestic and international) provide much smaller shares of total revenues. Thus, as Figure 23.6 also shows, private philanthropy—from individuals, corporations,

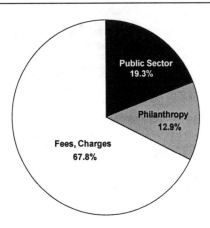

Figure 23.6   Sources of nonprofit revenue in Peru, 1995

and foundations combined—accounts for 12.9 percent of nonprofit income in Peru, while public sector cash payments account for 19.3 percent. [8]

- **Revenue structure with volunteers.** This pattern of nonprofit revenue does not change significantly when volunteers are factored into the picture. One of the main reasons for this is that most of the volunteer work involved in this sector is in community-based organizations, in which the imputed value for this effort is the opportunity cost in the labor market, which is very low. In fact, as shown in Figure 23.7, when volunteer work is included, the private philanthropy share increases only modestly from 12.9 percent to 14.0 percent, and public sector support declines from 19.3 percent to 19.0 percent. Self-generated income, however, is still the dominant revenue source.

- **Revenue structure with in-kind contributions.** A shift does occur, however, when in-kind contributions are taken into account. Interestingly, it is the public sector share that shows a relatively dramatic increase, from 19.3 percent without in-kind contributions to 26.7 percent with them. Thus, while cash support from the public sector is modest, in-kind contributions of food and other items, mainly to the previously mentioned *comedores populares* and *comités de vaso de leche,* make a major difference. Meanwhile, the private philanthropy share remains about the same (12.7 percent), while the fee share declines to 60.6 percent.

- **Similar to other Latin American countries.** The pattern of nonprofit finance evident in Peru is quite similar to that elsewhere in Latin America. Thus, as shown in Figure 23.8, as in Peru, the nonprofit organiza-

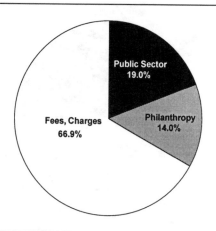

Figure 23.7   Sources of nonprofit revenue in Peru, with volunteers, 1995

tions in the other Latin American countries included in this project also derived the majority of their revenues from fees and charges. In fact, the share of total nonprofit income coming from fees and charges stood at 74.0 percent for all five Latin American countries, well above the Peruvian figure of 67.8 percent. The public sector and philanthropic shares of nonprofit revenue in Peru deviated slightly from the regional average, with public sector (domestic and international) support stronger in Peru than for the region as a whole (19.3 percent vs. 15.5 percent on average) and private giving slightly more prevalent (12.9 percent vs. 10.4 percent).

- **Deviation from the global average.** While the revenue structure of the Peruvian nonprofit sector generally mirrors that in other Latin American countries, it differs considerably from that evident elsewhere in the world. Thus, as Figure 23.8 also shows, while fees and charges are the dominant element in the financial base of the nonprofit sector globally, its dominance is considerably less pronounced elsewhere than it is in Peru (49.4 percent of total revenue compared to 67.8 percent in Peru). By contrast, public sector payments generally comprise a considerably larger share of nonprofit income in these other countries (40.1 percent vs. 19.3 percent in Peru).

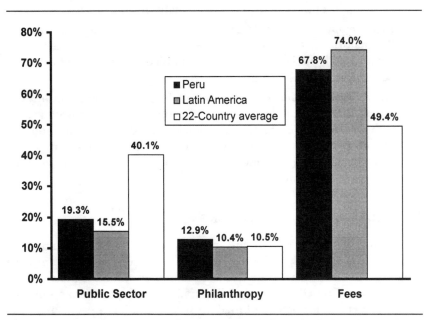

Figure 23.8   Sources of nonprofit cash revenue in Peru, Latin America, and 22-country average, 1995

- **Important support from international sources.** International aid is an important source of the total cash revenues of nonprofit organizations in Peru, representing around 20 percent. This is important to stress because 13.1 percent of the total revenues comes from public international support (multilateral and bilateral organizations). This means that the domestic public sector is the source of only 6.2 percent of total cash revenue. Something similar occurs with private giving: international private giving (e.g., CARE) represents 7 percent of the total cash revenues and domestic private giving only 5.9 percent. In other words, the actual amount of domestic public sector and philanthropic support for nonprofit organizations in Peru is relatively limited.
- **Variations by subsector.** Where reliable data on revenue by subsector are available, they indicate the existence of three distinct patterns of nonprofit finance in Peru, as shown in Figure 23.9:

  Fee-dominant fields. Fee income is the dominant source of income in three fields of nonprofit action for which data were collected: cultural and sport associations, educational institutions, and social service agencies. In the case of cultural and sport associations, membership dues are the primary source of income. Educational institutions receive fees for the services they provide, while social service agencies, especially the *comedores populares* and *comités de vaso de leche*, depend for at least part of their livelihood on payments for the meals they serve.

  Philanthropy-dominant field. Health-related nonprofit agencies receive the majority (57.9 percent) of their resources from private philanthropy.[9] Still, public sector payments also constitute a significant portion (37.4 percent) of their income.

  International aid-dominant fields. International aid (public and private) is the dominant source of income in three fields of nonprofit activity included in these estimates: environment, development and housing, and civic and advocacy. This is not surprising because the predominant organizations in these fields are NGOs, which rely heavily on international assistance to operate.

CONCLUSIONS AND IMPLICATIONS

In a society marked by extreme and persistent poverty, social injustice, and a historically weak and authoritarian state, ordinary Peruvians have long organized in diverse ways to try to meet their own basic material and spiritual needs. Based on longstanding traditions of solidarity and mutual self-help, Peru today boasts a broad array of private, nonprofit organizations whose relative economic and social impact approach that of more "developed" countries in the Latin American region and beyond.

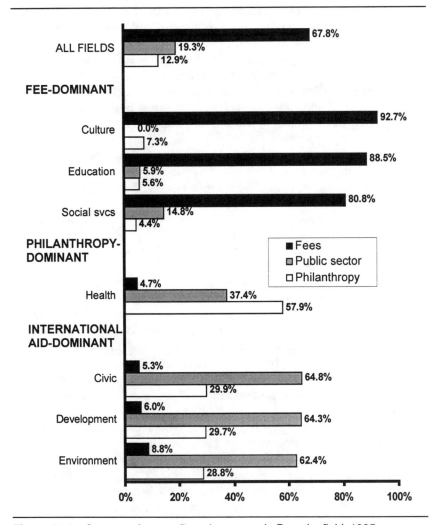

Figure 23.9 Sources of nonprofit cash revenue in Peru, by field, 1995

At the same time, the Peruvian nonprofit sector remains extremely heterogeneous and relatively fragmented, a fact that poses challenges for its consolidation and future impact. To overcome this situation, a number of steps are needed:

- **Increasing awareness of this sector.** The "third sector" in Peru is still an elusive concept that has not gained sufficient recognition in academic or policy circles or among public opinion more generally. Greater efforts thus are needed to bridge the divide that exists between the various components of the nonprofit sector and foster a common understanding of a sector sharing similar interests and needs. The emergence of the concept of civil society has been useful in this regard, but more research, dialogue, and interaction will be required.

- **Capacity building and empowerment.** One way to foster a sense of a distinctive nonprofit sector in Peru is to invest in the capacity of this sector through improved training of nonprofit leaders and strengthening of organizations.
- **Strengthening state-society relations.** As the data and historical analysis presented here show, the state has not been a firm supporter of the development of a nonprofit sector in Peru, although it has not been the main obstacle either. In fact, the relationship between the state and diverse forms of nonprofit organization has been complex and varied, ranging from open hostility to forms of populist co-optation, to more recent forms of collaboration in public policy formation and implementation.

  In the current context, it is important to promote increased public-private partnership, but this must be based on a reasonable degree of autonomy for the nonprofit partners, as well as greater delegation of power and responsibility. It is not sufficient for nonprofits to be simply implementers or "transmission belts" for public policies or programs, but rather they should be involved in the definition of the policy agenda per se (through mechanisms of consultation and participation), the design and definition of program methodologies, and the evaluation of programs and projects.

  Furthermore, it is important to establish a more coherent legal and tax framework for nonprofits in Peru, one that rewards private initiative in philanthropy and social organization. For example, the current tax framework provides few incentives for the creation of nonprofit organizations, and inhibits the mobilization of greater private resources for development and for the establishment of lasting philanthropic institutions.

- **Promoting greater philanthropy and volunteerism.** The building of a more secure domestic fiscal base for nonprofits is critical to their future development in Peru, particularly for those human rights, advocacy, development, and environmental organizations that have played an important part in the development of a new type of nonprofit presence in Peruvian society. The dependence of many NGOs on foreign sources of income leaves them vulnerable to policy changes made outside Peru, while the dependence of grassroots community groups on the fees and volunteer labor of the very poor leaves them with a chronically limited financial base. In effect, it is important to encourage greater private giving in Peru, both individual and institutional, as well as to promote greater voluntary activity and active organizational membership among the middle classes and professional groups.

Important changes are under way in Peruvian society at the present time as memories of the political violence and economic crisis of the 1980s have subsided and greater economic stability has taken root. Among the more hopeful developments in this country today is precisely the emergence of a definable nonprofit sector, a set of institutions outside the market and the state through which citizens can join together to pursue a wide variety of social, political, and economic objectives.

ENDNOTES

1. The work in Peru was coordinated by Felipe Portocarrero and Cynthia Sanborn who served as local associates. They were assisted by Hanny Cueva, Armando Millán, and Gastón Yalonetzky. The team was aided, in turn, by a local advisory committee (see Appendix D for a list of committee members). The Johns Hopkins project was directed by Lester M. Salamon and Helmut K. Anheier and the Latin American portion of the work overseen by Regina List.

2. The Peruvian team was able to secure additional information about two fields of activity (grant-making foundations and professional and trade associations/unions) only after the comparative dataset used in this volume was tallied. Where possible, this new information will be provided in endnotes.

3. The inclusion of grant-making foundations and professional associations would add approximately $82 million in expenditures and bring the nonprofit sector's expenditures to the equivalent of 2.2 percent of GDP.

4. Grant-making foundations and professional associations would add another 6,500 FTE jobs, and increase the sector's share of total nonagricultural employment to 2.5 percent.

5. Centro de Investigación de la Universidad del Pacífico, *Encuesta sobre donaciones y trabajo voluntario en el Perú [Survey on giving and volunteering in Peru]*, Lima: 1998. This exercise in projection is limited by two factors: that the survey was conducted among adults in only four major cities and that it is based on self-reporting of hours contributed.

6. When paid employment in foundations and professional associations is included, education is only slightly less dominant (70.8 percent).

7. The development field's share is 13.8 percent if paid employment in foundations and professional associations are included. This figure is still significantly higher than the Latin American and 22-country averages.

8. With the new revenue data on professional associations and foundations, the revenue mix changes little. Given the membership-based character of professional associations, it should not be surprising that the fees and charges share is slightly higher at 69.8 percent, the private giving share is 12.2 percent, and the public sector share is 18.1 percent.

9. A recent health finance study confirms that private giving is the largest source of income for health-related organizations; however, there is no indication of what portion is domestic and what portion is international.

APPENDIX A

Methodology and Approach

OVERVIEW

The Johns Hopkins Comparative Nonprofit Sector Project sought to develop a common base of data about a similar set of "nonprofit" or "voluntary" institutions in a disparate set of countries. This required that we resolve five critical methodological and conceptual challenges:

- first, to select a set of countries that differed enough along key dimensions to allow us to test some of the major theories in this field;
- second, to define more precisely and more concretely what we meant by "nonprofit" or "voluntary" organizations to be sure that we were examining the same phenomenon in all of the countries;
- third, to develop a classification scheme that could differentiate the various types of entities that share the resulting common features;
- fourth, to identify the most meaningful, but still feasible, aspects of these organizations to focus on for data-gathering purposes; and
- fifth, to devise a way to collect reliable data on these aspects in a cost-efficient fashion.

This Appendix discusses how we went about these five tasks. Appendix C provides more detail on the actual sources of data used in the various countries.

1. Country selection

Central to this project has been the desire to collect a comparable body of data about the nonprofit sector in a broad cross-section of countries. This required that we give careful attention to the selection of target countries. Of particular concern was to make sure that we included countries that differed from each other along dimensions that prior theories suggested might translate into different patterns of nonprofit activity. Only in this way would it be possible to subject these theories to serious empirical testing.

More specifically, prior theory led us to choose countries that differed along the following dimensions:

- their level of economic development;
- their level of government social welfare spending;
- the legal framework they provide for nonprofit action;
- their religious and broader socio-cultural diversity; and
- their social and economic histories.

Also relevant to the selection process was our ability to identify financial support to carry out the work in the given country since only limited central funding was available.

Ultimately, we targeted 28 countries for this phase of the work and were able to generate resources and carry out the needed data-gathering in 22 of them (plus preliminary efforts in a twenty-third country, Poland). Fortunately, these countries offer a considerable range of variation on all five of these dimensions. They represent five of the seven continents, many of the world's major religious traditions, widely disparate patterns of social welfare provision, and divergent levels of overall economic and social development. At the same time, several countries began the data-gathering process much later than these others, and a number of key areas and regions ultimately could not be included. A Phase IIB of the project, focusing on Africa, the Arab Middle East, and South Asia, is now under way to fill in these gaps in coverage.

2. Defining the nonprofit sector: Project coverage

In order to ensure that this project focused on a similar range of entities in all project countries, significant effort went into the development of a common "working definition" of the "nonprofit" sector that could be used in all project sites. This was done by first asking the team of local associates we assembled to collaborate with us on the project to describe the range of organizations and similar entities commonly regarded as nonprofit organizations or part of the "third sector" in their respective countries, and then comparing these descriptions across countries to identify the common elements. A similar process was then repeated when additional countries were added to the project, and adjustments were made to accommodate types of organizations not encountered previously.

Out of this process emerged five key structural and operational characteristics that seemed to define the range of entities most commonly associated with the nonprofit or voluntary sector in countries throughout the world. This "structural-operational" definition then became the working definition of the nonprofit sector for purposes of our project. To be covered by the project under this definition, therefore, an entity had to be:

- **Organized**, i.e., institutionalized to some extent. What is important is not that the organization be registered or legally recognized, but that it have some institutional reality. This can be signified by some degree of internal organizational structure; relative persistence of goals, structure, and activities; meaningful organizational boundaries; as well as a legal charter of incorporation. Both formal and informal organizations are covered by this definition. Excluded are purely ad hoc and temporary gatherings of people with no real structure or organizational identity.
- **Private**, i.e., institutionally separate from government. This does not mean that nonprofit organizations may not receive significant government support or even that government officials cannot sit on their boards. Rather, they must be "nongovernmental" in the sense of being structurally separate from the instrumentalities of government, and they do not exercise governmental authority.
- **Non-profit-distributing**, i.e., not returning profits generated to their owners or directors. Nonprofit organizations may accumulate surplus in a given year, but the profits must be plowed back into the basic mission of the agency, not distributed to the organizations' owners, members, founders, or governing board. The fundamental question is: how does the organization handle profits? If they are reinvested or otherwise applied to the stated purpose of the organization, the organization would qualify as a nonprofit institution.
- **Self-governing**, i.e., equipped to control their own activities. Some organizations that are private and nongovernmental may nevertheless be so tightly controlled either by governmental agencies or private businesses that they essentially function as parts of these other institutions even though they are structurally separate. To meet this criterion, organizations must control their activities to a significant extent, have their own internal governance procedures, and enjoy a meaningful degree of autonomy.
- **Voluntary**, i.e., involving some meaningful degree of voluntary participation. This involves two different, but related, considerations: First, the organization must engage volunteers in its operations and management, either on its board or through the use of volunteer staff and

voluntary contributions. Second, "voluntary" also carries the meaning of "non-compulsory." Organizations in which membership is required or otherwise stipulated by law are excluded from the nonprofit sector. These include some professional associations that require membership in order to be licensed to practice a trade or profession.

As reflected in the classification discussion below, this definition embraces a rather broad set of institutions. Included are trade and professional associations, traditional charitable organizations, organizations involved in religious worship, so-called nongovernmental organizations (NGOs) engaged in development work, grassroots development organizations, higher education institutions, hospitals, and organized social movements, among others. At the same time, both practical considerations and definitional issues complicated the treatment of some types of organizations. Two broad classes of these deserve special mention here:

- *Religious worship organizations.* Churches, synagogues, mosques, and other religious worship organizations are included within the project's definition, and data were sought on them. However, such data could not be collected for all project countries. Accordingly, the religious data are reported separately here. Religiously-affiliated service organizations (e.g., schools, hospitals, day care centers, clinics) were covered everywhere. Such organizations are included in the appropriate service field in which they primarily operate (e.g., education, health, etc.) rather than in "Religion," however, as noted in "Fields of Activity" below.
- *Cooperatives, mutuals, and self-help groups.* Certain types of organizations occupy a "gray area" so far as the project definition is concerned. For example, most cooperatives, mutual societies, and economic self-help groups would be excluded from the project's coverage because they generally would not meet the "non-profit-distributing" criterion. However, it was determined that those cooperatives, mutuals, and similar organizations for which the profit motive is secondary and the primary intent is to offer services that benefit the broader local community could be included.

For further information about the structural-operational definition and how it applies in various country settings, see Salamon, Lester M. and Helmut K. Anheier, eds., *Defining the nonprofit sector: A cross-national analysis.* Manchester: Manchester University Press, 1997; and the collection of "definition working papers" published as part of the Johns Hopkins Comparative Nonprofit Sector Project Working Paper Series, available through the

Johns Hopkins Institute for Policy Studies at the address indicated on the back of this volume's title page.

3. Fields of activity: The classification system

Once the definition of the nonprofit sector was set, a similar effort was undertaken to construct a classification system that could be used to differentiate the various types of organizations covered by this definition. Because we hoped eventually to have the data developed by this project integrated into the regular national income accounting carried out by economic statistics agencies throughout the world, we decided to model our classification system on the one used in regular national income accounting, namely the International Standard Industrial Classification (ISIC) system. This classification scheme differentiates various entities in terms of their principal "economic activity" or field of work (e.g., health, education, social services). Thus, for example, a nonprofit organization that mainly provides health services, but also conducts research as a secondary activity, would be classified as a health-related organization, rather than an educational one. Similarly a religious congregation whose main economic activity is operating a primary school would be classified under education, not religion. Because it is not always feasible to do this on an organization-by-organization basis, such determination often had to be made for entire classes of organizations.

Because the level of differentiation of entities in the fields where nonprofit organizations are active seemed rather limited in the existing ISIC system, however, we drew on the experience of the project countries as reported by our local associates to amplify the ISIC structure somewhat. The result was the development of an International Classification of Nonprofit Organizations (ICNPO) that was tested against the experience of the various project countries. This typology, too, was reviewed when new countries entered the project, and adaptations were made where necessary.

As outlined in Table A.1 below, the resulting classification scheme breaks the nonprofit sector down into twelve "major groups" ranging from arts and culture to "not elsewhere classified." Each "major group" is then further divided into subgroups. Altogether, 27 subgroups are identified. Generally speaking, data limitations made it impossible to differentiate organizations at the subgroup level but more confidence can be placed in the data at the level of the major groups.

A more detailed outline of the types of entities included within each ICNPO major group and subgroup is provided at the end of this appendix. For further clarification, please see Salamon, Lester M. and Helmut K. Anheier, "The International Classification of Nonprofit Organizations:

Table A.1   International Classification of Nonprofit Organizations (ICNPO):
Major Groups and Subgroups

GROUP 1:	CULTURE AND RECREATION	GROUP 6:	DEVELOPMENT AND HOUSING
1 100	Culture and Arts	6 100	Economic, Social and Community Development
1 200	Sports		
1 300	Other Recreation and Social Clubs	6 200	Housing
GROUP 2:	EDUCATION AND RESEARCH	6 300	Employment and Training
2 100	Primary and Secondary Education	GROUP 7:	LAW, ADVOCACY AND POLITICS
2 200	Higher Education	7 100	Civic and Advocacy Organizations
2 300	Other Education	7 200	Law and Legal Services
2 400	Research		
GROUP 3:	HEALTH	7 300	Political Organizations
3 100	Hospitals and Rehabilitation	GROUP 8:	PHILANTHROPIC INTERMEDIARIES AND VOLUNTARISM PROMOTION
3 200	Nursing Homes		
3 300	Mental Health and Crisis Intervention		
3 400	Other Health Services	GROUP 9:	INTERNATIONAL
GROUP 4:	SOCIAL SERVICES	GROUP 10:	RELIGION
4 100	Social Services		
4 200	Emergency and Relief	GROUP 11:	BUSINESS AND PROFESSIONAL ASSOCIATIONS, UNIONS
4 300	Income Support and Maintenance		
GROUP 5:	ENVIRONMENT		
5 100	Environment	GROUP 12:	[NOT ELSEWHERE CLASSIFIED]
5 200	Animal Protection		

ICNPO-Revision 1, 1996," *Working Papers of the Johns Hopkins Comparative Nonprofit Sector Project,* No. 19. Baltimore: The Johns Hopkins Institute for Policy Studies, 1996; and Salamon, Lester M., and Helmut K. Anheier, "In Search of the Nonprofit Sector II: The Question of Classification," in Salamon, Lester M. and Helmut K. Anheier, eds., *Defining the nonprofit sector: A cross-national analysis.* Manchester: Manchester University Press, 1997.

4. Key variables

A major objective of this project, and the one that is the principal focus of this book, was to document the scale of the nonprofit sector in the countries covered and the revenue sources used to support it. For these purposes, we focused on four key variables. The significance of these variables and the various terms we use to discuss them are described below.

- **Expenditures.** In this book, the term "expenditures" is used as a shorthand for "operating expenditures," i.e., the costs incurred in the general operations of an organization. These include salaries, fringe benefits, and other personnel costs; purchases of non-capital goods, supplies, and services; and any fees and charges paid. However, "operating expenditures" excludes "capital expenditures," i.e., costs incurred in land acquisition, building construction, and purchase of major equipment and vehicles, since these are typically paid for over time.
- **Employment.** Because of cross-national differences in wage rates and other costs, employment seemed a better basis for comparing the scale of the nonprofit sector across countries than expenditures. To facilitate cross-national comparisons, however, it was necessary to translate the number of employees working for nonprofit organizations into "full-time equivalent (FTE) employees" because many nonprofit employees work part-time. This was done by using national standards of full-time equivalent work. Throughout the text, "employment," "employees," and "jobs" refer to "full-time equivalent" (FTE) paid employment or jobs. Where specifically noted, moreover, full-time equivalent volunteer employment is also included. Nonprofit employment is generally computed as a share of total nonagricultural employment, though when volunteers are included they are added to the denominator as well.
- **Volunteers.** In addition to the number of paid workers, we also attempted to gather data on the number of volunteers working for nonprofit organizations in our target countries. These data were generally compiled through population surveys. As with employment data, volunteer inputs were converted into full-time equivalent jobs and calculated as a share of total nonagricultural FTE paid and volunteer labor. We also calculated the imputed value of this volunteer labor for use mainly in our revenue estimates. This was done by multiplying the number of FTE volunteers by the average wage in the particular industry.
- **Revenues.** In addition to measuring the expenditures and employment of nonprofit organizations, we also attempted to estimate the sources

of the revenues supporting these expenditures and levels of activity. For this purpose, we treated revenues as inflows of spendable resources received by the organization during the year. We further distinguished cash revenues from in-kind revenues, which include the imputed value of volunteer labor, and sought data on both. Unless otherwise noted in the text, revenue data typically refer to cash revenues. More specifically, we differentiated three main sources of such revenue:

Fees and charges, which include membership dues; service charges paid directly by the client in exchange for services; investment income; and income from the sale of goods and services whether or not they are related to the organization's mission.

Public sector payments, which refer to revenues coming from all branches of government (administrative, judicial, and legislative) as well as quasi-governmental entities such as social insurance funds at all levels (national, departmental, municipal, etc.). In essence, we use "public sector" and "governmental" synonymously. Public sector revenues include grants and contracts in support of specific organizational activities or services; statutory transfers mandated by law in support of an organization's general mission or activities; and third party payments, i.e., indirect government payments for reimbursement to another organization for services rendered to individuals.

Philanthropy, or private giving, which includes revenues received from at least four types of sources: (a) individual contributions; (b) private foundation grants; (c) corporate donations, including those from corporate foundations; and (d) contributions channeled through federated giving funds or programs.

5. Data collection and assembly strategy

A central premise of this project has been that far more data exist on some of these key dimensions of the nonprofit sector in each country than is widely recognized. Such data are often collected as part of the process of national income accounting, which is used to build up estimates of overall national income and product and its distribution among different industries. However, these sources often group data on nonprofit organizations together with data on other types of organizations, or provide information in a form that is hard to translate into the variables of interest without further work, all of which make it difficult to gather the information that is needed directly on the nonprofit sector.

The first step in each country therefore has been to conduct an inventory of existing statistical data sources that contain information on the nonprofit sector or its parts. The next step, and a central task of the project, has been to devise ways to take advantage of these existing data sources and use them to develop reasonable estimates of the various dimensions of the nonprofit sector of interest to us. This often required "building up" from data elements that were available to the ones that we ideally wanted. On occasion, when no existing data source provided sufficient information on a particular activity group or variable of interest, the research teams have conducted targeted surveys using, for the most part, common survey instruments developed by the project. Ultimately, the data assembly strategies have differed from country to country depending on the nature of the specific data sources. These strategies and sources are briefly outlined in the individual country chapters above and Appendix C below. Finally, once the data were assembled, each country team entered them into a dedicated computer-based data entry program and, subsequently, submitted the completed data tables to the Johns Hopkins core team for cross-checking and comparison.

ATTACHMENT TO APPENDIX A

INTERNATIONAL CLASSIFICATION OF NONPROFIT ORGANIZATIONS

Detailed Table

Group 1: Culture and Recreation

1 100 Culture and Arts

Media and communications. Production and dissemination of information and communication; includes radio and TV stations; publishing of books, journals, newspapers, and newsletters; film production; and libraries.

Visual arts, architecture, ceramic art. Production, dissemination, and display of visual arts and architecture; includes sculpture, photographic societies, painting, drawing, design centers, and architectural associations.

Performing arts. Performing arts centers, companies, and associations; includes theater, dance, ballet, opera, orchestras, chorals, and music ensembles.

Historical, literary, and humanistic societies. Promotion and appreciation of the humanities, preservation of historical and cultural artifacts, and commemoration of historical events; includes historical societies, poetry and literary societies, language associations, reading promotion, war memorials, and commemorative funds and associations.

Museums. General and specialized museums covering art, history, sciences, technology, and culture.

Zoos and aquariums.

1 200 Sports

Provision of amateur sport, training, physical fitness, and sport competition services and events; includes fitness and wellness centers.

1 300 Other Recreation and Social Clubs

Recreation and social clubs. Provision of recreational facilities and services to individuals and communities; includes playground associations, country clubs, men's and women's clubs, touring clubs, and leisure clubs.

Service clubs. Membership organizations providing services to members and local communities, for example: Lions, Zonta International, Rotary Club, and Kiwanis.

Group 2: Education and Research

2 100 Primary and Secondary Education

Elementary, primary, and secondary education. Education at elementary, primary, and secondary levels; includes pre-school organizations other than day care.

2 200 Higher Education

Higher education. Higher learning, providing academic degrees; includes universities, business management schools, law schools, medical schools.

2 300 Other Education

Vocational/technical schools. Technical and vocational training specifically geared towards gaining employment; includes trade schools, paralegal training, secretarial schools.

Adult/continuing education. Institutions engaged in providing education and training in addition to the formal educational system; includes schools of continuing studies, correspondence schools, night schools, and sponsored literacy and reading programs.

2 400 Research

Medical research. Research in the medical field; includes research on specific diseases, disorders, or medical disciplines.

Science and technology. Research in the physical and life sciences, and engineering and technology.

Social sciences, policy studies. Research and analysis in the social sciences and policy area.

Group 3: Health

3 100 Hospitals and Rehabilitation

Hospitals. Primarily inpatient medical care and treatment.

Rehabilitation. Inpatient health care and rehabilitative therapy to individuals suffering from physical impairments due to injury, genetic defect, or disease and requiring extensive physiotherapy or similar forms of care.

3 200 Nursing Homes

Nursing homes. Inpatient convalescent care, residential care, as well as primary health care services; includes homes for the frail elderly and nursing homes for the severely handicapped.

3 300 Mental Health and Crisis Intervention

Psychiatric hospitals. Inpatient care and treatment for the mentally ill.

Mental health treatment. Outpatient treatment for mentally ill patients; includes community mental health centers, and halfway homes.

Crisis intervention. Outpatient services and counsel in acute mental health situations; includes suicide prevention and support to victims of assault and abuse.

3 400 Other Health Services

Public health and wellness education. Public health promotion and health education; includes sanitation screening for potential health hazards, first aid training and services, and family planning services.

Health treatment, primarily outpatient. Organizations that provide primarily outpatient health services—e.g., health clinics and vaccination centers.

Rehabilitative medical services. Outpatient therapeutic care; includes nature cure centers, yoga clinics, and physical therapy centers.

Emergency medical services. Services to persons in need of immediate care; includes ambulatory services and paramedical emergency care, shock/trauma programs, lifeline programs, and ambulance services.

Group 4: Social Services

4 100 Social Services

Child welfare, child services, and day care. Services to children, adoption services, child development centers, foster care; includes infant care centers and nurseries.

Youth services and youth welfare. Services to youth; includes delinquency prevention services, teen pregnancy prevention, drop-out prevention, youth centers and clubs, and job programs for youth; includes YMCA, YWCA, Boy Scouts, Girl Scouts, and Big Brothers/Big Sisters.

Family services. Services to families; includes family life/parent education, single parent agencies and services, and family violence shelters and services.

Services for the handicapped. Services for the handicapped; includes homes, other than nursing homes, transport facilities, recreation, and other specialized services.

Services for the elderly. Organizations providing geriatric care; includes in-home services, homemaker services, transport facilities, recreation, meal programs, and other services geared towards senior citizens. (Does not include residential nursing homes.)

Self-help and other personal social services. Programs and services for self-help and personal development; includes support groups, personal counseling, and credit counseling/money management services.

4 200 Emergency and Relief

Disaster/emergency prevention and control. Organizations that work to prevent, predict, control, and alleviate the effects of disasters, to educate or otherwise prepare individuals to cope with the effects of disasters, or to provide relief to disaster victims; includes volunteer fire departments, life boat services, etc.

Temporary shelters. Organizations providing temporary shelters to the homeless; includes travelers aid and temporary housing.

Refugee assistance. Organizations providing food, clothing, shelter, and services to refugees and immigrants.

4 300 Income Support and Maintenance

Income support and maintenance. Organizations providing cash assistance and other forms of direct services to persons unable to maintain a livelihood.

Material assistance. Organizations providing food, clothing, transport, and other forms of assistance; includes food banks and clothing distribution centers.

Group 5: Environment

5 100 Environment

Pollution abatement and control. Organizations that promote clean air, clean water, reducing and preventing noise pollution, radiation control, treatment of hazardous wastes and toxic substances, solid waste management, and recycling programs.

Natural resources conservation and protection. Conservation and preservation of natural resources, including land, water, energy, and plant resources for the general use and enjoyment of the public.

Environmental beautification and open spaces. Botanical gardens, arboreta, horticultural programs and landscape services; organizations promoting anti-litter campaigns; programs to preserve the parks, green spaces, and open spaces in urban or rural areas; and city and highway beautification programs.

5 200 Animal Protection

Animal protection and welfare. Animal protection and welfare services; includes animal shelters and humane societies.

Wildlife preservation and protection. Wildlife preservation and protection; includes sanctuaries and refuges.

Veterinary services. Animal hospitals and services providing care to farm and household animals and pets.

Group 6: Development and Housing

6 100 Economic, Social, and Community Development

Community and neighborhood organizations. Organizations working towards improving the quality of life within communities or neighborhoods, e.g., squatters' associations, local development organizations, poor people's cooperatives.

Economic development. Programs and services to improve economic infrastructure and capacity; includes building of infrastructure like roads; and financial services such as credit and savings associations, entrepreneurial programs, technical and managerial consulting, and rural development assistance.

Social development. Organizations working towards improving the institutional infrastructure and capacity to alleviate social problems and to improve general public well being.

6 200 Housing

Housing associations. Development, construction, management, leasing, financing, and rehabilitation of housing.

Housing assistance. Organizations providing housing search, legal services, and related assistance.

6 300 Employment and Training

Job training programs. Organizations providing and supporting apprenticeship programs, internships, on-the-job training, and other training programs.

Vocational counseling and guidance. Vocational training and guidance, career counseling, testing, and related services.

Vocational rehabilitation and sheltered workshops. Organizations that promote self-sufficiency and income generation through job training and employment.

Group 7: Law, Advocacy, and Politics

7 100 Civic and Advocacy Organizations

Advocacy organizations. Organizations that protect the rights and promote the interests of specific groups of people, e.g., the physically handicapped, the elderly, children, and women.

Civil rights associations. Organizations that work to protect or preserve individual civil liberties and human rights.

Ethnic associations. Organizations that promote the interests of, or provide services to, members belonging to a specific ethnic heritage.

Civic associations. Programs and services to encourage and spread civic mindedness.

7 200 Law and Legal Services

Legal services. Legal services, advice, and assistance in dispute resolution and court-related matters.

Crime prevention and public policy. Crime prevention to promote safety and precautionary measures among citizens.

Rehabilitation of offenders. Programs and services to reintegrate offenders; includes halfway houses, probation and parole programs, prison alternatives.

Victim support. Services, counsel, and advice to victims of crime.

Consumer protection associations. Protection of consumer rights, and the improvement of product control and quality.

7 300 Political Organizations

Political parties and organizations. Activities and services to support the placing of particular candidates into political office; includes dissemination of information, public relations, and political fundraising.

Group 8: Philanthropic Intermediaries and Voluntarism Promotion

8 100 Philanthropic Intermediaries and Voluntarism Promotion

Grant-making foundations. Private foundations; including corporate foundations, community foundations, and independent public-law foundations.

Volunteerism promotion and support. Organizations that recruit, train, and place volunteers and promote volunteering.

Fund-raising organizations. Federated, collective fundraising organizations; includes lotteries.

Group 9: International

9 100 International Activities

Exchange/friendship/cultural programs. Programs and services designed to encourage mutual respect and friendship internationally.

Development assistance associations. Programs and projects that promote social and economic development abroad.

International disaster and relief organizations. Organizations that collect, channel, and provide aid to other countries during times of disaster or emergency.

International human rights and peace organizations. Organizations which promote and monitor human rights and peace internationally.

Group 10: Religion

10 100 Religious Congregations and Associations

Congregations. Churches, synagogues, temples, mosques, shrines, monasteries, seminaries, and similar organizations promoting religious beliefs and administering religious services and rituals.

Associations of congregations. Associations and auxiliaries of religious congregations and organizations supporting and promoting religious beliefs, services and rituals.

Group 11: Business and Professional Associations, and Unions

11 100 Business and Professional Associations, and Unions

Business associations. Organizations that work to promote, regulate, and safeguard the interests of special branches of business, e.g., manufacturers' association, farmers' association, bankers' association.

Professional associations. Organizations promoting, regulating, and protecting professional interests, e.g., bar association, medical association.

Labor unions. Organizations that promote, protect, and regulate the rights and interests of employees.

Group 12: [Not Elsewhere Classified]

12 100 N.E.C.

APPENDIX B

Comparative Data Tables

Table B.1   Nonprofit sector FTE employment excluding religious worship, by country and field of activity, 1995

Region	Country	Culture	Education	Health	Social Svcs	Environment	Development	Advocacy	Phil. Intermediaries	International	Professional	Other/n.e.c.	Total Nonprofit Employment	Nonprofit Share of Total** Employment
Western Europe	Austria	8.4%	8.9%	11.6%	64.0%	0.4%	0.0%	4.5%	0.0%	0.8%	1.4%	0.0%	143,637	4.5%
	Belgium	4.9%	38.8%	30.4%	13.8%	0.5%	9.9%	0.4%	0.2%	0.2%	0.9%	0.0%	357,802	10.5%
	Finland	14.2%	25.0%	23.0%	17.8%	1.0%	2.4%	8.7%	0.0%	0.3%	7.2%	0.3%	62,848	3.0%
	France	12.1%	20.7%	15.5%	39.7%	1.0%	5.5%	1.9%	0.0%	1.8%	1.8%	0.0%	959,821	4.9%
	Germany	5.4%	11.7%	30.6%	38.8%	0.8%	6.1%	1.6%	0.4%	0.7%	3.9%	0.0%	1,440,850	4.9%
	Ireland	6.0%	53.7%	27.6%	4.5%	0.9%	4.3%	0.4%	0.1%	0.3%	2.2%	0.0%	118,664	11.5%
	Netherlands	4.1%	27.8%	41.8%	19.2%	1.0%	2.6%	0.6%	0.4%	0.6%	2.0%	0.0%	652,829	12.6%
	Spain	11.8%	25.1%	12.2%	31.8%	0.3%	11.2%	3.4%	0.1%	2.0%	1.8%	0.3%	475,179	4.5%
	U.K.	24.5%	41.5%	4.3%	13.1%	1.3%	7.6%	0.7%	0.7%	3.8%	2.6%	0.0%	1,415,743	6.2%
	Western Europe Avg.*/Total	10.1%	28.1%	21.9%	27.0%	0.8%	5.5%	2.5%	0.2%	1.2%	2.6%	0.1%	5,627,372	7.0%
Other Developed Countries	Australia	16.4%	23.3%	18.6%	20.1%	0.5%	10.8%	3.2%	0.1%	0.2%	4.3%	2.6%	402,574	7.2%
	Israel	5.9%	50.3%	27.0%	10.9%	0.8%	1.0%	0.4%	2.0%	0.1%	1.8%	0.0%	145,396	9.2%
	Japan	3.1%	22.5%	47.1%	16.6%	0.4%	0.3%	0.2%	0.2%	0.4%	5.0%	4.3%	2,140,079	3.5%
	U.S.	7.3%	21.5%	46.3%	13.5%	0.0%	6.3%	1.8%	0.3%	0.0%	2.9%	0.0%	8,554,900	7.8%
	Other Developed Avg.*/Total	8.2%	29.4%	34.8%	15.3%	0.4%	4.6%	1.4%	0.6%	0.2%	3.5%	1.7%	11,242,949	6.9%
	All Developed Avg.*/Total	9.5%	28.5%	25.9%	23.4%	0.7%	5.2%	2.1%	0.3%	0.8%	2.9%	0.6%	16,870,321	7.0%
Central Europe	Czech Rep.	31.0%	14.6%	13.6%	11.2%	3.7%	7.4%	3.1%	2.0%	1.1%	12.3%	0.0%	74,196	1.7%
	Hungary	38.1%	10.0%	4.5%	11.1%	2.0%	13.2%	1.0%	3.3%	0.8%	16.1%	0.0%	44,938	1.3%
	Romania	34.0%	17.9%	13.1%	20.7%	0.7%	3.6%	4.4%	0.8%	1.3%	3.6%	0.0%	37,353	0.6%
	Slovakia	36.7%	28.5%	1.9%	5.2%	6.8%	1.1%	2.9%	4.9%	0.9%	10.4%	0.8%	16,196	0.9%
	Central Europe Avg.*/Total	34.9%	17.7%	8.3%	12.0%	3.3%	6.3%	2.8%	2.8%	1.0%	10.6%	0.2%	172,683	1.1%
Latin America	Argentina	15.1%	41.2%	13.4%	10.7%	0.3%	5.7%	0.4%	0.2%	1.3%	6.8%	4.9%	395,315	3.7%
	Brazil	17.0%	36.9%	17.8%	16.4%	0.2%	1.1%	0.6%	0.0%	0.4%	9.6%	0.0%	1,034,550	2.2%
	Colombia	9.4%	26.1%	17.5%	14.6%	0.8%	13.1%	1.3%	0.9%	0.1%	15.1%	1.2%	286,861	2.4%
	Mexico	7.7%	43.2%	8.1%	8.7%	0.7%	0.5%	0.3%	0.3%	0.0%	30.5%	0.0%	93,809	0.4%
	Peru	4.0%	74.5%	4.2%	1.2%	0.6%	14.5%	0.8%	0.1%	0.0%	0.0%	0.0%	126,988	2.4%
	Latin America Avg.*/Total	10.6%	44.4%	12.2%	10.3%	0.5%	7.0%	0.7%	0.3%	0.4%	12.4%	1.2%	1,937,524	2.2%
	Grand Average/Total	14.4%	30.2%	19.6%	18.3%	1.1%	5.8%	1.9%	0.8%	0.8%	6.5%	0.7%	18,980,528	4.8%

* Unweighted averages, calculated on the assumption that missing values equal zero.

** Nonagricultural FTE employment.

Source: The Johns Hopkins Comparative Nonprofit Sector Project, Phase II

Table B.2   Nonprofit sector FTE employment with volunteers, excluding religious worship, by country and field of activity, 1995

Region	Country	Culture	Education	Health	Social Svcs	Environment	Development	Advocacy	Phil. Intermediaries	International	Professional	Other /n.e.c	Total Nonprofit Employment	Nonprofit Share of Total** Employment
Western Europe	Austria	6.5%	6.9%	9.1%	49.9%	0.3%	0.0%	3.5%	0.0%	0.6%	1.1%	22.1%	184,323	5.7%
	Belgium	11.1%	30.5%	23.9%	22.9%	0.5%	8.3%	0.5%	0.3%	0.4%	1.5%	0.0%	456,901	13.0%
	Finland	32.6%	12.4%	13.1%	15.5%	0.7%	1.6%	16.8%	0.2%	0.4%	6.2%	0.4%	137,599	6.3%
	France	30.0%	14.6%	9.2%	27.4%	5.0%	4.7%	1.9%	0.6%	2.4%	4.3%	0.0%	1,981,476	9.6%
	Germany	19.7%	7.6%	21.8%	27.2%	2.8%	4.4%	3.3%	1.0%	1.6%	4.2%	6.4%	2,418,924	8.0%
	Ireland	10.5%	43.0%	23.3%	13.0%	0.9%	5.7%	0.5%	0.7%	0.4%	1.7%	0.3%	150,314	14.2%
	Netherlands	17.3%	23.3%	28.9%	20.5%	2.0%	1.7%	3.0%	0.2%	1.2%	1.8%	0.0%	1,042,929	18.7%
	Spain	15.2%	20.6%	10.5%	30.8%	3.0%	9.2%	5.9%	0.1%	2.6%	1.8%	0.2%	728,778	6.8%
	U.K.	27.5%	25.4%	8.0%	16.0%	2.4%	12.5%	1.8%	1.3%	2.4%	1.5%	1.2%	2,536,026	10.6%
Western Europe Avg.*/Total		**19.0%**	**20.5%**	**16.4%**	**24.8%**	**2.0%**	**5.4%**	**4.1%**	**0.5%**	**1.3%**	**2.7%**	**3.4%**	**9,637,270**	**10.3%**
Other Developed Countries	Australia	22.7%	17.9%	14.9%	23.6%	1.4%	10.4%	2.9%	0.2%	0.4%	3.3%	2.4%	579,722	10.1%
	Israel	8.6%	41.4%	27.2%	16.0%	0.6%	0.8%	2.0%	1.6%	0.1%	1.6%	0.0%	176,657	11.0%
	Japan	5.5%	18.5%	37.3%	17.3%	0.7%	1.9%	0.5%	1.1%	1.6%	5.0%	10.7%	2,835,176	4.6%
	U.S.	9.0%	18.5%	34.2%	22.1%	1.0%	4.0%	4.9%	1.0%	0.3%	3.9%	1.1%	13,549,062	11.9%
Other Developed Avg.*/Total		**11.5%**	**24.1%**	**28.4%**	**19.7%**	**0.9%**	**4.3%**	**2.6%**	**1.0%**	**0.6%**	**3.4%**	**3.6%**	**17,140,617**	**9.4%**
All Developed Avg.*/Total		**16.6%**	**21.6%**	**20.1%**	**23.2%**	**1.6%**	**5.0%**	**3.6%**	**0.6%**	**1.1%**	**2.9%**	**3.4%**	**26,777,887**	**10.0%**
Central Europe	Czech Rep.	35.8%	10.6%	11.9%	13.1%	6.1%	6.7%	3.5%	2.2%	1.4%	8.6%	0.0%	115,056	2.7%
	Hungary	36.8%	8.9%	4.7%	15.1%	2.2%	11.3%	2.3%	3.7%	1.0%	14.0%	0.0%	54,816	1.6%
	Romania	28.6%	15.1%	8.5%	32.2%	2.2%	2.4%	3.8%	1.0%	4.0%	2.4%	0.0%	83,861	1.3%
	Slovakia	37.0%	20.4%	1.9%	10.1%	9.0%	1.1%	3.8%	5.6%	0.9%	9.1%	1.1%	23,047	1.2%
Central Europe Avg.*/Total		**34.5%**	**13.8%**	**6.7%**	**17.6%**	**4.9%**	**5.4%**	**3.4%**	**3.1%**	**1.8%**	**8.5%**	**0.3%**	**276,780**	**1.7%**
Latin America	Argentina	13.8%	31.5%	9.8%	13.5%	1.6%	15.7%	1.8%	0.1%	0.8%	8.2%	3.2%	659,425	6.0%
	Brazil	15.1%	35.1%	17.5%	19.2%	0.2%	3.0%	0.7%	0.0%	0.4%	8.6%	0.3%	1,173,766	2.5%
	Colombia	7.5%	20.2%	15.3%	18.7%	0.8%	18.5%	1.6%	1.5%	0.1%	14.9%	0.9%	377,617	3.1%
	Mexico	6.4%	30.7%	8.4%	16.3%	1.8%	1.2%	0.8%	0.8%	0.0%	33.6%	0.0%	141,024	0.7%
	Peru	3.4%	62.0%	3.5%	17.7%	0.6%	12.1%	0.7%	0.1%	0.0%	0.0%	0.0%	153,374	2.9%
Latin America Avg.*/Total		**9.2%**	**35.9%**	**10.9%**	**17.1%**	**1.0%**	**10.1%**	**1.1%**	**0.5%**	**0.2%**	**13.0%**	**0.9%**	**2,505,207**	**3.0%**
Grand Average/Total		**18.2%**	**23.4%**	**15.6%**	**20.8%**	**2.1%**	**6.2%**	**3.0%**	**1.1%**	**1.0%**	**6.2%**	**2.3%**	**29,559,875**	**6.9%**

* Unweighted averages, calculated on the assumption that missing values equal zero.
** Nonagricultural FTE employment.
Source: The Johns Hopkins Comparative Nonprofit Sector Project, Phase II

Table B.3 Nonprofit revenues (with and without volunteer input), excluding religious worship, by country and revenue source, 1995

Region	Country	Excluding Volunteer Input			Total Cash Revenue	Including Volunteer Input			Total Cash Revenue and Volunteer Input
		Share of Revenue from:				Share of Revenue from:			
		Public Sector	Private Giving	Fees, Charges	millions US $	Public Sector	Private Giving	Fees, Charges	millions US $
Western Europe	Austria	50.4%	6.1%	43.5%	6,262	41.3%	23.1%	35.6%	7,643
	Belgium	76.8%	4.7%	18.6%	25,576	65.9%	18.1%	16.0%	29,773
	Finland	36.2%	5.9%	57.9%	6,064	25.2%	34.6%	40.3%	8,722
	France	57.8%	7.5%	34.6%	57,304	33.4%	46.6%	20.0%	99,234
	Germany	64.3%	3.4%	32.3%	94,454	42.5%	36.2%	21.3%	142,887
	Ireland	77.2%	7.0%	15.8%	5,017	67.6%	18.6%	13.8%	5,732
	Netherlands	59.0%	2.7%	38.3%	60,400	46.0%	24.1%	29.9%	77,427
	Spain	32.1%	18.8%	49.0%	25,778	25.2%	36.3%	38.5%	32,833
	U.K.	46.7%	8.8%	44.6%	78,220	36.4%	28.8%	34.8%	100,196
	Western Europe Average*/Total	55.6%	7.2%	37.2%	359,074	42.6%	29.6%	27.8%	504,447
Other Developed Countries	Australia	31.1%	6.4%	62.5%	20,227	25.4%	23.4%	51.2%	24,712
	Israel	63.9%	10.2%	25.8%	10,947	59.1%	17.0%	23.9%	11,842
	Japan	45.2%	2.6%	52.1%	258,959	41.5%	10.7%	47.8%	282,314
	U.S.	30.5%	12.9%	56.6%	566,960	25.6%	26.9%	47.4%	675,973
	Other Developed Average*/Total	42.7%	8.0%	49.3%	857,094	37.9%	19.5%	42.6%	994,841
	All Developed Average/Total*	51.6%	7.5%	40.9%	1,216,168	41.2%	26.5%	32.4%	1,499,288
Central Europe	Czech Rep.	39.4%	14.0%	46.6%	860	32.1%	30.0%	37.9%	1,056
	Hungary	27.1%	18.4%	54.6%	1,433	26.2%	21.1%	52.7%	1,483
	Romania	45.0%	26.5%	28.5%	130	20.5%	66.5%	13.0%	285
	Slovakia	21.9%	23.3%	54.9%	295	21.3%	25.1%	53.5%	302
	Central Europe Average*/Total	33.3%	20.5%	46.1%	2,718	25.0%	35.7%	39.3%	3,126
Latin America	Argentina	19.5%	7.5%	73.1%	13,321	16.2%	23.0%	60.8%	16,014
	Brazil	15.5%	10.7%	73.8%	11,390	14.5%	16.3%	69.2%	12,144
	Colombia	14.9%	14.9%	70.2%	1,719	13.1%	24.9%	62.0%	1,948
	Mexico	8.5%	6.3%	85.2%	1,554	7.5%	17.9%	74.7%	1,774
	Peru	19.3%	12.9%	67.8%	1,190	19.0%	14.0%	66.9%	1,206
	Latin America Average*/Total	15.5%	10.4%	74.0%	29,173	14.1%	19.2%	66.7%	33,085
	Grand Average*/Total	40.1%	10.5%	49.4%	1,248,659	32.1%	26.5%	41.4%	1,535,499

* Unweighted averages.
** Volunteer input has been included in the Private Giving column.
Source: The Johns Hopkins Comparative Nonprofit Sector Project, Phase II

Table B.4 Nonprofit sector FTE employment with religious worship, by country and field of activity, 1995

Region	Country	Culture	Education	Health	Social Svcs	Environment	Development	Advocacy	Phil. Inter-mediaries	International	Religious Worship	Professional	Other n.e.c.	Total Nonprofit Employment	Nonprofit Share of Total** Employment
Western Europe	Austria	8.0%	8.5%	11.1%	61.1%	0.4%	0.0%	4.3%	0.0%	0.7%	4.5%	1.4%	0.0%	150,425	4.7%
	Finland	13.5%	23.8%	21.9%	16.9%	1.0%	2.2%	8.3%	0.0%	0.2%	4.8%	6.9%	0.3%	66,043	3.1%
	France	11.9%	20.4%	15.2%	39.1%	0.9%	5.4%	1.9%	0.0%	1.8%	1.5%	1.7%	0.0%	974,867	5.0%
	Germany	5.2%	11.3%	29.8%	37.8%	0.8%	5.9%	1.6%	0.4%	0.7%	2.7%	3.8%	0.0%	1,480,850	5.1%
	Ireland	5.7%	50.7%	26.1%	4.3%	0.9%	4.0%	0.4%	0.1%	0.3%	5.5%	2.1%	0.0%	125,584	12.2%
	Netherlands	4.1%	27.5%	41.4%	18.9%	1.0%	2.5%	0.6%	0.4%	0.6%	1.1%	1.9%	0.0%	660,299	12.7%
	U.K.	23.5%	39.8%	4.1%	12.6%	1.2%	7.3%	0.7%	0.7%	3.6%	3.9%	2.5%	0.0%	1,473,443	6.4%
Western Europe Avg.*/Total		10.3%	26.0%	21.4%	27.2%	0.9%	3.9%	2.5%	0.2%	1.1%	3.5%	2.9%	0.0%	4,931,512	7.0%
Other Developed Countries	Australia	15.9%	22.5%	18.0%	19.4%	0.4%	10.5%	3.1%	0.1%	0.2%	3.1%	4.2%	2.5%	415,651	7.5%
	Israel	5.8%	49.7%	26.7%	10.7%	0.7%	1.0%	0.4%	1.9%	0.1%	1.2%	1.8%	0.0%	147,166	9.3%
	Japan	2.9%	21.0%	44.1%	15.6%	0.4%	0.3%	0.2%	0.2%	0.3%	6.5%	4.7%	4.0%	2,287,993	3.7%
	U.S.	6.5%	19.1%	41.1%	12.0%	0.0%	5.6%	1.6%	0.2%	0.0%	11.2%	2.6%	0.0%	9,634,600	8.8%
Other Developed Avg.*/Total		7.8%	28.1%	32.5%	14.4%	0.4%	4.3%	1.3%	0.6%	0.2%	5.5%	3.3%	1.6%	12,485,411	7.3%
All Developed Avg.*/Total		9.4%	26.8%	25.4%	22.6%	0.7%	4.1%	2.1%	0.4%	0.8%	4.2%	3.0%	0.6%	17,416,923	7.1%
Central Europe	Czech Rep.	29.5%	13.8%	12.9%	10.6%	3.5%	7.0%	2.9%	1.9%	1.0%	5.1%	11.7%	0.0%	78,200	1.8%
	Romania	33.4%	17.6%	12.9%	20.3%	0.6%	3.6%	4.3%	0.8%	1.3%	1.6%	3.5%	0.0%	37,974	0.6%
	Slovakia	31.5%	24.4%	1.6%	4.5%	5.8%	0.9%	2.5%	4.2%	0.7%	14.3%	8.9%	0.7%	18,888	1.0%
Central Europe Avg.*/Total		31.4%	18.6%	9.1%	11.8%	3.3%	3.8%	3.2%	2.3%	1.0%	7.0%	8.0%	0.2%	135,062	1.2%
Latin America	Argentina	12.9%	35.1%	11.4%	9.1%	0.3%	4.8%	0.3%	0.2%	1.1%	14.8%	5.8%	4.2%	464,214	4.4%
	Brazil	15.6%	33.8%	16.3%	15.0%	0.2%	1.0%	0.6%	0.0%	0.4%	8.3%	8.8%	0.0%	1,128,387	2.4%
Latin America Avg.*/Total		14.2%	34.5%	13.9%	12.1%	0.2%	2.9%	0.5%	0.1%	0.7%	11.6%	7.3%	2.1%	1,592,601	3.4%
Grand Average/Total		14.1%	26.2%	20.9%	19.2%	1.1%	3.9%	2.1%	0.7%	0.8%	5.6%	4.5%	0.7%	19,144,585	5.6%

* Unweighted averages, calculated on the assumption that missing values equal zero.

** Nonagricultural FTE employment.

Source: The Johns Hopkins Comparative Nonprofit Sector Project, Phase II

Table B.5 Nonprofit sector FTE employment with volunteers and religious worship, by country and field of activity, 1995

Region	Country	Culture	Edu-cation	Health	Social Svcs	Environ-ment	Develop-ment	Advo-cacy	Phil. Inter-mediaries	Inter-national	Religious Worship	Profes-sional	Other /n.e.c	Total Nonprofit Employment	Nonprofit Share of Total** Employment
Western Europe	Austria	6.3%	6.7%	8.7%	48.1%	0.3%	0.0%	3.4%	0.0%	0.6%	3.6%	1.1%	21.3%	191,111	5.9%
	Finland	31.9%	12.1%	12.8%	15.2%	0.7%	1.6%	16.4%	0.2%	0.4%	2.3%	6.1%	0.4%	140,794	6.4%
	France	28.4%	13.9%	8.7%	25.9%	4.7%	4.5%	1.8%	0.6%	2.3%	5.2%	4.1%	0.0%	2,089,683	10.1%
	Germany	17.7%	6.8%	19.6%	24.4%	2.5%	4.0%	2.9%	0.9%	1.4%	10.2%	3.8%	5.7%	2,692,324	8.8%
	Ireland	9.9%	40.6%	22.0%	12.3%	0.8%	5.4%	0.4%	0.6%	0.4%	5.6%	1.6%	0.3%	159,274	15.0%
	Netherlands	16.6%	22.4%	27.8%	19.7%	2.0%	1.6%	2.9%	0.2%	1.2%	4.0%	1.7%	0.0%	1,085,853	19.4%
	U.K.	22.2%	20.5%	6.5%	12.9%	2.0%	10.1%	1.4%	1.0%	1.9%	19.2%	1.2%	0.9%	3,137,446	12.8%
Western Europe Avg.*/Total		19.0%	17.6%	15.2%	22.7%	1.9%	3.9%	4.2%	0.5%	1.2%	7.1%	2.8%	4.1%	9,496,486	11.2%
Other Developed Countries	Australia	20.7%	16.4%	13.6%	21.6%	1.3%	9.5%	2.6%	0.1%	0.3%	8.6%	3.0%	2.2%	634,003	11.0%
	Israel	8.5%	40.7%	26.8%	15.8%	0.6%	0.8%	2.0%	1.6%	0.1%	1.6%	1.5%	0.0%	179,571	11.1%
	Japan	5.0%	16.7%	33.7%	15.6%	0.6%	1.7%	0.5%	1.0%	1.4%	9.7%	4.5%	9.7%	3,138,257	5.1%
	U.S.	7.2%	14.9%	27.5%	17.7%	0.8%	3.2%	4.0%	0.8%	0.3%	19.7%	3.1%	0.9%	16,881,456	14.5%
Other Developed Avg.*/Total		10.4%	22.2%	25.4%	17.7%	0.8%	3.8%	2.2%	0.9%	0.5%	9.9%	3.1%	3.2%	20,833,288	10.4%
All Developed Avg.*/Total		15.9%	19.2%	18.9%	20.8%	1.5%	3.9%	3.5%	0.6%	0.9%	8.1%	2.9%	3.8%	30,329,774	10.9%
Central Europe	Czech Rep.	33.3%	9.9%	11.1%	12.2%	5.7%	6.3%	3.3%	2.0%	1.3%	6.9%	8.0%	0.0%	123,600	2.9%
	Romania	27.4%	14.5%	8.1%	30.9%	2.1%	2.3%	3.6%	0.9%	3.8%	4.0%	2.3%	0.0%	87,391	1.4%
	Slovakia	32.7%	18.0%	1.7%	8.9%	8.0%	1.0%	3.3%	4.9%	0.8%	11.8%	8.0%	1.0%	26,121	1.4%
Central Europe Avg.*/Total		31.1%	14.1%	7.0%	17.3%	5.2%	3.2%	3.4%	2.6%	2.0%	7.6%	6.1%	0.3%	237,111	1.9%
Latin America	Argentina	10.7%	24.3%	7.5%	10.4%	1.2%	12.1%	1.4%	0.1%	0.6%	22.9%	6.3%	2.5%	855,257	7.7%
	Brazil	12.1%	28.1%	14.1%	15.4%	0.2%	2.4%	0.6%	0.0%	0.3%	19.8%	6.9%	0.2%	1,463,485	3.2%
Latin America Avg.*/Total		11.4%	26.2%	10.8%	12.9%	0.7%	7.2%	1.0%	0.0%	0.4%	21.3%	6.6%	1.3%	2,318,742	5.4%
Grand Average/Total		18.2%	19.1%	15.6%	19.2%	2.1%	4.1%	3.2%	0.9%	1.1%	9.7%	4.0%	2.8%	32,885,628	8.5%

* Unweighted averages, calculated on the assumption that missing values equal zero.
** Nonagricultural FTE employment.
Source: The Johns Hopkins Comparative Nonprofit Sector Project, Phase II

Table B.6   Nonprofit revenues (with and without volunteer input), including religious worship, by country and revenue source, 1995

Region	Country	Excluding Volunteer Input				Including Volunteer Input**			
		Share of Revenue from:			Total Cash Revenue	Share of Revenue from:			Total Cash Revenue and Volunteer Input
		Public Sector	Private Giving	Fees, Charges	millions US $	Public Sector	Private Giving	Fees, Charges	millions US $
Western Europe	Austria	47.3%	5.7%	47.0%	6,771	39.3%	21.6%	39.1%	8,151
	Finland	36.0%	7.1%	56.8%	6,302	25.4%	35.6%	40.0%	8,959
	France	57.1%	8.5%	34.4%	58,016	31.9%	48.8%	19.2%	103,769
	Germany	64.8%	3.4%	31.8%	95,966	39.8%	40.6%	19.6%	156,114
	Ireland	74.5%	10.3%	15.2%	5,201	65.0%	21.6%	13.3%	5,956
	Netherlands	58.5%	3.4%	38.1%	60,938	44.8%	25.9%	29.2%	79,501
	U.K.	45.2%	11.3%	43.5%	81,647	32.3%	36.6%	31.1%	114,290
Western Europe Average*/Total		54.8%	7.1%	38.1%	314,841	39.8%	33.0%	27.4%	476,741
Other Developed Countries	Australia	29.9%	9.2%	60.9%	20,978	23.7%	28.1%	48.2%	26,506
	Israel	63.5%	10.5%	26.0%	11,100	58.7%	17.3%	24.0%	12,011
	Japan	40.9%	3.6%	55.5%	286,703	37.2%	12.3%	50.5%	315,271
	U.S.	27.4%	21.2%	51.3%	631,599	21.9%	37.0%	41.1%	789,783
Other Developed Average*/Total		40.4%	11.1%	48.4%	950,379	35.4%	23.7%	40.9%	1,143,571
All Developed Average/Total*		49.6%	8.6%	41.9%	1,265,221	38.2%	29.6%	32.3%	1,620,312
Central Europe	Czech Rep.	39.5%	15.0%	45.6%	923	31.8%	31.4%	36.7%	1,144
	Romania	45.1%	26.5%	28.4%	134	20.6%	66.4%	13.0%	294
	Slovakia	22.1%	23.7%	54.2%	327	21.6%	25.5%	53.0%	334
Central Europe Average*/Total		35.5%	21.7%	42.7%	1,384	24.7%	41.1%	34.2%	1,773
Latin America	Argentina	17.2%	18.6%	64.2%	15,155	14.1%	33.4%	52.5%	18,521
	Brazil	14.4%	17.0%	68.6%	12,249	12.8%	26.1%	61.1%	13,752
Latin America Average*/Total		15.8%	17.8%	66.4%	27,404	13.4%	29.7%	56.8%	32,273
Grand Average*/Total		42.7%	12.2%	45.1%	1,294,008	32.6%	31.8%	35.7%	1,654,358

* Unweighted averages.
** Volunteer input has been included in the Private Giving column.

Source: The Johns Hopkins Comparative Nonprofit Sector Project, Phase II

Table B.7   Monetary conversion rates, 1995

Region	Country	Currency Name	Conversion Rate
			1 US $ =
Western Europe	Austria	Austrian Schilling	10.08
	Belgium	Belgian Franc	29.51
	Finland	Finnish Markka	4.59
	France	French Franc	5.00
	Germany	German Mark	1.43
	Ireland	Irish Pound	0.62
	Netherlands	Dutch Guilder	1.61
	Spain	Spanish Peseta	124.73
	U.K.	British Pound	0.63
Other Developed Countries	Australia	Australian Dollar	1.33
	Israel	New Israeli Shekel	3.01
	Japan	Japanese Yen	102.91
	U.S.	US Dollar	1.00
Central Europe	Czech Rep.	Czech Koruna	26.20
	Hungary	Hungarian Forint	125.70
	Romania	Romanian Leu	2,033.00
	Slovakia	Slovak Crown	30.60
Latin America	Argentina	Argentine Peso	1.00
	Brazil	Brazilian Real	1.00
	Colombia	Colombian Peso	912.89
	Mexico	Mexican Peso	6.80
	Peru	Peruvian Nuevo Sol	2.25

Appendix C

Data Sources

OVERVIEW

Noted below are summaries of the major data sources cited by the project teams in developing the basic empirical data reported here. More detailed information on these sources can be secured directly from the local associate in each site, identified in the notes to each chapter. Contact information can be obtained from the Johns Hopkins Comparative Nonprofit Sector Project (CNP). Access to these data varies considerably by site and data source.

WESTERN EUROPE

Belgium

Most of the Belgian data reported in this volume have been extrapolated from a detailed pilot study covering two well-defined geographical areas: the territory of the town of Liège, representative of the nonprofit sector in Wallonia, and the town of Hasselt, representative of the nonprofit sector in Flanders. As far as the nonprofit sector in the Brussels region is concerned, no specific study was carried out; rather, it was estimated through a combination of weighted means from the Wallonia and Flanders results.

Before initiating the main survey, the Belgian team precisely defined the population to be studied. The National Register of Legal Entities, edited by the Home Office and constituted on the basis of the statutes and other essential acts required of Associations Without Profit Purpose (AWPPs), enabled the team to determine the exact number of associations maintaining a legal personality and to identify those established in Liège and Hasselt. Within AWPP populations in Liège (3,074 entities) and Hasselt (993 entities), two random samples were formed (702 in Liège and 684 in Hasselt). However, hospitals and nonprofit private schools were excluded from the survey because these two groups, highly structured and closely monitored by the corresponding and competent Ministries, are the objects of regular statistical analyses.

From within the samples, the AWPPs in operation then were differentiated from the inactive AWPPs. Only the former were the focus of a face-to-face survey conducted over the course of 1996. Among the active associations, those employing paid staff and those that depended entirely on volunteer staff were identified. The results obtained from the Liège and Hasselt associations were then extrapolated to a regional level by using a simple rule of three based on the number of associations in each region. [For the Brussels region the same extrapolations were constructed from the Liège and Hasselt realities on the basis of linguistic distribution (20 percent Dutch speakers and 80 percent French speakers).] Finally, to obtain national level estimates, the regional results were added together and complemented with data relative to the two activity groups not covered by the survey.

Finland

Because the classification system used in official Finnish statistics is inconsistent with the Comparative Nonprofit Sector Project's International Classification of Nonprofit Organizations (ICNPO) system, it was impossible to rely solely on official data for this study. For this reason, the Finnish project team relied primarily on survey data, pulling information from official statistics only to the extent that it was available.

The nonprofit organization database for Finland is composed of three separate sources: a questionnaire survey distributed to local level associations, a survey distributed to national associations, and a sample of private foundations. By far the most comprehensive data were gathered from the questionnaire survey sent to local associations. Approximately 8,700 associations, nearly thirteen per cent of all registered associations, received the questionnaire. Almost half of them (47 percent) returned it. Another survey based on a sample (of every fifteen units) consisting of confederations, unions, and district-level associations constituted the second data source. The sample covered 310 items, and 160 associations answered the questionnaire. Both surveys were completed in 1997 and were based on the data from 1996. The questionnaires mapped membership, organizational structure, revenues, operating and capital expenditures, employment, and volunteering. The data on foundations were collected from the Register of Foundations. Every tenth one of 1,800 actually operating foundations was included in the analysis.

France

In essence, the same methodology was used in France in this second phase of the project as was used in the 1990 study (Phase I). The main data source was the registry of public and private entities known as SIRENE (*Systeme de repertoire des enterprises et des etablissments*), from which the French team was able to disaggregate most nonprofit organizations in France. The SIRENE file provided data on employment, expenditures, and industrial classification codes that were matched with the ICNPO.

Revenue data came from several sources. For education, health, and international activities, satellite accounts, social security statistics, and the Ministry of Cooperation data were used. For other fields, the French team used a survey of nonprofit organizations at the municipal level, conducted by Vivianne Tchernonong. The data on individual giving and volunteering came from a population survey conducted by E. Archambault and J. Boumendil (Paris: ISL, Fondation de France, Laboratoire d'Economie Sociale, 1997). The giving and volunteering data are for 1996.

Germany

The use of existing data sources for project purposes in Germany proved somewhat problematic, since the basic data sources useful for an analysis of the nonprofit sector remain somewhat limited. While official statistics include a category labeled "organizations without profit motive" (*Organisationen ohne Erwerbscharakter*), this category is frequently subsumed under either the public sector or private households categories. So far, the official statistics have proved to be ineffective in representing the nonprofit sector in the context of overall economic accounts. Moreover, in the context of the harmonization of official statistics in the European Union, it seems likely that the already limited data sources will be further curtailed in the future.

Given this complex situation, the German project team faced the task of assembling a basic data set from a variety of different sources in partial, but useful, cooperation with the Federal Statistical Office. These included data from the national accounts and special surveys provided by official statistics, the Federal Labor Office, as well as a number of other surveys, directories, and member information provided by nonprofit or industry umbrella groups or professional associations. Remaining data gaps were filled with additional surveys organized and conducted by the project team, including an organizational survey and a population survey on giving and volunteering.

Ireland

There is no nationally-available complete or representative database of nonprofit organizations in Ireland. In general, data on nonprofit organizations are neither collected nor reported, and although component data can be tracked through the national accounting system, other methods of data collection had to be employed in order to start building up a composite map of the nonprofit sector in Ireland. The Labor Force Survey (which is a sample survey) and the Population Census collect and report on a category entitled, respectively, "Welfare and Charitable Services" or "Social Work and Related Activities," which are both categories for nonprofit organizations included in most of the ICNPO groups. The Irish team decided to investigate this further with the aid of the Central Statistics Office (CSO). Meanwhile, data on education, health, and the activity of nonprofit organizations in those categories are also available from the CSO, although these may not be available publicly.

To derive operating expenditures, annual reports were used, as were informed opinions from practitioners within the Irish nonprofit sector. These provided "guesstimates" that could be applied, as appropriate, to each ICNPO group. Volunteering figures were taken from a 1994 survey on volunteering conducted among a random sample of the population (Ruddle, H. & Mulvihill, R., *Reaching Out: Charitable Giving and Volunteering in the Republic of Ireland*, Dublin: Policy Research Centre, 1995). The survey data were re-analyzed in order to fit them into the appropriate ICNPO group. Average hourly wages were calculated from CSO data for many ICNPO groups.

To assess the revenue of the nonprofit sector in Ireland, a "top-down" approach was adopted. The National Accounts for 1995 were used for government grants, statutory transfers, and third party payments. Details of European Union funding were obtained from the annual reports of government departments. Third party payments were cross checked against the annual reports of statutory bodies which support the nonprofit sector such as FAS (the state training agency), Combat Poverty Agency, and the National Social Service Board and also through individual inquiries with these offices for further details.

Very little information is available to date on the amount of funding given by businesses to nonprofit organizations. A survey of the top 1,000 companies in Ireland is still underway at the Policy Research Centre, but the findings were not available for this publication. The figures for individual giving were compiled from a 1997 survey on individual donations to charity, the results of which are still being analyzed. A sample of 1,200 people was surveyed throughout 1997. The results were grossed up to allow for giving in the total population aged over 18 and were then adjusted using the Consumer Price Index for 1997 and 1996 to give figures for 1995. The Household Budget Survey 1995 conducted by the CSO provided details on household spending for religion as this was deemed to be possibly a more reliable estimate than that available from the survey on individual giving.

The Netherlands

Despite the size and prominence of the nonprofit sector in the Netherlands, the data situation is not ideal. Information on nonprofits is scattered and, if available, assembled for different purposes. The Dutch team's job was to bring the data together to draw up estimates for the entire nonprofit sector in the Netherlands within the framework of the Comparative Nonprofit Sector Project.

The basic approach was to gather data at the highest available level of aggregation. If the data were not available at one level, the Dutch team looked one step down. The main levels are: the nonprofit sector as a whole, specific subfields (such as education, religion, and health care), specific types of activities within subfields (primary education, museums, and hospitals), and finally individual organizations. In practice, data were often only available at the third level (specific types of activities within subfields). These were then allocated according to the ICNPO. If possible at all, the team wanted to refrain from collecting data by means of surveys or by the meticulous process of reviewing individual organizations. The first of the less-preferred strategies could be avoided, while the second unfortunately not.

The national accounts were the most obvious starting point for data on nonprofits, but, despite U.N. guidelines, the Dutch statistics office never published separate figures for nonprofits serving households. Nevertheless, the national accounts were of great value for estimations of professional organizations and for assessing ratios between wages and operating expenditures.

Industry reports were among the major sources used. The statistics office collects data and produces excellent reports on specific activities such as hospitals, sport clubs, museums, and homes for the elderly. In some cases the reports offered a break down between type of organization. In other cases the most difficult task was to separate the share of nonprofits in the activities by using other sources. A second set of important sources was (national) umbrella organizations. The information obtained from them on, for instance, residential health care, social services, fundraising and churches was invaluable and a *sine qua non* for drawing up a complete picture of these activities. The third main sources were annual (financial) reports of individual organizations, especially those involved in environmental, political, and philanthropic activities.

Spain

There was no single source of data that covered all, or even most, of the types of organizations in the nonprofit sector in Spain. The Spanish research team, therefore, culled information on employment, expenditures, and revenues from a number of different sources, mainly coming from governmental agencies or ministries, including the Ministries of Education and Culture, of Social Affairs, and of Health, the national statistics institute, and the statistics institutes for the Basque country and Cataluña. The resulting data were pieced together to estimate first the totals for the entire nonprofit sector and then were disaggregated to the various fields of activity.

United Kingdom

The U.K. estimates were established primarily through secondary analysis of a wide range of large data sets at the Personal Social Services Research Unit (PSSRU) at the London School of Economics. In each case, detailed re-analysis of data collected for other purposes was undertaken, and careful account was taken of the varying approaches to coverage and definition. Two of the most important sources, which were exhaustively and comprehensively examined, were:

- Surveys of registered charities conducted in 1992/93 and 1995/96, and subsequent analyses of registered charities' accounts, conducted by the National Council for Voluntary Organisations (NCVO) on behalf of the Office for National Statistics (ONS). The most recent survey involved a gross sample size of 4,038, generating 1,271 useable returns. For further details, see Hems, L. & and Passey, A., *The UK Voluntary Sector Almanac 1998/99* (London: NCVO Publications, 1998).
- The U.K. Labour Force Survey, undertaken by ONS, which is the primary source of labor market data in the U.K. Pooled data for 1995 relating to around 2,000 people who (on a subjective definition) were employed in the voluntary sector (out of a total sample of 96,000 households included overall) were analyzed.

In addition, a special re-analysis of a major survey of volunteering undertaken in 1997 by the National Centre for Volunteering was conducted on behalf of PSSRU by BMRB. These data fed into estimates across a number of fields of activity in a variety of ways. In addition, specialist data sources were used in developing estimates for particular fields. Some of the most important of these were the Museum & Galleries Commission's DOMUS database; published and unpublished data from the Department for Education and Employment, the Higher Education Statistical Agency, the Further Education Funding Council, and the Office for Science and Technology; data reported in *Laing's Review of Private Health Care* (London: Laing and Buisson, 1996); and the Housing Corporation database. Where these databases only provided data on England, or England and Wales, equivalent data were sought for Scotland and for Northern Ireland [with the help of the Northern Ireland Council for Voluntary Action (NICVA)] through a range of official and other sources, in order to build consolidated U.K. estimates.

It was possible to construct estimates of income, expenditure, paid employment and volunteering by creatively combining these and other sources of information in all fields, with the exception of financial and paid employment estimates for recreation. To estimate the scale and scope of activity in this field, special surveys were undertaken of sports and social clubs in three locales: Kent (the basis for estimates in Great Britain apart from London), London, and Northern Ireland (undertaken by NICVA).

Finally, the only subcategory identified in the ICNPO not fully covered in these estimates was political parties. These organizations' paid staff and volunteers are included for the category "law, advocacy and politics" for the "broad nonprofit sector" in 1995 using the sources referred to above. However, it was not possible to include their income and expenditure in the financial estimates.

OTHER DEVELOPED COUNTRIES

Australia

Most of the data were gathered from the Australian Bureau of Statistics (ABS) special industry surveys and from a special survey of nonprofit organizations and several industries that would not be covered otherwise by the regular surveys. Where a survey collected data for a year either side of the target 1995/96 year, financial data were adjusted using the Consumer Price Index. These data were supplemented by data from the economy-wide survey (for religious organizations), by data collected for administrative purposes (such as for schools) by government departments, and by data collected through surveys conducted by the Australian Nonprofit Data Project (ANDP) or estimates made by ANDP staff from other survey or administrative data. Data on volunteering were taken from the ABS 1995 survey of voluntary work.

Israel

The basic CNP approach led the Israeli team to establish cooperation with the National Accounts Division of the Central Bureau of Statistics (CBS) and with the Department for Non-Profit and Public Institutions of the Income Tax Division. The data are, in principle, based on CBS surveys conducted for the State of Israel National Accounts. However, these surveys presented a number of problems in connection with CNP: 1) the data had to be adapted to the ICNPO categories, which require greater detail than National Accounts classification; 2) the surveys did not include organizations with less than two employees, which are included in the Hopkins project scheme; and 3) the CBS analysis of third sector financing did not distinguish between donations from individuals, business, foundations, and other sources, as requested by the project.

To solve the first and second problems, the Israeli team classified all the nonprofit institutions that appeared in the Income Tax records according to the ICNPO categories. This classification (which distinguished among small, medium, and large organizations) provided the key for breaking down the broader CBS categories to the more specific ICNPO categories. Organizations with less than two employees were added to this classification in 1995, sorted according to the pattern of categories for 1991 (when a detailed survey was conducted with ICNPO categories).

A survey of a representative sample of the adult Israeli population provided information on patterns of volunteering and donating by Israelis, completing the National Accounts data in this regard. The extent of volunteering found in the sample was used to calculate the total annual Israeli adult volunteer hours in all third sector fields. The volunteer units were converted to full-time equivalents (FTEs) by dividing the total number of volunteer hours into full-time positions according to CBS definitions.

Japan

The main data source was the Survey on Private Nonprofit Institutions, conducted by the Japanese government's Economic Planning Agency and used by the System of National Accounting in estimating the scale of the nonprofit sector in Japan. Since the survey uses a classification system that is considerably different from the ICNPO and does not cover all fields of activity, the Japanese team used other data sources to supplement the missing information. The supplementary data sources include data published by the Ministry of Education, Culture and Science and the Ministry of Health and Welfare in the respective activity fields. The limitation of these sources is that they focus on corporations providing public goods and services, while seriously under-reporting purely voluntary associations.

Other supplementary data sources include the *Directory of Grant-making Foundations*, published by the Foundation Center of Japan, the *Directory of Trusts* published by the Charitable Trust Association, and the directory of international entities published by the Japanese NGO Center for International Cooperation.

United States

Data on nonprofit employment in the United States were derived mainly from workplace surveys conducted for the U.S. Bureau of Labor Statistics (BLS) and published in *Employment and Earnings*. However, this source does not differentiate nonprofit from for-profit employment. To make this breakdown, ratios were developed based on data available from the U.S. Census of Service Industries, which was conducted every five years. To go from employment and wages to total expenditures, various industry ratios were applied based on the *Service Annual Survey* and the *Survey of Current Business*. These estimates have been developed for the "charitable" portion of the American nonprofit sector [so-called 501(c)(3) and (c)(4) organizations] for selected years by Virginia Hodgkinson and Murray Weitzman et al. at Independent Sector and published in *Nonprofit Almanac: Dimensions of the Independent Sector 1996–1997* (San Francisco: Jossey-Bass Publishers, 1996). These data were extrapolated to the base year used in this project. Data on the fields not covered in the *Almanac* were estimated directly from BLS data, *Service Annual Survey*, and *Employment and Earnings*.

Revenue data come from a variety of different subsector sources and from surveys conducted by the American Association of Fund-raising Counsel as reported in annual editions of *Giving USA*; the Foundation Center (foundation giving) as reported in annual editions of *Foundation Giving*; Independent Sector (on giving and volunteering); and *America's Nonprofit Sector: A Primer* by Lester M. Salamon (New York: The Foundation Center, 1999).

CENTRAL AND EASTERN EUROPE

Czech Republic

In the Czech Republic, statistical information on the nonprofit sector that is available in the system of national accounts (SNA) remains limited and proved insufficient for the purposes of this project. In addition, certain important variables on voluntary organizations and church institutions are not covered in the national accounts at all. For this reason, it was necessary to identify and gather a broad range of supplementary information outside the framework of national accounts to estimate key aspects of the structure and importance of nonprofit organizations in society. Additional official data sources that were utilized included population and household censuses that are regularly carried out by the Central Statistical Office as well as information provided by a number of ministerial agencies, including the Research Institute of Labor and Social Affairs, the Institute of Health Care Information and Statistics, the Institute for Information in Education, the Institute of Economy of the Czech National Bank, and the Grant Agency of the Academy of Sciences. Beyond these official sources, the project team also utilized databases and other research available from a wide range of nonprofit groups and market research firms, as well as university-based research projects.

Hungary

The main data source on the Hungarian nonprofit sector is an annual survey carried out by the Hungarian Central Statistical Office (CSO). In 1996, more than 40,000 foundations and associations were sent a questionnaire asking them about their economic activities and social background in 1995. As in previous years, approximately 50 percent of the organizations filled and returned the forms to the CSO. This amount of data made it possible to develop estimates for the whole nonprofit sector. To do this, the Hungarian team hypothesized that organizations of the same legal form, working in the same field of activity and having their seat in communities of the same type, have more or less the same characteristics as far as their financial base and public sector support are concerned. It also was assumed that changes within these groupings among the organizations that returned the questionnaires (data-providing organizations) are similar to those of the ones that did not (non-data-providing organizations). If one accepts these hypotheses—and preliminary calculations already proved that these hypotheses were acceptable—it is possible to make estimates that are valid for the whole nonprofit sector.

The results of the CSO's annual survey provided most of the information needed for the Comparative Project. When not, the Hungarian team was able to rely on other surveys or data sources to produce the missing figures. The 1990 and 1995 data are fully comparable since the survey methodology was basically the same. The only important difference is that the 1995 data are much more reliable because the sample used in 1990 was quite small.

Poland

The employment data presented in the Polish chapter were calculated primarily on the basis of a spring 1998 census (SOF) of associations, foundations, labor unions, employers' organizations, political parties, and professional and business associations conducted by the Polish Central Statistical Office (GUS). Of the 38,398 organizations surveyed, 69 percent returned completed questionnaires, 16 percent refused to provide information, 5 percent declared themselves inactive, and the remaining 10 percent did not respond at all to the survey for unknown reasons. The GUS released full-time equivalent employment data for only the 69 percent of organizations that provided information. The Polish project team then estimated employment data for the 16 percent of organizations that refused to return the questionnaires. Since it is not known what proportion (if any) of the ten percent of organizations that did not respond at all are still economically active, it was assumed that all of these organizations were defunct for the purpose of a conservative estimate. The employment data reported here only relate to employees hired on the basis of employment contracts in 1997. Thus, other types of employment, such as independent contractor-type working relationships, are not covered by labor statistics in Poland, although they are a very important source of employment in the Polish nonprofit sector. In addition, certain types of nonprofit organizations, mostly church-based social service, health care, and educational institutions, were not covered in the GUS survey, but employment data on these organizations were pulled from other official surveys (Z-01).

Volunteer employment data are based on a Time Use Survey of a representative, random sample of 1,000 households organized by the Central Statistical Office in October 1996 and on the Giving and Volunteering Survey of a representative, random sample of 1,153 adult respondents carried out by the Polish team in June 1998. The Time Use Survey data were used to establish the total number of hours volunteered for nonprofit organizations and then translated into full-time equivalent employment. The Giving and Volunteering Survey data—generally less reliable than time use surveys—were used to differentiate between religious and non-religious volunteering.

Romania

With insufficient official data on the nonprofit sector available in Romania, the main source of information was a census of nonprofit organizations conducted by the Civil Society Development Foundation in Bucharest. A detailed questionnaire was administered in the fall of 1996 to the approximately 12,000 organizations identified in the central register of the Ministry of Justice. Organizations were asked to report on 1995 as the base year. After adjusting for defunct organizations, the response rate was 25 percent. Key variables were first estimated at the sector level and then broken down to the subgroups of the ICNPO. The estimates reported in the Romanian chapter are essentially based on this census, supplemented with data that were provided ultimately by official statistical sources, including the National Commission for Statistics and various ministries and central governmental agencies. In addition, the Civil Society Development Foundation commissioned representative population surveys on giving and volunteering and a survey of corporate giving to fill remaining data gaps.

Slovakia

The basic strategy in Slovakia was to work closely with the Statistical Office of the Slovak Republic (SOSR), which maintains a statistical register of organizations that allows identification of nonprofit legal entities and can serve as a sampling frame. Using this register, the SOSR had already launched a limited survey of the nonprofit sector in 1995 for national accounting purposes, sampling 6 percent of the organizations with a response rate of 26 percent. A second survey in 1996 sampled 25 percent of the total universe of more than 18,000 registered nonprofit organizations with a response rate of approximately 30 percent. The stratified survey covered all large organizations, but only sampled smaller organizations. In addition, federations and umbrella groups were required to provide statistical information for all of their subsidiaries.

Although the key purpose of the surveys was the generation of national accounts data, the 1996 survey incorporated the ICNPO and covered all key variables necessary for CNP. The estimation of project data followed the standard techniques and procedures of the Statistical Office. In addition to the survey, the Slovak project team utilized additional information from the register of organizations, labor force surveys, and the national accounts. Supplementary data sources also included the Ministry of Finance (public sector financial accounts and budget information on nonprofits), other ministerial sources, and social and health insurance companies.

LATIN AMERICA

Argentina

Argentina's starting point was the *Censo Nacional Económico* (CNE 94-National Economic Census), which covered 1993 and was published in 1994. Conducted by the National Statistics and Census Bureau, CNE 94 provided information on all main employment and expenditure variables, as well as some revenue variables, for all major ICNPO groups and subgroups, except unions, for which a separate source was used. Because CNE 94 used a classification system other than the ICNPO (ISIC rev.3), some 19,000 records had to be reviewed one-by-one in order to place organizations in the proper ICNPO groups. Employment data were updated to 1995 using the 1995 Household Survey, and other adjustments to employment and expenditure figures were made using ratios and standards approved by the Argentine National Accounts Office.

Revenue data provided in CNE 94 required disaggregation by the Argentine research team. The researchers used a 1998 Survey on Giving and Volunteering conducted by Gallup as the basis for estimating variables such as the amount of individual giving and the number of hours volunteered. Furthermore, a database of community-based and other nonprofit organizations assembled by the *Centro de Organizaciones Comunitarias* (CENOC-Center for Community Organizations) and the results of an organizational survey conducted by the *Fundación Juan Minetti* and the *Universidad Nacional de Córdoba* in the city of Córdoba were used to fill in gaps in revenue, volunteering, and membership data.

Brazil

The principal source of employment and wage data was the 1991 Population Census, since no economic census had been conducted in the last decade. The Population Census, assembled by the *Instituto Brasileiro de Geografia e Estatística* (IBGE-Brazilian Institute of Geography and Statistics), provided data on the number of people employed in paid and unpaid jobs, the branch of activity in which they were employed, and their average wages. For certain activity groups, especially health and education, the Brazilian team relied on other sources of information (a 1992 health sector survey, a 1997 school census, etc.) to determine the proportion of nonprofit entities among all organizations. Finally, a 1995 Microcensus (household survey) was used to bring the resulting estimates of employment and wages up to CNP's 1995 base year.

On the revenue side, the Brazilian team used data pulled from the Treasury Secretariat's *Sistema de Administração Financeira* (SIAFI-Financial Administration System) for estimates of federal government support, from a survey conducted by IBGE for state-level support, and from SAFEM, a subset of SIAFI, for municipal government funding. Private giving estimates were derived from a giving and volunteering survey, conducted for the Brazilian project team by IBOPE, and from corporate tax returns available through the Finance Ministry.

Colombia

No single information source in Colombia provided sufficient coverage of all the organizations or all the variables that are part of this project. To estimate employment, the Colombian research team first consolidated data from a survey conducted in 1991 by the *Centro de Información de Entidades Sin Animo de Lucro* (CIDESAL-Nonprofit Information Center) under the auspices of Fundación Social, and the latest National Economic Census taken in 1990 by the *Departamento Administrativo Nacional de Estadística* (DANE-National Administrative Department for Statistics). These data were projected to the larger universe of nonprofit organizations on the basis of a listing compiled from directories and other information sources. To project employment from 1990/91 to 1995, the team used the average rate of growth for employment in "community, social and personal services" as determined through quarterly employment surveys conducted by the National Planning Department. Operating expenditures were estimated mainly using data from the Colombian tax authority DIAN. Where reliable information on employment and expenditures was available on a specific type of organization such as family compensation funds, family welfare homes, schools, and universities, the specific data replaced census estimates.

Revenue data, like employment and expenditure data, were derived from a variety of sources. A survey conducted in 1997 by PROCALI, an association of NGOs in the city of Cali, provided the broad outline of the revenue structure, and personal interviews of a number of nonprofit leaders helped fill gaps and verify information.

Information on volunteering again was compiled from various data sources. The two main sources were the CIDESAL survey mentioned above and a survey of nonprofit organizations in the city of Antioquia conducted in 1995 by the NGO Codesarrollo.

Mexico

Mexico's primary source of data was the 1993 Economic Census, conducted by the *Instituto Nacional de Estadística Geográfica e Informática* (INEGI-National Institute of Geographic Statistics and Informatics) and published in 1994. The Census provided information on all main employment and expenditure variables, as well as partial revenue data. A small survey was conducted to disaggregate the data on ICNPO Groups 5 to 9 (environment, development and housing, civic/advocacy, and philanthropic intermediaries) which had been lumped together in the Census. Because available resources did not permit a separate giving and volunteering survey, the Mexican team used data on "non-paid employment" as a proxy for volunteering.

The revenue data provided in the Census were identified only as "internal," i.e., income from fees, sales, and other self-generated income, and "external," which included all other income whether from government sources or private donations. To disaggregate the "external" revenue data into the desired categories for the project, the Mexican team obtained information from federations of organizations in some cases and from a telephone survey of organizations in other cases.

Peru

In Peru, the general workplace census taken in 1993 (*Censo Nacional Económico*-CENEC) could not be used for the entire range of nonprofit organizations or variables, although it was useful for filling gaps and calculating ratios. Thus, to compile the basic estimates of employment and operating expenditures, the Peruvian team first identified a number of other studies undertaken by various national government ministries that provided broad and reliable coverage of specific "industries," including the National Education Census (1993), the National Census of Universities (1995), and the National Census of Sanitary Infrastructure (1995). Directories of nongovernmental organizations (NGOs), including an "official" directory (1996) compiled by *Secretaría Ejecutiva de Cooperación Técnica Internacional* (SECTI-Executive Secretariat for International Technical Cooperation) and PACT (Private Agencies Collaborating Together), and another compiled by DESCO (1995), a national-level NGO, offered information on the subset of nonprofit organizations that work in various fields. In addition, a National Census of Municipalities (1994) contained information on the number of two of the most widespread types of community-based organizations, *comites de vaso de leche* (Glass of Milk committees) and *comedores populares* (community soup kitchens). Information about their members, volunteers, and expenditures was derived from other studies that focused on these organizations. Finally, the CENEC and other official statistics were used generally to fill in selected data gaps and calculate key ratios.

Estimates of the Peruvian nonprofit sector's revenue structure were derived, in part, from the CENEC and a different SECTI study on international aid and other forms of technical cooperation in Peru (1997). Additional information was taken from a 1996 health sector finance survey, official reports from the government's *Programa Nacional de Asistencia Alimentaria* (PRONAA-National Food Assistance Program), and an NGO survey conducted by SASE and Instituto APOYO.

Finally, the Peruvian team conducted a small population survey on giving and volunteering practices in four major cities (Centro de Investigación de la Universidad del Pacífico, *Encuesta sobre donaciones y trabajo voluntario en el Peru*, Lima: 1998). The survey results were used to calculate the number of hours volunteered for certain fields of activity. Other information about unpaid labor was taken from the CENEC, and more specific sources were used when available.

APPENDIX D

Advisory Committees

INTERNATIONAL ADVISORY COMMITTEE

Nicole Alix, UNIOPSS; *Farida Allaghi,* AGFUND; *Manuel Arango,* CEMEFI; *Mauricio Cabrera Galvis,* Fundación FES; *John Clark,* The World Bank; *Pavol Demeš,* SAIA; *Barry Gaberman,* Ford Foundation; *Cornelia Higginson,* American Express Company; *Stanley Katz,* Princeton University; *Miklós Marschall,* Hungary; *Kumi Naidoo,* CIVICUS; *John Richardson,* European Foundation Centre; *S. Bruce Schearer,* The Synergos Institute.

LOCAL ADVISORY COMMITTEES

Western Europe

Belgium
Each of the following agencies has one representative: Banque Nationale de Belgique (Chair); Fondation Roi Baudoin; Confédération des entreprises non marchandes; Ministère de l'emploi et de l'environnement; Ministère des affaires sociales; Ministère de la Région wallonne; Ministère de la Région Bruxelles-Capitale; Ministère de la Communauté flamande; Ministère de la Communauté française; Comission Communautaire Commune.

Finland
Krister Sthåhlberg (Chair), Åbo Akademi University; *Olavi Borg,* University of Tampere; *Maija Innanen,* Finnish Sport Federation; *Leila Kurki,* Finnish

Confederation of Salaried Employees; *Kari-Pekka Mäkiluoma,* Federation of Finnish Municipalities; *Rolf Myhrman,* Ministry of Social Affairs and Health; *Martti Siisiäinen,* University of Lapland; *Hannu Uusitalo,* Academy of Finland; *Jouko Vasama,* Association of Voluntary Health, Social and Welfare Organizations.

France

Laurence Delmotte (Chair), Fondation de France; *Jean Bastide,* CNVA; *Chantal Bruneau,* Ministère de la Jeunesse et des Sports; *Marie-Thérèse Cheroutre,* *Olivier Dargnies,* Délégation à la qualité de la vie, Ministère de l'Environment; *Anne David,* FONDA; *Mireille Delbeque,* Délégation Formations et Développement, Ministère de la Culture; *Léon Dujardin,* Secours Populaire Français; *Ghislaine Esquiague,* Délégation interministérielle à la ville; *Hugues Feltesse,* UNIOPSS; *Francis Lacloche,* Caisse des Dépots et Consignations; *Jacqueline Lauriau,* Ministère de la Recherche; *Jacqueline Mengin,* CELAVAR; *Marie Dominique Monferrand,* Réseau Information Gestion; *Guy Neyret,* INSEE; *Claudine Padieu,* Direction de l'Action Sociale, Ministère des Affaires Sociales; *Guy Pailler,* Association des Paralysés de France; *Daniel Rault,* Délégation interministérielle à l'innovation sociale et à l'économie sociale; *Jean Pierre Reisman,* Ministère de la Culture; *Philippe Saint Martin,* Ministère du Travail et des Affaires socials, Direction de l'action sociale; *Denis Tzarevcan,* Fondation d'enterprise du crédit Coopératif.

Germany

Rupert Graf Strachwitz (Chair), Maecenata Institut für Dritter-Sektor-Forschung; *Ulli Arnold,* Universität Stuttgart; *Klaus Balke,* Nationale Kontakt und Informationsstelle zu Anregung und Unterstützung von Selbsthilfegruppen; *Rudolph Bauer,* Universität Bremen; *Hans-Jochen Brauns,* DPWV Landesverband Berlin; *Peter-Claus Burens,* Stiftung Deutsche Sporthilfe; *Marita Haibach,* *Albert Hauser,* Caritasverband der Erzdiözese München und Freising; *Christoph Mecking,* Bundesverband Deutscher Stiftungen; *Bernd Meyer,* Deutscher Städtetag; *Klaus Neuhoff,* Universität Witten/Herdecke; *Eckart Pankoke,* Universität der Gesamthochschule Essen; *Heide Pfarr,* Hans-Böckler-Stiftung; *Peter Philipp,* Daimler Chrysler AG; *Stephanie Rüth,* BfS-Service GmbH; *Gabriele Schulz,* Deutscher Kulturrat; *Wolfgang Seibel,* Universität Konstanz; *Marlehn Thieme,* Deutsche Bank Stiftung Alfred Herrhausen Hilfe zur Selbsthilfe; *Gerhard Trosien,* Deutscher Sportbund; *Olaf Werner,* Friedrich-Schiller-Universität Jena; *Wolfgang Zapf,* Wissenschaftszentrum Berlin für Sozialforschung.

Ireland

Joyce O'Connor (Chair), National College of Ireland; *Roger Acton,* Disability Federation of Ireland; *Mel Cousins,* Barrister-at-Law and Personal Advisor to Minister for Social, Community and Family Affairs; *Raymond Jordan*, Department of Education; *Bernadette Kinsella*, Secretariat of Secondary Schools; *Mick Lucey*, Central Statistics Office; *Paul Marron*, Central Statistics Office; *Ernest Sterne*, Secondary Education Committee; *James Williams*, Economic and Social Research Institute.

Netherlands
Th. van Oosten (Chair), Juliana Welzijn Fonds; *B.M. Jansen*, Algemeen Bureau Katholiek Onderwijs; *J.H.L. Meerdink*, Prins Bernhard Fonds; *L. Roosendaal*, Centraal Bureau voor de Statistiek; *A.J.P. Schrijvers*, Universiteit Utrecht; *A.J. Spee*, Ministerie van Onderwijs, Cultuur en Wetenschappen; *Th.J. van Loon*, Nederlandse Organisaties Vrijwilligerswerk; *W. Woertman*, Ministerie van Volksgezondheid Welzijn en Sport.

United Kingdom
Ian Bruce (Chair), Royal National Institute for the Blind; *Michael Brophy*, Charities Aid Foundation; *Richard Corden*, Charity Commission; *Paul Fredericks*, Head of Communications, Charity Commission; *Les Hems*, The Johns Hopkins University; *Janet Novak*, Voluntary and Community Services, Department of National Heritage; *Cathy Pharaoh*, Charities Aid Foundation; *Roger Ward*, ONS.

Other Developed

Australia
Margaret Bell, Australian Council of Volunteering; *Steven Bowman*, Australian Society of Association Executives Limited; *Jeff Byrne*, Industry Commission; *Elizabeth Cham*, Australian Association of Philanthropy; *Gabrielle Gelly*, Australian Conservation Foundation; *Steve Haynes*, Confederation of Australian Sport; *Betty Hounslow*, Australian Council of Social Service; *Philip Hughes*, Christian Research Association; *Richard Madden*, Australian Institute of Health and Welfare; *Russel Roggers*, Australian Bureau of Statistics; *Fergus Thomson*, National Council of Independent Schools' Associations; *David Throsby*, Macquarie University.

Israel
Ya'acov Kop (Chair), Center for Social Policy Research; *J. Aviad*, K.R.B. Foundation; *H. Ayalon*, Amal Network; *Yehoshua David*, Income Tax Commission; *S.N. Eisenstadt*, Hebrew University; *Yoram Gabbai*, Bank HaPoalim; *Y. Galnoor*, Hebrew University; *D. Lehman-Messer*, Ministry of Justice; *A. Mantver*, Joint Distribution Committee-Israel; *Moshe Sikron*, Central Bureau of Statistics.

Central and Eastern Europe

Czech Republic

Fedor Gál (Chair), Business Leader; *Helena Ackermannová*, Donors Forum; *Milan Damohorský*, ISS Charles University; *Ivan Gabal*, Gabal Consulting; *Petr Háva*, ISS Charles University; *Miroslav Purkrábek*, ISS Charles University; *Jana Ryšlinková*, ICN.

Hungary

Marianna Török (Chair), Centre for Nonprofit Information and Education (NIOK); *János Bocz*, Central Statistical Office; *Beatrix Göz*, Ministry of Finance; *Gábor Gyorffy*, PHARE Program; *Béla Jagasics*, Landorhegy Foundation-Nonprofit Service Centre; *Anikó Kaposvári*, Foundation for the Education on Human Rights and Peace; *Judit Monostori*, Central Statistical Office; *László Sík*, Ministry of Finance.

Poland

Alina Baran, Central Statistical Office; *Natalia Bolgert*, Bank of Socio-Economical Initiatives & Forum of Non-governmental Initiatives Association; *Janusz Gałęziak*, Ministry of Labor and Social Policy; *Helena Góralska*, Member of Parliment, Public Finance Commission; *Mirosława Grabowska*, Institute of Sociology, University of Warsaw; *Hubert Izdebski*, Faculty of Law, University of Warsaw; *Wojciech Lazewski*, Caritas-Poland; *Piotr Marciniak*, "NGOs and Legislation" Project; *Krzysztof Ners*, Deputy Minister of Finance; *Joanna Staręga-Piasek*, Member of Parliament, Public Finance Commission; *Edmund Wnuk-Lipiński*, Institute of Social Policy, Polish Academy of Science; *Zbigniew Woźniak*, University of Poznań; *Mirosław Wyrzykowski*, Institute for Public Affairs; *Witold Zdaniewicz*, Catholic Church Statistics Institute.

Romania

Sorin Antohi, Central European University; *Aurora Liiceanu*, University of Bucharest; *Dan Manoleli*, Romanian Parliament Expert; *Liviu Matei*, Ministry of National Education; *Mihaela Miroiu*, National School for Political and Administrative Studies; *Dumitru Sandu*, University of Bucharest; *Ancuta Vamesu*, Civil Society Development Foundation; *Mihaela Vlasceanu*, University of Bucharest.

Slovakia

Pavol Demeš (Chair), Slovak Academic Information Agency; *Martin Bútora*, Milan Simecka Foundation; *Olga Cechová*, Institute for Law Approximation; *Katarína Koštálová*, Slovak Academic Information Agency; *Milan Olexa*, Statistical Office of the Slovak Republic.

Latin America

Argentina

Heber Camelo, U.N. Economic Commission for Latin America (CEPAL); *Marita Carballo,* GALLUP-Argentina; *Juana Ceballos,* Cáritas (formerly); *Ricardo Ferraro,* Fundación YPF (formerly); *Ernesto Gore,* Universidad de San Andrés; *María Herrera Vegas,* Fundación Bunge y Born; *Rafael Kohanoff,* Gobierno de la Ciudad Autónoma de Buenos Aires; *María Rosa Martíni,* Foro del Sector Social; *Dolores Olmos de Taravella,* Fundación Juan Minetti; *Beatriz Orlowski de Amadeo,* CENOC, Secretaría de Desarrollo Social; *Catalina Smulovitz,* Universidad Torcuato Di Tella; *Andrés Thompson,* W.K. Kellogg Foundation.

Colombia

Inés de Brill, CCONG; *Mauricio Cabrera,* FES; *Marco Cruz,* Fundación Antonio Restrepo Barco; *Mauricio Londoño,* National Department of Planning; *Jose Bernardo Toro,* Fundación Social; *Olga Lucia Toro,* Centro Colombiano de Filantropía.

Mexico

Marie Claire Acosta Urquidi, Comisión Mexicana de Defensa y Promoción de Derechos Humanos; *Sergio Aguayo Quezada,* El Colegio de Mexico; *Rubén Aguilar Valenzuela,* Causa Ciudadana; *Luis F. Agullar Villanueva,* Secretaría de Gobernación; *Manuel Arango Arias,* CEMEFI; *Vicente Arredondo Ramírez,* Fundación Demos; *Manuel Canto Chac,* Universidad Autónoma Metropolitana; *Alfonso Castillo Sánchez,* Unión de Esfuerzos por el Campo; *Norman Collins,* Ford Foundation; *Julio Faesler Carlisle,* Consejo para la Democracia; *Rosa María Fernández Rodriguez,* Consultant; *Sergio García,* Foro de Apoyo Mutuo; *Jesús Luis García Garza,* Universidad Iberoamericana; *Claudio X. González Guajardo,* Oficina de la Presidencia de la República; *Ricardo Govela Autrey,* Philos; *Luis Hernández Navarro,* Coordinadora Nacional de Organizaciones Cafetaleras; *Alonso Lujambio,* Instituto Tecnológico Autónomo de México; *María Angélica Luna Parra,* México Ciudad Humana; *Dionisio Pérez Jácome,* Unidad de Promoción de Inversiones; *Federico Reyes Heroles,* Revista Este País; *Rafael Reygadas Robles-Gil,* Convergencia; *Alejandra Sánchez Gabito,* Consultant; *Jairo Sánchez Méndez,* Banco Interamericano de Desarrollo; *Martha Smith de Rangel,* CEMEFI; *Guillermo Soberón Acevedo,* Fundación Mexicana para la Salud; *Ekart Wild,* Fundación Frederich Ebert; *Alfonso Zárate,* Grupo Consultor Interdiciplinario.

Peru

Federico Arnillas, Asociación Nacional de Centros (ANC); *Cecilia Blondet,* Instituto de Estudios Peruanos (IEP); *Baltazar Caravedo,* Seguimiento, Análisis y

Evaluación para el Desarrollo (SASE); *Elizabeth Dasso*, Banco Mundial; *Javier Díaz Albertini*, Universidad de Lima; *Estuardo Marrou*, Escuela de Posgrado de la Universidad del Pacífico; *Kris Merschrod*, Private Agencies Collaborating Together (PACT); *María Jesús Reinafarje*, Secretaría de Cooperación Técnica Internacional, Ministerio de la Presidencia (MIPRE-SECTI); *María Isabel Remy*, Centro de Investigación y Promoción del Campesino (CIPCA); *Mario Ríos*, Cáritas Perú; *Manuel Sotomayor*, Perú 2021; *Mariano Valderrama*, Centro Peruano de Estudios Sociales (CEPES).

APPENDIX E

Local Associates

Phase II

Argentina
Mario Roitter
CEDES

Australia
Mark Lyons/Susan Hocking
UTS-CACOM

Austria
Christoph Badelt
Wirtschaftsuniversität Wien

Belgium
Jacques Defourny
Centre D'Économie Sociale
Universite de Liège au Sart-
   Tilman
Jozef Pacolet
Katholieke Universiteit Leuven

Brazil
Leilah Landim
Instituto de Estudos da Religião

Colombia
Rodrigo Villar
Confederación Colombiana de
   ONGs

Czech Republic
Martin Potůček/Pavol Frič
Charles University
Institute of Sociological Studies

Finland
Voitto Helander
Åbo Akademi

France
Édith Archambault
Universite de Paris I-Sorbonne
Laboratoire D'Économie Social

Germany
Eckhard Priller
Wissenschaftszentrum Berlin
Annette Zimmer
Westfälische Wilhems-Universität
   Münster

507

Hungary
Éva Kuti/István Sebestény/Agnes Vajda
Civitalis

Ireland
Joyce O'Connor/Freda Donoghue
National College of Ireland

Israel
Benjamin Gidron
Ben Gurion University of the Negev
Israeli Center for Third-sector
    Research

Italy
Paolo Barbetta
Istituto per la Ricerca Sociale

Japan
Naoto Yamauchi/Masaaki Homma
Osaka School of International
    Public Policy

Mexico
CEMEFI
Principal Investigator:
Gustavo Verduzco
El Colegio de Mexico, A.C.

The Netherlands
Paul Dekker/Ary Burger
Social and Cultural Planning Office

Norway
Hakon Lorentzen
Institutt for Samfunnsforskning
Per Selle
Norwegian Research Centre in
    Organization and Management

Peru
Felipe Portocarrero/Cynthia Sanborn
Centro de Investigación de la
    Universidad del Pacífico

Poland
Ewa Leś
University of Warsaw
Institute of Social Policy
Jan Jakub Wygnański
KLON/JAWOR

Romania
Daniel Saulean
Civil Society Development
    Foundation

Russia
Oleg Kazakov
Nonprofit Sector Research
    Laboratory

Slovakia
Helena Woleková
S.P.A.C.E. Foundation

South Africa
Mark Swilling/Hanlie van Dyk
University of Witwatersrand

Spain
José Ignacio Ruiz Olabuénaga
CINDES

United Kingdom
Jeremy Kendall/Martin Knapp
PSSRU
London School of Economics
Department of Social
    Administration

United States
Lester M. Salamon/
    S. Wojciech Sokolowski
The Johns Hopkins University

Venezuela
Rosa Amelia Gonzalez
IESA